DISSERTATIONS IN HISTORY
Volume II

Warren F. Kuehl

DISSERTATIONS IN HISTORY

An Index to Dissertations
Completed in History Departments
of United States & Canadian Universities
1961 - June 1970

The University Press of Kentucky

To Marshall & Paul

ISBN: 0-8131-1264-8

Library of Congress Catalog Card Number: 75-183351

Copyright © 1972 by The University Press of Kentucky

A statewide cooperative scholarly publishing agency
serving Berea College, Centre College of Kentucky,
Eastern Kentucky University, Kentucky Historical Society,
Kentucky State College, Morehead State University, Murray
State University, University of Kentucky, University of
Louisville, and Western Kentucky University.

Editorial and Sales Offices: Lexington, Kentucky 40506

CONTENTS

PREFACE

The highly favorable response to the index to dissertations for the period 1876 through 1960[1] stimulated the compiling of the present volume. I hope it will serve as a useful guide both in providing materials to researchers and as an indication of subjects explored. This volume covers the period from 1961 through the June commencement of 1970. It also incorporates a few titles of the earlier period which were missed, particularly for those departments where previous records were incomplete.[2]

This volume follows the same format as the earlier one. The standards for inclusion and exclusion are the same, and the same rationale prevails.[3] Only dissertations completed in formally organized departments of history and for which a doctor of philosophy degree was granted are included. No dissertations from inter-disciplinary or non-history departments have been knowingly listed.

A distinctive feature of this volume, however, is the more complete index section. The index to the first volume included topics indicated in or implicit in the dissertation titles. For this volume it was possible to use published abstracts, and the result is a larger and more useful index. While *Dissertation Abstracts* proved useful in the indexing process, it is not a complete source for all dissertations. Neither the University of Chicago nor Harvard, both large producers of dissertations in history, subscribes to the service. Furthermore, many studies completed in the period just prior to 1971 have not yet appeared in abstract form, and a surprising number of others have never been printed in *Dissertation Abstracts*. Approximately one-fourth of the studies have therefore been indexed solely from their titles or subjects implicit in their titles. Since it is difficult for any one person to perceive all of the possible relationships implicit in subjects covering all time periods, nations, and topics related to history, such an index cannot be perfect. I hope, however, that sufficient index headings have been provided so that any researcher with imagination will be able to discover what has been done on particular topics.

Users of this work should also examine the index compiled for *Dissertation Abstracts* volumes 1 through 29. This computer compilation, based upon key words in the titles, reveals the major shortcomings of such a process, yet it serves as a limited guide to studies completed in other departments which might be useful to historians.

One might wish, indeed plead, that future authors follow the common-sense rule of embodying in their titles a clear indication of the subject matter. This would make future bibliographical studies, which will have to be more computer oriented, much more complete and useful. Such titles as "The Problem of the Internal Senses in the Fourteenth Century" and "Scholars of the Urban-Industrial Frontier, 1880-1889" provide few clues to even an informed and imaginative indexer. Unfortunately, many similar examples could be cited.

It is also evident that the service provided by the American Historical Association through its pamphlets on "Dissertations in Progress" is not fully utilized in two ways. First, a surprising number of dissertations are never listed. Second, the usual duplication of topics, as the index section reveals, still exists. It should be noted, however, that such instances seem to be less obvious than in the first volume. A comparison of this volume with the previous one shows fewer examples of overlap.

The sources of information used in compiling the list of titles were varied, but files of departments of history and library records proved to be the most useful. Initially, I requested lists from history departments. These were checked against the annual volumes of *American Doctoral Dissertations* and *Dissertation Abstracts*. This operation revealed so many discrepancies that the lists for each university were sent to libraries where the card catalogs presumably have accurate titles. Thus while the cooperation of chairmen and graduate advisors was fully appreciated, it still appears that most historians are not conscientious keepers of their own records. The titles of completed dissertations submitted to the American Historical Association and published in mimeographed form and its annual reports also revealed a significant number of variations in titles. Again it would be helpful if departments, in transmitting such information, would strive for a higher degree of accuracy.

[1] Warren F. Kuehl, *Dissertations in History: An Index to Dissertations Completed in History Departments of United States and Canadian Universities, 1873-1960* (Lexington: University of Kentucky Press, 1965).

[2] See tabular summary, pp. ix-x, especially notes.

[3] Kuehl, *Dissertations, 1873-1960*, ix.

This volume would not have been possible without the cooperation of many persons in history departments and university libraries who checked titles for accuracy and completeness. My thanks to them is exceedingly great. Several students, graduate and undergraduate, have also devoted hundreds of hours to the project, and their contribution should be acknowledged. I am particularly indebted to Farajollah Ardalan and Denise Shamberger, but Valerie Dapp assumed an even greater responsibility in mastering the details of the operation. Diane Markley typed the manuscript with accuracy and care, and Pat Godfrey also aided in the typing. I am also indebted to nearly all of my colleagues in the Department of History at the University of Akron who patiently responded to queries on obscure subjects. Boris Blick and Vincent Cassidy were especially helpful in this respect. Don R. Gerlach, who read the entire index section, aided greatly in improving its accuracy. As usual, I am indebted to the members of my family, especially my wife Olga, for the patience and understanding they have shown.

NUMERICAL SUMMARY OF UNITED STATES AND CANADIAN DOCTORAL DEGREES IN HISTORY, 1873-JUNE 1970

Institution	Date 1st Degree	1873-1960	1961-1970	Total
Alabama, U. of	1952	10	31	41
Alberta, U. of	1964	0	4	4
American U.	1922	49[1]	39	88
Arizona, U. of	1963	0	17	17
Arkansas, U. of [2]	1954	1	0	1
Ball State U.	1964	0	17	17
Boston Col.	1933	20	6	26
Boston U.	1926	42	71	113
Brigham Young U.	1966	0	6	6
British Columbia	1968	0	7	7
Brown U.	1889	27	24	51
Bryn Mawr Col.	1896	36	18	54
Buffalo, U. of[3]	1949			
Calif., U. of (Berkeley)	1908	419[1]	248	667
Calif., U. of (Davis)	1967	0	5	5
Calif., U. of (L.A.)	1939	109	122	231
Calif., U. of (Riverside)	1966	0	4	4
Calif., U. of (Santa Barbara)	1963	0	28	28
Case W. Reserve[4]	1896	42	50	92
Catholic U. of America	1909	186[1]	61	247
Chicago, U. of	1895	428	155	583
Cincinnati, U. of	1965	0	11	11
Claremont	1955	5	27	32
Clark U.	1916	76	16	92
Col. of the Pacific[5]	1960	0	0	0
Colorado, U. of	1929	52	70	122
Columbia U.	1883	797	366	1163
Connecticut, U. of	1967	0	16	16
Cornell U.	1890	196	87	283
Delaware, U. of	1964	0	12	12
Denver, U. of	1964	0	28	28
Duke U.	1929	110[1]	139	249
Emory U.	1952	18	33	51
Florida, U. of	1952	20[1]	37	57
Florida State U.	1962	0	35	35
Fordham U.	1925	100	41	141
George Peabody Col.	1926	25	18	43
George Washington U.	1895	34	17	51
Georgetown U.	1923	106	81	187
Georgia, U. of	1939	2	85	87
Harvard U.[6]	1873	712[1]	327	1039
Hawaii, U. of	1964	0	8	8
Idaho, U. of	1965	0	6	6
Illinois, U. of	1906	203	86	289
Indiana U.	1913	113	139	252
Iowa, State U. of	1909	159[7]	70	229
Johns Hopkins	1878	216[1]	65	281
Kansas, U. of	1921	18	45	63
Kansas State U.	1967	0	2	2
Kent State U.	1966	0	16	16
Kentucky, U. of	1933	30	41	71
Laval U.	1948	3	12	15
Lehigh U.	1954	3	10	13
Louisiana State U.	1936	25[1]	30	55
Loyola U. (Chicago)	1939	23[1]	25	48
McGill U.	1939	13	22	35
Maine, U. of	1966	0	8	8
Manitoba, U. of	1968	0	3	3
Marquette U.[2]	1924	7	0	7
Maryland, U. of	1937	17	57	74
Massachusetts, U. of	1965	0	4	4
Miami U.	1968	0	1	1
Michigan State U.	1952	6	62	68
Michigan, U. of	1884	223	103	326
Minnesota, U. of	1888	144	101	245
Mississippi, U. of	1963	0	11	11
Mississippi, U. of Southern	1969	0	4	4
Mississippi State U.	1962	0	26	26
Missouri, U. of	1935	51	69	120
Montana, U. of	1970	0	1	1
Nebraska, U. of	1903	61	32	93
New Mexico, U. of	1948	18	55	73
New York, City U. of	1967	0	13	13
New York, State U. (Binghamton)	1970	0	1	1
New York, State U. (Buffalo)	1949	1	16	17
New York U.	1899	91	121	212
Niagara U.[2]	1936	7	0	7
North Carolina, U. of	1926	150	117	267
North Dakota, U. of[8]	1935	4	2	6
Northern Illinois U.	1966	0	5	5
Northwestern U.	1918	86	99	185
Notre Dame, U. of	1928	19[1]	38	57
Ohio State U.	1925	134	102	236
Oklahoma, U. of	1930	43	62	105
Oregon, U. of	1936	15	48	63
Ottawa, U. d'	1953	6	13	19
Pennsylvania State U.	1952	7[1]	25	32
Pennsylvania, U. of	1891	309	111	420
Pittsburgh, U. of	1930	62	29	91
Princeton U.	1894	96[1]	90	186
Radcliffe[6]	1906	70	6	76
Rice U.	1933	6	18	24
Rochester, U. of	1954	21	56	77
Rutgers—State U.	1946	2	64	66
St. John's U. (N.Y.)	1942	25	44	69
St. Louis U.	1925	56[1]	83	139
South Carolina, U. of	1929	13	28	41
Southern California, U. of	1931	108[1]	74	182
Stanford U.	1910	182	102	284
Syracuse U.	1883	18	25	43
Temple U.	1970	0	2	2
Tennessee, U. of	1965	0	8	8
Texas, U. of	1927	184	92	276
Texas Christian U.	1967	0	16	16
Texas Technological Col.	1954	6	17	23

Institution	Date 1st Degree	1873-1960	1961-1970	Total
Toronto, U. of	1925	41[1]	49	90
Tulane U.	1950	14	62	76
Utah, U. of	1949	5	20	25
Vanderbilt U.	1899	80	40	120
Virginia, U. of	1904	68	85	153
Washington, U. of	1922	41[1]	95	136
Washington State U.[5]	1936	0	0	0
Washington U. (St.L.)	1926	18	12	30
Wayne State U.	1961	0	19	19
West Virginia U.	1933	14	8	22
Western Reserve U.[4]	1896			
Wisconsin, U. of	1893	432	354	786
Yale U.	1882	306	140	446
Total		7,695[9]	5,884[10]	13,579

[1] Includes dissertations not listed in 1873-1960 volume but included in 1961-1970 volume, as follows:

American U. (2) A141, F135

Calif., U. of (Berkeley) (2) F215, R35

Catholic U. of America (37) A33, B184, B213, B299, B382, B442, B459, B513, B531, B537, C294, C364, E78, F186, G135, G255, H186, H336, L105, L241, L245, M12, M16, M29, M88, M117, M127, M484, N28, N79, O22, R217, S544, T22, T73, W54, W325

Duke U. (3) H29, P105, S466

Florida, U. of (1) L201

Harvard U. (1) A64

Johns Hopkins (1) A42

Louisiana State U. (1) D124

Loyola U. (Chicago) (3) P64, R182, T18

Notre Dame, U. of (4) B52, C155, F168, G222

Pennsylvania State U. (1) D109

Princeton U. (1) B430

St. Louis U. (1) L35

Southern California, U. of (1) G136

Toronto, U. of (1) M33

Washington, U. of (8) B176, C154, C226, H407, S442, T146, W262, W309

[2] Once offered doctorate in history but none conferred since 1960.

[3] *See* New York, State U. (Buffalo).

[4] Western Reserve and Case Institute of Technology merged in 1967 as Case Western Reserve. The data here include only dissertations completed before and after the merger in the Department of History of what was Western Reserve University. Dissertations completed at Case before and since the merger are in the Department of the History of Science and Technology and are therefore not included. Data now listed under Case Western Reserve.

[5] The 1873-1960 volume included six titles for Washington State and one for College of the Pacific. This was erroneous because the degrees conferred at Washington were in American Studies rather than history and because the College of the Pacific has no doctoral program in history. Figures are corrected accordingly.

[6] In 1963 Radcliffe and Harvard combined their programs. The Harvard figure includes all Radcliffe data for 1963 and after.

[7] Corrected because of duplicate listing since discovered in 1873-1960 volume.

[8] Doctor of Philosophy program now discontinued.

[9] Total revised from that listed in 1873-1960 volume (see notes 1, 5, 7).

[10] Does not include 68 pre-1961 dissertations included in 1961-1970 volume (see note 1).

A

A1 Abarca, Ramón E. Bourbon "Revanche" against England: The Balance of Power, 1763-1770. Notre D 1965

A2 Abbott, Albert. Shadows of the Schism: Pitt's Circular Dispatch and the Genesis of Enforcement. Georgetown 1962

A3 Abbott, Richard H. Cobbler in Congress: Life of Henry Wilson, 1812-1875. Wis 1965

A4 Abele, Charles A. The Grand Indian Council and Treaty of Prairie du Chien, 1825. Loyola 1969

A5 Abella, Irving M. The Struggle for Industrial Unionism in Canada: The CIO, the Communist Party and the Canadian Congress of Labour, 1936-1956. Toronto 1969

A6 Aberbach, Alan D. Samuel Latham Mitchill: A Romantic Nationalist in the Age of Jefferson. Fla U 1962

A7 Abosch, David. Katō Hiroyuki and the Introduction of German Political Thought in Modern Japan, 1868-1883. Cal, Berkeley 1964

A8 Abou-El-Haj, Rifa'at Ali. The Reisülküttab and Ottoman Diplomacy at Karlowitz. Princeton 1963

A9 Abrahams, Paul P. The Foreign Expansion of American Finance and Its Relationship to the Foreign Economic Policies of the United States, 1907-1921. Wis 1967

A10 Abrahamse, Dorothy Z. Hagiographic Sources for Byzantine Cities, 500-900 A.D. Mich U 1967

A11 Abramoske, Donald J. The *Chicago Daily News*: A Business History, 1875-1901. Chicago 1963

A12 Abrams, Richard M. Massachusetts Politics, 1900-1912: Conservatism in a Progressive Era. Columbia 1962

A13 Abu Ghazaleh, Adnan M. Arab Cultural Nationalism in Palestine, 1919-1948. NYU 1967

A14 Accinelli, Robert D. The United States and the World Court, 1920-1927. Cal, Berkeley 1968

A15 Ackerman, Robert K. South Carolina Colonial Land Policies. SC 1965

A16 Acrea, Kenneth C., Jr. Wisconsin Progressivism: Legislative Response to Social Change, 1891 to 1909. Wis 1968

A17 Adams, David K. The Voyage to Sparta: Political Ideas in Selected Writings of Maurice Barrès. Ind 1962

A18 Adams, Frederick C. The Export-Import Bank and American Foreign Policy, 1934-1939. Cornell 1968

A19 Adams, Glen W. The UNESCO Controversy in Los Angeles, 1951-1953: A Case Study of the Influence of Right-Wing Groups on Urban Affairs. S. Cal 1970

A20 Adams, Graham, Jr. Age of Industrial Violence: Social Conflict in America as Revealed by U. S. Commission on Industrial Relations, 1912-1916. Columbia 1962

A21 Adams, Jeremy Y. D. Sense of Community in the Early Middle Ages: Populus and Other Sociopolitical Terms in the Works of Jerome, Augustine, and Isidore of Seville. Harvard 1967

A22 Adams, Rita G. Brigadier-General John Adams, C.S.A.: Biography of a Frontier American (1825-1864). St. L 1964

A23 Addington, Larry H. General Franz Halder and the German Army and General Staff, 1938-1941. Duke 1962

A24 Adelson, Judah. The Vermont Press and the French Revolution, 1789-1799. NYU 1961

A25 Adewoye, Omoniyi. The Legal Profession in Southern Nigeria, 1863-1943. Columbia 1968

A26 Adler, Leslie K. The Red Image: American Attitudes toward Communism in the Cold War Era. Cal, Berkeley 1970

A28 Adriance, Thomas J. The Mobilization and Concentration of the French Army in 1870. Columbia 1968

A29 Adshead, Samuel A. M. The Modernization of the Chinese Salt Administration, 1900-1920. Harvard 1968

A30 Afferica, Joan M. The Political and Social Thought of Prince M. M. Shcherbatov (1733-1790). Harvard 1967

A31 Agócs, Sándor. The Party of God: Pope Pius X and the Social Doctrine of the Church. Rochester 1970

A32 Ahern, Wilbert H. Laissez Faire versus Equal Rights: Liberal Republicans and the Negro, 1861-1877. Northwestern 1968

A33 Aherne, Consuelo Maria, Sister. Valeiro of Bierzo: An Ascetic of the Late Visigothic Period. Cath 1949

A34 Ahlin, John H. New England Rubicon: A Study of Eastern Maine during the American Revolution. Boston U 1962

A35 Aho, Ilma R. A Record of the Activities of the Lutheran Evangelical Association of Finland in Japan, 1900-1946. Cal, Berkeley 1969

A36 Aiken, John R. Utopianism and the Emergence of the Colonial Legal Profession: New York, 1664-1710, a Test Case. Rochester 1967

A37 Airo-Farulla, Joseph A. The Political Opposition of the Huguenots to Henry IV, 1589 to 1598. Wash U 1969

A38 Akerman, Robert H. The Triumph of Moderation in Florida Thought and Politics: A Study of the Race Issue from 1954 to 1960. Am 1967

A39 Akhtar, Mushtaq A. The Royal Titles Bill: Public Opinion in the United Kingdom, India and Canada. McGill 1969

A40 Alagoa, Ebiegberi J. The Settlement of the Niger Delta: Ijo Oral Traditions. Wis 1966

A41 Albee, Parker B., Jr. American and Allied Policies at the Paris Peace Conference: The Drawing of the Polish-German Frontier. Duke 1968

A42 Albrecht, Frank M. The New Psychology in America, 1880-1895. JH 1960

A43 Albro, Ward S., III. Ricardo Flores Magón and the Liberal Party: An Inquiry into the Origins of the Mexican Revolution of 1910. Ariz 1967

A44 Alder, Douglas D. Otto Bauer's Opposition Policy, 1918-1927. Ore 1966

A45 Aldred, Francis K. The Brussels Conference: A Study of Efforts during 1937 to Formulate a Joint Anglo-American Far Eastern Policy. Va 1967

A46 Aldrich, James M. The Revolutionary Legislature in Pennsylvania: A Roll Call Analysis. Maine 1969

A47 Aldridge, Frederick S. Organization and Administration of the Militia System of Colonial Virginia. Am 1964

A48 Aldstadt, David P. The Radical Movement in England, 1806-1814. Case W Reserve 1968

A49 Alexander, Charles C., Jr. Invisible Empire in the Southwest: The Ku Klux Klan in Texas, Louisiana, Oklahoma, and Arkansas, 1920-1930. Tex U 1962

A50 Alexander, James W. Herbert de Losinga, Bishop of Norwich, 1091-1119. JH 1964

A51 Alexander, John T. The Russian Government and Pugachev's Revolt, 1773-1775. Ind 1966

A51a Alexander, Michael Van Cleave. A Biography of Sir Richard Weston, First Earl of Portland (1577-1635), until His Appointment as Lord Treasurer in July 1628. NC 1969

A52 Alexander, Thomas G. The Federal Frontier: Interior Department Financial Policy in Idaho, Utah, and Arizona, 1863-1896. Cal, Berkeley 1965

A53 Alexeev, Wassilij. The Russian Orthodox Church under German Occupation, 1941-1945. Minn 1967

A54 Alfonso, Oscar M. The Presidential Leadership of Theodore Roosevelt in Philippine Policy. Chicago 1966

A55 Alford, Terry L. Western Desert Images in American Thought, 1800-1860. Miss S 1970

A56 Algier, Keith W. Feudalism of New Spain's Northern Frontier: Valle de San Bartolomé, a Case Study. NM 1966

A56a Algrem, Beverly S. Mendeleev: The Third Service. 1834-1882. Brown 1968

A57 Ali, Agha Ashraf. Theories of Americanization Operative in Gary Schools, 1907-1917. Ball State 1964

A58 Alksnis, Gunnar. Ludwig Klages and His Attack on Rationalism. Kans S 1970

A59 Allard, Dean C., Jr. Spencer Fullerton Baird and the United States Fish Commission: A Study in the History of American Science. Geo W 1967

A60 Allardyce, Gilbert D. The Political Transition of Jacques Doriot, 1926-1936. Ia 1966

A61 Allen, Alexander R. The Crest and Crisis of the Social Gospel in Canada, 1916-1927. Duke 1967

A62 Allen, Donald R. French Views of America in the Nineteen-Thirties. Boston U 1970

A63 Allen, E. John B. The Diplomatic Courier in Europe: 1559-1598. Brigham Young 1969

A64 Allen, Frederick S. The British Army, 1860-1900: A Study of the Cardwell Manpower Reforms. Harvard 1960

A65 Allen, James B. The Company Town as a Feature of Western American Development. S Cal 1964

A66 Allen, Samuel E., Jr. The Zemstvo as a Force for Social and Civic Regeneration in Russia: A Study of Selected Aspects, 1864-1905. Clark 1969

A67 Allen, William S. Thalburg: The Nazi Seizure of Power in a Single German Town, 1930 to 1935. Minn 1962

A68 Allison, George R. Imperialism and Appeasement: A Study of the Ideas of the Round Table Group. Harvard 1965

A69 Allmendinger, David F., Jr. Indigent Students and Their Institutions, 1800-1860. Wis 1968

A70 Allswang, John M. The Political Behavior of Chicago's Ethnic Groups, 1918-1932. Pitt 1967

A71 Alltmont, René C. Belgian Overseas Expansion during the Nineteenth Century. Del 1969

A72 Almaraz, Felix D., Jr. The Administration of Manuel Maria de Salcedo of Texas: 1808-1813. NM 1968

A73 Alston, Patrick L. State Education and Social Change in the Russian Empire, 1871-1914. Cal, Berkeley 1961

A74 Altman, Albert. The Emergence of the Press in Meiji Japan. Princeton 1965

A75 Altschul, Michael. The Clare Family, 1263-1314. JH 1962

A76 Alvarez, Eugene. Travel on Antebellum Southern Railroads. Ga 1966

A77 Amacher, Melchior P. The Influence of the Neuroanatomy, Neurophysiology and Psychiatry of Freud's Teachers on His Psychoanalytic Theories. Wash U 1962

A77a Amaru, Betsy H. Arminianism in England, 1595-1629. Mass 1969

A78 Amato, Joseph A. Emmanuel Mounier and Jacques Maritain: A French Catholic Understanding of the Modern World. Rochester 1970

A79 Ambler, Effie K. A. S. Suvorin from Nihilist to *Mrakobes,* 1861-1881. Ind 1968

A80 Ambrose, Stephen E. Upton and the Army. Wis 1963

A81 Ambrosius, Lloyd E. The United States and the Weimar Republic, 1918-1923: From the Armistice to the Ruhr Occupation. Ill 1967

A82 Ames, William E. A History of the *National Intelligencer,* 1800-1869. Minn 1962

A83 Amin, Abdul A. British Interests in the Persian Gulf, 1747-1788. Md 1962

A84 Ammerman, David L. The First Continental Congress and the Coming of the American Revolution. Cornell 1966

A85 Amos, Virginia. A Mexican Positivist: Gabino Barreda, His Life and Work. Tex C 1969

A86 Amundson, Richard J. The American Life of Henry Shelton Sanford. Fla S 1963

A87 Anchor, Robert. Community and History in Johann Gottfried Herder. Rochester 1965

A88 Anderle, Josef. The Slovak Issue in the Munich Crisis of 1938. Chicago 1961

A89 Anderson, Adrian N. Albert Sidney Burleson: A Southern Politician in the Progressive Era. Tex Tech 1967

A90 Anderson, James C. The Caldeirão Movement: A Case Study in Brazilian Messianism, 1926-1938. Geo W 1970

A91 Anderson, James L. The Governor's Council of Colonial America: A Study of Pennsylvania and Virginia, 1660-1776. Va 1967

A92 Anderson, James R. The New Deal Career of Frances Perkins, Secretary of Labor, 1933-1939. Case W Reserve 1968

A93 Anderson, Jane J. Political Necessity in the Literature of the French Enlightenment: Diderot and the *Encyclopédie.* Brown 1962

A94 Anderson, Philip J. The Simple Builders: The Shakers, Their Villages and Architecture. St L 1969

A95 Anderson, Richard G. Benito Gerónimo Feijóo y Montenegro, Champion of Experimental Science. Tex C 1970

A96 Anderson, Richard L. The Rise and Fall of Middle-Class Loyalty to the Roman Empire: A Social Study of Velleius Paterculus and Ammianus Marcellinus. Cal, Berkeley 1962

A97 Anderson, Robert M. A Social History of the Early 20th Century Pentecostal Movement. Columbia 1969

A98 Anderson, Ruth T. A Study of the Career of Theodore II, Emperor of Ethiopia, 1855-1868. Ohio 1966

A99 Anderson, Thomas P. The French Intelligentsia and the Spanish Civil War, 1936-1939. Loyola 1965

A100 Andrade, Ernest, Jr. United States Naval Policy in the Disarmament Era, 1921-1937. Mich S 1966

A101 Andrea, Alfred J. Pope Innocent III as Crusader and Canonist: His Relations with the Greeks of Constantinople, 1198-1216. Cornell 1969

A102 Andrews, Avery D., II. The Turkish Threat to Venice, 1453-1463. Penn U 1962

A103 Andrews, Herbert D. Bismarck's Foreign Policy and German Historians, 1919-1945. Northwestern 1964

A104 Andrews, Richard A. Years of Frustration: William T. Sherman, the Army, and Reform, 1869-1883. Northwestern 1968

A105 Andrews, Thomas F. The Controversial Career of Lansford Warren Hastings, Pioneer California Promoter and Emigrant Guide. S Cal 1970

A106 Andriette, Eugene A. The Counties of Devon and Exeter in the Civil War Period, 1640-1646. Wis 1968

A107 Anglin, Jay P. The Court of the Archdeacon of Essex, 1571-1609: An Institutional and Social Study. UCLA 1965

A108 Anna, Timothy E. Mexico City in the War of Independence, 1810-1821. Duke 1969

A109 Annunziata, Frank A. The Attack on the Welfare State: Patterns of Anti-Statism from the New Deal to the New Left. Ohio 1968

A110 Ansel, Bernard D. The Beginning of the Modern Jewish Community in Argentina, 1852-1891. Kans U 1969

A110a Antone, George P., Jr. Willis Duke Weatherford: An Interpretation of His Work in Race Relations, 1906-1946. Vanderbilt 1969

A111 Anzulovic, James V., Jr. The Russian Record of the Winter War, 1939-1940: An Analytical Study of Soviet Records of the War with Finland from 30 November 1939 to 12 March 1940. Md 1968

A112 Applebaum, Wilbur. Kepler in England: The Reception of Keplerian Astronomy in England, 1599-1687. SUNY, Buffalo 1969

A113 Appleby, Joyce O. An American Pamphlet in Paris. Claremont 1966

A114 Applegate, Howard L. Constitutions like Iron: The Life of the American Revolutionary War Soldiers in the Middle Department, 1775-1783. Syracuse 1966

A115 Aprahamian, Ashod R. The Mayoral Politics of Detroit, 1897 through 1912. NYU 1969

A116 Apt, Leon J. Louis-Philippe de Ségur: An Intellectual in a Revolutionary Age. Chicago 1965

A117 Arbagi, Martin G. Byzantium in Latin Eyes, 800-1204. Rutgers 1969

A118 Arceneaux, William. The Venezuelan Experience: 1958 and the Patriotic Junta. LSU 1969

A119 Archer, Julian P. W. The First International and the Lyon Revolutionary Movement, 1864-1871. Wis 1970

A120 Archer, Mary Urban, Sister. Woodrow Wilson: The Post Presidential Years. St L 1963

A121 Archer, Richard L. New England Federalism and the Hartford Convention. Cal, Santa Barbara 1968

A122 Argersinger, Peter H. Populism and Politics: William Alfred Peffer and the People's Party. Wis 1970

A123 Armand, Laura M. Protestantism in La Rochelle, 1755-1830: The Consequences of Bourgeois Rule. Harvard 1969

A124 Armeson, Robert B. Origins and Effects of the National Service Law of December 5, 1916: A Study of Manpower Policy in Imperial Germany during World War I. Cal, Berkeley 1961

A125 Armitstead, Paul T. Retired Military Leaders in American Business. Tex U 1967

A126 Armour, David A. The Merchants of Albany, New York, 1686-1760. Northwestern 1965

A127 Armstrong, Frederick H. Toronto in Transition: The Emergence of a City, 1828-1838. Toronto 1965

A128 Armstrong, John B. Harrisville: A New Hampshire Mill Town in the Nineteenth Century. Boston U 1962

A129 Armstrong, Warren B. The Organization, Function, and Contribution of the Chaplaincy in the United States Army, 1861-1865. Mich U 1964

A130 Arnold, Eric A., Jr. Administrative Leadership in a Dictatorship: The Position of Joseph Fouché in the Napoleonic Police, 1800-1810. Columbia 1969

A131 Arnold, Joseph L. The New Deal in the Suburbs: The Greenbelt Town Program, 1935-1952. Ohio 1968

A132 Arnstein, Walter L. The Bradlaugh Case: A Study in Late Victorian Opinion and Politics. Northwestern 1961

A133 Arthur, Charles B. The Revolution in British Naval Strategy, 1800-1801. Harvard 1966

A134 Arthur, David T. "Come Out of Babylon": A Study of Millerite Separatism and Denominationalism, 1840-1865. Rochester 1970

A135 Artigiani, Philip R. The Functional Self: A Study of the Effects of the Philosophy and Practice of Science on the Scientist's Self-Image during the Nineteenth and Twentieth Centuries. Am 1969

A136 Asado, Sadao. Japan and the United States, 1915-1925. Yale 1963

A137 Ashby, Darrel L. Senator William E. Borah and Progressivism in the 1920's. Md 1966

A138 Asher, Harvey. The Kornilov Affair: A History and Interpretation. Ind 1967

A139 Askew, Thomas A., Jr. The Liberal Arts College Encounters Intellectual Change: A Comparative Study of Education at Knox and Wheaton Colleges, 1837-1925. Northwestern 1969

A140 Astorino, Samuel J. The Decline of the Republican Dynasty in Pennsylvania, 1929-1934. Pitt 1962

A141 Athearn, Clarence R. Woodrow Wilson's Philosophy. Am 1931

A142 Atherton, Herbert M. Political Prints in the Age of Walpole, the Pelhams, and Bute: A Study of the Ideographic Representation of Politics. Yale 1968

A143 Athey, Louis L. The Consumers' Leagues and Social Reform, 1890-1923. Del 1965

A144 Atkins, Richard A. British Policy towards Egypt, 1876 to 1882. Cal, Berkeley 1968

A145 Atlas, Jerrold. Organization of the Kingdom of Jerusalem under Amalric I (1163-1174). NYU 1969

A146 Atwell, John W., Jr. The Jury System and Its Role in Russia's Legal, Social, and Political Development from 1857 to 1914. Princeton 1970

A147 Atwell, Priscilla A. Freedom and Diversity: Continuity in the Political Tradition of Thomas Jefferson and John C. Calhoun. UCLA 1967

A148 Auerbach, Jerold S. The La Follette Committee: Labor and Civil Liberties in the New Deal. Columbia 1965

A149 Augustine, Wilson R. The Economic Attitudes and Opinions Expressed by the Russian Nobility in the Great Commission of 1767. Columbia 1969

A150 Auld, John W. The Pro-Boer Liberals in Britain at the Time of the Boer War. Stanford 1970

A151 Auld, Leona R. Discontent with the Spanish System of Control in Upper Peru, 1730-1809. UCLA 1963

A152 Aurand, Harold W. The Anthracite Mine Workers, 1869-1897: A Functional Approach to Labor History. Penn S 1969

A153 Ausmus, Harry J. Christoph of Württemberg's Attempts to Unify Protestantism, 1555-1568. Ohio 1969

A154 Austen, Ralph A. Native Policy and African Politics: Indirect Rule in Northwest Tanzania, 1889-1939. Harvard 1966

A155 Austensen, Roy A. The Early Career of Count Buol, 1837-1852. Ill 1969

A156 Austin, Alan K. The Role of the Anglican Church and Its Clergy in the Political Life of Colonial Virginia. Ga 1969

A157 Austin, Mary Teresita, Sister. The Political, Economic, and Social Aspects of Edward VI's Reign as Viewed through the Sermons and Letters of Hugh Latimer. Mich S 1961

A158 Auten, Arthur H. Charles Francis Adams, Jr., Historian: An Appraisal. Case W Reserve 1965

A159 Avrich, Paul H. The Russian Revolution and the Factory Committees. Columbia 1961

A160 Axeen, David L. Romantics and Civilizers: American Attitudes toward War, 1898-1902. Yale 1969

A161 Axford, Hiram W. Gilpin County Gold: The Life and Career of Peter B. McFarlane. Denver 1969

A162 Azkoul, Michael S. *Peri Oikonomia Theou:* The Meaning of History According to the Greek Fathers. Mich S 1968

B

B1 Baader, Heinz G. Class and Status as Viewed by Feudal Aristocrat and Peasant. Cal, Berkeley 1965

B2 Babcock, Robert H. The A.F.L. in Canada, 1896-1908: A Study in American Labor Imperialism. Duke 1970

B3 Baby, Ampat K. Communist Rule in Kerala. Ind 1964

B4 Bacharach, Jere L. A Study of the Correlation between Textual Sources and Numismatic Evidence for Mamlūk Egypt and Syria, A.H. 784-872/A.D. 1382-1468. Mich U 1967

B5 Bachman, James R. Theodore Lothrop Stoddard: The Bio-Sociological Battle for Civilization. Rochester 1967

B6 Bachman, Van C. Peltries or Plantations? The Economic Policies of the Dutch West India Company in New Netherland, 1623-1639. JH 1965

B7 Bachrach, Bernard S. Merovingian Military Organization and the Beginnings of Feudalism. Cal, Berkeley 1966

B8 Backor, Joseph. M. N. Katkov: Introduction to His Life and His Russian National Policy Program, 1818-1870. Ind 1966

B9 Bader, Louis. Gas Illumination in New York City, 1823-1863. NYU 1970

B10 Bader, Thomas M. A Willingness to War: A Portrait of the Republic of Chile during the Years Preceding the War of the Pacific. UCLA 1967

B11 Bader, William B. A Communist Failure: Occupied Austria, 1945-1950. Princeton 1964

B12 Baehr, George B. The Attempt at a Transportation Empire in New England: The New York, New Haven and Hartford Railroad, 1872-1913. Notre D 1969

B13 Baer, George W. The Coming of the Italo-Ethiopian War. Harvard 1965

B14 Baggs, Albert E. Social Evangel as Nationalism: A Study of the Salvation Army in Japan, 1895-1940. SUNY, Buffalo 1966

B15 Bahney, Robert S. Generals and Negroes: Education of Negroes by the Union Army, 1861-1865. Mich U 1965

B16 Bailey, Benjamin F. Warfare and History as Interpreted by Three Twentieth-Century British Military Historians. Fla S 1966

B17 Bailey, Charles R. The College at Moulins, 1761-1780: An Example of the Former Jesuit Colleges outside Paris but within the Jurisdiction of the Parlement of Paris. Chicago 1968

B18 Bailey, David C. The Cristero Rebellion and the Religious Conflict in Mexico, 1926-1929. Mich S 1969

B19 Bailey, John A., Jr. Lion, Eagle, and Crescent: The Western Allies and Turkey in 1943: A Study of British and American Diplomacy in a Critical Year of the War. Georgetown 1969

B20 Bailey, John B. Some Sources of American Constitutionalism: A Study in the History of Ideas. Ga 1964

B21 Bailey, Stephen. Erich Ludendorff as Quartermaster General of the German Army, 1916-1918. Chicago 1966

B22 Baillargeon, Noel. *Histoire du Séminarie de Québec sous l'épiscopat de Mgr de Laval,* 1663-1688. Laval 1969

B23 Baily, Samuel L., III. Nationalism and Organized Labor in Argentina: 1890-1955. Penn U 1964

B24 Bair, Henry M., Jr. Carl Peters and German Colonialism: A Study in the Ideas and Actions of Imperialism. Stanford 1969

B25 Baird, Jay W. German Home Propaganda, 1941-1945, and the Russian Front. Columbia 1966

B26 Baird, Thomas R. The Napoleonic Counts and Barons, 1808-1814: A Political and Social Study. NYU 1968

B27 Baird, W. David. Peter Pitchlynn: Choctaw Delegate. Okla 1969

B28 Bakalis, Michael J. Ninian Edwards and Territorial Politics in Illinois, 1775-1818. Northwestern 1966

B29 Baker, Abner S. The Oregon Pioneer Tradition in the Nineteenth Century: A Study of Recollection and Self-Definition. Ore 1968

B30 Baker, Donald N. Revolutionism in the French Socialist Party between the World Wars: The Revolutionary *Tendances*. Stanford 1965

B31 Baker, George R. F. The Political Economy of Sallustio Bandini. NYU 1966

B32 Baker, George T., III. Mexico City and the War with the United States: A Study in the Politics of Military Occupation. Duke 1970

B33 Baker, George W., Jr. The Caribbean Policy of Woodrow Wilson, 1913-1917. Colo 1961

B34 Baker, Robert P. A Regional Study of Working Class Organization in France: Socialism in the Nord, 1870-1924. Stanford 1967

B35 Baker, Thomas H., III. The Memphis *Commercial Appeal*, 1865-1941. Tex U 1965

B36 Bakken, Gordon M. Rocky Mountain Constitution-Making, 1850-1912. Wis 1970

B37 Balawyder, Aloysius. Canadian-Soviet Relations, 1920-1935. McGill 1966

B38 Balcer, Jack M. From Confederate Freedom to Imperial Tyranny: A Study of the Restrictions Imposed by Athens on the Political Self-Determination of the Member States in the Delian Confederacy, 478-431 B.C. Mich U 1964

B39 Baldrige, Edwin R., Jr. Talleyrand in the United States, 1794 to 1796. Lehigh 1963

B40 Baldwin, Donald N. A Historical Study of the Western Origin, Application and Development of the Wilderness Concept, 1919-1933. Denver 1965

B41 Baldwin, Fred D. The American Enlisted Man in World War I. Princeton 1964

B42 Balfe, Richard G. Charles P. Neill and the United States Bureau of Labor: A Study in Progressive Economic Social Work and Public Administration. Notre D 1956

B43 Ball, Larry D., Sr. The Office of the United States Marshal in the Arizona and New Mexico Territories, 1851-1912. Colo 1970

B44 Ballard, Brook B., Jr. Colonial Reformers as an Imperial Factor, 1815-1855. Ill 1967

B45 Balsama, George D. The Controversy over French Quietism during the Reign of Louis XIV: Doctrine and Politics, 1686-1700. Brown 1970

B46 Balsamo, Larry T. Theodore G. Bilbo and Mississippi Politics, 1887-1932. Mo 1967

B47 Baltimore, Lester B. Southern Nationalists and Southern Nationalism, 1850-1870. Mo 1968

B48 Bank, Bruce H. Where Terms Begin: Giambattista Vico and the Natural Law. Harvard 1966

B49 Banks, Ronald F. The Separation of Maine from Massachusetts, 1785-1820. Maine 1966

B50 Banner, James M., Jr. To the Hartford Convention: Chapters in the History of Massachusetts Federalism, 1800-1815. Columbia 1968

B51 Banner, Lois W. The Protestant Crusade: Religious Missions, Benevolence, and Reform in the U. S., 1790-1840. Columbia 1970

B52 Barbato, Mary Bernard, Sister. The Isolationist Impulse in European Inter-Nation Conflicts as Evidenced in American Diplomatic Correspondence from Europe, 1920-1925. St L 1964

B52a Barbeau, Arthur E. The Black American Soldier in World War I. Pitt 1970

B53 Barber, Henry E. The History of the Florida Cross-State Canal. Ga 1969

B54 Barber, William D. The West in National Politics, 1784-1804. Wis 1961

B55 Barcio, Robert. Tobias Mullen and the Diocese of Erie, 1869-1899. Case W Reserve 1965

B56 Barcroft, John H. Buckingham and the Central Administration, 1616-1628. Minn 1963

B57 Bardsley, Virginia O. James Rogan: Hill Country Pioneer. Miss S 1961

B58 Barefield, James P. The King's Bishop: The Role of Peter des Roches in the Royal Administration, 1197-1216. JH 1967

B59 Barfield, Claude E., Jr. The Democratic Party in Congress, 1909-1913. Northwestern 1965

B60 Barger, Bob D. Raymond Haight, California's "Angry" Young Man: The Biography of a Political Activist. S Cal 1967

B61 Baringer, Richard L. Inquiry Differences in Selected Current Senior High School United States History Textbooks and an Instrument for Their Comparative Education. Geo P 1969

B62 Barkan, Elliott R. Portrait of a Party: The Origins and Development of the Whig Persuasion in New York State. Harvard 1969

B63 Barker, John C. The Reputation of Blaise Pascal in England and America in the Eighteenth and Early Nineteenth Centuries. Toronto 1967

B63a Barker, John W., Jr. Manuel II Palaeologues, 1391-1425: A Study in Late Byzantine Statesmanship. Rutgers 1961

B64 Barker, Verlyn L. John W. Nevin: His Place in American Intellectual Thought. St L 1970

B65 Barker-Benfield, Graham J. The Horrors of the Half-Known Life: Aspects of the Exploitation of Women by Men. UCLA 1968

B66 Barkin, Kenneth D. The Controversy over German Industrialization. Brown 1966

B67 Barlow, William R. Congress during the War of 1812. Ohio 1961

B68 Barnard, Virgil J. The Conscience of a College: A Study of Oberlin, 1866-1902. Chicago 1964

B69 Barnes, Howard A. Horace Bushnell: An American Christian Gentleman. Ia 1970

B70 Barnes, Robert P. The Scottish Revolution of 1689. S Cal 1967

B71 Barnett, Richard C. The Household and Secretariat of William Cecil, Lord Burghley. NC 1963

B72 Baron, Harold M. Economic Development and American Foreign Policy, 1865-1892. Chicago 1963

B73 Barone, Louis A. Republican House Minority Leader Bertrand H. Snell and the Coming of the New Deal, 1931-1939. SUNY, Buffalo 1969

B74 Barr, Chester A. Texas Politics, 1876-1906. Tex U 1966

B75 Barrett, Gwynn W. John M. Bernhisel, Mormon Elder in Congress. Brigham Young 1968

B76 Barrett, John W. A Study of British and American Foreign Relations with Spain, 1942-1945. Georgetown 1970

B77 Barrier, Norman G. Punjab Politics and the Disturbances of 1907. Duke 1966

B78 Barron, William S., Jr. The Controversy between Martin Bucer and Bartholemew Latomus (1543-1546). Cath 1966

B79 Barrow, Robert M. Newspaper Advertising in Colonial America, 1704-1775. Va 1967

B80 Barrow, Thomas C. The Colonial Customs Service, 1660-1775. Harvard 1961

B81 Barrows, Floyd D. The House of Commons of 1685: A Study of the Membership and Politics of the Only Parliament of King James II. UCLA 1967

B82 Barsky, Arthur. The Thoughts of Coleridge on the Events of His Times with Some Possible Influence of His Thoughts on History. UCLA 1964

B83 Barsness, Richard W. The Maritime Development of San Pedro Bay, California, 1821-1921. Minn 1963

B84 Bartee, Wayne C. Theodor von Schoen and the Prussian Reform Era, 1793-1809. Columbia 1966

B85 Barth, Gunther P. Bitter Strength: A History of the Chinese in the United States, 1850-1870. Harvard 1962

B86 Bartholomew, Francis M., Jr. The Petrashevskii Circle. Princeton 1969

B87 Bartley, Numan V., Jr. The Rise of Massive Resistance: Race and Politics in the South during the 1950's. Vanderbilt 1968

B88 Bartlow, Robert M. The Low-Church Movement in Elizabethan Anglicanism. Chicago 1967

B89 Barton, Hildor A. Count Hans Axel von Fersen: A Political Biography to 1800. Princeton 1962

B90 Barton, Tom K. Politics and Banking in Republican Kentucky, 1805-1824. Wis 1968

B91 Bartus, M. Raimonde, Sister. The Presidential Election of 1836. Fordham 1967

B92 Barzillay, Phyllis. Stephanus de Lingua-tonte: Studies in the Sermons of Stephen Langton (*ca.* 1155-1228). Columbia 1966

B93 Basalla, George. Science and Government in England, 1800-1870. Harvard 1964

B94 Basil, John D. Political Decisions Made by the Menshevik Leaders in Petrograd during the Revolution of 1917. Wash U 1966

B95 Bassett, John H. The Purchase System in the British Army, 1660-1871. Boston U 1969

B96 Bassett, Michael E. R. The Socialist Party of America, 1912-1919: Years of Decline. Duke 1964

B97 Bassler, Gerhard P. The Origins of German Communism, 1900-1917. Kans U 1966

B98 Bast, Benjamin F. The Soviet Leaders and Planning, 1928-1934. Pitt 1963

B99 Batinski, Michael C. Jonathan Belcher of Massachusetts, 1682-1741. Northwestern 1969

B100 Batman, Richard D. The Road to the Presidency: Hoover, Johnson, and the California Republican Party, 1920-1924. S Cal 1966

B101 Battick, John. Cromwell's Navy and the Foreign Policy of the Protectorate, 1653-1658. Boston U 1967

B102   Batzel, Victor M.   Sir Henry James Sumner Maine: A Study in Naturalistic Law. Ia 1967

B103   Bauer, Arnold J.   Chilean Rural Society in the Nineteenth Century. Cal, Berkeley 1969

B104   Bauer, Wolfred.   The Shipment of American Strategic Raw Materials to Nazi Germany: A Study in United States Economic Foreign Policy, 1933-1939. Wash U 1964

B105   Baughman, James P.   The Maritime and Railroad Interests of Charles Morgan, 1837-1885: A History of the "Morgan Line." Tulane 1962

B106   Baum, Emmi.   Empress Leopoldina: Her Role in the Development of Brazil, 1817-1826. NYU 1965

B107   Bauman, Harold.   The Historiography of Carl L. Becker. Ia 1964

B108   Bauman, John F.   The City, the Depression, and Relief: The Philadelphia Experience, 1929- 1939. Rutgers 1969

B109   Baumgardner, James L.   Andrew Johnson and the Patronage. Tenn 1968

B110   Bausum, Henry S.   Primitivism in English Books on the New World, 1511-1626. Chicago 1963

B111   Baxter, Colin F.   Admiralty Problems during the Second Palmerston Administration, 1859-1865. Ga 1965

B112   Baxter, Craig.   The Jana Sangh: A Biography of an Indian Political Party. Penn U 1967

B113   Baydo, Gerald R.   Cattle Ranching in Territorial New Mexico. NM 1970

B114   Bayor, Ronald H.   Ethnic Conflict in New York City, 1929-1941. Penn U 1970

B115   Bazillion, Richard J.   Karl Biedermann: The Making of a National Liberal, 1837-1871. Wis 1970

B116   Beach, Frank.   The Transformation of California, 1900-1920: The Effects of the Westward Movement on California's Growth and Development in the Progressive Period. Cal, Berkeley 1963

B117   Beal, Annabel L.   The Populist Party in Custer County, Nebraska: Its Role in Local, State, and National Politics, 1889-1906. Neb 1965

B118   Beal, Tarcísio.   *Os Jesuítas, A Universidade de Coimbra e a Igrija* Brasileira: *Subsídios para a História do Regalismo em Portugal e no Brasil, 1750-1850.* Cath 1969

B119   Bean, Geraldine B.   Charles Boettcher: A Study in Pioneer Western Enterprise. Colo 1970

B120   Beardsley, Edward H.   Portrait of a Scientist: The Professional Career of Harry Luman Russell. Wis 1966

B121   Beasley, Paul W.   The Life and Times of Isaac Shelby, 1750-1826. Ky 1968

B122   Beasley, Troy W.   Anglo-American Relations during the Second Gladstone Administration, 1880-1885. Ga 1965

B123   Beattie, Donald W.   Sons of Temperance: Poineers in Total Abstinence and "Constitutional" Prohibition. Boston U 1966

B124   Beatty, David P.   The Canada-United States Permanent Joint Board on Defense. Mich S 1969

B125   Beatty, Hubert I.   Why Form a More Perfect Union? A Study of the Origins of the Constitutional Convention 1787. Stanford 1962

B126   Beaver, Roy D.   A Progressive at War: Newton D. Baker and the American War Effort, 1917-1918. Northwestern 1962

B127   Beck, Kathryn Jane.   The Early Career of the Fifth Duke of Newcastle, 1833-1852. Case W Reserve 1961

B128   Beck, Paul L.   Daniel Drake and the Interior Valley. Neb 1961

B129   Becker, Christopher B.   The Church School in Tsarist Social and Educational Policy, from Peter to the Great Reforms. Harvard 1965

B130   Becker, Seymour.   Russia's Central Asian Protectorates: Bukhara and Khiva, 1865-1917. Harvard 1963

B131   Becker, William H.   The Wholesalers of Hardware and Drugs, 1870-1900. JH 1969

B132   Beckham, Stephen D.   George Gibbs, 1815-1873: Historian and Ethnologist. UCLA 1969

B133   Beddow, James B.   Economic Nationalism or Internationalism: Upper Midwestern Response to New Deal Tariff Policy, 1934-1940. Okla 1969

B134   Bedford, Henry F.   The Socialist Movement in Massachusetts, 1890-1913. Mass 1965

B135   Beecher, Jonathan F.   Charles Fourier and His Early Writings, 1800-1820. Harvard 1968

B136   Beeman, Richard R.   The Old Dominion and the New Nation, 1788-1801. Chicago 1968

B137 Beer, Barrett L. A Study of John Dudley, Duke of Northumberland and His Family. Northwestern 1965

B137a Beesley, David. The Politics of Bankruptcy in the United States, 1837-1945. Utah 1968

B138 Beezley, William H. Revolutionary Governor: Abraham González and the Mexican Revolution in Chihuahua, 1909-1913. Neb 1968

B139 Begnaud, Allen E. British Operations in the Caribbean and the American Revolution. Tulane 1966

B140 Behrends, Frederick O. Bishop Fulbert and the Diocese of Chartres (1006-1028). NC 1962

B141 Behrman, Cynthia F. The Mythology of British Imperialism, 1880-1914. Boston U 1965

B142 Beier, A. Leon. Studies in Poverty and Poor Relief in Warwickshire, 1540-1680. Princeton 1969

B143 Beik, William H. Governing Languedoc: The Practical Functioning of Absolutism in a French Province, 1633-1685. Harvard 1969

B144 Beinfeld, Solon. Guizot, Metternich and the Conservative Entente, 1846-1848. Harvard 1961

B145 Beisel, David R. The Bavarian Nobility in the Seventeenth Century: A Socio-Political Study. NYU 1969

B146 Beisner, Robert L. The Anti-Imperialist Impulse: The Mugwumps and the Republicans, 1898-1900. Chicago 1965

B147 Beitscher, Jane K. Feudal Society in the Limousin, 850-1124. Wis 1969

B148 Beitzell, Robert E. Major Strategic Conferences of the Allies, 1941-1943: Quadrant, Moscow, Sextant and Eureka. NC 1967

B149 Bell, John D. The Agrarian Movement in Bulgaria, 1899-1918. Princeton 1970

B150 Bell, John L. Constitutions and Politics: Constitutional Revision in the South Atlantic States, 1864-1902. NC 1970

B151 Bell, John P. The Costa Rican Revolution of 1948. Tulane 1968

B152 Bell, Leland V. Anatomy of a Hate Movement: The German American Bund, 1936-1941. W Va 1968

B153 Bell, Robert G. James C. Malin: A Study in American Historiography. UCLA 1968

B154 Bell, Rudolph M. Politics and Factions, 1789-1801. CUNY 1969

B155 Bell, Sidney. Woodrow Wilson and the Evolution of the New Diplomacy. Wis 1969

B156 Bellot, Leland J. Mr. Secretary Knox: A Biographical Study of an Eighteenth-Century Civil Servant. Tex U 1967

B157 Belz, Herman J. Reconstructing the Union: Conflicts of Theory and Policy during the Civil War. Wash U 1966

B158 Benert, Richard R. Inferior Magistrates in Sixteenth-Century Political and Legal Thought. Minn 1967

B159 Benincasa, Frederick A. An Analysis of the Historical Development of the Tennessee Valley Authority from 1933 to 1961. St John's 1961

B160 Benjamin, Philip S. The Philadelphia Quakers in the Industrial Age, 1865-1920. Columbia 1967

B161 Bennet, Douglas J., Jr. The Idea of Kingship in 17th Century Russia. Harvard 1968

B162 Bennett, David H. The Demagogues' Appeal in the Depression: The Origins and Activities of the Union Party, 1932-1936. Chicago 1963

B163 Bennett, Edward M. Franklin D. Roosevelt and Russian-American Relations, 1933-1939. Ill 1961

B164 Bennett, James D., II. Struggle for Power: The Relationship between the Tennessee Valley Authority and the Private Power Industry. Vanderbilt 1969

B165 Bennett, Norman R. The Arab Power of Tanganyika in the Ninteenth Century. Boston U 1961

B166 Bennish, Leroy J. The Stamp Act Congress. Duke 1967

B167 Benowitz, Elliot. B. N. Chicherin: Rationalism and Liberalism in Nineteenth-Century Russia. Wis 1966

B168 Benson, Maxine F. Edwin James: Scientist, Linguist, Humanitarian. Colo 1968

B169 Benson, Sumner. Boris Chicherin and the Dilemma of Russian Liberalism. Harvard 1968

B170 Bensusan, H. Guy. The Spanish Struggle against Foreign Encroachment in the Caribbean, 1675-1697. UCLA 1970

B171 Bentley, Elna-Jean. The Formulary of Thomas Hoccleve. Emory 1965

B172 Benton, William A. The Whig-Loyalists: An Aspect of Political Ideology in the American Revolutionary Era. Penn U 1965

B173 Berberet, William G. The Evolution of a New Deal Agricultural Program: Soil Conservation Districts and Comprehensive Land and Water Development in Nebraska. Neb 1970

B174 Berdahl, Robert M. The Transformation of the Prussian Conservative Party, 1866-1876. Minn 1965

B175 Berg, Meredith W. The United States and the Breakdown of Naval Limitation, 1934-1939. Tulane 1966

B176 Berg, Walter L. Nathaniel Southgate Shaler: A Critical Study of an Earth Scientist. Wash U 1957

B177 Berge, Dennis E. Mexican Response to United States' Expansionism, 1841-1848. Cal, Berkeley 1965

B178 Berge, William H. The Impulse for Expansion: John W. Burgess, Alfred Thayer Mahan, Theodore Roosevelt, Josiah Strong, and the Development of a Rationale. Vanderbilt 1969

B179 Bergen, Madelyn U. The *Sachsenspiegel:* A Preliminary Study for a Translation. Ohio 1966

B180 Berger, Carl C. The Vision of Grandeur: Studies in the Ideas of Canadian Imperialism, 1867-1914. Toronto 1967

B181 Berger, Henry W. Union Diplomacy: American Labor's Foreign Policy in Latin America, 1932-1955. Wis 1966

B182 Berger, Martin E. War, Armies, and Revolution: Friedrich Engels' Military Thought. Pitt 1969

B183 Bergeron, Paul H. The Jacksonian Party on Trial: Presidential Politics in Tennessee, 1836-1856. Vanderbilt 1965

B184 Bergkamp, Joseph U. Dom Jean Mabillon and the Benedictine Historical School of St. Maur. Cath 1928

B185 Bergman, Andrew L. Depression America and Its Movies. Wis 1970

B186 Bergmann, Joyce M. The Provincial Assemblies of Roman Africa. Md 1967

B187 Bergquist, Harold E., Jr. Russian-American Relations, 1820-1830: The Diplomacy of Henry Middleton, American Minister at St. Petersburg. Boston U 1970

B188 Bergquist, James M. The Political Attitudes of the German Immigrant in Illinois, 1848-1860. Northwestern 1966

B189 Beringer, Richard E. Political Factionalism in the Confederate Congress. Northwestern 1966

B190 Berkman, Joyce A. Pacificism in England, 1914-1939. Yale 1967

B191 Berlatsky, Joel A. The Social Structure of the Elizabethan Episcopacy, 1558-1603. Northwestern 1970

B192 Berlin, Ira. Slaves Who Were Free: The Free Negro in the Upper South, 1776-1861. Wis 1970

B193 Berls, Janet W. The Elementary School Reforms of Maria Theresa and Joseph II in Bohemia. Columbia 1970

B194 Berman, Myron. The Attitude of American Jewry towards East European Jewish Immigration, 1881-1914. Columbia 1963

B195 Berman, Sylvan M. Hitler: A Study of Ideology and "Realpolitik" in German-Soviet Relations, 1938-1941. Am 1962

B196 Berman, William C. The Politics of Civil Rights in the Truman Administration. Ohio 1963

B197 Bernath, Stuart. Squall across the Atlantic: American Civil War Prize Cases and Diplomacy. Cal, Santa Barbara 1968

B198 Berner, Samuel J. The Florentine Patriciate in the Transition from Republic to Principato, 1530-1610. Cal, Berkeley 1969

B199 Bernhard, Winfred E. A. Fisher Ames, Spokesman of Federalism, 1758-1797. Columbia 1961

B200 Bernstein, Alvin H. The Rural Crisis in Italy and the *Lex Agraria* of 133 B. C. Cornell 1969

B201 Bernstein, Arthur I. The Rise of the Democratic-Republican Party in New York City, 1789-1800. Columbia 1964

B202 Bernstein, Barton J. The Truman Administration and the Politics of Inflation. Harvard 1964

B202a Bernstein, David A. New Jersey and the American Revolution: The Establishment of a Government Amid Civil and Military Disorder, 1770-1781. Rutgers 1970

B203 Bernstein, David J. Youth and Society in Elizabethan London. Harvard 1970

B204 Bernstein, Gail L. Kawakami Hajime: Portrait of a Reluctant Revolutionary. Harvard 1968

B205 Bernstein, John A. Beauty and the Law: Shaftesbury's Relation to Christianity and the Enlightenment. Harvard 1970

B206 Bernstein, Leonard H. Alexander Hamilton and Political Factions in New York to 1787. NYU 1970

B206a   Bernstein, Richard M.   The *Anschluss* Question in Weimar Politics. Princeton 1969

B207   Berrigan, Joseph R., Jr.   Benzo D'Alessandria and the Cities of Italy. Tulane 1963

B208   Berrol, Selma C.   Immigrants at School: New York City, 1898-1914. CUNY 1967

B209   Berry, Charles R.   The Reform in the Central District of Oaxaca, 1856-1867: A Case Study. Tex U 1967

B210   Berry, M. Frances, Sister.   The Negro Soldier Movement and the Adoption of National Conscription, 1652-1865. Mich U 1966

B211   Berry, M. Francis, Sister.   Exposition of British Welfare Liberalism. St L 1966

B213   Bertels, Thomas More, Sister.   The National Grange: Progressives on the Land, 1900-1930. Cath 1962

B214   Bertrand, Charles L.   Revolutionary Syndicalism in Italy, 1912-1922. Wis 1969

B215   Berwanger, Eugene H.   Western Anti-Negro Sentiment and Laws, 1846-1860: A Factor in the Slavery Extension Controversy. Ill 1964

B216   Best, Henry B. M.   George-Étienne Cartier. Laval 1969

B217   Betanzos, Ramon J.   Franz von Baader's Philosophy of Love. Mich U 1968

B218   Betcherman, Lita-Rose.   Balthazar Gerbier: A Renaissance Man in Early Stuart England. Toronto 1969

B219   Betten, Neil B.   Catholicism and the Industrial Worker during the Great Depression. Minn 1968

B220   Beuttenmuller, Paul A.   The Secularization of Divine Providence in the Cartesian Age. St L 1964

B221   Beveridge, Charles E.   Frederick Law Olmstead: The Formative Years, 1822-1865. Wis 1966

B222   Beyer, Barry K.   Thomas E. Dewey, 1937-1947: A Study in Political Leadership. Rochester 1962

B223   Beyerl, Richard F.   The National Liberals and the Socialist Law in 1878. Ind 1969

B224   Bezucha, Robert J.   Association and Insurrection: The Republican Party and the Worker Movement in Lyon, 1831-1835. Mich U 1968

B225   Bibber, Joyce K.   The Chinese Communists as Viewed by the American Periodical Press, 1920-1937. Stanford 1969

B226   Bicha, Karel D.   Canadian Immigration Policy and the American Farmer, 1896-1914. Minn 1963

B227   Bienvenu, Richard T.   Work Humanized and Man. Regenerated: The Idea of Work in Saint-Simon, the Saint-Simonians and Fourier. Harvard 1965

B228   Bigler, Robert M.   The Political Leaders of the Protestant Clergy in Prussia, 1815-1847. Cal, Berkeley 1964

B229   Bikle, George B., Jr.   The New Jerusalem: Aspects of Utopianism in the Thought of Kagawa Toyohiko. Cal, Berkeley 1968

B230   Bilderback, Dean L.   The Membership of the Council of Basle. Wash U 1966

B231   Billings, Warren M.   "Virginias Deploured Condition," 1660-1676: The Coming of Bacon's Rebellion. N Ill 1968

B232   Billingsley, Edward B.   The United States Navy and the Independence of Latin America: Chile and Peru, 1817-1825. NC 1965

B233   Bilstein, Roger E.   Prelude to the Air Age: Civil Aviation in the United States, 1919-1929. Ohio 1965

B234   Binder, John F.   The Social Context of Selected English Periodicals, 1760-1815: A Quantitative Profile of Their Contributors and Content. Northwestern 1970

B235   Bindler, Norman.   American Socialism and the First World War. NYU 1970

B236   Binford, Joseph N.   The Politics of Horace Walpole. Ky 1966

B237   Bing, John D.   A History of Cilicia during the Assyrian Period. Ind 1969

B238   Binning, Francis W.   Henry Clay Warmoth and Louisiana Reconstruction. NC 1969

B239   Birchler, Allen B.   The Influence of the Scottish Clergy on Politics, 1616-1638. Neb 1966

B240   Birdsell, Dale.   United States Army Chemical Warfare Service Logistics Overseas, World War II. Penn U 1962

B241   Birn, Donald S.   Britain and France at the Washington Conference, 1921-1922. Columbia 1964

B242   Birn, Raymond F.   Pierre Rousseau and the *Philosophes* of Bouillon. Ill 1961

B243   Birnbaum, Lucille T.   Behaviorism: John Broadus Watson and American Social Thought, 1913-1933. Cal, Berkeley 1964

B244 Birnbaum, Norman. Communist China's Policy toward Her Minority Nationalities, 1950-1965. St John's 1970

B245 Bisceglia, Louis R. Norman Angell: Knighthood to Nobel Prize, 1931-1935. Ball State 1967

B246 Bischoff, Henry C. The Reformers, the Workers, and the Growth of Positive Government: A History of the Labor Legislation Movement in New York State, 1865-1915. Chicago 1964

B247 Bischoff, William L. Artists, Intellectuals, and Revolution: Munich, 1918-1919. Harvard 1970

B248 Bishop, David W. Railroad Decisions of the Interstate Commerce Commission, 1887-1950: Their Guiding Principles. Cath 1962

B249 Bittle, George C. In the Defense of Florida: The Organized Florida Militia from 1821 to 1920. Fla S 1965

B250 Bitton, Ronald D. The French Nobility as Seen by Contemporaries, 1560-1630. Princeton 1961

B251 Bjelovucic, Harriet T. The Ragusan Republic: Victim of Napoleon and Its Own Conservatism. Columbia 1964

B252 Bjorgan, G. Rudolph. The Success Story of an Immigrant. Minn 1967

B253 Black, Anthony R. An Edition of the Cavendish Irish Parliamentary Diary, 1776-1778. Notre D 1969

B254 Black, Frederick R. The Last "Lords Proprietors" of West Jersey: The West Jersey Society, 1692-1702. Rutgers 1964

B255 Black, John B. The Changing Place of the Monarchy in British National Life in the Last Third of the Nineteenth Century. Columbia 1965

B256 Black, Joseph L. N. M. Karamzin as an Historian. McGill 1968

B257 Blackburn, Charles B. Military Opposition to Official State Department Policy Concerning the Mexican Intervention, 1862-1867. Ball State 1969

B258 Blackey, Robert A. The Political Career of George Montagu Dunk, 2nd Earl of Halifax, 1748-1771: A Study of an Eighteenth Century English Minister. NYU 1968

B259 Blackmon, Dora E. The Care of the Mentally Ill in America, 1604-1812, in the Thirteen Original Colonies. Wash U 1964

B260 Blackmon, Joab L., Jr. Judge Samuel Sewall, 1652-1730: A Biography. Wash U 1964

B261 Blackmore, John T. The Life Work and Influence of Ernst Mach. UCLA 1970

B262 Blaine, Bradford B. The Application of Waterpower to Industry during the Middle Ages. UCLA 1965

B263 Blair, Leon B. Western Window in the Arab World. Tex C 1968

B264 Blakely, Brian L. The Colonial Office, 1870-1890. Duke 1966

B265 Blakey, Arch F. A History of the Florida Phosphate Industry, 1888-1966. Fla S 1967

B266 Blakey, George T., Jr. Historians on the Homefront: Propagandists for the Great War. Ind 1970

B267 Blanco, Enrique G. The Rule of the Military Order of St. James. Chicago 1967

B268 Bland, James E. The Oliver Wolcotts of Connecticut: The National Experience, 1775-1800. Harvard 1970

B269 Blanke, Richard D. Prussian Polish Policy and the Polish Minority in Prussia under Bismarck and Caprivi, 1886-1894. Cal, Berkeley 1970

B270 Blankenship, Warren M. Progressives and the Progressive Party in Oregon, 1906-1916. Ore 1966

B271 Blanshei, Sarah R. Perugia: A Study of Medieval Urban Growth. Bryn Mawr 1970

B272 Blanton, Silas W., Jr. Virginia in the 1920's: An Economic and Social Profile. Va 1969

B273 Blantz, Thomas E. Francis J. Haas: Priest in Government Service. Columbia 1968

B274 Blazsik, Gloria E. Theodore Roosevelt's Far Eastern Policy and the T'ang Shao-yi Mission. Georgetown 1969

B275 Blecker, Paulin M. The Two Laws and Benedictine Monasticism: A Study in Benedictine Government, 1198-1216. Wis 1964

B276 Bledsoe, Wayne M. Problems in Medieval Historiography: A Selective Study. Mich S 1969

B277 Bledstein, Burton J. Cultivation and Custom: The Idea of Liberal Culture in Post-Civil War America. Princeton 1967

B278 Bleser, Carol R. The South Carolina Land Commission: A Study of a Reconstruction Institution. Columbia 1966

B279 Blewett, Peter F. The Gallicanism of L.-E. Du Pin. Boston C 1969

B280   Block, John M.   British Opinion of Prussian Policy, 1854-1866. Wis 1969

B281   Block, Robert H.   Southern Opinion of Woodrow Wilson's Foreign Policies, 1913-1917. Duke 1968

B282   Blocker, Jack S., Jr.   From Party to League: Changes within the American Prohibition Movement, 1890-1913. Wis 1970

B283   Blodgett, Geoffrey T.   Massachusetts Democrats in the Cleveland Era. Harvard 1961

B284   Blomquist, Thomas W.   Trade and Commerce in Thirteenth Century Lucca. Minn 1966

B285   Bloom, Florence T.   The Political Career of William Bourke Cockran. CUNY 1970

B286   Bloom, Jeanne G.   Sir Edmund Andros: A Study in Seventeenth Century Colonial Administration. Yale 1962

B287   Bloomberg, Paula.   Hermann Rauschning and the German Emigration. NM 1967

B288   Bloomfield, Edith.   Soviet Historiography of 1905 as Reflected in Party Histories of the 1920's. Wash U 1966

B289   Bloomfield, Maxwell H., III.   The American Mind as Reflected in Representative American Magazines, 1900-1914. Tulane 1962

B290   Blue, Frederick J.   A History of the Free Soil Party. Wis 1966

B291   Blum, George P.   German Social Democracy in the Reichstag, 1890-1914. Minn 1962

B292   Blumenthal, Michael D.   The Economic Good Neighbor: Aspects of United States Economic Policy toward Latin America in the Early 1940's as Revealed by the Activities of the Office of Inter-American Affairs. Wis 1968

B293   Boatman, Ellis G.   Evolution of a President: The Political Apprenticeship of Warren G. Harding. SC 1966

B294   Boba, Imre.   Nomads in the Formation of the Kievan State. Wash U 1962

B295   Bocage, Leo J.   The Public Career of Charles R. Crane. Fordham 1962

B296   Bock, Edward C.   Wilhelm Emmanuel Von Ketteler: His Social and Political Philosophy. Okla 1967

B297   Bockelman, Wayne L.   Continuity and Change in Revolutionary Pennsylvania: A Study of County Government and Officeholders. Northwestern 1969

B298   Bode, Frederick A.   Southern White Protestantism and the Crisis of the New South: North Carolina, 1894-1903. Yale 1969

B299   Bodenstedt, M. Immaculate, Sister.   The Study of the *De Vita Christi* of Ludolphus the Carthusian. Cath 1944

B300   Bodet, Gerald P.   The Meaning of Treason in Seventeenth Century England. Tulane 1963

B301   Bödy, Paul.   Baron Joseph Eötvös and the Reconstruction of the Habsburg Monarchy, 1840-1867. Notre D 1964

B302   Boeck, George A.   An Early Iowa Community: Aspects of Economic, Social and Political Development in Burlington, Iowa, 1833-1866. Ia 1961

B303   Boerner, Barbara W.   The United States and Weimar Germany, 1919-1929. Wis 1961

B304   Bogue, James F.   Tiberius in the Reign of Augustus. Ill 1970

B305   Bohachevsky-Chomiak, Martha.   Sergei N. Trubetskoi: A Study in the Russian Intelligentsia. Columbia 1968

B306   Bohon, John W.   Reactionary Politics in Russia, 1905-1909. NC 1967

B307   Boles, John B.   The Religious Mind of the Old South: The Era of the Great Revival, 1787-1805. Va 1969

B308   Bolitho, Harold.   The Fudai Daimyo in the Tokugawa Settlement. Yale 1969

B309   Boll, Michael M.   The Social and Political Philosophy of Semen L. Frank: A Study in Prerevolutionary Twentieth-Century Russian Liberalism. Wis 1970

B310   Bolt, Ernest C., Jr.   The War Referendum Approach to Peace in Twentieth Century America: A Study in Foreign Policy and Military Defense Attitudes. Ga 1966

B311   Bolt, Robert.   A Biography of Donald M. Dickinson. Mich S 1963

B312   Bonadio, Felice A.   Ohio Politics during Reconstruction, 1865-1868. Yale 1964

B313   Bonar, James A.   Benjamin Rush and the Theory and Practice of Republican Education in Pennsylvania. JH 1965

B314   Bond, Gordon C.   The British Expedition to the Scheldt in 1809. Fla S 1966

B315   Bonds, William N.   Money and Prices in Medieval Genoa (1155-1255). Wis 1968

B316 Bone, Christopher. Literature of Political Commitment in Britain between the Wars: Michael Roberts, Stephen Spender, W. H. Auden. Chicago 1969

B317 Boney, Francis N. The Life of John Letcher, Virginia's Civil War Governor. Va 1963

B318 Bonnell, Robert A. The Career and Thought of Coluccio Salutati. Case W Reserve 1964

B319 Bonner, Robert E. Administration and Public Service under the Early Stuarts: Edward Viscount Conway as Secretary of State, 1623-1628. Minn 1968

B320 Bonomi, Patricia. A Factious People: Chapters in the History and Historiography of Colonial New York Politics. Columbia 1970

B321 Bonwick, Colin C. English Radicals and the American Revolution. Md 1969

B322 Bonwick, Mary H. R. The Radicalism of Sir Francis Burdett (1770-1844) and Early Nineteenth-Century "Radicalisms." Cornell 1967

B323 Booth, Alan R. Americans in South Africa, 1784-1870. Boston U 1964

B324 Boothe, Leon E. Woodrow Wilson's Cold War: The President, the Public, and the League Fight, 1919-1920. Ill 1966

B325 Borden, Philip J. Rite Words in Rote Order: Rankean History in America, 1870-1900. Wayne 1968

B326 Borg, Daniel R. The Politics of the Prussian Church, 1917-1927: A Study of the Political Thought and Action of German Protestants in the Weimar Republic. Yale 1963

B327 Borit, Gabor S. Lincoln and the Economics of the American Dream: The Whig Years, 1832-1854. Boston U 1968

B328 Born, John D., Jr. British Trade in West Florida, 1763-1783. NM 1963

B329 Borne, Lawrence R. Colonel James A. Ownbey and the Wootton Land and Fuel Company. Colo 1970

B330 Borza, Eugene N. *Diodorus Siculus:* A Study of the Seventeenth Book. Chicago 1966

B331 Bosch, Allan W. The Salvation Army in Chicago, 1885-1914. Chicago 1965

B332 Bosch, William J. Judgment on Nuremberg: American Attitudes toward the Major War Crimes Trials. NC 1966

B333 Boss, Ronald I. Rousseau's Answer to Bayle's Paradox: The Civil Religion and the Meaning of Belief. Columbia 1970

B334 Boss, Valentine J. Newton's Influence in Eighteenth Century Russia. Harvard 1962

B335 Bostic, Theodora P. English Foreign Policy, 1528-1534: The Diplomacy of the Divorce. Ill 1967

B336 Botond-Blazek, Joseph. Puritans and Sex: An Inquiry into the Legal Enforcement of Sexual Morality in 17th Century Massachusetts. UCLA 1962

B337 Bottigheimer, Karl S. The English Interest in Southern Ireland, 1641-1650. Cal, Berkeley 1965

B338 Bottino, Edward J. The Rambler Controversy: Positions of Simpson, Newman and Acton, 1856-1862. St John's 1970

B339 Boudreau, Joseph A. The Enemy Alien Problem in Canada, 1914-1921. UCLA 1965

B340 Boudreaux, Julianna L. A History of Philanthropy in New Orleans, 1835-1862. Tulane 1961

B341 Boughner, D. Terry, Jr. George Read and the Founding of the Delaware State, 1781-1798. Cath 1970

B342 Boulle, Pierre H. The French Colonies and the Reform of Their Administration during and following the Seven Years' War. Cal, Berkeley 1968

B343 Boullianne, Réal G. A Critical Appreciation and Catalogue of Correspondence of the Royal Institution for the Advancement of Learning in the Early 19th Century. McGill 1970

B344 Bourdon, Roger J. George Wharton James, Interpreter of the Southwest. UCLA 1965

B345 Bourguignon, Henry J. The First Federal Court: The History of the Continental Congress' Committees on Appeal and Its Court of Appeals in Cases of Capture, 1775-1787. Mich U 1968

B346 Bourke, Paul F. Culture and the Status of Politics, 1909-1917: Studies in the Social Criticism of Herbert Croly, Walter Lippmann, Randolph Bourne and Van Wyck Brooks. Wis 1967

B347 Bowers, Paul C., Jr. Richard Henry Lee and the Continental Congress, 1774-1779. Duke 1965

B348 Bowers, Richard H. Baronial Reaction and Rebellion: The King's Cause. Miss S 1965

B349 Bowers, William L. Farmers and Reformers in an Urban Age: The Country Life Movement and the "Rural Problem," 1900-1920. Ia 1968

B350 Bowling, Kenneth R. Politics in the First Congress, 1789-1791. Wis 1968

B351 Bowman, Clifford E. The Local Nebraska Press and National Politics, 1896-1908. Neb 1964

B352 Bowman, Larry G. Virginia and the Continental Association, 1774-1776. NM 1967

B353 Bowser, Frederick P., III. Negro Slavery in Colonial Perú, 1529-1650. Cal, Berkeley 1967

B354 Boxall, James A., Jr. Albert Gallatin and American Foreign Policy: A Study in Thought and Action. Mich S 1967

B355 Boxerman, Burton A. Reaction of the St. Louis Jewish Community to Anti-Semitism, 1933-1945. St L 1967

B356 Boxerman, Lawrence H. St. Louis Urban League: History and Activities. St L 1968

B357 Boyer, Hugh E. The Growth of the Fear of France in the Reign of Charles II. Ohio 1969

B358 Boyer, Paul S. The Vice-Society Movement and Book Censorship in America, 1873-1933. Harvard 1966

B359 Boyer, Richard E. English Declarations of Indulgence, 1687 and 1688, and the Revolution. Mo 1961

B360 Boyle, Hugh C. Weimar Defense Minister: Between Government and Reichswehr. Wis 1961

B361 Boyle, James M. The XXI Bomber Command: Primary Factor in the Defeat of Japan. St L 1964

B362 Boyle, John H. Japan's Puppet Regimes in China, 1937-1940. Stanford 1968

B363 Braatz, Werner E. Neo-Conservatism in Crisis at the End of the Weimar Republic: Franz von Papen and the Rise and Fall of the "New State," June to December, 1932. Wis 1969

B364 Brack, Gene M. Imperious Neighbor: The Mexican View of the United States, 1821-1846. Tex U 1967

B365 Bradbury, Miles L. Adventure in Persuasion: John Witherspoon, Samuel Stanhope Smith, and Ashbel Green. Harvard 1967

B366 Bradley, Harold C. Frank P. Walsh and Post War America. St L 1966

B367 Bradley, Robert I. Blacklo: An Essay in Counter-Reform. Columbia 1963

B368 Brady, Robert L. The Emergence of a Negro Class in Mexico, 1524-1640. Ia 1965

B369 Brady, Thomas A., Jr. Jacob Sturm and the Political Security of German Protestantism, 1525-1532. Chicago 1968

B370 Bragdon, Chandler. Canadian Attitudes to the Foreign Policy of the United States in the Period 1935-1939. Rochester 1961

B371 Bragdon, Earl D. The Federal Power Commission and the Regulation of Natural Gas: A Study in Administrative and Judicial History. Ind 1962

B372 Braje, Wilfried. The Foreign Policy of the German SDP, 1949-1957. Clark 1964

B373 Bramble, Max E. Alexander Hamilton and Nineteenth-Century American Historians: A Study of Selected Interpretations of Hamilton. Mich S 1968

B374 Branam, Donald A. Tory Opinion in the Early Nineteenth Century. Cal, Berkeley 1967

B375 Brand, Charles M. Byzantium and the West: Political Relations, 1180-1203. Harvard 1961

B376 Brand, Mary Vivian, Sister. The Social Catholic Movement in England, 1920-1955. St L 1963

B377 Brandes, Raymond S. Frank Hamilton Cushing: Pioneer Americanist. Ariz 1965

B378 Brandes, Stuart D. Welfarism in American Industry, 1880-1940. Wis 1970

B379 Brandfon, Robert L. Planters of the New South: An Economic History of the Yazoo-Mississippi Delta. Harvard 1962

B379a Brandon, Betty J. Alexander Jeffrey McKelway: Statesman of the New Order. NC 1969

B380 Branyan, Robert L. The Antimonopoly Activities during the Truman Administration. Okla 1961

B381 Brashares, Richard A. The Political Career of the Marquess Wellesley in England and Ireland. Duke 1968

B382 Brassel, Kathleen, Sister. The Clausulae in the Works of Gregory the Great. Cath 1939

B383 Bratton, Mary Jo J. John Esten Cooke: The Young Writer and the Old South, 1830-1861. NC 1969

B384 Brauer, Kinley J. Cotton *vs.* Conscience: Massachusetts Whig Politics and Southwestern Expansion, 1843-1848. Cal, Berkeley 1963

B385 Brazill, William J., Jr. The Young Hegelians. Yale 1967

B386 Brechka, Frank T. Gerard van Swieten and His World, 1700-1772. Cal, Berkeley 1968

B387 Breeden, James O. Joseph Jones: Confederate Surgeon. Tulane 1967

B388 Breen, Timothy H. The Character of the Good Ruler: A Study of Puritan Political Ideas in New England, 1630-1730. Yale 1968

B389 Breen, William J. The Council of National Defense: Industrial and Social Mobilization in the United States, 1916-1920. Duke 1968

B390 Breese, Donald H. Politics in the Lower South during Presidential Reconstruction, April to November, 1865. UCLA 1964

B391 Breese, Lauren W. Richard II, Duke of Normandy (996-1026). UCLA 1967

B392 Brehm, Donald L. Monarchy in the Political Thought of Alfonso X, El Sabio of Castile, 1252-1284. St L 1968

B393 Breiseth, Christopher N. British Conservatism and French Revolutions: John Wilson Croker's Attitudes to Reform and Revolution in Britain and France. Cornell 1964

B394 Brenman, Andrew H. Economic Reform in Neuzeit Austria, 1852-1859. Princeton 1966

B395 Brennan, James F. The Origins, Development and Failure of Russian Social-Democratic *Economism,* 1886-1903. Cal, Berkeley 1963

B396 Brennan, John A., Jr. The Senate Silver Bloc and the First New Deal. Colo 1967

B397 Brennan, John J. England in the Foreign Policy of Francis I, 1515-1525. Fordham 1969

B398 Brennan, John W. Liberal State and Italian Nation: England and the Unification of Italy, 1859-1860. Harvard 1966

B399 Brenner, Louis. The Shehus Kukawa: A History of the al-Kanemi Dynasty of Bornu. Columbia 1968

B400 Brenner, Robert P. Commercial Change and Political Conflict: The Merchant Community in Civil War London. Princeton 1970

B401 Brescia, Anthony M. Richard Rush and the French Revolution of 1848. St John's 1968

B402 Breslow, Boyd. The English Sheriff during the Reign of King Edward I. Ohio 1968

B403 Breslow, Marvin A. English Puritan Views of Foreign Nations, 1618 to 1640. Harvard 1963

B405 Brewer, James H. F. Politics in the French Army: The Aftermath of the Dreyfus Case, 1899-1905. Geo W 1967

B406 Brewer, Thomas B. The Formative Period of 140 American Manufacturing Companies, 1789-1929. Penn U 1962

B407 Briceland, Alan V. Ephraim Kirby, Connecticut Jeffersonian, 1757-1804: The Origin of the Jeffersonian Republican Party in Connecticut. Duke 1965

B408 Bridenhagen, Clement F. The Coalition of the North against Rosas. Colo 1970

B409 Bridges, Roger D. The Constitutional World of Senator John Sherman, 1861-1869. Ill 1970

B410 Briggs, Josiah M., Jr. D'Alembert: Mechanics, Matter, and Morals. Columbia 1962

B411 Briggs, Robert L. The Progressive Era in Cleveland, Ohio: Tom L. Johnson's Administration, 1901-1909. Chicago 1962

B412 Bright, Samuel R., Jr. Confederate Coast Defense. Duke 1961

B413 Brill, Earl H. Religion and the Rise of the University: A Study of the Secularization of American Higher Education, 1870-1910. Am 1969

B414 Brill, Reginald. An English Captain in the Later Hundred Years War: John, Lord Talbot, c. 1388-1444. Princeton 1966

B415 Brilliant, Ashleigh E. Social Effects of the Automobile in Southern California during the Nineteen-Twenties. Cal, Berkeley 1964

B416 Brinks, Herbert J. Peter White: A Career of Business and Politics in an Industrial Frontier Community. Mich U 1965

B417 Broder, Harry M. Robert Lowe, His Career and Ideas. Case W Reserve 1962

B418 Brodhead, Michael J. Judge Frank Doster: Kansas Populist and Reform Ideologue. Minn 1967

B419 Broesamle, John J. William Gibbs McAdoo: Businessman in Politics, 1863-1917. Columbia 1969

B420 Brogden, Neal H. French Military Reform after the Defeat of 1870-1871. UCLA 1961

B421 Brooks, Courtney G. American Aeronautics as Spectacle and Sport. Tulane 1969

B422 Brooks, E. Willis. D. A. Miliutin: Life and Activity to 1856. Stanford 1970

B423 Brooks, George E., Jr. America's Legitimate Trade with West Africa, 1789-1914. Boston U 1962

B424 Brooks, Robin. Melancton Smith: New York Anti-Federalist, 1744-1798. Rochester 1964

B425 Brookshire, Jerry H. British Labour Recovering: Labour between the General Election of 1931 and 1935. Vanderbilt 1970

B426 Broussard, James H. The Federalist Party in the South Atlantic States, 1800-1812. Duke 1968

B427 Browder, George C. SIPO and SD, 1931-1940: Formation of an Instrument of Power. Wis 1968

B428 Brower, Daniel R., Jr. The French Communist Party and the Popular Front, 1934-1938. Columbia 1963

B429 Brown, Ben F. Sidney Sonnino, 1847-1922: The Stranger in Two Worlds. Harvard 1966

B430 Brown, Charles R. The Northern Confederacy According to the Plans of the Essex Junto, 1796-1814. Princeton 1913

B431 Brown, D. Peter. The Economic Views of Illinois Democrats, 1836-1861. Boston U 1970

B432 Brown, Dorothy M. Party Battles and Beginnings in Maryland, 1786-1812. Georgetown 1962

B433 Brown, Elizabeth A. R. Charters and Leagues in Early Fourteenth Century France: The Movement of 1314 and 1315. Radcliffe 1961

B434 Brown, Emily C. Har Dayal: A Portrait of an Indian Intellectual. Ariz 1967

B435 Brown, Frederick D. The British Conservative Unionist Party, Tariff Reform, and the Election of 1906: An Interpretation. Penn U 1967

B436 Brown, H. Haines III. Archbishop Hincmar of Rheims (ca. 806-882): His Idea of *Ministerium* in Theory and *Praxis*. Mich S 1968

B437 Brown, Harold O. J. John Laski, A Theological Biography: A Polish Contribution to the Protestant Reformation. Harvard 1967

B438 Brown, Ian. The Anglican Evangelicals in British Politics, 1780-1833. Lehigh 1965

B439 Brown, Irene Q. Politics and Renaissance Educational Reform: Toulouse and the Founding of Its Municipal *Collège*, 1500-1565. Harvard 1969

B440 Brown, Jerome F. Five Somerset Families, 1590-1640. Cal, Berkeley 1966

B441 Brown, John E. Business and the Education of a Gentleman in Late Victorian England. Stanford 1966

B442 Brown, John L. The *Methodus ad Facilem Historiarum Cognitionem* of Jean Bodin: A Critical Study. Cath 1939

B443 Brown, Katharine B. L. The Role of Presbyterian Dissent in Colonial and Revolutionary Virginia, 1740-1785. JH 1969

B444 Brown, Lawrence H. The Grafton and North Cabinets, 1766-1775. Toronto 1963

B445 Brown, Letitia W. Free Negroes in the Original District of Columbia. Harvard 1966

B446 Brown, Mark N. George Savile, Marquis of Halifax, 1633-1695. Harvard 1964

B447 Brown, Martha F. The Foreign Policy of Henry VIII, 1536-1547. Northwestern 1970

B448 Brown, Michael J. The Life of Sir Thomas Roe, 1580-1644. Emory 1964

B449 Brown, Nicolette F. Ultra-Royalist Deputies in the *Chambre Introuvable,* 1815-1816. Duke 1969

B450 Brown, Norman D. Edward Stanly: Federal Whig. NC 1963

B451 Brown, Richard D. The Boston Committee of Correspondence in the Revolution, 1772-1774. Harvard 1966

B452 Brown, Robert C. Canadian-American Relations in the Latter Part of the Nineteenth Century. Toronto 1962

B453 Brown, Roger G. The Dreyfus Affair and Fashoda: A Study of the Interaction of Domestic and International Politics, 1893-1898. Cal, Berkeley 1968

B454 Brown, Spencer H. A History of the People of Lagos, 1852-1886. Northwestern 1964

B455 Brown, Wallace. The Structure of Loyalism during the American Revolution. Cal, Berkeley 1964

B456 Brown, Wilburt S. The Amphibious Campaign for New Orleans, 1814-1815. Ala 1963

B457 Brown, William A. The Caliphate of Hamdullahi, *ca.* 1818-1864: A Study in African History and Tradition. Wis 1969

B458 Brownback, Annadrue H. Congressional and Insular Opposition to Puerto Rican Autonomy. Ala 1966

B459 Browne, Patrick W. Beginnings of the Catholic Church in the United States. Cath 1922

B460 Brownell, Blaine A. The Urban Mind in the South: The Growth of Urban Consciousness in Southern Cities, 1920-1927. NC 1969

B461 Browning, Reed S. The Duke of Newcastle and the King of the Romans Election Plan, 1749-1754. Yale 1965

B462   Brownlee, Wilson E.   Progressivism and Economic Growth: The Wisconsin Income Tax, 1911-1929. Wis 1969

B463   Brownsword, Alan W.   Connecticut Political Patterns, 1817-1828. Wis 1962

B464   Bruchey, Eleanor S.   The Business Elite in Baltimore, 1880-1914. JH 1967

B465   Brückmann, John J.   English Coronations, 1216-1308: The Edition of the Coronation *Ordines*. Toronto 1964

B466   Brundage, Anthony L.   The Landed Interest and the Establishment of the New Poor Law in Northamptonshire. UCLA 1970

B467   Brunet, Joseph, Jr.   Science and the Early École Polytechnique, 1794-1806: The Impact of the Early Polytechniciens on the Science of the Eighteenth Century and on the Industrial Revolution in the Nineteenth Century. Ky 1969

B468   Brunk, Gerald R.   The Bishops in Parliament, 1559-1601. Va 1968

B469   Bryan, Anthony T.   Mexican Politics in Transition, 1900-1913: The Role of General Bernardo Reyes. Neb 1970

B470   Bryant, Keith L.   "Alfalfa Bill" Murray: Apostle of Agrarianism. Mo 1965

B471   Brynn, Edward P.   Decline of the Prostestant Ascendancy: The Church of Ireland in the Age of Catholic Emancipation. Stanford 1968

B472   Brynteson, William E.   Roman Law and Legislation in the Middle Ages. Wis 1963

B473   Bryson, Thomas A.   Woodrow Wilson, the Senate, Public Opinion, and the Armenian Mandate Question, 1919-1920. Ga 1965

B474   Buchanan, John N.   Charles I and the Scots, 1637-1649. Toronto 1966

B475   Buckhout, Gerard L.   The Concept of the State in Modern Germany. Northwestern 1962

B476   Buckley, James M.   Diplomatic Background for Byzantine Support of the Papacy at Ferrara Florence, 1438-1439. Geo W 1970

B477   Buckley, Thomas H.   The United States and the Washington Conference, 1921-1922. Ind 1961

B478   Buder, Stanley.   Pullman: An Experiment in Industrial Order and Community Planning, 1880-1930. Chicago 1966

B479   Buel, Richard V., Jr.   Studies in the Political Ideas of the American Revolution, 1760-1776. Harvard 1962

B480   Buenker, John D.   The Adoption of the Income Tax Amendment: Case Study of a Progressive Reform. Georgetown 1964

B481   Bugbee, Bruce W.   The Early American Law of Intellectual Property: The Historical Foundations of the United States Patent and Copyright Systems. Mich U 1961

B482   Buhite, Russell D.   Nelson T. Johnson and American Policy toward China, 1925-1941. Mich S 1965

B483   Buhl, Lance C.   The Smooth Water Navy: American Naval Policy and Politics, 1865-1876. Harvard 1969

B483a   Buice, Sammy D.   The Civil War and the Five Civilized Tribes: A Study in Federal-Indian Relations. Okla 1970

B484   Bujarski, George T.   Polish Liberalism, 1815-1831: The Misplaced Discourse. Harvard 1967

B485   Buker, George E.   Riverine Warfare: Naval Combat in the Second Seminole War, 1835-1842. Fla U 1969

B486   Bukey, Evan B.   The Guelph Movement in Imperial Germany, 1866-1918. Ohio 1969

B487   Bullough, William A.   Urban Education in the Gilded Age, 1876-1906. Cal, Santa Barbara 1970

B488   Bumsted, John M.   The Pilgrims' Progress: The Ecclesiastical History of the Old Colony, 1620-1775. Brown 1965

B489   Buni, Andrew.   The Negro in Virginia Politics, 1902-1950. Va 1965

B490   Buntin, Arthur R.   The Indian in American Literature, 1680 to 1760. Wash U 1961

B491   Bunting, Marie de Chantal, Mother.   Liturgy and Politics in Ninth Century Gaul. Fordham 1967

B492   Burch, Franklin W.   Alaska's Railroad Frontier: Railroads and Federal Development Policy, 1898-1915. Cath 1965

B493   Burdick, Walter E., Jr.   Elite in Transition: From Alienation to Manipulation. N Ill 1969

B494   Burg, Barry R.   Richard Mather (1596-1669): The Life and Work of a Puritan Cleric in New England. Colo 1967

B495   Burggraaff, Winfield J.   Civil-Military Relations in Venezuela: 1935-1959. NM 1967

B496   Burgwin, Howard J., Jr.   Continuity versus Change in Italian Policy toward France, 1932-1936. Pitt 1968

B497 Burke, Albie. Federal Regulation of Congressional Elections in Northern Cities, 1871-1894. Chicago 1968

B498 Burke, Bernard V. American Diplomats and Hitler's Rise to Power, 1930-1933: The Mission of Ambassador Sackett. Wash U 1966

B499 Burke, Frank G. Prince Henry of Prussia and the Revolutionary Era. Chicago 1969

B500 Burke, Gerard F. The Viceroyalty of Lord William Fitzwilliam: A Crisis in Anglo-Irish Political History. Am 1968

B501 Burke, James L. The Public Career of Judson Harmon. Ohio 1969

B502 Burke, John G. The Establishment and Early Development of the Science of Crystallography. Stanford 1962

B503 Burke, Joseph C. William Wirt: Attorney General and Constitutional Lawyer. Ind 1965

B503a Burke, Joseph H. Spain's Attitude toward the War for American Independence. Cath 1909

B504 Burke, Richard T. The German *Panzerwaffe,* 1920-1939: A Study in Institutional Change. Northwestern 1969

B505 Burke, Robert L. Franklin D. Roosevelt and the Far East, 1913-1941. Mich S 1969

B506 Burlingham, Katherine L. "The Necessity of Sound Doctrine": A Study of Calvinism and Its Opponents as Seen in American Religious Periodicals, 1800-1825. Ore 1965

B507 Burner, David B. The Democratic Party in Transition, 1918-1928. Columbia 1965

B508 Burnett, Robert A. Georges Clemenceau in the Paris Peace Conference, 1919. NC 1968

B509 Burnette, Rand. The Quest for Union in the American Colonies, 1689-1701. Ind 1967

B510 Burns, Augustus M., III. North Carolina and the Negro Dilemma, 1930-1950. NC 1969

B511 Burns, E. Bradford. The Unwritten Alliance: Brazilian-American Relations during the Rio-Branco Era, 1902-1912. Columbia 1965

B512 Burns, Helen M. The American Banking Community and New Deal Banking Reform, 1933-1935. NYU 1965

B513 Burns, John F. Controversies between Royal Governors and Their Assemblies in the Northern American Colonies. Cath 1923

B514 Burns, M. François, Sister. Maurice Barrès: Myth-Maker of Modern French Nationalism. Cath 1968

B515 Burns, Paul E. Liberalism without Hope: The Constitutional Democratic Party in the Russian Revolution, February-July, 1917. Ind 1967

B516 Burns, Robert E. The Rise of John Fitzgibbon, 1776-1789: A Study of Anglo-Irish Politics during the Age of the American Revolution. Harvard 1961

B517 Burns, Roy G., Jr. American-Japanese Relations, 1920-1925. Mo 1962

B518 Burnside, Ronald D. The Governorship of Coleman Livingston Blease of South Carolina, 1911-1915. Ind 1963

B519 Burris, Craven A. Arthur James Balfour as a Political Leader: Party, Power, and the Constitution, 1891-1905. Duke 1965

B520 Burton, Robert E. A History of the Democratic Party in Oregon, 1900-1956. Ore 1969

B521 Busch, Briton C. British Policy in the Persian Gulf, 1894-1914. Cal, Berkeley 1965

B522 Buschen, John J. The Making of the Medieval French Constitution, 1180-1314. Ind 1966

B523 Buser, John E. After Half a Generation: The South of the 1880's. Tex U 1968

B524 Bush, John M., III. Disillusioned New Dealers. Miss S 1964

B525 Bush, John W. Napoleon III and the Redeeming of Venetia, 1864-1866. Fordham 1961

B526 Bush, Martin H. Philip Schuyler: The Revolutionary War Years. Syracuse 1966

B527 Bush, Mary T. Representative Nineteenth Century New England Historians View Manifest Destiny. Ottawa 1963

B528 Bush, Robert D. Individualism and the Role of the Individual in British and French Socialism: The Early Years, 1800-1848. Kans U 1969

B529 Bustos-Videla, Cesar. Church and State in Ecuador: A History of Politico-Ecclesiastical Relations during the Age of Gabriel García Moreno, 1860-1875. Georgetown 1966

B530 Butters, Avery J. New Hampshire History and the Public Career of Meshech Weare, 1713 to 1786. Fordham 1961

B531 Buttimer, Charles H. *Didascalicon de Studio Legendi.* Cath 1939

B532   Buzicky, Charles W.   C.C.C.C. MS. 415: An Edition and an Identification. Minn 1967

B533   Byerly, Benjamin F.   Military Administration in Thirteenth Century England: A Study Emphasizing the Contributions of the Wardrobe in the Wars of Henry III and Edward I, 1216-1307. Ill 1965

B534   Bylsma, John R.   Political Issues and Party Unity in the House of Commons, 1852-1857: A Scalogram Analysis. Ia 1968

B535   Bynum, Caroline W. *Docere Verbo et Exemplo:* An Aspect of Twelfth Century Spirituality. Harvard 1969

B536   Byrd, Edward L., Jr.   Paul Déroulède, Revanchist. Tex Tech 1969

B537   Byrne, Mary of the Incarnation, Sister.   The Nun Tradition in Medieval England. Cath 1932

B538   Byrne, Venard J.   Alexander Komulovic, Papal Diplomat, 1593-1598. Fordham 1961

B539   Byrnes, Don R.   The Pre-Revolutionary Career of Provost William Smith, 1751-1780. Tulane 1969

C

C1   Cady, David B.   The Influence of the Garden City Ideal on American Housing and Planning Reform, 1900-1940. Wis 1970

C2   Cahow, Clark R.   The History of the North Carolina Mental Hospitals, 1848-1960. Duke 1967

C3   Caine, Philip D.   The American Periodical Press and Military Preparedness during the Hoover Administration. Stanford 1966

C4   Caine, Stanley P.   Railroad Regulation in Wisconsin, 1903-1910: An Assessment of a Progressive Reform. Wis 1967

C5   Calbert, Jack L.   James Edward and Miriam Amanda Ferguson, the "Ma" and "Pa" of Texas Politics. Ind 1968

C6   Calhoon, Robert M.   Critics of Colonial Resistance in the Pre-Revolutionary Debate, 1763-1776. Case W Reserve 1964

C7   Calhoun, Dougald T.   The Deputies and Revolution: New Views of French Revolutionary Problems, 1789-1791. NC 1969

C8   Calkins, Kenneth R.   Hugo Haase, a Political Biography. Chicago 1966

C9   Calkins, Mary Ann.   The Political Career of Maurice Barrès, 1888-1923: The Trial of a Nationalist Ideology. Bryn Mawr 1968

C10   Call, Paul.   The Revolutionary Activities of the *Kolokol* Group among the Raskolniks. Ind 1964

C11   Callahan, Daniel F.   Benedictine Monasticism in Aquitaine, 935-1030. Wis 1968

C12   Callahan, Marie.   The Gallicanism of Claude Fleury. Boston C 1970

C13   Callahan, Raymond A., Jr.   The Reorganization of the East India Company's Armies, 1784-1798. Harvard 1967

C14   Callahan, William J., Jr.   The Crown and the Promotion of Industry in Eighteenth Century Spain. Harvard 1964

C15   Callow, Alexander B.   A History of the Tweed Ring. Cal, Berkeley 1961

C16   Calmes, Alan R.   Indian Cultural Traditions and European Conquest of the Georgia-South Carolina Coastal Plain, 3000 B.C.-1733 A.D.: A Combined Archaeological and Historical Investigation. SC 1968

C17   Calton, Jerry M.   The Party That Never Was: A Study of the Failure of the Campaign for Political Integration among Left-Wing and Radical Groups in Britain, 1929-1939. Wash U 1970

C18   Calvert, Monte A.   The Professionalization of the American Mechanical Engineer, 1830-1910. Pitt 1965

C19   Calvert, Robert A.   The Southern Grange: The Farmer's Search for Identity in the Gilded Age. Tex U 1969

C20   Camfield, Thomas M.   Psychologists at War: The History of American Psychology and the First World War. Tex U 1969

C21   Camp, Richard L.   The Papal Ideology of Social Reform: A Study in Historical Development, 1878-1963. Columbia 1965

C22   Campbell, Ballard C.   Political Parties, Cultural Groups, and Contested Issues: Voting in the Illinois, Iowa and Wisconsin House of Representatives, 1886-1895. Wis 1970

C23   Campbell, Clarice T.   A History of Tougaloo College. Miss U 1970

C24   Campbell, Fenton G., Jr.   Czechoslovak-German Relations during the Weimar Republic, 1918-1933. Yale 1967

C25   Campbell, Gregg M.   Walter Lippmann: An Intellectual and Biographical Analysis of *A Preface to Politics*. Minn 1969

C26   Campbell, Hugh G.   The Radical Right in Mexico, 1929-1949. UCLA 1968

C27   Campbell, James W.   The Influence of the Revolutions of 1848 on Great Britain. Ga 1963

C28   Campbell, John.   The Walloon Community in Canterbury, 1625-1649. Wis 1970

C29   Campbell, John P.   Republican Leadership and International Arbitration, 1910-1913. Yale 1961

C30   Campbell, Leon G., Jr.   The Military Reform in the Viceroyalty of Peru, 1762-1800. Fla U 1970

C31   Campbell, Leslie C.   History of Pharmacy in Mississippi. Miss U 1967

C32   Campbell, M. Anne Francis, Sister.   Bishop England's Sisterhood, 1829-1929. St L 1968

C33   Campbell, Miles W.   The Ascendancy of the Earls of Wessex, 1018-1066. S Cal 1963

C34   Campbell, Penelope.   Maryland in Africa: The Maryland State Colonization Society, 1831-1857. Ohio 1967

C35   Campbell, Randolph B.   Henry Clay and the Emerging Nations of Spanish America, 1815-1829. Va 1966

C36   Campbell, Stanley W.   Enforcement of the Fugitive Slave Law, 1850-1860. NC 1967

C37   Campbell, Stuart L.   Historical Objectives and Objective History: Perspectives on the Historiography of the Second Empire. Rochester 1969

C38   Campbell, Thomas F.   Daniel E. Morgan: The Good Citizen in Politics. Case W Reserve 1965

C39   Campbell, Thomas M., Jr.   The Role of Edward R. Stettinius, Jr., in the Founding of the United Nations. Va 1964

C40   Campbell, William B.   William Gordon, Priest and Commissary, Tex U 1965

C41   Campion, Loren K.   Behind the Modern *Drang nach Osten:* Baltic Émigrés and Russophobia in Nineteenth-Century Germany. Ind 1966

C42   Canedy, Charles R., III.   An Entrepreneurial History of the New York Frontier, 1739-1776. Case W Reserve 1967

C43   Cann, Marvin L.   Burnet Rhett Maybank and the New Deal in South Carolina, 1931-1941. NC 1967

C44   Cannon, Donald Q.   Christoph D. Ebeling: A German Geographer of America. Clark 1967

C45   Cantor, Louis.   The Creation of the Modern National Guard: The Dick Militia Act of 1903. Duke 1963

C46   Capowski, Vincent J.   The Making of a Jacksonian Democrat: Levi Woodbury, 1789-1831. Fordham 1966

C47   Cappelluti, Frank J.   The Life and Thought of Giulio Douhet. Rutgers 1967

C48   Carageorge, Ted.   An Evaluation of Hoke Smith and Thomas E. Watson as Georgia Reformers. Ga 1963

C49   Carballosa, Evis L.   Attitude of the Refugees toward Economic Changes in Cuba since Castro. Tex C 1970

C50   Cardon, Louis B.   The Economic Bases of Franco-German Rivalry in Morocco, 1906-1909. Cal, Berkeley 1966

C51   Cardoso, Joaquin J.   Hinton Rowan Helper: A Nineteenth-Century Pilgrimage. Wis 1967

C52   Carey, James L.   A History of the Indiana Penitentiary System, 1821-1933. Ball State 1966

C53   Carey, John J., Jr.   Progressives and the Immigrant, 1885-1915. Conn 1968

C54   Carl, George E.   British Commercial Interest in Venezuela during the Nineteenth Century. Tulane 1968

C55   Carleton, Mark T.   The Political History of the Louisiana State Penitentiary, 1835-1968. Stanford 1970

C56   Carlisle, Rodney P.   The Political Ideas and Influence of William Randolph Hearst, 1928-1936. Cal, Berkeley 1965

C57   Carlson, Arvid J.   The Bishops and the Queen: A Study of "Puritan" Episcopal Activity in Early Elizabethan England, 1558-1566. Princeton 1962

C58   Carlson, Charles P., Jr.   Justification and the Sacraments: A Study in Medieval Interpretations of St. Paul's Theology. Colo 1964

C59   Carlson, Donald A.   Great Britain and the Abolition of the Slave Trade to Latin America. Minn 1964

C60   Carlson, Lewis H.   J. Parnell Thomas and the House Committee on Un-American Activities, 1938-1948. Mich S 1967

C61   Carlson, Martin E.   The Development of Irrigation in Nebraska, 1854-1910: A Descriptive Survey. Neb 1963

C61a   Carlton, Charles H.   The Court of Orphans: A Study in the History of Urban Institutions with Special Reference to London, Bristol, and Exeter in the Sixteenth and Seventeenth Centuries. UCLA 1970

C62   Carpenter, Luther P.   G. D. H. Cole: An Intellectual Biography. Harvard 1967

C63   Carper, N. Gordon.   The Convict-Lease System in Florida, 1866-1923. Fla S 1964

C64   Carr, Lois G.   County Government in Maryland, 1689-1709. Harvard 1968

C65   Carr, Wendell R., Jr.   The Early Thought of John Stuart Mill, 1822-1840. Harvard 1967

C66   Carrell, William D.   Social, Political and Religious Involvements of American College Professors, 1750-1800. Geo P 1968

C67   Carrier, Fred J.   Jacques Doriot: A Political Biography. Wis 1968

C68   Carrier, Maurice.   *Le libéralisme de Jean-Baptiste Eric Dorion.* Laval 1967

C69 Carrigan, D. Owen. Martha Moore Avery: The Career of a Crusader. Maine 1966

C70 Carrigan, Jo Ann. The Saffron Scourge: A History of Yellow Fever in Louisiana, 1796-1905. LSU 1961

C71 Carriker, Robert C. Fort Supply, Indian Territory: Frontier Outpost on the Southern Plains, 1868-1894. Okla 1967

C72 Carroll, Charles F. The Forest Civilization of New England: Timber, Trade, and Society in the Age of Wood, 1600-1688. Brown 1970

C73 Carroll, Daniel B. Henri Mercier in Washington, 1860-1863. Penn U 1968

C74 Carroll, Genevieve C. The German Confederation of 1815 and the North German Confederation of 1867: A Study in Continuity. Ky 1967

C75 Carroll, Peter N. Puritanism and the Wilderness: The Intellectual Significance of the New England Frontier, 1629-1675. Northwestern 1968

C76 Carroll, Rosemary F. The Impact of the Great Depression on American Attitudes towards Success: A Study of the Programs of Norman Vincent Peale, Dale Carnegie, and Johnson O'Connor. Rutgers 1969

C77 Carroll, Roy. The Parliamentary Representation of Yorkshire, 1625-1660. Vanderbilt 1964

C78 Carroll, Sharon A. Elitism and Reform: Some Antislavery Opinion Makers in the Era of Civil War and Reconstruction. Cornell 1970

C79 Carrott, Montgomery B., Jr. The Expansion of the Fourteenth Amendment to Include Personal Liberties, 1920-1941. Northwestern 1966

C80 Carson, David M. A History of the Reformed Presbyterian Church in America to 1871. Penn U 1964

C81 Carson, Donald K. Richard Olney, Secretary of State, 1895-1897. Ky 1969

C82 Carter, Charles H. Intelligence from England: Spanish Hapsburg Policymaking and Its Informational Base, 1598-1625. Columbia 1962

C83 Carter, Dan T. The Scottsboro Case, 1931-1950. NC 1967

C84 Carter, Edward C., II. The Political Activities of Mathew Carey, Nationalist, 1760-1814. Bryn Mawr 1962

C85 Carter, George E. The Use of the Doctrine of Higher Law in the American Anti-Slavery Crusade, 1830-1860. Ore 1970

C86 Carter, Purvis M. Congressional and Public Reaction to Wilson's Caribbean Policy, 1913-1917. Colo 1970

C87 Caruthers, Sandra T. Charles Legendre, American Diplomacy and Expansion in Meiji Japan. Colo 1966

C88 Cary, Lorin L. Adolph Germer: From Labor Agitator to Labor Professional. Wis 1968

C89 Casagrande, Ronald B. Nietzsche and Wagner: Their Relationship. Syracuse 1963

C90 Casais, John A. The New York State Constitutional Convention of 1821 and Its Aftermath. Columbia 1967

C91 Casambre, Napoleon J. Francis Burton Harrison: His Administration in the Philippines, 1913-1921. Stanford 1969

C92 Cash, Joseph H. Labor in the West: The Homestake Mining Company and Its Workers, 1877-1942. Ia 1966

C93 Cash, Philip P. Aesculapius Becomes a Rebel: Medical Men and Problems of the Massachusetts and Continental Armies at the Siege of Boston, April, 1775 to April, 1776. Boston C 1968

C94 Cashdollar, Charles D. American Church Attitudes toward Social Catastrophe: The Panic of 1873 as a Case Study. Penn U 1969

C95 Cashin, Edward L. Thomas E. Watson and the Catholic Laymen's Association of Georgia. Fordham 1962

C96 Cashman, Richard I. The Politics of Mass Recruitment: Attempts to Organize Popular Movements in Maharashtra, 1891-1908. Duke 1969

C97 Caspary, Gerard E. The King and the Two Laws: A Study of the Influence of Roman and Canon Law on the Development of Ideas on Kingship in Fourteenth Century England. Harvard 1962.

C98 Cassar, George H. The Dardanelles Operation: The French Role. McGill 1968

C99 Cassell, Frank A. Samuel Smith: Merchant Politician, 1792-1812. Northwestern 1968

C100 Cassels, Alan. Mussolini's Foreign Policy: The First Years, 1922-1924. Mich U 1961

C101 Cassidy, Rita M. Britain and Basutoland: A Study of Men and Policies from the Gun War to the Anglo-Boer War. UCLA 1967

C102 Casteel, James D. Professors and Applied Ethics: Higher Education in a Revolutionary Era, 1750-1800. Geo P 1964

C103 Caster, James G., Jr. The Earliest Spanish Explorations to the Pacific Northwest. NM 1969

C104 Cavaioli, Frank J. West Point and the Presidency. St John's 1961

C105 Cavanagh, John C. The Military Career of Major General Benjamin Lincoln in the War of the American Revolution, 1775-1781. Duke 1969

C106 Cavanaugh, Gerald J. Vauban, D'Argenson, Turgot: From Absolutism to Constitutionalism in Eighteenth Century France. Columbia 1967

C107 Cave, Alfred A. The Jacksonian Movement in American Historiography. Fla U 1961

C108 Cazier, Stanford O. CARE: A Study in Cooperative Voluntary Relief. Wis 1964

C109 Cease, Ronald C. Areawide Local Government in the State of Alaska: The Genesis, Establishment, and Organization of Borough Government. Claremont 1965

C110 Cecil, Lamar J. R., Jr. Albert Ballin: Merchant of Hamburg. JH 1962

C111 Cederberg, Herbert R., Jr. An Economic Analysis of English Settlement in North America, 1583 to 1635. Cal, Berkeley 1968

C112 Cell, John W. British Colonial Policy in the 1850's: A Study of the Decision-Making Process. Duke 1965

C113 Celms, Peter. A. H. L. Heeren: His Life and His Idea of History. Northwestern 1967

C114 Cerillo, Augustus, Jr. Reform in New York City: A Study of Urban Progressivism. Northwestern 1969

C115 Cesari, Gene S. American Arms-Making Machine Tool Development, 1798-1855. Penn U 1970

C116 Chace, Russell E., Jr. The African Impact on Colonial Argentina. Cal, Santa Barbara 1969

C117 Chadwin, Mark L. Warhawks: The Interventionists of 1940-1941. Columbia 1965

C118 Chaffin, Robert J. Prologue to War: The Townshend Acts and the American Revolution, 1767-1770. Ind 1967

C119 Chalk, Frank R. The United States and the International Struggle for Rubber, 1914-1941. Wis 1970

C120 Chalmers, Leonard. Tammany Hall and New York City Politics, 1853-1861. NYU 1967

C121 Chambers, Henry E. *Exempla virtutis* in Themistius and the Latin Panegyrists. Ind 1968

C122 Chambliss, William J. Chiaraijima Village: Land Tenure, Taxation, and Local Trade, 1818-1884. Mich U 1963

C123 Chamlee, Roy Z., Jr. The Sabbath Crusade: 1810-1920. Geo W 1968

C124 Champie, Ellmore A. Voltaire, Fossils, and the World Machine. Harvard 1967

C125 Chan, Hok Lam W. Liu Chi (1311-1375): The Dual Image of a Chinese Imperial Advisor. Princeton 1967

C126 Chandler, Billy J. The Inhamuns: A Community in the *Sertão* of Northeast Brazil, 1707-1930. Fla U 1967

C127 Chaney, William A. The Cult of Kingship in Anglo-Saxon England: The Transition from Paganism to Christianity. Cal, Berkeley 1961

C128 Chang, Aloysius. The Chinese Community of Nagasaki in the First Century of the Takugawa Period (1603-1688). St John's 1970

C129 Chang, Hsu-Hsin. The Kuomintang's Foreign Policy, 1925-1928. Wis 1967

C130 Chang, Richard T. Fujita Tōko and Sakuma Shōzan: Bakumatsu Intellectuals and the West. Mich U 1964

C131 Channing, Steven A. Crisis of Fear: Secession in South Carolina, 1859-1860. NC 1968

C132 Chapin, Seymour L. Astronomy and the Paris Academy of Sciences during the Eighteenth Century. UCLA 1964

C133 Chappell, John E., Jr. Huntington and His Critics: The Influence of Climate on Civilization. Kans U 1968

C134 Chappius, Charles W. Anglo-German Relations, 1929-1933: A Study of the Role of Great Britain in the Achievement of the Aims of German Foreign Policy. Notre D 1966

C135 Chardkoff, Richard B. Communist Toehold in the Americas: A History of Official United States Involvement in the Guatemalan Crisis, 1954. Fla S 1967

C136 Charlton, Thomas L. The Development of St. Louis as a Southwestern Commercial Depot, 1870-1920. Tex U 1969

C137 Chary, Fredrick B. Bulgaria and the Jews: "The Final Solution," 1940 to 1944. Pitt 1968

C138 Chase, James S. The Emergence of the National Nominating Convention, 1816-1832. Chicago 1962

C139 Chastain, James G. French *Kleindeutsch* Policy in 1848. Okla 1967

C140 Chatfield, E. Charles, Jr. Pacifism and American Life, 1914 to 1941. Vanderbilt 1965

C141 Chavarría, Jesús. José Carlos Mariátegui: Revolutionary Nationalist: The Origins and Crisis of Modern Peruvian Nationalism, 1870-1930. UCLA 1967

C142 Chavis, John M. T. James Couzens: Mayor of Detroit, 1919-1922. Mich S 1970

C143 Chay, Jongsuk. The United States and the Closing Door in Korea: American-Korean Relations, 1894-1905. Mich U 1965

C144 Chazan, Robert L. Thirteenth-Century Jewry in Northern France: An Economic and Political History. Columbia 1967

C145 Cheaney, Henry E. Attitudes of the Indiana Pulpit and Press toward the Negro, 1860-1880. Chicago 1961

C146 Cheek, William F., III. Forgotten Prophet: The Life of John Mercer Langston. Va 1961

C147 Chen, Joseph T. The May Fourth Movement in Shanghai. Cal, Berkeley 1964

C148 Ch'en, Ta-tuan. Sino-Liu-ch'iuan Relations in the Nineteenth Century. Ind 1963

C149 Cheng, Emily H. United States Policy during the Chinese Revolution. SC 1963

C150 Cheng, Shelley H. The T'ung-Meng-Hui: Its Organization, Leadership and Finances, 1905-1912. Wash U 1962

C151 Chenoweth, Lawrence E. The American Dream of Success and the Search for the Self, 1917-1955. Cal, Berkeley 1969

C152 Chepaitis, Joseph B. The First Federal Social Welfare Measure: The Sheppard-Towner Maternity and Infancy Act 1918-1932. Georgetown 1968

C153 Chester, Edward W. Trends in Recent European Thought on America. Pitt 1961

C154 Chiang, Siang-tseh. The Organization of the Nien Rebellion and the Struggle between the Nien and Loyalists (1851-1868). Wash U 1951

C155 Chiao, Joseph Ming-shun. The Beginning of the American-Chinese Diplomatic Relations: The Cushing Mission and the Treaty of Wanghia of 1844. Notre D 1954

C156 Chickering, Roger P. Pacifism in Germany, 1900-1914: A Study of Nationalism and Wilhelmine Society. Stanford 1968

C157 Chipman, Donald E. History of the Province of Pánuco in New Spain, 1518-1533. NM 1962

C158 Chi Sung-chun, Madeleine, Sister. The Chinese Question during the First World War. Fordham 1968

C159 Chodorow, Stanley A. The Ecclesiology of Gratian. Cornell 1968

C160 Chojnacki, Stanley J. The Making of the Venetian Renaissance State: The Achievement of a Noble Political Consensus, 1378 - 1420. Cal, Berkeley 1968

C161 Chrisman, Miriam U. The Impact of the Reformation on the City of Strasbourg, 1480-1548. Yale 1962

C162 Christen, Robert J. King Sears: Politician and Patriot in a Decade of Revolution. Columbia 1968

C163 Christensen, Carl C. The Nuernberg City Council as a Patron of the Fine Arts, 1500-1550. Ohio 1965

C164 Christensen, William E. Splendid Old Roman: The Political and Journalistic Career of Edgar Howard. Neb 1967

C165 Christianson, James R. A Study of Osage History Prior to 1876. Kans U 1968

C166 Christianson, John R. *Cloister and Observatory:* Herrevad Abbey and Tycho Brahe's Uraniborg. Minn 1964

C167 Christie, Jean. Morris Llewellyn Cooke: Progressive Engineer. Columbia 1963

C168 Christofferson, Thomas R. The Revolution of 1848 in Marseille. Tulane 1968

C169 Christopherson, Archie J. The Establishment of Roman Government in the Three Gauls. Md 1966

C170 Chu, Yung-deh R. An Introductory Study of the White Lotus Sect in Chinese History with Special Reference to Peasant Movements. Columbia 1967

C171 Chudacoff, Howard P. Men in Motion: Residential Mobility in Omaha, Nebraska, 1880-1920. Chicago 1969

C172 Chumney, James R., Jr. Don Carlos Buell, Gentleman General. Rice 1964

C173 Churgin, Naomi H. Major John Cartwright: A Study in Radical Parliamentary Reform, 1774-1824. Columbia 1963

C174 Ciccarelli, Orazio A. The Sánchez Cerro Regimes in Peru, 1930-1933. Fla U 1969

C175 Cienciala, Anna Maria. Polish Foreign Policy and the Western Powers, January 1938-April 1939. Ind 1962

C176 Cinclair, Richard J. Will H. Hays: Republican Politician. Ball State 1969

C177 Clancy, John J., Jr. David Humphreys: A Forgotten American. St John's 1970

C178 Clancy, Manus J., III. Senator George W. Norris: An Analysis and Evaluation of His Role of Insurgency during the Hoover Years. St John's 1965

C179 Clanton, Orval G. The Kansas Populists: A Study of the Leadership and Ideology of the Kansas People's Party. Kans U 1967

C180 Clapham, Noel P. Anglo-French Influence on Hitler's Northern Policy, September, 1939-April, 1940. Neb 1968

C181 Clardy, Jesse. The Philosophical Ideas of Alexander N. Radishchev. Mich U 1961

C182 Clarfield, Gerard H. Timothy Pickering and American Foreign Policy, 1795-1800. Cal, Berkeley 1965

C183 Clark, Aubert J. The Movement for International Copyright in Nineteenth Century America. Cath 1961

C184 Clark, Charles H. The Railroad Safety Movement in the United States: Origins and Development, 1869 to 1893. Ill 1966

C185 Clark, John Dennis J. The Adjustment of Irish Immigrants to Urban Life: The Philadelphia Experience, 1840-1870. Temple 1970

C186 Clark, Eugene V. Catholic Liberalism and Ultramontanism, Freedom and Duty: A Study of the Quarrel over the Control of Catholic Affairs in England, 1858-1866. Notre D 1965

C187 Clark, John G. The Development of the Grain Trade in the East North Central States of the United States from 1815 to 1960. Stanford 1963

C188 Clark, Linda L. Social Darwinism and French Intellectuals, 1860-1915. NC 1968

C189 Clark, Lovell C. A History of the Conservative Administrations, 1891-1896. Toronto 1968

C190 Clark, Malcolm C. The Coastwise and Caribbean Trade of the Chesapeake Bay, 1696-1776. Georgetown 1970

C191 Clark, Michael D. American Patricians as Social Critics, 1865-1914. NC 1965

C192 Clark, Norman H. Liquor Reform and Social Change: A History of the Prohibition Movement in the State of Washington. Wash U 1964

C193 Clark, Truman R. Puerto Rico and the United States, 1917-1933: A Failure of Imperial Tutelage. Bryn Mawr 1970

C194 Clarke, George W. The Unionist Party and Tariff Reform, 1903-1906. NC 1964

C195 Clarke, Jeffrey J. Military Technology in Republican France: The Evolution of the French Armored Force, 1917-1940. Duke 1969

C196 Clary, Norman J. French Antisemitism during the Years of Drumont and Dreyfus, 1886-1906. Ohio 1970

C197 Clausner, Marlin D. Rural Santo Domingo: Settled, Unsettled, and Resettled. Temple 1970

C198 Clauss, Errol M. The Atlanta Campaign, 18 July-2 September, 1864. Emory 1965

C199 Claxton, Robert H. Lorenzo Montúfar: Central American Liberal. Tulane 1970

C200 Clay, William W. H. Kentucky: The Awful Path to Statehood, 1782-1792. Ky 1966

C201 Claypool, James C. The Early Political Career of Aristide Briand, 1902-1914. Ky 1968

C202 Clayton, Bruce L. Southern Critics of the New South, 1890-1914. Duke 1966

C203 Clayton, James L. The American Fur Company: The Final Years. Cornell 1964

C204 Cleary, Robert E. Executive Agreements in the Conduct of United States Foreign Policy: A Case Study: The Destroyer-Base Deal. Rutgers 1969

C205 Clemens, Diane. Soviet Diplomacy at Yalta. Cal, Santa Barbara 1966

C206 Clements, Valiant M. The Rise and Extinction of Jansenism in France. Colo 1961

C207 Clemmer, Robert R. Enlightenment Church History in the United States, 1800-1850. Penn U 1961

C208 Cliatt, James E., III. Lindamood and Puckett, Trading as Columbus Brick Company. Miss S 1967

C209 Clifford, John G. The Plattsburg Training Camp Movement, 1913-1917. Ind 1969

C210 Clifford, Nicholas R. British Policy in the Far East, 1937-1941. Harvard 1961

C211 Clinch, Thomas A. Populism and Bimetallism in Montana. Ore 1964

C212 Cline, Peter K. Political Aspects of Economic Policy of British Governments, 1918-1923: A Study in the Politics of the Economic and Social Transition Following the Great War. Stanford 1969

C213 Clines, Virginia Theresa, Sister. The Role of Charles Francis Adams as American Minister to Great Britain during the Civil War. St John's 1964

C214 Clokey, Richard M. The Life of William H. Ashley. Wis 1969

C215 Clouse, Robert G. The Influence of John Henry Alsted on English Millenarian Thought in the Seventeenth Century. Ia 1963

C216 Clowse, Converse D. The Charleston Export Trade, 1717-1737. Northwestern 1963

C217 Clubb, Jerome M. Congressional Opponents of Reform, 1901-1913. Wash U 1963

C218 Clutts, Betty C. Country Life Aspects of the Progressive Movement. Ohio 1962

C219 Coady, Joseph W. Franklin D. Roosevelt's Early Washington Years (1913-1920). St John's 1968

C220 Coate, Charles E. Water, Power, and Politics in the Central Valley Project, 1933-1967. Cal, Berkeley 1969

C221 Coats, George Y. The Philippine Constabulary, 1901-1917. Ohio 1968

C222 Cobb, William H. French Diplomatic Relations with Spain, 1632-1635. Tulane 1970

C223 Coben, Stanley. The Political Career of A. Mitchell Palmer. Columbia 1961

C224 Cochran, John P. The Virginia Agricultural and Mechanical College: The Formative Half Century, 1872-1919, of Virginia Polytechnic Institute. Ala 1961

C225 Cochran, John S. Henry Villard and Oregon's Transportation Development, 1863-1881. Harvard 1961

C226 Cody, Cecil E. A Study of the Career of Itagaki Taisuke (1837-1919), a Leader of the Democratic Movement in Meiji Japan. Wash U 1955

C227 Coe, Stephen H. Indian Affairs in Pennsylvania and New York, 1783-1794. Am 1968

C228 Coger, Dalvan M. The International Politics of Apartheid: South Africa and the United Nations, 1945-1962. SC 1970

C229 Coghlan, Francis A. James Bryce: Intellectual Architect of the Anglo-American Entente. Bryn Mawr 1966

C230 Cohen, Alfred. The Kingdom of God in Puritan Thought: A Study of the English Puritan Quest for the Fifth Monarchy. Ind 1961

C231 Cohen, David K. The Social Theory of Auguste Comte (1819-1826). Rochester 1961

C232 Cohen, Henry. Business and Politics from the Age of Jackson to the Civil War: A Study from the Life of W. W. Corcoran. Cornell 1965

C233 Cohen, Ira. The Auction System in the Port of New York, 1817-1837. NYU 1969

C234 Cohen, Joel A. Rhode Island and the American Revolution: A Selective Socio-Political Analysis. Conn 1967

C235 Cohen, Marshall J. Self and Society: Charles Horton Cooley and the Idea of Social Self in American Thought. Harvard 1967

C236 Cohen, Norman S. William Allen: Chief Justice of Pennsylvania, 1704-1780. Cal, Berkeley 1966

C237 Cohen, Ronald D. Colonial Leviathan: New England Foreign Affairs in the Seventeenth Century. Minn 1967

C238 Cohen, Sheldon S. The Connecticut Colony Government and the Polity of the Congregational Churches, 1708-1760. NYU 1963

C239 Cohen, Sidney L. Viking Fortresses of the Trelleborg Type. Yale 1962

C240 Cohen, Warren I. Revisionism between World Wars: A Study in American Diplomatic History. Wash U 1962

C241 Cohen, William. James Miller McKim: Pennsylvania Abolitionist. NYU 1968

C242 Cohen, William B. Rulers of Empire: The French Colonial Service in Africa, 1880-1960. Stanford 1969

C243 Coifman, Victoria B. History of the Wolof State of Jolof until 1860, Including Comparative Data from the Wolof State of Walo. Wis 1969

C244 Coker, William S. United States-British Diplomacy over Mexico, 1913. Okla 1965

C245 Colahan, Thomas S. The Cautious Revolutionaries: The Scottish Middle Classes in the Making of the Scottish Revolt, 1637-1638. Columbia 1962

C246 Colbert, Edward P. The Martyrs of Cordoba (850-859): A Study of the Sources. Cath 1963

C247 Cole, Douglas L. The Better Patriot: John S. Ewart and the Canadian Nation. Wash U 1968

C248 Cole, John R. Moralistic Classicism in the Political Literature of the French Enlightenment. Harvard 1970

C249   Cole, Phillip A. The British Image of the French Third Republic, 1870-1882. Boston U 1963

C250   Cole, Richard G. Eberlin von Günzburg and the German Reformation. Ohio 1963

C251   Cole, William R. Brockton, Massachusetts: A History of the Decline of a Shoe Manufacturing City, 1900-1933. Boston U 1968

C252   Colebank, Kenneth B. Civil Rights Legislation, 1866-1875. Ky 1969

C253   Coleman, Bevley R. A History of State Parks in Tennessee. Geo P 1963

C254   Coleman, John P. In Pursuit of Harmony: A Study of the Thought of Jesse Macy. Ia 1968

C255   Colish, Marcia L. The Mirror of Language: A Study in the Medieval Theory of Knowledge. Yale 1965

C256   Collier, James G. The Political Career of James McDowell, 1830-1851. NC 1963

C257   Collins, George W. United States-Moroccan Relations, 1904-1912. Colo 1965

C258   Collins, Jacquelin. The Scottish Episcopacy, 1596-1638. Ill 1964

C259   Collins, William. Overland Journeys in Oregon and California of the United States Navy Exploring Expedition. NM 1966

C260   Colman, Gould P. A History of Agricultural Education at Cornell University. Cornell 1962

C261   Colt, Avery M. Problems of Early Colonial Government: South Carolina, 1670-1680. Chicago 1962

C262   Combs, Jerald A. Power Politics and Ideology: A Case Study of the Jay Treaty. UCLA 1964

C263   Comerford, Robert J. The American Liberty League. St John's 1967

C264   Comfort, Richard A. The Politics of Labor in Hamburg, 1918-1924. Princeton 1962

C266   Condon, Richard H. The Reform of English Prisons, 1773-1816. Brown 1962

C267   Condon, Richard W. The Moscow Parenthesis: A Study of Finnish-German Relations, 1940-1941. Minn 1969

C268   Condon, Thomas J. The Commercial Origins of New Netherland. Harvard 1962

C269   Congleton, Betty C. George D. Prentice and His Editorial Policy in National Politics, 1830-1861. Ky 1962

C270   Conheady, Eileen C., Sister. The Saints of the Merovingian Dynasty: A Study of Merovingian Kingship. Chicago 1967

C271   Conklin, Rosalind. Medieval English Minstrels, 1216-1485. Chicago 1964

C272   Conley, Patrick T. Rhode Island Constitutional Development, 1636-1841: Prologue to the Dorr Rebellion. Notre D 1970

C273   Colin, Joseph R. The Wobblies: A Study of the Industrial Workers of the World before World War I. Wis 1966

C274   Conlon, Frank F. The Emergence of the Saraswat Brahmans, 1830-1930: A Study of Caste and Social Change in Modern India. Minn 1969

C275   Connell, Charles W. Western Views of the Tartars, 1240-1340. Rutgers 1969

C276   Connell, Joan. The Roman Catholic Church in England, 1553-1850: A Study in Internal Politics. Chicago 1969

C277   Connelly, James L., Jr. The Movement to Create a National Gallery of Art in Eighteenth-Century France. Kans U 1962

C278   Connelly, Joan. The Tragic Week: A Study of Anticlericalism in Spain. Bryn Mawr 1964

C279   Connelly, Thomas L. Metal, Fire and Forge: The Army of Tennessee, 1861-1862. Rice 1963

C280   Connick, George P. The United States and Central America, 1823-1850. Colo 1969

C281   Connors, James J. Poets and Politics: A Study of the Careers of C. Day Lewis, Stephen Spender and W. H. Auden in the 1930's. Yale 1967

C282   Conrad, David E. The Forgotten Farmers: The AAA and the Southern Tenants, 1933-1936. Okla 1962

C283   Conrad, Robert E. The Struggle for the Abolition of the Brazilian Slave Trade, 1808-1853. Columbia 1967

C284   Conrad, Roderick H. Spanish-United States Relations, 1868-1874. Ga 1969

C285   Constable, John W. Johann Brenz's Role in the Sacramentarian Controversy of the Sixteenth Century. Ohio 1967

C286   Constantelos, Demetrius J. Philanthropia and Philanthropic Institutions in the Byzantine Empire, A.D. 330-1204. Rutgers 1965

C287   Contee, Clarence G. W. E. B. DuBois and African Nationalism, 1914-1945. Am 1969

C288 Contreras, Belisario R. The New Deal Treasury Department Art Programs and the American Artist, 1933 to 1943. Am 1967

C289 Conway, Jill K. The First Generation of American Women Graduates. Harvard 1969

C290 Conway, Thomas G. The Extension of the Poor Law to Ireland. Loyola 1969

C291 Coode, Thomas H. Georgia Congressmen and the New Deal, 1933-1938. Ga 1966

C292 Cook, Bernard A. The Impact of the Paris Commune upon German Socialism, 1871-1875. St L 1970

C293 Cook, Blanche W. Woodrow Wilson and the Antimilitarists, 1914-1917. JH 1970

C294 Cook, Genevieve Marie, Sister. The Life of Saint Epiphanius by Ennodius: A Translation with an Introduction and Commentary. Cath 1942

C295 Cook, John F. A History of Liberal Education at the University of Wisconsin,1862-1918. Wis 1970.

C296 Cook, Marjorie H. Restoration and Innovation: Alabamians Adjust to Defeat, 1865-1867. Ala 1968

C297 Cook, Philip C. EFTA: The Origins and History of the European Free Trade Association. Ga 1968

C298 Cook, Philip L. Zion City, Illinois: Twentieth Century Utopia. Colo 1965

C299 Cook, Wendell H., Jr. The Schleswig-Holstein Question and Anglo-German Relations, March, 1848 to July, 1849. NM 1970

C300 Cooke, James J. Eugène Etienne and New French Imperialism, 1880-1910. Ga 1969

C301 Cooke, John W. Some Aspects of the Concept of the Free Individual in the United States, 1800-1860. Vanderbilt 1967

C302 Cooke, Raymond M. British Evangelicals, Native Peoples and the Concept of Empire, 1837-1852. Ore 1963

C303 Cooling, Benjamin F., III. Benjamin Franklin Tracy: Lawyer, Soldier, Secretary of the Navy. Penn U 1969

C304 Coombs, F. Alan. Joseph Christopher O'Mahoney: The New Deal Years. Ill 1968

C305 Coombs, Norman R. The Doctrine of the Incarnation and Christian Socialism. Wis 1961

C306 Coons, Ronald E. Steamships and Statesmen: Austria and the Austrian Lloyd, 1836-1848. Harvard 1966

C307 Cooper, David. Capital Punishment within Prisons Bill, 1868. NYU 1969

C308 Cooper, Donald B. Epidemic Disease in Mexico City, 1761-1813. Tex U 1963

C309 Cooper, Elias O. Gotthald Ephraim Lessing and the Idea of Toleration in the Enlightenment. Columbia 1969

C310 Cooper, James L. Interests, Ideas, and Empires: The Roots of American Foreign Policy, 1763-1779. Wis 1964

C311 Cooper, James N. The Predecessors of Militant Dissent: English Evangelical Dissent in Its Relations with Church and State, 1832-1841. Harvard 1970

C312 Cooper, John M., Jr. The Vanity of Power: American Isolationism and the First World War, 1914-1917. Columbia 1968

C313 Cooper, Robert I. William Rhinelander Stewart and the Expansion of Public Welfare Services in New York State, 1882-1929. CUNY 1969

C314 Cooper, Sandi E. Peace and Internationalism: European Ideological Movements behind the Two Hague Conferences (1889 to 1907). NYU 1967

C315 Cooper, William J. The Conservative Regime in South Carolina, 1877-1890. JH 1966

C316 Cope, Esther S. Parliament and Proclamations, 1604-1629. Bryn Mawr 1969

C317 Copeland, Henry J. The Resistance and Post-Liberation French Politics, 1940-1946. Cornell 1966

C318 Copenhaver, Brian P. Symphorien Champier and the Reception of the Occultist Tradition in Renaissance France. Kans U 1970

C319 Copp, Nelson G. "Wetbacks" and *Braceros:* Mexican Migrant Laborers and American Immigration Policy. Boston U 1963

C320 Coppa, Frank J. Giolitti and Industrial Italy: An Analysis of the Interrelationship between Giolitti's Economic Policy and His Political Progress. Cath 1966

C321 Copps, Michael J. Gilded Age America and the Pursuit of Reality. NC 1967

C322 Corbett, Theodore G. The Elements of Reform in Early Seventeenth Century Spain. S Cal 1970

C323 Cordier, Sherwood S. Erwin Rommell as Commander: The Decisive Years, 1940-1942. Minn 1963

C324 Corkran, David H., III. The New England Colonists' English Image, 1550-1714. Cal, Berkeley 1970

C325 Cornebise, Alfred E. Some Aspects of the German Response to the Ruhr Occupation, January-September 1923. NC 1965

C326 Corrigan, M. Saint Pierre, Sister. William Jones of the Second Bank of the United States: A Reappraisal. St L 1966

C327 Cortada, Rafael L. The Government of Spain under Joseph Bonaparte, 1808-1814. Fordham 1968

C328 Cortés, Carlos E. The Role of Rio Grande do Sul in Brazilian Politics, 1930-1967. NM 1969

C329 Cosgrove, Richard A. Sir Eyre Crowe and the English Foreign Office, 1905-1914. Cal, Riverside 1967

C330 Cosmas, Graham A. An Army for Empire: The United States Army in the Spanish-American War, 1898-1899. Wis 1969

C331 Costello, David R. Prime Minister Kokovtsev and the Duma: A Study in the Disintegration of the Tsarist Regime, 1911-1914. Va 1970

C332 Costello, Lawrence. The New York City Labor Movement, 1861-1873. Columbia 1967

C333 Cotroneo, Ross R. The History of the Northern Pacific Land Grant, 1900-1952. Idaho 1967

C334 Coughlan, Neil P. Dewey and the University. Wis 1968

C335 Coughlin, Magdalen, Sister. Boston Merchants on the Coast, 1787-1821: An Insight into the American Acquisition of California. S Cal 1970

C336 Coulter, Thomas C. A History of Woman Suffrage in Nebraska, 1856-1920. Ohio 1967

C337 Couse, Gordon S. The Historical Consciousness of the Doctrinaires as Represented by Pierre Paul Royer-Collard, François Guizot, and Victor Cousin. Chicago 1965

C338 Couturier, Edith B. Hacienda of Hueyapan: A History of a Mexican Social and Economic Institution, 1550-1940. Columbia 1965

C339 Covert, James T. Mandell Creighton and English Education. Ore 1967

C340 Cowan, Richard O. Mormonism in National Periodicals. Stanford 1961

C341 Cox, Henry B. To the Victor: A History of the French Spoliation Claims Controversy, 1793-1955. Geo W 1967

C342 Cox, Joseph W. Robert Goodloe Harper: The Evolution of a Southern Federalist Congressman. Md 1967

C343 Cox, Marvin R. The Legitimists under the Second French Republic. Yale 1966

C344 Cox, Thomas R. Sails and Sawmills: The Pacific Lumber Trade to 1900. Ore 1969

C345 Cox, William A. The Art World and *Mir Iskusstva:* Studies in the Development of Russian Art, 1890-1905. Mich U 1970

C346 Coy, Richard D. Cushman K. Davis and American Foreign Policy, 1887-1900. Minn 1965

C347 Coyle, Mary E. Sir Richard Rich, First Baron Rich (1496-1567), a Political Biography. Harvard 1967

C348 Coyle, Walter A. The Clarendonian Dilemma: A Constitutional Crisis. Colo 1969

C349 Coyner, Martin B., Jr. John Hartwell Cocke of Bremo: Agriculture and Slavery in the Ante-Bellum South. Va 1961

C350 Crabtree, Loren W. Christian Colleges and the Chinese Revolution, 1840-1940: A Case Study in the Impact of the West. Minn 1969

C351 Cragan, Thomas M. Thomas Jefferson's Early Attitudes toward Manufacturing, Agriculture, and Commerce. Tenn 1965

C352 Crahan, Margaret E. Clerical Immunity in the Viceroyalty of Peru, 1684-1692: A Case Study of Civil-Ecclesiastical Relations. Columbia 1967

C353 Crane, Philip M. Governor Jo Wright: Hoosier Conservative. Ind 1963

C354 Crangle, John V. The Decline and Survival of British Anti-Imperialism (1878-1885). SC 1968

C355 Cranston, John W. German Unification and the Liberal Ideal in the *Preussische Jahrbücher*, 1858-1877. Wis 1970

C356 Crapol, Edward P. "America for Americans": Economic Nationalism and Anglophobia, 1876-1896. Wis 1968

C357 Craven, Nancy L. Kuhlmann or Ludendorff? Failure of a Bureaucracy, 1917-1918. Chicago 1969

C358 Cravens, Hamilton. American Scientists and the Heredity-Environment Controversy, 1883-1940. Ia 1969

C359   Crawford, Charles W.   A History of the R. F. Learned Lumber Company, 1865-1900. Miss U 1968

C360   Crawford, Frederic M., Jr.   The *Mercure historique et politique,* 1715-1781: A Critical Analysis. Ky 1969

C361   Crawford, Robert B.   The Life and Thought of Chang Chü-cheng, 1525-1582. Wash U 1961

C362   Crean, Eileen M.   The Governor-Generalship of Turkestan under K. P. von Kaufmann, 1867-1882. Yale 1970

C363   Creekmore, Marion V., Jr.   The German Reichstag Election of 1928. Tulane 1968

C364   Creighton, Andrew J.   Anticlaudien: A Thirteenth Century French Adaptation of the Anticlaudianus of Alain de Lille, by Ellebaut, Edited, with an Introduction, Commentary, and Glossary. Cath 1944

C365   Creighton, John K.   Georges-Jacques Danton: A Re-evaluation of Aspects of His Political Career from August 10, 1792 to April 5, 1794. Colo 1965

C366   Cripps, Thomas R.   The Lily White Republicans: The Negro, the Party, and the South in the Progressive Era. Md 1967

C367   Croal, Ralph F.   The Idea of the *École spéciale militaire* and the Founding of Saint-Cyr. Ariz 1970

C368   Croce, Lewis H.   The Lincoln Administration. Md 1968

C369   Crockett, Norman L.   The Middlewestern Wool Manufacture, 1860-1914. Mo 1966

C370   Crofts, Daniel W.   The Blair Bill and the Elections Bill: The Congressional Aftermath to Reconstruction. Yale 1968

C371   Croizier, Ralph C.   Chinese Medicine in the Twentieth Century Intellectual Revolution: The Tensions of Cultural Choice. Cal, Berkeley 1965

C372   Cromwell, Richard S.   The Free Democratic Party in German Politics, 1945-1956: A Historical Study of a Contemporary Liberal Party. Stanford 1961

C373   Cronenberg, Allen T.   The *Volksbund für das Deutschtum im Ausland:* Völkisch Ideology and German Foreign Policy, 1881-1939. Stanford 1970

C374   Crook, David H.   Louis Sullivan, the World's Columbian Exposition, and American Life. Harvard 1964

C375   Crooks, James B.   Politics and Progress: The Rise of Urban Progressivism in Baltimore, 1895 to 1911. JH 1964

C376   Crosby, Alfred W., Jr.   America, Russia, Hemp and Napoleon: A Study of Trade between the United States and Russia, 1783-1814. Boston U 1961

C377   Crosby, Travis L.   English Agricultural Politics, 1815-1825. JH 1965

C378   Cross, Michael S.   The Dark Druidical Groves: The Lumber Community and the Commercial Frontier in British North America, to 1854. Toronto 1968

C379   Cross, Truman B.   Viktor Chernov: Reason and Will in a Morality for Revolution. Ind 1968

C380   Crouch, Thomas W.   The Making of a Soldier: The Career of Frederick Funston, 1865-1902. Tex U 1969

C381   Crouse, Maurice A.   The Manigault Family of South Carolina, 1685-1783. Northwestern 1964

C382   Crow, Herman L.   A Political History of the Texas Penal System, 1829-1951. Tex U 1964

C383   Crowder, Daniel B.   Profile in Progress: A Study of Local #287, UAW-CIO. Ball State 1969

C384   Crowgey, Henry G.   The Formative Years of Kentucky's Whiskey Industry. Ky 1968

C385   Crowley, Florence J.   The Conservative Thought of José Vasconcelos. Fla U 1963

C386   Crowley, John E.   Industry, Frugality, and Community: The Persuasion of Work in Early America. JH 1970

C387   Crowley, Weldon S.   Erastianism in England, 1640-1662. Ia 1966

C388   Crummey, Robert O.   The Old Believers and the World of Anti-Christ: The Social and Economic Development of the Raskol in the Olonets Region, 1654-1744. Chicago 1964

C389   Crump, Gary A.   Ammianus Marcellinus as a Military Historian. Ill 1969

C390   Crunican, Paul E.   The Manitoba School Question and Canadian Federal Politics, 1890-1896: A Study in Church-State Relations. Toronto 1968

C391   Cubberly, Ray E.   The Committee of General Security during the Reign of Terror. Wis 1967

C392   Cubby, Edwin A.   The Transformation of the Tug and Guyandot Valleys: Economic Development and Social Change in West Virginia, 1888-1921. Syracuse 1962

C393 Cuddigan, John D. Three Puritan Peers: Their Religious Beliefs and Activities in the Puritan Revolution. Minn 1969

C394 Cuddy, Joseph E. Irish-Americans and National Isolationism, 1914-1920. SUNY, Buffalo 1965

C395 Cuff, Robert D. Business, Government and the War Industries Board. Princeton 1966

C396 Culley, John J. Muted Trumpets: Four Efforts to Better Southern Race Relations, 1900-1919. Va 1967

C397 Cullop, Charles P. Confederate Propaganda in Europe, 1861-1865. Va 1962

C398 Culpepper, Jack M., III. The Legislative Origins of Peasant Bondage in Muscovy. Columbia 1965

C399 Cummings, Charles M. Seven Ohio Confederate Generals: Case Histories of Defection. Ohio 1963

C400 Cummings, Raymond L. France and the Fall of the Kingdom of the Two Sicilies, 1860. Penn U 1964

C401 Cummins, Lejeune. The Origin and Development of Elihu Root's Latin American Diplomacy. Cal, Berkeley 1964

C402 Cunningham, Otis E. Shiloh and the Western Campaign of 1862. LSU 1966

C403 Cunningham, Raymond J. Ministry of Healing: The Origins of the Psychotherapeutic Role of the American Churches. JH 1965

C404 Cunsolo, Ronald S. Enrico Corradini and Italian Nationalism, 1896-1923. NYU 1962

C405 Curl, Donald W. Murat Halstead, Editor and Politician. Ohio 1964

C406 Curran, Daniel J. Hendrick B. Wright: A Study in Leadership. Fordham 1962

C407 Curran, Michael W. Vladimir Stasov and the Development of Russian National Art, 1850-1906. Wis 1965

C408 Curran, Thomas J. Know-Nothings of New York. Columbia 1963

C409 Currey, Cecil B. Benjamin Franklin and the Radicals, 1765-1775. Kans U 1965

C410 Currie, Gary R. Latin America and the Era of Disarmament: The First Stage, 1920-1925. Minn 1970

C411 Curry, Earl R. The United States and the Dominican Republic, 1924-1933: Dilemma in the Caribbean. Minn 1966

C412 Curry, Leonard P. The Thirty-Seventh Congress: Blueprint for Modern America. Ky 1961

C413 Curry, Richard O. A House Divided: A Study of Statehood Politics and the Copperhead Movement in West Virginia during the Civil War. Penn U 1961

C414 Curtis, Bruce E. The Middle Class Progressivism of William Graham Sumner. Ia 1964

C415 Curtis, George M., III. The Virginia Courts during the Revolution. Wis 1970

C416 Curtis, James C. The Heritage Imperiled: Martin Van Buren and the Presidency, 1837-1841. Northwestern 1967

C417 Curtis, Julia B. The Organized Few: Labor in Philadelphia, 1857-1873. Bryn Mawr 1970

C418 Cusack, John B. The American Weekly Humor Magazine in the Nineteenth Century. Boston U 1969

C419 Cushman, Joseph D., Jr. The Episcopal Church in Florida: 1821-1892. Fla S 1962

C420 Cusimano, Richard C. Albertino Mussato and the Politics of Early *Trecento* Padua: A Prehumanist in the Transition from Commune to *Signoria*. Ga 1970

C421 Cuthbert, Julie S. The Anatomy of a Society: A Portrait of the English Aristocracy, 1702-1760. Ore 1969

C422 Cuthbertson, William W. William Allen White and the *Emporia Gazette*, 1895-1944. Rochester 1962

C423 Cutler, Allan H. Catholic Missions to the Moslems to the End of the First Crusade (1100). S Cal 1963

C424 Cutler, Kenneth E. The House of Godwine, 1009-1066. Ind 1965

C425 Cutler, Robert S. Carolingian Italian Policies, 739-780. Mich S 1970

D

D1 Dabrowski, Stanislaw. The Peace Treaty of Riga, 1921. Kent 1968

D2 Daetweiler, Robert C. Richard Bland, Conservator of Self-Government in Eighteenth-Century Virginia. Wash U 1969

D3 Dain, Norman. Insanity: Changing Concepts in the United States, 1789-1865. Columbia 1961

D4 Dalfiume, Richard M. Desegregation of the United States Armed Forces, 1939-1953. Mo 1966

D5 D'Allaire, Micheline. *Histoire Sociale d'une Communauté en Nouvelle-France: L'Hôpital-Général de Québec, 1692-1764.* Ottawa 1968

D6 Dallek, Robert. Roosevelt's Ambassador: The Public Career of William E. Dodd. Columbia 1964

D7 Dalstrom, Harl A. Kenneth S. Wherry. Neb 1965

D8 Daly, James W. The Royalist Constitutional Position, 1641-1645. Toronto 1963

D9 Daly, John M., Sister. Mary Anderson, Pioneer Labor Leader. Georgetown 1968

D10 Daly, Lawrence J. Themistius: A "Mandarin" of Late Antiquity. Loyola 1970

D11 Danahar, David C. Austria-Hungary and the Triple Alliance System, 1887-1897. Mass 1970

D12 Daniel, Charles E., Jr. The Significance of the Sermons of Wenzeslaus Linck. Ohio 1968

D13 Daniel, E. Randolph. Joachim of Flora and the Joachite Tradition of Apocalyptic Conversion in the Later Middle Ages. Va 1966

D14 Daniel, James C. Peonage in the New South. Md 1970

D15 Daniell, Jere R. New Hampshire Politics and the American Revolution, 1741-1790. Harvard 1964

D16 Daniels, Bruce C. Large Town Power Structures in Eighteenth Century Connecticut: An Analysis of Political Leadership in Hartford, Norwich and Fairfield. Conn 1970

D17 Daniels, George H. Baconian Science in America, 1815-1845. Ia 1963

D18 Daniels, James D. Amos Kendall: Cabinet-Politician, 1829-1841. NC 1968

D19 Daniels, Roger. The Politics of Prejudice: The Anti-Japanese Movement in California and the Struggle for Japanese Exclusion. UCLA 1961

D20 Danzer, Gerald A. America's Roots in the Past: Historical Publication in America to 1860. Northwestern 1967

D21 Danziger, Edmund J. The Peculiar Service: Problems in the Administration of Federal Indian Policy during the Civil War. Ill 1966

D22 Darcy, Cornelius P. The Encouragement of the Fine Arts in Lancashire, 1760-1860. Columbia 1970

D23 Dargo, George. Legal Codification and the Politics of Territorial Government in Jefferson's Louisiana, 1803-1808. Columbia 1970

D24 Das Gupta, Arun K. Acheh in Indonesian Trade and Politics, 1600-1641. Cornell 1962

D25 Daum, Paul S. Some Polish Boundary Problems and the United States Reaction, 1919-1945. Boston U 1966

D26 Dauphinee, Bede A. Church and Parliament in Brazil during the First Empire, 1823-1831. Georgetown 1965

D27 Davenport, Robert W. Fremont Older in San Francisco Journalism, A Partial Biography, 1856-1918. UCLA 1969

D28 Davids, Diana I. The Public Career of George William Frederick Howard, Seventh Earl of Carlisle, 1826-1852. Yale 1969

D29 Davids, Leonard R. Forces Governing Diplomatic Relations between Britain and Italy, 1930-1935. Georgetown 1961

D30 Davidson, David M. Rivers and Empire: The Madeira Route and the Incorporation of the Brazilian Far West, 1737-1808. Yale 1970

D31 Davidson, Gordon W. Henry Ford: The Formation and Course of a Public Figure. Columbia 1966

D32 Davidson, John. Trade and Politics in the Sherbro Hinterland, 1849-1890. Wis 1969

D33 Davidson, Kerry. The French Socialist Party and Parliamentary Efforts to Achieve Social Reform, 1906-1914. Tulane 1970

D34   Davies, David A.   V. A. Maklakov and the Problem of Russia's Westernization. Wash U 1968

D35   Davies, Richard O.   The Truman Housing Program. Mo 1963

D36   Davies, Robert B.   The International Operations of the Singer Manufacturing Company, 1854-1895. Wis 1967

D37   Davies, Thomas M., Jr.   Indian Integration in Peru: A Half Century of Experience, 1900-1948. NM 1970

D38   Davis, Calvin D.   The United States and the First Hague Peace Conference. Ind 1961

D39   Davis, Donald E.   Lenin's Theory of War. Ind 1969

D40   Davis, G. Cullom.   The Federal Trade Commission: Promise and Practice in Regulating Business, 1900-1929. Ill 1969

D41   Davis, George H.   The Dissolution of the Institute of Pacific Relations, 1944-1961. Chicago 1966

D42   Davis, Hugh C.   An Analysis of the Rationale of Representative Conservative Alabamians, 1874-1914. Vanderbilt 1964

D43   Davis, Hugh H.   The Reform Career of Joshua Leavitt, 1794-1873. Ohio 1969

D44   Davis, James R.   A History of the Evangelical United Brethren Church in California, 1849-1962. S Cal 1963

D45   Davis, John A.   The Ku Klux Klan in Indiana, 1920-1930: An Historical Study. Northwestern 1966

D46   Davis, John M.   The Image of Lincoln in the South: From Secession to Lincoln Centennial Year (1860-1909). Rice 1967

D47   Davis, John W.   Hitler and the Versailles Settlement. Wis 1964

D48   Davis, Lawrence B.   The Baptist Response to Immigration in the United States, 1880-1925. Rochester 1968

D49   Davis, Polly Ann.   Alben W. Barkley: Senate Majority Leader and Vice President. Ky 1963

D50   Davis, Richard H.   Nineteenth-Century African Education in the Cape Colony: A Historical Analysis. Wis 1969

D51   Davis, Richard W.   William Smith: A Study in the Politics of Dissent, 1784-1832. Columbia 1964

D52   Davis, Robert H.   Acosta, Caro, and Lleras: Three Essayists and Their Views of New Granada's National Problems, 1832-1853. Vanderbilt 1969

D53   Davis, Robert L.   The Search for Values: The American Liberal Climate of Opinion in the Nineteen Thirties and the Totalitarian Crisis of the Coming of the Second World War as Seen in the Thought of Charles Beard and Archibald MacLeish. Claremont 1970

D54   Davis, Robert R., Jr.   Manners and Diplomacy: A History of American Diplomatic Etiquette and Protocol during the Early National Period. Mich S 1967

D55   Davis, Rodney O.   Illinois Legislators and Jacksonian Democracy, 1834-1841. Ia 1966

D56   Davis, Roger G.   Conscientious Cooperators: The Seventh-Day Adventists and Military Service, 1860-1945. Geo W 1970

D57·   Davis, Ronald L.   A History of Resident Opera in the American West. Tex U 1961

D58   Davis, Ronald W.   Historical Outline of the Kru Coast, Liberia, 1500 to the Present. Ind 1968

D59   Davis, Sandra T. W.   Ono Azusa, A Meiji Intellectual. Penn U 1968

D60   Davis, Thomas W.   Arthur S. Colyar and the New South, 1860-1905. Mo 1962

D61   Davis, Virgil S.   Stephen Elliott: A Southern Bishop in Peace and War. Ga 1964

D62   Davis, Walter W.   Emperor Joseph II and the Austrian Netherlands, 1780-1787. Colo 1965

D63   Daws, Alan G.   Honolulu—The First Century: Influences in the Development of the Town to 1876. Hawaii 1966

D64   Dawson, Jerry F.   The Evolution of Friedrich Schleiermacher as a Nationalist. Tex U 1964

D65   Dawson, John P.   The Judges in the *Bailliages* and *Sénéchaussées*, 1763-1800: A Study of Middle-Class Office-Holders before and during the French Revolution. Harvard 1961

D66   Day, Charles R.   Freedom of Conscience and Protestant Education in France, 1815-1885. Harvard 1964

D67   Day, John.   *Les douanes de Gênes, 1376-1377, Ecole Practique des Hautes Études.* Columbia 1963

D68   Deák, Istvan.   Weimar Germany's "Homeless Left": The World of Carl von Ossietzky. Columbia 1964

D69 Dean, Warren K. São Paulo's Industrial Elite, 1890-1960. Fla U 1964

D70 Deaton, Thomas M. Atlanta during the Progressive Era. Ga 1969

D71 De Benedetti, Charles L. American Internationalism in the 1920's: Shotwell and the Outlawrists. Ill 1968

D72 DeBerry, John H. Confederate Tennessee. Ky 1967

D73 Debo, Richard K. George Chicherin: Soviet Russia's Second Foreign Commissar. Neb 1964

D74 DeBoe, David C. The United States and the Geneva Disarmament Conference, 1932-1934. Tulane 1969

D75 Decker, Joe F. Progressive Reaction to Selective Service in World War I. Ga 1969

D76 Decker, Leslie E. Railroads, Lands, and Politics: The Taxation of the Railroad Land Grants, 1864-1897. Cornell 1961

D77 Decker, Robert J. Jason Lee, Missionary to Oregon: A Re-evaluation. Ind 1961

D78 Decker, Robert O. The New London Merchants, 1645-1909: The Rise and Decline of a Connecticut Port. Conn 1970

D79 DeCola, Thomas G. Roosevelt and Mussolini: The Critical Years, 1938-1941. Kent 1967

D80 Dee, Bleeker. Duvalier's Haiti: A Case Study of National Disintegration. Fla U 1967

D81 De Giustino, David A. Phrenology in Britain, 1815-1855: A Study of George Combe and His Circle. Wis 1969

D82 de Graaf, Lawrence B. Negro Migration to Los Angeles, 1930-1950. UCLA 1962

D83 De Grand, Alexander J. The Italian Nationalist Association: Its Origins and Development, 1903-1915. Chicago 1968

D84 de Gryse, Louis M. The Reform of Flemish Judicial and Fiscal Administration in the Reign of Philip of Alsace (1157/63-1191). Minn 1969

D85 Dehmelt, Bernard K. Bülow's Moroccan Policy, 1902-1905. Penn U 1963

D86 Deierhoi, Tyler. The Conduct of German Policy at the General Disarmament Conference of 1932. Duke 1964

D87 Deiner, John T. ATLAS: A Labor Instrument of Argentine Expansionism under Perón. Rutgers 1969

D88 De Jong, John A. American Attitudes toward Evolution before Darwin. Ia 1962

D89 Delaney, Norman C. John McIntosh Kell: "Luff" of the *Alabama*. Duke 1967

D90 Del Duca, Gemma M., Sister. A Political Portrait: Félix Varela y Morales, 1788-1853. NM 1966

D91 D'Elia, Donald J. Benjamin Rush: An Intellectual Biography. Penn S 1965

D92 Dell, Harry J., Jr. The Illyrian Frontier to 229 B.C. Wis 1964

D93 Della Cava, Ralph. Miracle of Joaseiro: A Political and Economic History of a Popular Religious Movement in Brazil, 1889-1934. Columbia 1968

D94 Dellagrotte, Joseph A. Venetian Diplomacy and the Treaty of Carlowitz, 1698-1699. Syracuse 1965

D95 Delman, Barbara M. Liberty and Common Law in Eighteenth-Century England. Columbia 1969

D96 De Lorme, Roland L. The Shaping of a Progressive: Edward P. Costigan and Urban Reform in Denver, 1910-1911. Colo 1965

D97 Delp, Robert W. The Harmonial Philosopher, Andrew Jackson Davis, and the Foundation of Modern American Spiritualism. Geo W 1965

D98 Delpar, Helen V. The Liberal Party of Colombia, 1863-1903. Columbia 1967

D99 de Luna, Adolph F. The Republic of Cavaignac. Ia 1962

D100 DeMarce, Virginia M. E. The Official Career of Georg III Truchsess von Waldburg: A Study in the Administration of Religious Policy by a Catholic Government during the First Years of the Reformation. Stanford 1967

D101 Deme, Laszlo. The Radical Left in the Hungarian Revolution of 1848. Columbia 1969

D102 DeMichele, Michael D. The Glorious Revolution in Maryland: A Study of the Provincial Revolution of 1689. Penn S 1967

D103 Dennison, George M. The Constitutional Issues of the Dorr War: A Study in the Evolution of American Constitutionalism, 1776-1849. Wash U 1968

D104 Denton, Charles R. American Unitarians, 1830-1865: A Study of Religious Opinion on War, Slavery, and the Union. Mich S 1969

D105 Denton, Edgar, III. The Formative Years of the United States Military Academy, 1775-1833. Syracuse 1964

D106 DePauw, Linda G. The Eleventh Pillar: New York State and the Federal Constitution. JH 1964

D107 Derby, William E. A History of the Port of Milwaukee, 1835-1910. Wis 1963

D108 Derfler, A. Leslie. Reformism: The Socialist Years of Alexandre Millerand. Columbia 1962

D109 Derr, Emerson L. Simon Snyder, Governor of Pennsylvania, 1808-1817. Penn S 1960

D110 Desai, Santosh N. Hindu Elements in Thai Culture. St John's 1968

D111 Désilets, Andrée. *Un père de la Confédération canadienne, Hector Louis Langevin* (1826-1906). Laval 1967

D112 Desmarais, Ralph H. The Supply and Transport Committee, 1919-1926: A Study of the British Government's Method of Handling Emergencies Stemming from Industrial Disputes. Wis 1970

D113 Desmond, Lawrence A. The Statute Legislation of Edward I and Its Effect upon the English Cistercians to 1399. Fordham 1967

D114 Despalatovic, Elinor M. Ljudevit Gaj and the Illyrian Movement (to 1843). Columbia 1969

D115 Detert, Mary Xavier, Sister. Catholic Political Activity in France, 1892-1914. Cath 1963

D116 Dethloff, Henry C. Populism and Reform in Louisiana. Mo 1964

D117 Detrick, Robert H. Henry Andrea Burgevine in China: A Biography. Ind 1968

D118 Detzer, David W. The Politics of the Payne-Aldrich Tariff of 1909. Conn 1970

D119 Devadanam, Chebrolu. The Development of Provincial Autonomy in India, 1919-1949. NYU 1964

D120 Devanesen, Chandran D. S. The Making of the Mahatma: An Interpretive Study of M.K. Gandhi's First Forty Years. Harvard 1962

D121 Devine, Joseph A., Jr. The British North American Colonies in the War of 1739-1748. Va 1968

D122 De Vore, Blanche B. The Influence of Antonio Díaz Soto y Gama on the Agrarian Movement in Mexico. S Cal 1963

D123 Dew, Charles B. Southern Industry in the Civil War Era: Joseph Reid Anderson and the Tredegar Iron Works, 1859-1867. JH 1964

D124 Dew, Lee A. The Racial Ideas of the Authors of the Fourteenth Amendment. LSU 1960

D125 Dewing, Rolland L. Teacher Organizations and Desegregation, 1954-1964. Ball State 1967

D126 Diamondstone, Judith M. The Philadelphia Corporation, 1701-1776. Penn U 1969

D127 DiBacco, Thomas V. Return to Dollar Diplomacy? American Business Reaction to the Eisenhower Foreign Aid Program, 1953-1961. Am 1965

D128 Dibner, Ursula R. B. The History of the National Socialist German Student League. Mich U 1969

D129 Dick, William M. Labor and Socialism in America: The Gompers Era. Toronto 1966

D130 Dickerman, Edmund H. The Kings' Men: The Ministers of Henry III and Henry IV, 1574-1610. Brown 1965

D131 Dickinson, John N. The Canal at Sault Ste. Marie, Michigan: Inception, Construction, Early Operation, and the Canal Grant Lands. Wis 1968

D132 Dickinson, William C. Sidney Godolphin, Lord Treasurer, 1702-1710. NC 1967

D133 Dickison, Edward H. The United States Merchant Marine as an Arm of National Policy. St L 1968

D134 Dicks, Samuel E. The Question of Peace: Anglo-French Diplomacy, A.D. 1439-1449. Okla 1966

D135 Dickson, John L. The Judicial History of the Cherokee Nation from 1721 to 1835. Okla 1964

D136 Dieker, M. Alberta, Sister. The Diplomatic Background of the *Reichskondat* of 1933. Ore 1968

D137 Dietrich, Donald J. German Idealism and the German Catholic Theological Response—Hermes, Möhler, Staudenmaier and Günther: 1815-1860. Minn 1969

D138 Dietz, Anthony G. The Prisoner of War in the United States during the War of 1812. Am 1964

D139 Diggins, John P. Mussolini's Italy: The View from America. S Cal 1964

D140 Dilkes, Thomas P., Jr. Values in the Historiography of Vasilii Osipovich Kliuchevskii. Ia 1964

D141 Dillingham, George A., Jr. Peabody Normal College in Southern Education, 1875-1909. Geo P 1970

D142 DiMeglio, Peter M. The United States and the Second Hague Peace Conference: The Extension of the Use of Arbitration. St John's 1968

D143 Dingman, Roger V. Power in the Pacific: The Evolution of American and Japanese Naval Policies, 1918-1921. Harvard 1969

D144 Dinkin, Robert J. Provincial Massachusetts: A Deferential or a Democratic Society? Columbia 1968

D145 Dinnerstein, Leonard. The Leo Frank Case. Columbia 1966

D146 DiNunzio, Mario R. Lyman Trumbull, United States Senator. Clark 1964

D147 Dinwoodie, David H. Expedient Diplomacy: The United States and Guatemala, 1898-1920. Colo 1966

D148 Di Scala, Spencer M. Filippo Turati and Factional Strife in the Italian Socialist Party, 1892-1912. Columbia 1969

D149 Dixon, Joseph M. Gregor Strasser and the Organization of the Nazi Party, 1925-1932. Stanford 1966

D150 Dizikes, John. Britain, Roosevelt and the New Deal, 1932-1938. Harvard 1964

D151 Dobbert, Guido A. The Disintegration of an Immigrant Community: The Cincinnati Germans, 1870-1920. Chicago 1965

D152 Dobney, Fredrick J. The Papers of Will Clayton. Rice 1970

D153 Dobson, John M. The Mugwump Protest in the Election of 1884. Wis 1966

D154 Dobson, Paul G. David Hume's Theory of History: A Study in the Relationship between His Philosophical, Sociological, and Historical Methodology. NYU 1965

D155 Dodd, Donald B. Unionism in Confederate Alabama. Ga 1969

D156 Dodd, Thomas J., Jr. The United States in Nicaraguan Politics: Supervised Elections, 1927-1932. Geo W 1966

D157 Dodge, Robert H. The Moscow Zemstvo and Elementary Education, 1868-1910. Syracuse 1970

D158 Dodge, Stephen C. The History of the Development of the Venezuelan Guayana Region. Minn 1968

D159 Doenecke, Justus D. American Public Opinion and the Manchurian Crisis, 1931-1933. Princeton 1966

D160 Doherty, Robert W. Alfred H. Love and the Universal Peace Union. Penn U 1962

D161 Dohse, Michael A. American Periodicals and the Palestine Triangle, April, 1936 to February, 1947. Miss S 1966

D162 Doig, Ivan C. John J. McGilvra: The Life and Times of an Urban Frontiersman, 1827-1903. Wash U 1969

D163 Dolan, G. Phillip. Major General William Heath and the First Years of the American Revolution. Boston U 1966

D164 Dolkart, Ronald H. Manuel A. Fresco, Governor of the Province of Buenos Aires, 1936-1940. UCLA 1961

D165 Dollar, Charles M. The Senate Progressive Movement, 1921-1933: A Roll Call Analysis. Ky 1966

D166 Dolman, Arthur. The Third Reich and Japan: A Study in Nazi Cultural Relations. NYU 1966

D167 Domer, Marilyn A. The Development of Federated Fund Raising in Muncie, Indiana, 1925-1957. Ball State 1968

D168 Domínguez T., Mauricio. The Development of the Technological and Scientific Coffee Industry in Guatemala, 1830-1930. Tulane 1970

D170 Donahoe, Bernard F. New Dealers, Conservatives and the Democratic Nominees of 1940. Notre D 1965

D171 Donald, Aida (DiPace). Prelude to Civil War: The Decline of the Whig Party in New York, 1848-1852. Rochester 1961

D172 Donathan, Carl D. Lucas Alamán and Mexican Foreign Affairs, 1821-1833. Duke 1968

D173 Donlon, Walter J. Lebaron Bradford Prince, Chief Justice and Governor of New Mexico Territory, 1879-1893. NM 1967

D174 Donnelly, James B. Prentiss Bailey Gilbert, the League Council, and the Manchurian Crisis of 1931. Va 1969

D174a Donoghue, Francis J. The Economic and Social Policies of John C. Calhoun. Columbia 1969

D175 Donovan, Robert K. Opposition to Roman Catholic Relief in Scotland, 1778-1782. Harvard 1965

D176 Donovan, Therese Anna, Sister. Americans and Englishmen through Each Other's Eyes, 1850-1860: A Study in National Spirit. Boston C 1963

D177 Doolen, Richard M. The Greenback Party in the Great Lakes Middlewest. Mich U 1969

D178 Doran, William A. The Development of the Industrial Spirit in Tennessee, 1910-1920. Geo P 1965

D179 Dorley, Albert J., Jr. The Role of Congress in the Establishment of Bases in Spain. St John's 1969

D180 Dormon, James H., Jr. The Theater in the Ante-Bellum South, 1815-1861. NC 1966

D181 Dorn, Jacob H., III. Washington Gladden: Prophet of the Social Gospel, 1836-1918. Ore 1965

D182 Dorotich, Daniel. History in the Soviet School, 1917-1937: Changing Policy and Practice. McGill 1964

D183 Dorsett, Lyle W. A History of the Pendergast Machine. Mo 1965

D184 Dosher, Harry R. The Concept of the Ideal Prince in French Political Thought, 800-1760. NC 1969

D185 Dotson, John E. Shipping Practices and Freight Rates in the Medieval Mediterranean. JH 1970

D186 Dotson, Lloyd C. The Diplomatic Mission of Baron Hyde de Neuville to the United States, 1816-1822. Ga 1970

D187 Doty, Charles S. Maurice Barrès and the Fate of Boulangism: The Political Career of Maurice Barrès (1888-1906). Ohio 1964

D188 Dougherty, John E. Mexico and Guatemala: 1856-1872: A Case Study in Extra-Legal International Relations. UCLA 1969

D189 Dougherty, Mark E. The Diplomacy of Decadence: Don Luis de Haro and the Peace of the Pyrenees. Ga 1970

D190 Doughty, Sylvia J. K. The German Science of Politics in the American University, Civil War to World War I. JH 1969

D191 Douglas, Donald M. The Early Ortsgruppen: The Development of National Socialist Local Groups, 1919-1923. Kans U 1968

D192 Douglas, Mary R. The Political Career of Archbishop John Williams, 1621-1640. Harvard 1967

D192a Downard, William L. The Cincinnati Brewing Industry, 1811-1933: A Social and Economic History. Miami U 1969

D193 Downes, Alan J. Optimism and Pessimism in American Magazines, 1850-1960. Wash U 1961

D194 Downey, Matthew T. The Rebirth of Reform: A Study of Liberal Reform Movements, 1865-1872. Princeton 1963

D194a Downing, Marvin L. Hugh R. Wilson and American Relations with the League of Nations, 1927-1937. Okla 1970

D195 Downs, Charles L. Britain and the Council of Europe. Ga 1969

D196 Downs, Jacques M. The American Community in Canton, 1784-1844. Georgetown 1961

D197 Dowty, Alan. The United States and the Crimean War: A Reappraisal of Nineteenth Century U.S. Isolation. Chicago 1963

D198 Doxsee, Gifford B. British Policy toward Palestine, 1914-1939. Harvard 1966

D199 Doyle, James T. James Edwin Campbell: Conservative Democratic Congressman, Governor and Statesman. Ohio 1967

D200 Doyle, Joseph J. Venezuela 1958: Transition from Dictatorship to Democracy. Geo W 1967

D201 Dozier, Robert R. Ministerial Efforts to Combat Revolutionary Propaganda, 1789-1793. Cal, Berkeley 1969

D202 Drache, Hiram M. The Day of Bonanza: A History of Bonanza Farming in the Red River Valley of the North. ND 1963

D203 Drake, Edson J. Bulgaria at the Paris Peace Conference: A Diplomatic History of the Treaty of Neuilly-Sur-Seine. Georgetown 1967

D204 Drake, Frederick C. "The Empire of the Seas": A Biography of Robert Wilson Shufeldt, USN. Cornell 1970

D205 Drake, Harold A. *Semper victor eris:* Evidence for the Policy and Belief of Constantine I Contained in Eusebius' *Tricennial Oration.* Wis 1970

D206 Draughon, Ralph B., Jr. William Lowndes Yancey: From Unionist to Secessionist, 1814-1852. NC 1968

D207 Drayer, Robert E. J. Hampton Moore: An Old Fashioned Republican. Penn U 1961

D208 Dreher, Robert E. Arthur de Gobineau: An Intellectual Portrait. Wis 1970

D209 Drescher, Nuala M. The Opposition to Prohibition, 1900-1919: A Social and Institutional Study. Del 1964

D210 Drimmer, Melvin. Nietzsche in American Thought, 1895-1925. Rochester 1965

D211 Driscoll, William D. Benjamin F. Butler: Lawyer and Regency Politician. Fordham 1965

D212 Droppers, Garrett. The *Questiones de spera* of Nicole Oresme: Latin Text with English Translation, Commentary and Variants. Wis 1966

D213 Drouin, Emeric O. *La Colonie Saint-Paul-des-Metis, Alberta (1896-1909).* Ottawa 1962

D214 Drozdowski, Eugene C. Edwin M. Stanton, Lincoln's Secretary of War: Toward Victory. Duke 1964

D215 Druks, Herbert. Harry S. Truman and the Russians, 1945-1953. NYU 1964

D216 Drummond, Gordon D. The Military Policy of the German Social Democratic Party, 1949-1960. Stanford 1968

D217 Drzewieniecki, Walter M. Polish Historiography from 1945 to 1958, with Special Attention to the History of the Period 1772-1815. Chicago 1963

D218 Dubbert, Joseph L. The Puritan in Babylon: William Allen White. Minn 1967

D220 Duff, John B. The Politics of Revenge: The Ethnic Opposition to the Peace Policies of Woodrow Wilson. Columbia 1964

D221 Duffy, Edward G. Politics of Expediency: Diplomatic Relations between the United States and Venezuela during the Juan Vicente Gómez Era. Penn S 1969

D222 Duffy, John J. Charleston Politics in the Progressive Era. SC 1963

D223 Dugas, Vera L. A Social and Economic History of Texas in the Civil War and Reconstruction Periods. Tex U 1963

D224 Duggan, Paul R. Currents of Administrative Reform in Germany, 1907-1918. Harvard 1969

D225 Duiker, William J., III. Ts'ai Yuan-p'ei and the Intellectual Revolution in Modern China. Georgetown 1968

D226 Dukes, Jack R. Helgoland, Zanzibar, East Africa: Colonialism in German Politics, 1884-1890. Ill 1970

D227 Dull, Jack L. A Historical Introduction to the Apocryphal (Ch'an-wei) Texts of the Han Dynasty. Wash U 1966

D228 Duly, Leslie C. British Land Policy at the Cape, 1795-1844. Duke 1965

D229 Dumin, Frederick. Background of the Austro-German *Anschluss* Movement. Wis 1963

D230 Duncan, Eva S. The Government of Bearn, 1472-1494. Emory 1968

D231 Duncan, Richard R. The Social and Economic Impact of the Civil War on Maryland. Ohio 1963

D232 Duncan, T. Bentley. Uneasy Allies: Anglo-Portuguese Commercial, Diplomatic, and Maritime Relations, 1642-1662. Chicago 1967

D233 Dunham, Chester G. The Diplomatic Career of Christopher Hughes. Ohio 1968

D234 Dunkak, Harry M. John Morin Scott and the Whig Politics in New York City (1752-1769). St John's 1968

D235 Dunn, Dennis J. Stalinism and the Vatican. Kent 1970

D236 Dunn, Edward T. Tutor Henry Flynt of Harvard College, 1675-1760. Rochester 1968

D237 Dunn, Fabius. The Administration of Don Antonio Cordero, Governor of Texas, 1805-1808. Tex U 1962

D238 Dunn, Patrick P. V. G. Belinskii: The Road to Reality, 1811-1841. Duke 1969

D239 Dunn, Ross E. The Colonial Offensive in Southeastern Morocco, 1881-1912: Patterns of Response. Wis 1969

D240 Duram, James C. Press Attitudes towards the Role of the Supreme Court in the 1930's. Wayne 1968

D241 Duran, Elizabeth C. The NAM's Opposition to the Gardner Eight-Hour Bill, 1902-1912: A Study in Lobbying. Ill 1963

D242 Durham, Robert J., Jr. In Search of the Council, 1585-1615. Yale 1969

D243 Dusenbury, Richard B. Truth and Technique: A Study of Sociology and the Social Survey Movement, 1895-1930. Wis 1969

D244 Dutra, Francis A. Matias de Albuquerque: A Seventeenth Century *Capitão Mor* of Pernambuco and Governor-General of Brazil. NYU 1968

D245 Duus, Peter. The Kenseikai and the Politics of Taisho Japan. Harvard 1965

D246 Dyck, Harvey L. German-Soviet Relations, 1926-1933: A Study in the Diplomacy of Instability. Columbia 1963

D247 Dykstra, Robert R. The Cattle Town Experience: Social Process and the Kansas Cattle-trading Centers, 1867-1885. Ia 1964

D248 Dyson, Lowell K. The Farm Holiday Movement. Columbia 1968

E

E1 Eagles, Keith D. Ambassador Joseph E. Davies and American-Soviet Relations, 1937-1941. Wash U 1966

E2 Eakins, David W. The Development of Corporate Liberal Policy Research in the United States, 1885-1965. Wis 1966

E3 Earl, John L., III. Talleyrand in America: A Study of His Exile in the United States, 1794-1796. Georgetown 1964

E4 Earnest, Grace E. City Life in the Old South: The British Travelers' Image. Fla S 1966

E5 Eastman, Lloyd E. Reactions of Chinese Officials to Foreign Aggression: A Study of the Sino-French Controversy, 1880-1885. Harvard 1963

E6 Eastwood, Bruce S. The Geometrical Optics of Robert Grosseteste. Wis 1964

E7 Eaton, Henry L. Early Russian Censuses and the Population of Muscovy, 1550-1650. Ill 1970

E8 Eaves, Richard G. Anglo-Scottish Relations during the Duke of Albany's Regency, 1515-1524. Ala 1970

E9 Eblen, Jack E. The Governor in the United States System of Territorial Government. Wis 1966

E10 Eckenrode, Thomas R. Original Aspects in Venerable Bede's Tidal Theories with Relation to Prior Tidal Observations. St L 1970

E11 Eckert, Edward K. William Jones and the Role of the Secretary of the Navy in the War of 1812. Fla U 1969

E12 Eckes, Alfred E., Jr. Bretton Woods: America's New Deal for an Open World. Tex U 1969

E13 Edelstein, Melvin A. *La Feuille Villageoise:* Communication and Rural Modernization in the French Revolution. Princeton 1965

E14 Edelstein, Tilden G. Strange Enthusiasm: Thomas Wentworth Higginson, 1823-1877. JH 1961

E15 Eder, Donald G. The Tannenbaum Thesis: A New Black Legend. Ohio 1970

E16 Edgar, Frank T. R. Sir Ralph Hopton, the "King's Man in the West," 1642-1652: A Study in Character and Command. Cal, Berkeley 1966

E17 Edgar, Walter B. The Libraries of Colonial South Carolina. SC 1969

E18 Edmondson, Clifton E. The Heimwehr and Austrian Politics, 1918-1934. Duke 1966

E19 Edmondson, Nelson. The Fichte Society: A Chapter in Germany's Conservative Revolution. Harvard 1964

E20 Edmondson, William D. Fundamentalist Sects of Los Angeles, 1900-1930. Claremont 1969

E21 Edmunds, John B., Jr. Francis W. Pickens: A Political Biography. SC 1967

E22 Edsall, Nicholas C. The New Poor Law and Its Opponents, 1834-1844. Harvard 1966

E23 Edwards, David W. Orthodoxy during the Reign of Tsar Nicholas I: A Study in Church-State Relations. Kans S 1967

E24 Edwards, Frank T. The United States Consulate in the Bahamas during the American Civil War: A Study of Its Function within a Naval and Diplomatic Context. Cath 1968

E25 Edwards, Glenn T. The Department of the Pacific in the Civil War Years. Ore 1963

E26 Edwards, Jerome E. Foreign Policy Attitudes of the *Chicago Tribune,* 1929-1941. Chicago 1966

E27 Edwards, Paul E., Jr. Lewis Mumford's Search for Values. Am 1970

E28 Edwards, Rhoda D. K. The Seventy-Eighth Congress on the Home Front: Domestic Economic Legislation, 1943-1944. Rutgers 1967

E29 Egan, Clifford L. Franco-American Relations, 1803-1814. Colo 1969

E30 Egan, David R. The Origin of the 1810 State Council and Its Functioning during the Reign of Alexander I. SUNY, Binghamton 1970

E31 Egbert, Arch O. Marriner S. Eccles and the Banking Act of 1935. Brigham Young 1967

E32 Egbuonu, Ndukwe N. Indirect Rule and Its Application in Southeastern Nigeria: A Study in the Techniques of British Colonial Administration. Columbia 1964

E33 Egerton, Cecil B. Rufus King and the Missouri Question: A Study in Political Mythology. Claremont 1968

E34 Ehret, Christopher P. The Southern Nilotes to 1600 A.D.: A Linguistic Approach to East African History. Northwestern 1969

E35 Eickhoff, Harold W. The Organization and Regulation of Medicine in Missouri, 1883-1901. Mo 1964

E36 Eid, Leroy V. Lincoln and the Coming of the Civil War. St John's 1961

E37 Eidson, William G. John Alexander Logan: Hero of the Volunteers. Vanderbilt 1967

E38 Eiklor, John L. Bavaria, the *Landtag,* and the War of 1866. Northwestern 1963

E39 Eisan, Leslie G. Lord Althorp: A Study of His Political Life with Special Reference to the Years 1830-1834. Chicago 1962

E40 Eisenberg, Bernard. James Weldon Johnson and the National Association for the Advancement of Colored People, 1916-1934. Columbia 1968

E41 Eisenberg, Peter L. The Sugar Industry of Pernambuco, 1850-1889. Columbia 1969

E42 Eisenstein, Hester. Victor Cousin and the War on the University of France. Yale 1968

E43 Eissenstat, Bernard W. M. N. Pokrovsky and Soviet Historiography. Kans U 1967

E44 Eisterhold, John A. Lumber and Trade in the Seaboard Cities of the Old South, 1607-1860. Miss U 1970

E44a Ekberg, Carl J. From Dutch War to European War: French Foreign Policy during 1673. Rutgers 1970

E45 Ekechi, Felix K. Missionary Enterprise in Igboland, 1857-1914. Wis 1969

E46 Elam, Robert V. Appeal to Arms: The Army and Politics in El Salvador, 1931-1964. NM 1968

E47 Elbert, Elmer D. Southern Indiana Politics on the Eve of the Civil War, 1858-1861. Ind 1967

E48 Elder, A. Jean. A Study of the Beauforts and Their Estates, 1399-1450. Bryn Mawr 1964

E49 Elder, James P., Jr. The Public Career of Henry Coventry: Statesman and Politician in the Reign of Charles II. NC 1970

E50 Eldot, Paula. Alfred Emanuel Smith, Reforming Governor. Yale 1961

E51 Elenbaas, Jack D. Detroit and the Progressive Era: A Study of Urban Reform, 1900-1914. Wayne 1968

E52 Elkin, Robert E. The Interactions between the Irish Rebellion and the English Civil Wars. Ill 1961

E53 Ellefson, Clinton A. The County Courts and the Provincial Court in Maryland, 1733-1763. Md 1963

E54 Ellenburg, Martha A. Reconstruction in Arkansas. Mo 1967

E55 Ellery, Suzanne C. From Sentimentalism to Sophistication: Best Sellers and Changing American Attitudes and Values, 1914-1945. JH 1970

E56 Ellinwood, DeWitt C., Jr. Lord Milner's "Kindergarten," the British Round Table Group, and the Movement for Imperial Reform, 1910-1918. Wash St L 1962

E57 Ellis, Donald W. Music in the Third Reich: National Socialist Aesthetic Theory as Governmental Policy. Kans U 1970

E58 Ellis, Jack D. French Socialist and Syndicalist Approaches to Peace, 1904-1914. Tulane 1967

E59 Ellis, John H. Yellow Fever and the Origins of Modern Public Health in Memphis, Tennessee, 1870-1900. Tulane 1962

E60 Ellis, Joseph A. Francisco Pimentel: His Life and Times. Columbia 1961

E61 Ellis, Joseph J., III. The Puritan Mind in Transition: The American Samuel Johnson (1696-1772). Yale 1969

E62 Ellis, L. Tuffly. The Texas Cotton Compress Industry: A History. Tex U 1964

E63 Ellis, Richard E. The Jeffersonian Crisis: Courts and Politics in the Young Republic. Cal, Berkeley 1969

E64 Ellis, Richard N. General John Pope and the Development of Federal Indian Policy, 1862-1886. Colo 1967

E64a Elovitz, Paul H. "Airy and Salubrius Factories" or "Dark Satanic Mills"? Some Early Reactions to the Impact of the Industrial Revolution on the Condition of the English Working Classes. Rutgers 1969

E65 Elrod, Richard B. The Venetian Question in Austrian Foreign Relations, 1860-1866. Ill 1967

E66 Elsmere, Mary Jane S. The Impeachment Trial of Justice Samuel Chase. Ind 1962

E67 Eluwa, Gabriel I. C. The Colonial Office and the Emergence of the National Congress of British West Africa. Mich S 1967

E68 Elwitt, Sanford H. The Radicals Enter French Politics, 1870-1875. Cornell 1963

E69 Elwood, Ralph C. The RSDRP in the Underground: A Study of the Russian Social Democratic Labor Party in the Ukraine, 1907-1914. Columbia 1969

E70 Emery, Harold W., Jr. The Mission of Albert Billot in Rome, 1890-1898, and the Franco-Italian Rapprochement. Penn U 1964

E71 Emmons, David M. The Boomers' Frontier: Land Promotion and the Settlement of the Central Plains, 1854-1893. Colo 1969

E72 Emmons, Terence L. The Russian Landed Gentry and the Peasant Emancipation of 1861. Cal, Berkeley 1966

E73 Enck, Henry S., III. The Burden Borne: Northern White Philanthropy and Southern Black Industrial Education, 1900-1915. Cincinnati 1970

E74 Enders, Calvin W. The Vinson Navy. Mich S 1970

E75 Endress, Charles A. The Republican-Radical and Radical-Socialist Party in the French Popular Front. Tulane 1968

E76 Engelder, Conrad J. The Churches and Slavery. A Study of the Attitudes toward Slavery of the Major Protestant Denominations. Mich U 1964

E77 Engelhardt, Carroll L. The Common School and the Ideal Citizen: Iowa, 1876-1921. Ia 1969

E78 Ennis, Gratia, Sister. The Vocabulary of the Institutions of Cassiodorus. Cath 1939

E79 Ensley, Philip C. The Political and Social Thought of Elmer Davis. Ohio 1965

E80 Enstam, Mary Elizabeth Y. The "Khaki" Election of 1900 in the United Kingdom. Duke 1968

E81 Enteen, George M. M. N. Pokrovskii and the Society of Marxist Historians. Geo W 1965

E82 Entner, Marvin L. Russia and Persia, 1890-1912. Minn 1963

E83 Epstein, David M. The Role of Mirabeau in the French Revolution. Neb 1967

E84 Epstein, Joel J. The Parliamentary Career of Francis Bacon, 1581-1614. Rutgers 1966

E85 Epstein, Laurence B. The American Philosophy of War, 1945-1967. S Cal 1967

E86 Erickson, Carolly. Francis Conformed to Christ: Bartholomew of Pisa's *De Conformitate* in Franciscan History. Columbia 1968

E87 Erickson, Erling A. Banks and Politics before the Civil War: The Case of Iowa, 1836-1865. Ia 1967

E88 Erickson, Nancy L. The Early Colonial Humorist. NC 1970

E89 Erickson, Norma N. A Dispute between a Priest and a Knight. Wash U 1966

E90 Erlebacher, Albert. Herman L. Ekern, the Quiet Progressive. Wis 1965

E91 Ernest, Welden A. Reclamation and Colonization by Immigrants from the Netherlands in the Archdiocese of Hamburg-Bremen during the Twelfth and Thirteenth Centuries. Harvard 1967

E92 Ernst, Eldon G. The Interchurch World Movement of North America, 1919-1920. Yale 1968

E93 Ernst, Joseph A. Currency in the Era of the American Revolution: A History of Colonial Paper Money Practices and British Monetary Policies, 1764-1781. Wis 1962

E94 Ershkowitz, Herbert. New Jersey Politics during the Era of Andrew Jackson, 1820-1837. NYU 1965

E95 Esler, Anthony J. The Aspiring Mind of the Elizabethan Younger Generation. Duke 1961

E96 Esper, Thomas. The Land and Government of Muscovy. Chicago 1964

E97 Essefian, Srpouhie-Anna. Medieval Monarchies of Armenia: The Last Phase. Georgetown 1970

E98 Essin, Emmett M., III. The Cavalry and the Horse. Tex C 1968

E99 Estes, James M. Johannes Brenz and the Problem of Church Order in the German Reformation. Ohio 1964

E100 Etheridge, Elizabeth W. The Strange Hunger: A Social History of Pellagra in the South. Ga 1966

E101 Etulain, Richard W. The Literary Career of a Western Writer: Ernest Haycox, 1899-1950. Ore 1966

E102 Eubanks, David L. Dr. J. G. M. Ramsey of East Tennessee: A Career of Public Service. Tenn 1965

E103 Eulie, Joseph A., Jr. Politics and Administration in Ireland, 1760-1766. Fordham 1965

E104 Evans, Anna M. Oliver Mowat and Ontario, 1872-1896: A Study in Political Success. Toronto 1967

E105 Evans, Frank B. Pennsylvania Politics, 1872-1877: A Study in Leadership without Responsibility. Penn S 1962

E106   Evans, Geraint N.D.   North American Soldier, Hydrographer, Governor: The Public Careers of J.F.W. DesBarres, 1721-1824. Yale 1965

E107   Evans, John L.   Petrashevskii and the Petrashevtsy. NC 1968

E108   Evans, Tony H.   Oregon Progressive Reform, 1902-1914. Cal, Berkeley 1966

E109   Evans, William B.   "Revolutionist Thought" in the *Daily Worker,* 1919-1939. Wash U 1965

E110   Evans, William M.   Ballots and Fence Rails: Reconstruction on the Lower Cape Fear. NC 1965

E111   Evanson, Philip N.   The Liberal Party and Reform in Brazil, 1860-1889. Va 1969

E112   Everett, Miles C.   Chester Harvey Rowell, Pragmatic Humanist and California Progressive. Cal, Berkeley 1966

E113   Everett, Robert B.   Race Relations in South Carolina, 1900-1932. Ga 1969

E114   Evers, Joseph C.   The History of the Southern Illinois Conference of the Methodist Church. Boston U 1962

E115   Ezell, Macel D.   The Evangelical Protestant Defense of Americanism, 1945-1960. Tex C 1969

E116   Ezergailis, Andrew.   The Bolshevik Revolution in Latvia, March to August, 1917. NYU 1968

F

F1 Fabiano, Thomas A. Venetian Foreign Policy from the Descent of Charles VIII to the Occupation of the Duchy of Milan (1495-1499). Syracuse 1967

F3 Fackler, Jon B. An End to Compromise: The Kansas-Nebraska Bill of 1854. Penn S 1969

F4 Factor, Robert L. The Archdiocese of Color: Cause, Casuistry and Organization in Black America. Wis 1968

F5 Fagan, Ann. Great Britain and Nazi Germany, 1933: The Origins of Appeasement. Bryn Mawr 1969

F6 Fagerlie, Joan M. Late Roman and Byzantine Solidi Found in Scandinavia. Wash U 1965

F7 Fagg, Jane B. Adam Ferguson: Scottish Cato. NC 1968

F8 Fahey, David M. Historical Interpretations of the English Civil War, Particularly since the Middle of the Eighteenth Century. Notre D 1964

F9 Fair, John D. The Role of the Conference in British Politics, 1884-1918. Duke 1970

F10 Fairfield, Leslie P. The Historical Thought of John Bale (1495-1563). Harvard 1969

F11 Fajn, Max. The *Journal des Hommes Libres de tous les pays.* Chicago 1969

F12 Falconeri, Gennaro. Reactions to Revolution: Japanese Attitudes and Foreign Policy toward China, 1924-1927. Mich U 1967

F13 Falk, Joyce D. The Concept of the Ideal Prince in the Literature of the French Enlightenment (1700-1780). S Cal 1969

F14 Fallaw, Walter R., Jr. The Rise of the Whig Party in New Jersey. Princeton 1967

F15 Fallis, Laurence S., Jr. The Idea of Progress in the Province of Canada, 1841-1867. Mich U 1966

F16 Falls, James S. The Justiciarship of Rannulf de Glanville, 1180-1189. Miss S 1967

F17 Falzone, Vincent J. Terence V. Powderly: Mayor and Labor Leader, 1849-1893. Md 1970

F18 Fan, Carol C. The Geographic Distribution of Leadership in China, 1875-1937. UCLA 1965

F19 Fann, Willerd R. The Consolidation of Bureaucratic Absolutism in Prussia, 1817-1827. Cal, Berkeley 1965

F20 Fargo, Mumtaz A. Arab-Turkish Relations from the Emergence of Arab Nationalism to the Arab Revolt, 1848-1916. Utah 1969

F21 Farmer, Donald W. Charles Howard of Effingham, Lord High Admiral of England: An Appreciative Re-evalution. Georgetown 1965

F22 Farmer, Harry F., Jr. The Hookworm Eradication Program in the South, 1909-1925. Ga 1970

F23 Farnell, James E. The Politics of the City of London (1649-1657). Chicago 1963

F24 Farnham, Thomas J. The State and the Nation: The History of the Federal-State Issue in American Diplomacy, 1789-1860. NC 1964

F25 Farrar, Marjorie M. French Blockade Policy, 1914-1918: A Study in Economic Warfare. Stanford 1968

F26 Farrar, Robert E. The Opposition of the Seventeenth Century Commonwealthsmen to the Cromwellian Protectorate. Ind 1969

F27 Farrell, John C. "Beloved Lady": A History of Jane Addams' Ideas on Reform and Peace. JH 1965

F28 Farrell, Richard T. Cincinnati in the Early Jackson Era, 1816-1834: An Economic and Political Study. Ind 1967

F29 Faulk, Odie B. The Last Years of Spanish Texas, 1778-1821. Tex Tech 1962

F30 Faulkner, Barbara L. Adin Ballou and the Hopedale Community. Boston U 1965

F31 Fedewa, Philip C. Abel Stearns in Transitional California, 1848-1871. Mo 1970

F32 Fehrenbach, Charles W. A Study of Spanish Liberalism: The Revolution of 1820. Tex U 1961

F33 Fein, Albert. Frederick Law Olmsted: His Development as a Theorist and Designer of the American City. Columbia 1969

F34 Feinberg, Harvey M. Elmina, Ghana: A History of Its Development and Relationship with the Dutch in the Eighteenth Century. Boston U 1969

F35   Feingold, Henry L. The Politics of Rescue: A Study of American Diplomacy and Politics Related to the Rescue of Refugees, 1938-1944. NYU 1966

F36   Feinstein, Marnin. The First Twenty-five Years of Zionism in the United States, 1882-1906. Columbia 1963

F37   Feldberg, Michael J. The Philadelphia Riots of 1844: A Social History. Rochester 1970

F38   Feldman, Gerald D. Army, Industry and Labor in Germany, 1914-1918. Harvard 1964

F39   Feldman, Leon A. Studies in the Life and Times of R. Nissim b. Reuben Gerondi of Barcelona, 1340-1380. Columbia 1967

F40   Feldman, Robert S. Between War and Revolution: The Russian General Staff, February–July 1917. Ind 1967

F41   Feldstein, Stanley. The Slave's View of Slavery. NYU 1969

F42   Felix, David. Walter Rathenau and the Politics of Reparations. Columbia 1970

F43   Feller, John Q., Jr. Theodore Roosevelt, the Department of Justice, and the Trust Problem: A Study in Presidential Policy. Cath 1968

F44   Fellman, Anita C. The Fearsome Necessity: Nineteenth Century British and American Strike Novels. Northwestern 1969

F45   Fellman, Michael D. The Unbounded Frame: Freedom and Community in Nineteenth Century American Utopianism. Northwestern 1969

F46   Felt, Thomas E. The Rise of Mark Hanna. Mich S 1961

F47   Fenichel, Allen H. Quantitative Analysis of the Growth and Diffusion of Steam Power in Manufacturing in the United States, 1838-1919. Penn U 1964

F48   Fennell, Thomas R. Commitment to Change: A History of Malayan Educational Policy, 1945-1957. Hawaii 1968

F49   Fenner, Francis E. Disraeli's Indian Policy. St John's 1966

F50   Fenner, Judith Anne G. Confederate Finances Abroad. Rice 1969

F51   Fenyo, Mario D. Horthy, Hitler, and Hungary: A Contribution to the Study of German-Hungarian Relations from June 1941 to the Fall of the Horthy Regime in October 1944. Am 1969

F52   Fenz, Emanuel G. South Tyrol, 1919-1939: A Study in Assimilation. Colo 1967

F53   Ferguson, J. Wilson. The Personal Reign of James V, King of Scots, 1528-1542. Princeton 1961

F54   Ferguson, Walter K. L. Geological Surveys in Texas, 1845-1909: An Institutional Study of Texas Politics. Tex U 1967

F54a   Fernández, José A. The Problem of War in Early Sixteenth-Century European Thought. Ind 1970

F55   Ferrell, Henry C., Jr. Claude A. Swanson of Virginia. Va 1964

F56   Ferrell, John R. Water Resource Development in the Arkansas Valley: A History of Public Policy to 1950. Okla 1968

F57   Ferrer, James. United States-Argentine Economic Relations, 1900-1930. Cal, Berkeley 1964

F58   Ferrer, José. The Armed Forces in Argentine Politics to 1930. NM 1966

F59   Ferrill, Arther L. Seneca: The Rise to Power. Ill 1964

F60   Ferris, Norman B. Tempestuous Mission, 1861-1862: The Early Diplomatic Career of Charles Francis Adams. Emory 1962

F61   Ferriss, William H. The Distortion of Pragmatism: How Practical-Minded Men, Including Philosophers, Translated an Epistemological Discipline into a Sociological Instrument. Vanderbilt 1965

F62   Ferroni, Charles D. The Italians in Cleveland: A Study in Assimilation. Kent 1969

F63   Fetter, Bruce S. Elisabethville and Lubumbashi: The Segmentary Growth of a Colonial City, 1910-1945. Wis 1968

F64   Fetzer, James A. Congress and China, 1941-1950. Mich S 1969

F65   Fiala, Robert D. George III in the Pennsylvania Press: A Study in Changing Opinions, 1760-1776. Wayne 1967

F66   Fichtner, Paula S. Dynast and Defender: Ferdinand I of Austria, 1522-1532. Penn U 1964

F67   Fick, George H. The Austrian Lands in Imperial Politics, 1198-1250. Harvard 1967

F68   Fickle, James E. The Origins and Development of the Southern Pine Association, 1883-1954. LSU 1970

F69   Field, Daniel. The End of Serfdom: Gentry and Bureaucracy in Russia, 1856-1861. Harvard 1969

F70 Fiering, Norman S. Moral Philosophy in America, 1700-1750, and Its British Context. Columbia 1969

F71 Filene, Peter G. American Attitudes toward Soviet Russia, 1917-1933. Harvard 1965

F72 Filippelli, Ronald L. The United Electrical, Radio and Machine Workers of America, 1933-1949: The Struggle for Control. Penn S 1970

F73 Finch, C. Herbert. Organized Labor in Louisville, Kentucky, 1880-1914. Ky 1966

F74 Fincher, John H. The Chinese Self-Government Movement, 1900-1912. Wash U 1969

F75 Findlay, James F., Jr. Dwight L. Moody, Evangelist of the Gilded Age, 1837-1899. Northwestern 1961

F76 Fine, John van A., Jr. The Bosnian Church: Its Place in Medieval Bosnia from the Twelfth to the Fifteenth Century. Harvard 1969

F77 Finger, John R. Henry L. Yesler's Seattle Years, 1852-1892. Wash U 1969

F78 Fingerhut, Eugene R. Assimilation of Immigrants on the Frontier of New York, 1764-1776. Columbia 1962

F79 Fink, Carole K. The Weimar Republic as the Defender of Minorities, 1919-1933: A Study of German Minorities Diplomacy and the League of Nations System for the International Protection of Minorities. Yale 1968

F80 Fink, Gary M. The Evolution of Social and Political Attitudes in the Missouri Labor Movement, 1900-1940. Mo 1968

F81 Finke, Hans-Joachim. "The Hanoverian Junta," 1714-1719. Del 1970

F82 Finlay, John L. The Origins of the Social Credit Movement. Manitoba 1968

F83 Finlayson, Michael G. Independency in Old and New England, 1630-1660: An Historiographical and Historical Study. Toronto 1968

F84 Finnegan, John P. Military Preparedness in the Progressive Era, 1911-1917. Wis 1969

F85 Finney, John D. A Study of Negro Labor during and after World War I. Georgetown 1967

F86 Fischer, David H. Federalists and Democracy, 1800-1816. JH 1962

F87 Fischer, Duane D. The John S. Owen Enterprizes. Wis 1964

F88 Fischer, Philip S. The French Theater and French Attitudes toward War, 1919-1939. Conn 1970

F89 Fischer, Roger A. The Segregation Struggle in Louisiana, 1850-1890. Tulane 1967

F90 Fischman, Jerome I. The Rise and Development of the Political Party in Puerto Rico under Spanish and American Rule and the Historical Significance of the Subsequent Emergence and Growth of the Popular Party. NYU 1962

F91 Fish, John O. Southern Methodism in the Progressive Era: A Social History. Ga 1969

F92 Fisher, Alan W. The Russian Annexation of the Crimea, 1774-1783. Columbia 1967

F93 Fisher, Craig B. The Beginnings of Communal Historiography in Central Italy. Cornell 1961

F94 Fisher, Joe A. No National School Board: The United States Supreme Court, Religion, and Public Education. Neb 1966

F95 Fisher, John E. Statesman of the Lost Cause: R. M. T. Hunter and the Sectional Controversy, 1847-1887. Va 1968

F96 Fitchen, Edward D. Alexis Everett Frye and the Reorganization of the Cuban School System, 1898-1902. Cal, Santa Barbara 1970

F97 Fithian, Floyd J. Soviet-American Economic Relations, 1918-1933: American Business in Russia during the Period of Nonrecognition. Neb 1964

F98 Fitts, James L. The Right to Riot: Aspects of the London High Church Riots, 1714-1723. UCLA 1970

F99 Fitzgerald, Richard A. Radical Illustrators of the *Masses* and *Liberator:* A Study of the Conflict between Art and Politics. Cal, Riverside 1969

F100 Fitzpatrick, Martha Ann, Sister. Richard Watson Gilder, Genteel Reformer. Cath 1966

F101 Fitzsimmons, Anne Marie, Sister. The Political Career of Daniel S. Lamont, 1870-1897. Cath 1965

F102 Flack, Bruce C. The Work of the American Youth Commission, 1935-1942. Ohio 1969

F103 Flack, James K. Formation of the Washington Intellectual Community, 1870-1898. Wayne 1968

F104 Flaherty, David H. Privacy in Colonial New England. Columbia 1967

F105   Flammer, Philip M.   *Primus Inter Pares:* A History of the Lafayette Escadrille. Yale 1963

F106   Flanagan, Vincent J.   Life of General Gouverneur Kemble Warren. CUNY 1969

F107   Flanders, Robert B.   Nauvoo: Kingdom on the Mississippi. Wis 1964

F108   Fleener, Charles J.   The Expulsion of the Jesuits from the Viceroyalty of New Granada, 1767. Fla U 1969

F109   Fleming, William F.   San Antonio: The History of a Military City, 1865-1880. Penn U 1963

F110   Flemion, Philip F.   Manuel José Arce and the Formation of the Federal Republic of Central America. Fla U 1969

F111   Fletcher, Allan W.   Appeasement Italian Style: The Italian Factor in British Foreign Policy, 1935-1939. Wash U 1970

F112   Fletcher, Marvin E.   The Negro Soldier and the United States Army, 1891-1917. Wis 1968

F113   Flickema, Thomas O.   The United States and Paraguay, 1845-1860: Misunderstanding, Miscalculation, and Misconduct. Wayne 1966

F114   Flood, Bruce P., Jr.   Macer Floridus: A Medieval Herbalism. Colo 1968

F115   Flood, Edward T.   Japan's Relations with Thailand, 1928-1941. Wash U 1967

F116   Florence, Ronald P.   Victor Adler: The Making of a Socialist. Harvard 1969

F117   Flores Caballero, Romeo R.   *Los Espanoles en la Vida Politica, Economica y Social de Mexico, 1804-1838.* Tex U 1968

F118   Flugel, Raymond R.   United States Air Power Doctrine: A Study of the Influence of William Mitchell and Guilio Douhet at the Air Corps Tactical School, 1921-1935. Okla 1965

F119   Flusche, Della M.   A Study of the Cabildo in Seventeenth Century Santiago, Chile, 1609-1699. Loyola 1969

F120   Flynn, George Q.   Franklin D. Roosevelt and American Catholicism, 1932-1936. LSU 1966

F121   Flynn, James T.   The Universities in the Russia of Alexander I: Patterns of Reform and Reaction. Clark 1964

F122   Flynn, John F.   Rife with Possibilities: The Irish Parliamentary Party and the South African War, 1899-1902. Columbia 1970

F123   Flynt, J. Wayne.   Duncan Upshaw Fletcher: Florida's Reluctant Progressive. Fla S 1965

F124   Fogarty, Gerald P.   Denis J. O'Connell: Americanist Agent to the Vatican, 1885-1903. Yale 1969

F125   Fogarty, Robert S.   The Oneida Community, 1848-1880: A Study in Conservative Christian Utopianism. Denver 1968

F126   Fogelson, Robert M.   Los Angeles: The Emergence of a Metropolis, 1850-1930. Harvard 1964

F127   Foley, M. Briant, Sister.   The Triumph of Militia Diplomacy: John Adams in the Netherlands, 1780-1782. Loyola 1968

F128   Foley, Michael F., Jr.   John Thurloe and the Foreign Policy of the Protectorate, 1654-1658. Ill 1967

F129   Foley, Vernard L.   The Invisible Hand: An Inquiry into the Nature and Causes of *The Wealth of Nations.* Cal, Berkeley 1970

F130   Foley, William E.   Territorial Politics in Frontier Missouri, 1804-1820. Mo 1967

F131   Folkman, David I., Jr.   Westward via Nicaragua: The United States and the Nicaragua Route, 1826-1869. Utah 1966

F132   Follis, Clifton G.   The Austrian Social Democratic Party, June 1914–November 1918. Stanford 1961

F133   Folmar, John K.   The Erosion of Republican Support for Congressional Reconstruction in the House of Representatives, 1871-1877: A Roll-Call Analysis. Ala 1968

F134   Folsom, Kenneth E.   Li Hung-chang: Friends, Guests, and Colleagues: A Study of the *Mu-fu* System in the Late Ch'ing Period. Cal, Berkeley 1964

F135   Fonbuena, Dedimo M.   Colonial Government under the United States Constitution. Am 1927

F136   Foner, Eric.   Free Soil, Free Labor, and Free Men: The Ideology of the Republican Party before the Civil War. Columbia 1969

F137   Foner, Jack D.   The United States Soldier between Two Wars: Army Life and Reforms, 1865-1898. Columbia 1968

F138   Foote, William A.   The American Independent Companies of the British Army, 1664-1764. UCLA 1966

F139   Forbes, Henry A. C.   A Study of Religious Melancholy and Seventeenth Century English Puritan Dissent. Harvard 1961

F140   Ford, Benjamin T.   A Duty to Serve: The Government Career of George Bruce Cortelyou. Columbia 1963

F141 Ford, Richard B. The Frontier in South Africa: A Comparative Study of the Turner Thesis. Denver 1966

F142 Forde, Nels W. The Sumerian Dam-kàr-e-ne of the Third Ur Dynasty. Minn 1964

F143 Forderhase, Rudolph E. Jacksonianism in Missouri, from Predilection to Party, 1820-1836. Mo 1968

F144 Forman, John P. Thomas Cranmer and the Foreign Princes: A Study in Reformation Diplomacy. St L 1969

F145 Forman, Paul. The Environment and Practice of Atomic Physics in Weimar Germany: A Study in the History of Science. Cal, Berkeley 1967

F146 Formisano, Ronald P. The Social Bases of American Voting Behavior: Wayne County, Michigan, 1837-1852, as a Test Case. Wayne 1966

F147 Fornara, Charles W. Strategia of Athens 501/0-405/4. UCLA 1961

F148 Fornari, Harry D. Mussolini's Gadfly: Roberto Farinacci. CUNY 1970

F149 Forness, Norman O. The Origins and Early History of the United States Department of the Interior. Penn S 1964

F150 Forrest, Jack L. United States Recognition of the Porfirio Diaz Government, 1876-1878. Okla 1967

F151 Forse, James H. The Political Career of Archbishop Bruno of Cologne: Ottonian Statesman of Tenth Century Germany. Ill 1967

F152 Forster, Cornelius P. Charles Townshend: A Study of His Political Conduct. Fordham 1963

F153 Forth, William S. Wesley L. Jones: A Political Biography. Wash U 1962

F154 Fortin, Roger A. The Decline of Royal Authority in Colonial Massachusetts. Lehigh 1969

F155 Foster, Claude R., Jr. Johannes Buenderlin: Radical Reformer of the Sixteenth Century. Penn U 1963

F156 Foster, Frank F. The Government of London in the Reign of Elizabeth I. Columbia 1968

F157 Foster, Mary C. Hampshire County, Massachusetts, 1729-1754: A Covenant Society in Transition. Mich U 1967

F158 Foster, Stephen. The Puritan Social Ethic: Class and Calling in the First Hundred Years of the Settlement in New England. Yale 1966

F159 Fotion, Janice C. Cabet and Icarian Communism. Ia 1966

F160 Foushee, Richard E. The Reciprocal Influence between Clergy and Laity on Social Issues: An Historical Investigation of Missouri's Presbyterian Clergy in Marion County on the Subject of Abolition, 1835-1845. St L 1969

F161 Fout, John C. Protestant Christian Socialism in Germany, 1848-1896: Wichern, Stoecker, Naumann: The Search for a New Social Ethic. Minn 1969

F162 Fowler, David H. Northern Attitudes towards Interracial Marriage: A Study of Legislation and Public Opinion in the Middle Atlantic States and the States of the Old Northwest. Yale 1963

F163 Fowler, Linda L. Suspect and Incapable Judges in Civilian and Canonist Thought. Wis 1968

F164 Fowler, Wilton B. Sir William Wiseman and the Anglo-American War Partnership, 1917-1918. Yale 1966

F165 Fox, Barry C. German Relations with Romania, 1933-1944. Case W Reserve 1964

F166 Fox, Daniel M. Simon Nelson Patten: Moralist of American Abundance. Harvard 1964

F167 Fox, Frank. French-Russian Commercial Relations in the Eighteenth Century and the French-Russian Commercial Treaty of 1787. Del 1966

F168 Fox, Mary Harrita, Sister. Peter E. Dietz and the American Catholic Social Movement: A Quarter Century of Leadership, 1900-1925. Notre D 1950

F169 Fox, Vivian C. Deviance in English Utopias in the 16th, 17th, and 18th Centuries. Boston U 1969

F170 Frakes, George E. The Origin and Development of the South Carolina Legislative Committee System, 1719-1776. Cal, Santa Barbara 1966

F171 France, Edward E. Some Aspects of the Migration of the Negro to the San Francisco Bay Area since 1940. Cal, Berkeley 1962

F172 Frank, Donald K. Twelfth Century Naturalism and the Troubadour Ethic. Wis 1961

F173 Frank, Douglas W. William Ernest Hocking and Twentieth Century International Tensions, 1914-1966. SUNY, Buffalo 1970

F174 Frank, Richard I. *Scholae Palatinae:* The Palace Guards of the Later Roman Empire. Cal, Berkeley 1965

F175　Frank, Robert H.　Hitler and the National Socialist Coalition, 1924-1932. JH 1970

F176　Frank, Sam H.　American Air Service Observation in World War I. Fla U 1961

F177　Frank, Wallace.　The History of Thoroughbred Racing in California. S Cal 1964

F178　Frank, Willard C., Jr.　Sea Power, Politics, and the Onset of the Spanish War, 1936. Pitt 1969

F179　Frankel, Benjamin A.　Venezuela and the United States, 1810-1888. Cal, Berkeley 1964

F180　Frankle, Barbara S.　The Genteel Family: High-Victorian Conceptions of Domesticity and Good Behavior. Wis 1969

F181　Frankle, Robert J.　Parliament, Crown, and Reform, 1689-1701. Wis 1970

F182　Franklin, Jimmie L.　Prohibition in Oklahoma, 1907-1959. Okla 1968

F183　Frantz, John B.　Revivalism in the German Reformed Church in America to 1850, with Emphasis on the Eastern Synod. Penn U 1961

F184　Fraser, Robert S.　The House of Lords in the First Parliament of Queen Victoria, 1837-1841. Cornell 1967

F185　Fraser, Walter J., Jr.　William Henry Ruffner: A Liberal in the Old and New South. Tenn 1970

F186　Frawley, M. Alphonsine, Sister.　Patrick Donahoe: Journalist. Cath 1946

F187　Frazee, Charles A.　The Orthodox Church of Greece from the Revolution of 1821 to 1852. Ind 1965

F188　Frederick, Duke.　The Second Confiscation Act: A Chapter of Civil War Politics. Chicago 1966

F189　Frederick, Peter J.　European Influences on the Awakening of the American Social Conscience, 1886-1904. Cal, Berkeley 1966

F190　Fredman, Lionel E.　The Australian Ballot as an American Reform. Tulane 1966

F191　Freed, John B.　The Mendicant Orders in German Society, 1219-1273. Princeton 1969

F192　Freehling, William W.　The Nullification Controversy in South Carolina. Cal, Berkeley 1964

F193　Freeman, John F.　French Humanists and Politics under Francis I. Mich U 1969

F194　Freeman, Keller C.　The Saints at War: A Study in Political Strategy, 1823-1833. Ga 1963

F195　Freeman, Rhoda G.　The Free Negro in New York City in the Era before the Civil War. Columbia 1966

F196　Freeman, Walden S.　Will H. Hays and the League of Nations. Ind 1967

F196a　Freidson, Marion F.　A Study of Medieval Queenship: Capetian France, 987-1237. Chicago 1964

F197　Freiwirth, Paul K.　Germany and Austria-Hungary as Allies, 1914-1916. Md 1961

F198　French, David C.　The Conversion of an American Radical: Elizur Wright, Jr., and the Abolitionist Commitment. Case W Reserve 1970

F199　French, Stanley G., Jr.　Some Theological and Ethical Uses of Mental Philosophy in Early Nineteenth Century America. Wis 1967

F200　Frey, Richard C.　John T. Flynn and the United States in Crisis, 1928-1950. Ore 1969

F201　Frey, Robert L.　A Technological History of Locomotives of the Northern Pacific Railway Company. Minn 1970

F202　Frey, Sylvia R.　The British Soldier in the American Revolution. Tulane 1969

F203　Fridell, Wilbur M.　The Policy of the Japanese Government toward Shinto Shrines at the Town and Village Level, 1894-1914. Cal, Berkeley 1966

F204　Friedland, Paul.　A Reconstruction of Early Tangut History. Wash U 1969

F205　Friedlander, Henry E.　The German Revolution, 1918-1919. Penn U 1968

F206　Friedlander, Robert A.　The July 1936 Military Rebellion in Spain: Background and Beginnings. Northwestern 1963

F207　Friedman, Lawrence J.　In Search of Uncle Tom: Racial Attitudes of Southern Leadership, 1865-1900. UCLA 1967

F208　Friedman, Saul S.　Official United States Policy toward Jewish Refugees, 1938-1945. Ohio 1969

F209　Fries, Donald O.　William Roy: A Study of Sixteenth-Century Protestant-Lollard Relationships. Mich S 1969

F210　Friesen, Abraham.　The Marxist Interpretation of the Reformation. Stanford 1967

F211　Frigulietti, James.　The Social and Religious Consequences of the French Revolutionary Calendar. Harvard 1966

F212   Frisch, Michael H.   From Town to City, Springfield, Massachusetts, and the Meaning of Community, 1840-1880. Princeton 1967

F213   Frost, Frank J.   The Scholarship of Plutarch: The Biographer's Contribution to the Study of Athenian History, 480-429 B.C. UCLA 1961

F214   Frost, Jerry W.   The Quaker Family in Colonial America: A Social History of the Society of Friends. Wis 1968

F215   Frost, Richard H.   The Mooney Case. Cal, Berkeley 1960

F216   Fry, Charles G.   Matthias Loy, Patriarch of Ohio Lutheranism, 1828-1915. Ohio 1965

F217   Fry, Nenah E.   Integral Socialism and the Third Republic (1883 to 1914). Yale 1964

F218   Fry, Richard T.   Community through War: A Study of Theodore Roosevelt's Rise and Fall as a Prophet and Hero in Modern America. Minn 1969

F219   Fuhrmann, Joseph T.   Foreign Entrepreneurs and the Origins of Capitalism in Russia: A Study of Industry and Progress in Seventeenth Century Russia. Ind 1968

F220   Fuller, Justin.   History of the Tennessee Coal, Iron, and Railroad Company, 1852-1907. NC 1966

F221   Fullington, Norbert L.   James Thomas Knowles and the *Nineteenth Century:* A Victorian Editor and His Periodical. Harvard 1966

F222   Fullinwider, S. Pendleton.   The Emancipation of Negro Thought, 1890-1930. Wis 1966

F223   Funigiello, Philip J.   A Political and Legislative History of the Public Utility Holding Company Act of 1935. NYU 1966

F224   Furay, Conal.   The Sick Society: A History of the Idea in Twentieth-Century American Self-Critical Literature. St L 1966

F225   Furdell, William J.   Cordell Hull and the London Economic Conference of 1933. Kent 1970

F226   Furer, Howard.   The Public Career of William Frederick Havemeyer. NYU 1963

F227   Furlong, Patrick J.   The Evolution of Political Organization in the House of Representatives, 1789-1801. Northwestern 1966

F228   Furstenberg, Barbara J.   The Emergence of Drama in the Curriculum: A Study of Contrasting Images of the University Professor. Wis 1968

F229   Furth, Charlotte D.   Ting Wen-chiang: An Intellectual under the Chinese Republic. Stanford 1966

F230   Fusco, Jeremiah N.   Diplomatic Relations between Italy and the United States, 1913-1917. Geo W 1969

F231   Futch, Jefferson D., III.   The United States and the Fall of the Weimar Republic: German-American Relations, 1930-1933. JH 1962

G

G1 Gabard, William M. Joseph Mackey Brown: A Study in Conservatism. Tulane 1963

G2 Gabel, Jack. Edward Morse Shepard: Militant Reformer. NYU 1967

G3 Gaboury, William J. Dissension in the Rockies: A History of Idaho Populism. Idaho 1966

G4 Gaddis, John L. The United States and the Origins of the Cold War, 1943-1946. Tex U 1968

G5 Gadol, Joan K. Leon Battista Alberti: The Renaissance of Geometric Space in Art and Science. Columbia 1963

G6 Gaeddert, Dale A. The Franco-Bavarian Alliance during the War of the Spanish Succession. Ohio 1969

G7 Gaffey, James P. The Life of Patrick W. Riordan, Second Archbishop of San Francisco, 1841-1914. Cath 1965

G8 Gagan, David P. "The Queen's Champion": The Life of George Taylor Denison III, Soldier, Author, Magistrate and Canadian Tory Patriot. Duke 1969

G9 Gagliano, Joseph A. A Social History of Coca in Peru. Georgetown 1961

G10 Gagliardo, John G. Agrarian Reform and the Peasant in German Historical and Political Literature, 1775-1840. Yale 1962

G11 Gagnon, Gregory O. Public Opinion and the Empire, 1855-1885: A Study of the Unofficial Mind of Victorian England. Md 1970

G12 Gahl, Daniel R. Indiana and the Sectional Pattern, 1828-1842. Northwestern 1963

G13 Gahn, Joseph A. The America of William Gropper, Radical Cartoonist. Syracuse 1966

G14 Galbraith, M. Rita Francis, Sister. The Arab-Jewish Conflict in a World Power Setting. St John's 1963

G15 Galishoff, Stuart. Public Health in Newark, 1832-1918. NYU 1969

G16 Gallagher, John P. Scranton: Industry and Politics, 1835-1885. Cath 1964

G17 Gallagher, Philip F. The Monastery of Mortemer-en-Lyons in the Twelfth Century: Its History and Its Cartulary. Notre D 1970

G18 Galloway, John A. John Barber White: Lumberman. Mo 1961

G19 Gambill, Edward L. Northern Democrats and Reconstruction, 1865-1868. Ia 1969

G20 Gannaway, Richard M. United States Representation at the Inter-American Conferences, 1889-1928. SC 1968

G21 Gannon, M. Anina, Sister. The Influence of the Permanent Mandates Commission in the Administration of the Class "A" Mandate. St John's 1969

G22 Gannon, Michael V. Augustin Verot and the Emergence of American Catholic Social Consciousness. Fla U 1962

G23 Ganyard, Robert L. North Carolina during the American Revolution: The First Phase, 1774-1777. Duke 1963

G24 Garber, Marilyn. A Liberal Revival of Natural Law in the United States, 1900-1945. UCLA 1967

G25 Garber, Morris W. The Silk Industry of Paterson, New Jersey, 1840-1913: Technology and the Origins, Development, and Changes in an Industry. Rutgers 1968

G26 Gard, William G. The Party and the Proletariat in Ivanovo-Voznesensk, 1892-1906. Ill 1967

G27 Gardner, H. Warren. The Dissenting Sects on the Southern Colonial Frontier, 1720-1770. Kans U 1969

G28 Gardner, James A. The Life of Moses Austin, 1761-1821. Wash St L 1963

G29 Gardner, Vivian P. Maurice Thorez: Policies and Practices of the French Communist Leader. S Cal 1966

G30 Garibaldi, David E. The Conservatives and the Development of the English Educational System, 1891-1902. Notre D 1970

G31 Garlid, George W. Politics in Minnesota and American Foreign Relations, 1921-1941. Minn 1967

G32 Garner, Reuben. Watchdogs of Empire: The French Colonial Inspection Service in Action, 1815-1913. Rochester 1970

G33 Garner, Richard L. Zacatecas, 1750-1821: The Study of a Late Colonial Mexican City. Mich U 1970

G34 Garosi, Frank J. The Ecclesiastical Policy of the Grand Duke Leopold of Tuscany, 1765-1790. Minn 1965

G35 Garrett, Clarke W. French Nationalism on the Eve of the French Revolution. Wis 1961

G36 Garrett, Shirley S. The Salvation of China: Urban Reform and the Chinese Y.M.C.A. Harvard 1966

G37 Garthwaite, Gene. The Bakhtiyāri Khāns: A Study in Tribal Disunity in Iran, 1880-1915. UCLA 1968

G38 Gasman, Daniel E. Social Darwinism in Ernst Haeckel and the German Monist League: A Study of the Scientific Origins of National Socialism. Chicago 1969

G39 Gáspár, Steven. Four Nineteenth-Century Hungarian Travelers in America. S Cal 1967

G40 Gasster, Michael. Currents of Thought in the T'ung-Meng-Hui. Wash U 1962

G41 Gaston, Paul M. The New South Creed, 1865-1900. NC 1961

G42 Gately, Michael O. The Development of the Russian Cotton Textile Industry in the Pre-Revolutionary Years, 1861-1913. Kans U 1968

G43 Gates, John M. An Experiment in Benevolent Pacification: The U.S. Army in the Philippines, 1898-1902. Duke 1967

G44 Gates, Robert A. The Economic Policies of the German Free Trade Unions and the German Social Democratic Party, 1930-1933. Ore 1970

G45 Gates, Rosalie P. The Tibetan Policy of George Nathaniel Curzon, Viceroy of India, January 1899-April 1904, December 1904-November 1905. Duke 1965

G46 Gavins, Raymond. Gordon Blaine Hancock, Southern Black Leader in a Time of Crisis, 1920-1954. Va 1970

G47 Gavronsky, Serge. The French Liberal Opposition and the American Civil War. Columbia 1965

G48 Gawalt, Gerard W. Massachusetts Lawyers: A Historical Analysis of the Process of Professionalization, 1760-1840. Clark 1969

G49 Gaworek, Norbert H. Allied Economic Warfare against Soviet Russia from November 1917 to March 1921. Wis 1970

G50 Gawronski, Donald V. Transcendentalism: An Ideological Basis for Manifest Destiny. St L 1964

G51 Gay, Albert C. The Daladier Administration, 1938-1940. NC 1970

G52 Gay, Thomas E., Jr. The Life and Political Career of J. Hoge Tyler, Governor of Virginia, 1898-1902. Va 1969

G53 Gazi, Stjepan. Stjepan Radic and the Croatian Question: A Study in Political Biography. Georgetown 1962

G54 Gebhard, Louis A., Jr. The Development of the Austro-Hungarian Navy, 1879-1914: A Study in the Operation of Dualism. Rutgers 1965

G55 Geer, Emily A. Lucy Webb Hayes: An Unexceptionable Woman. Case W Reserve 1962

G56 Geerken, John H. Heroic Virtue: An Introduction to the Origins and Nature of a Renaissance Concept. Yale 1968

G57 Geib, George W. A History of Philadelphia, 1776-1789. Wis 1969

G58 Geiger, Reed G. The Anzin Company: The History of a French Coal Mining Firm, 1800-1833. Minn 1965

G59 Geismar, Peter M. De Gaulle, the Army, and Algeria: The Civil-Military Conflict over Decolonization, 1958-1962. Columbia 1967

G60 Gellman, Irwin F. Good Neighbor Diplomacy and the Rise of Batista, 1933-1945. Ind 1970

G61 Gelsinger, Bruce E. Foreign Trade of the Medieval Icelandic Republic. UCLA 1969

G62 Gemorah, Solomon. Laurence Gronlund's Ideas and Influence, 1877-1899. NYU 1965

G63 Gendzier, Irene L. The Politics of Faith: Ya'queb Sanu' as *Abu Naddara*. Columbia 1964

G64 George, James H., Jr. United States Postwar Relief Planning: The First Phase, 1940-1943. Wis 1970

G65 George, Margaret Y. Appeasement: Crisis of British Conservatism. Pitt 1964

G66 George, Mary Karl, Sister. Zachariah Chandler: Radical Revisited. St L 1965

G67 George, William B. The Disestablishment of the Anglican Church in Wales. Columbia 1963

G68 Gerassi, Marysa. Argentine Nationalism of the Right: The History of an Ideological Development, 1930-1946. Columbia 1964

G69 Gerber, Richard A. The Liberal Republican Alliance of 1872. Mich U 1967

G70 Gericke, Robert W. German Commercial Policy and Party Politics, 1890-1903. Okla 1961

G71 Gerlach, Don R. Philip Schuyler: The Origins of a Conservative Patriot, 1733-1777. A Study in Provincial Politics and the American Revolution in New York. Neb 1961

G71a Gerlach, Larry R. Revolution or Independence? New Jersey, 1760-1776. Rutgers 1968

G72 German, James C. Taft's Attorney General: George W. Wickersham. NYU 1969

G73 Gerome, Frank A. United States-Mexican Relations during the Initial Years of the Mexican Revolution. Kent 1968

G74 Gerstein, Linda G. Nikolia Strakhov: The Modern Slavophile. Harvard 1966

G75 Gerteiny, Alfred G. The Concept of Positive Neutralism in the United Arab Republic. St John's 1963

G76 Gerteis, Louis S. From Contraband to Freedman: Federal Policy toward Southern Blacks, 1861-1865. Wis 1969

G77 Gerulaitis, Leonardas V. The Venetian Incunabula: Printers and Readers. Mich U 1969

G78 Gerus, Oleh W. The Reformed State Council, 1905-1917: A Phase in Russian Constitutionalism. Toronto 1970

G79 Ghelfi, Gerald J. European Opinions of American Republicanism during the "Critical Period," 1781-1789. Claremont 1968

G80 Ghezzi, Bertil W. *L'Univers* and the Definition of Papal Infallibility. Notre D 1969

G81 Gibbons, Edward J. The Attitude of American Economists toward the Labor Movement, 1919-1930. Notre D 1964

G82 Gibson, George H. The Development of Federal Policy toward Noncommercial Educational Broadcasting. NC 1961

G83 Gibson, William. A History of Family and Child Welfare Agencies in Baltimore, 1849-1943. Ohio 1969

G84 Gidney, James B. An American Mandate for Armenia. Case W Reserve 1963

G85 Gienapp, Ruth A. The Monism of Ernst Haeckel. Cornell 1968

G86 Giese, Dale F. Soldiers at Play: A History of Social Life at Fort Union, New Mexico, 1851-1891. NM 1969

G87 Giffin, Donald W. The Normal Years: Brazilian-American Relations, 1930-1939. Vanderbilt 1962

G88 Giffin, Frederick C. Russian Factory Legislation in the 1880's. Emory 1965

G89 Giffin, William W. The Negro in Ohio, 1914-1939. Ohio 1968

G90 Gifford, Jack J. The Northwest Indian War, 1784-1795. UCLA 1964

G91 Gifford, James F., Jr. A History of Medicine at Duke University, Volume I: Origins and Growth, 1865-1941. Duke 1970

G92 Gifford, Prosser. Framework for a Nation: An Economic and Social History of Northern Rhodesia, 1914-1939. Yale 1964

G93 Giglio, James N. The Political Career of Harry M. Daugherty. Ohio 1968

G94 Gignilliat, John L. The Thought of Douglas Southall Freeman. Wis 1968

G95 Gilbane, Brendan F. A Social History of Samuel Slater's Pautucket, 1790-1830. Boston U 1969

G96 Gilbert, Carl L., Jr. The Hirota Ministries: An Appraisal, Japan's Relations with China and the U.S.S.R., 1933-1938. Georgetown 1967

G97 Gilbert, James B. *Partisan Review* and the Decline of Literary Radicalism, 1912-1952. Wis 1966

G98 Gilcreast, Everett A. Richard Henry Pratt and American Indian Policy, 1877-1906: A Study of the Assimilation Movement. Yale 1967

G99 Gilderus, Mark T. The United States and the Mexican Revolution, 1915-1920: A Study of Policy and Interest. Neb 1968

G100 Giles, Charles B. Benjamin Colman: A Study of the Movement toward Reasonable Religion in the 17th Century. UCLA 1963

G101 Gill, Paul E. Sir John Fortescue: Chief Justice of the King's Bench, Polemicist on the Succession Problem, Governmental Reformer, and Political Theorist. Penn S 1968

G102 Gillaspie, William R. Juan de Ayala y Escobar, *Procurador* and Entrepreneur: A Case Study of the Provisioning of Florida, 1683-1716. Fla U 1961

G103 Gillespie, Neal C. George Frederick Holmes and the Philosophy of Faith: A Study in the Religious Crisis of American Orthodoxy in the Nineteenth Century. Duke 1964

G104 Gillette, J. William. The Power of the Ballot: The Politics of Passage and Ratification of the Fifteenth Amendment. Princeton 1963

G105 Gilley, Billy H. Social Trends as Reflected in American Fiction, 1870-1901. Ga 1966

G106 Gillgannon, M. McAuley, Sister. The Sisters of Mercy as Crimean War Nurses. Notre D 1962

G107 Gilliard, Frank D. The Social Origins of Bishops in the Fourth Century. Cal, Berkeley 1966

G108 Gillis, John R. The Prussian Bureaucracy, 1840-1860: A Study of Social and Political Transformation. Stanford 1965

G109 Gilmartin, Jeanine, Sister. An Historical Analysis of the Growth of the National Consumer Movement in the United States from 1947 to 1967. Georgetown 1970

G110 Gilsdorf, Aletha J. B. The Puritan Apocalypse: New England Eschatology in the Seventeenth Century. Yale 1965

G111 Gimelli, Louis B. Luther Bradish, 1783-1863. NYU 1964

G112 Ginsberg, Stephen F. The History of Fire Protection in New York City, 1800-1842. NYU 1968

G113 Ginter, Donald E. The Whig Party, 1783-1793: A Study in the Modern Party System. Cal, Berkeley 1964

G114 Girard, Charlotte, S. M. The Effects of Western Hemispheric Issues upon Franco-American Relations during the Second World War. Bryn Mawr 1968

G115 Gisselquist, Orloue N. The French Ambassador, Jean Antoine de Mesmes, Comte d'Avaux, and French Diplomacy at The Hague, 1678-1684. Minn 1968

G116 Gitman, Joseph. The Jews and Jewish Problems in the Polish Parliament, 1919-1939. Yale 1963

G117 Glas, Edward H. The Struggle for the Reform of the Court-Martial Procedure under Chancellor Hohenlohe, 1894-1898. Rutgers 1970

G118 Glascock, Melvin B. New Spain and the War for America, 1779-1783. LSU 1969

G119 Glaser, David P. Pacific Northwest Press Reaction to Wilson's Mexican Diplomacy, 1913-1916. Idaho 1965

G120 Glaser, William. Local Government and Life in Paris, 1914-1918. Mo 1962

G121 Glasrud, Bruce A. Black Texans, 1900-1930: A History. Tex Tech 1969

G122 Glauert, Earl T. Ricardo Rojas and the Emergence of Argentine Nationalism (1903-1933). Penn U 1962

G122a Glazer, Penina M. A Decade of Transition: A Study of Radical Journals of the 1940's. Rutgers 1970

G123 Glazer, Walter S. Cincinnati in 1840: A Community Profile. Mich U 1968

G124 Glazier, Ira A. The Foreign Trade of Lombardy and Venetia, 1815-1865. Harvard 1964

G125 Gleason, Abbott. European and Muscovite: A Life of Ivan V. Kireevskii. Harvard 1969

G126 Gleason, Elisabeth G. Cardinal Gasparo Contarini (1483-1542) and the Beginning of Catholic Reform. Cal, Berkeley 1963

G127 Gleissner, Richard A. The Establishment of Royal Government in Maryland: A Study of Crown Policy and Provincial Politics, 1680-1700. Md 1968

G128 Glenn, Virginia L. James Hamilton, Jr., of South Carolina: A Biography. NC 1964

G129 Glenski, Zoé, Sister. Lord Ashley in the House of Commons, 1826-1851. Fordham 1966

G130 Glick, Thomas F. Irrigation and Society in Medieval Valencia. Harvard 1968

G131 Glickman, Rose B. The Literary Raznochintsy in Mid-Nineteenth Century Russia. Chicago 1967

G132 Gliozzo, Charles A. The Anti-Christian Movement in Paris during the French Revolution, 1789-1794. SUNY, Buffalo 1966

G133 Gnizi, Haim. V. F. Calverton: Independent Radical. CUNY 1968

G134 Godbold, Edward S., Jr. Ellen Glasgow and the Woman Within. Duke 1970

G135 Godecker, Mary Salesia, Sister. Rt. Rev. Simon W. Gabriel Bruté de Rémur, First Bishop of Vincennes, Indiana: Part II, Priestly Career in Maryland, 1810-1834. Cath 1929

G136 Goff, John S. Robert Todd Lincoln in Politics and Diplomacy. S Cal 1960

G137 Goff, Richard D. Logistics and Supply Problems of the Confederacy. Duke 1963

G138   Goffart, Walter A.   The Le Mans Forgeries: An Inquiry into Their Date, Purpose, and Authorship. Harvard 1961

G139   Goheen, Robert B.   The Function of the Peers in Early Tudor Governance. Yale 1968

G140   Goist, Park D.   The City as Organism: Two Recent American Theories of the City. Rochester 1967

G141   Gold, Robert L.   The Transfer of Florida from Spanish to British Control, 1763-1765. Ia 1964

G142   Goldberg, Hannah F.   George Henry Lewes and the Secular Revelation. JH 1964

G143   Golden, Anne T.   Attitudes to the Soviet Union as Reflected in the American Press, 1944-1948. Toronto 1970

G144   Golden, Peter B.   The Q'azars: Their History and Language as Reflected in the Islamic, Byzantine, Caucasian, Hebrew and Old Russian Sources. Columbia 1970

G145   Goldenberg, Joseph A.   The Shipbuilding Industry in Colonial America. NC 1969

G146   Goldfield, David R.   The Triumph of Politics over Society: Virginia, 1851-1861. Md 1970

G147   Goldman, Aaron L.   Crisis in the Rhineland: Britain, France and the Rhineland. Ind 1967

G148   Goldman, Peter.   The Republic of Virtue and Other Essays on the Early National Period. Columbia 1970

G149   Goldman, Stuart D.   The Forgotten War: The Soviet Union and Japan, 1937-1939. Georgetown 1970

G150   Goldmann, William E.   International Confederation of Free Trade-Unions: History of an Organization, 1949-1962. S Cal 1967

G151   Goldstein, Kalman.   The Albany Regency: The Failure of Practical Politics. Columbia 1969

G152   Goldthwaite, Richard A.   Four Florentine Families in the Renaissance. Columbia 1965

G153   Goldwert, Marvin.   The Argentine Revolution of 1930: The Rise of Modern Militarism and Ultra-Nationalism in Argentina. Tex U 1962

G154   Goodfellow, Guy F.   Calvin Coolidge: A Study of Presidential Inaction. Md 1969

G155   Goodman, David M.   Apaches as Prisoners of War, 1886-1894. Tex C 1969

G156   Goodman, Paul.   The Democratic-Republicans of Massachusetts: Politics in a Young Republic. Harvard 1961

G157   Goodrich, Thomas D.   Sixteenth-Century Ottomas Americana: or a Study of *Tarih-i Hind-i Garbi.* Columbia 1968

G158   Goodrich, Wendel E.   Henry VI and the Decline of the German Monarchy: A Study of Personality and Politics in Late Twelfth Century Germany. Duke 1970

G159   Goodrum, Richard G.   The German Socialists and National Unification, 1859-1871. Wis 1969

G160   Goodsell, James N.   Cartagena de Indias: Entrepôt for a New World (1533-1597). Harvard 1966

G161   Goodstein, Judith R.   Sir Humphry Davy: Chemical Theory and the Nature of Matter. Wash U 1969

G162   Goodwin, Gerald J.   The Anglican Middle Way in Early Eighteenth-Century America: Anglican Religious Thought in the American Colonies, 1702-1750. Wis 1965

G163   Goodwin, Herbert M.   California's Growing Freeway System. UCLA 1969

G163a   Gordon, Bertram.   Catholic Social Thought in Austria, 1815-1848. Rutgers 1969

G164   Gordon, Evelyn B.   The Significance of Political Caricature during the Reign of Louis-Philippe, 1830-1835. Penn U 1970

G165   Gordon, Gerald R.   The AFL, the CIO, and the Quest for a Peaceful World, 1914-1946. Maine 1967

G166   Gordon, Irene L.   Revolutionary Banditry: An Interpretation of the Social Roles of the Ukrainian Cossacks in their First Rebellions, 1590-1596. Yale 1970

G167   Gordon, Jean.   The Fine Arts in Boston, 1815 to 1879. Wis 1965

G168   Gordon, Joseph F.   The History and Development of Irrigated Cotton on the High Plains of Texas. Tex Tech 1961

G169   Gordon, Leonard.   Formosa as an International Prize in the Nineteenth Century. Mich U 1961

G170   Gordon, Leonard A.   Bengal and the Indian National Movement: A Study of Regionalism, Politics, and Thought. Harvard 1969

G171   Goren, Arthur A.   The New York Kehillah, 1908-1922. Columbia 1966

G172 Gorman, David J. Frank Hayward Severance: Historian of the Niagara Frontier. Notre D 1966

G173 Gorman, Joseph B. Estes Kefauver: A Partial Biography, 1903-1952. Harvard 1970

G174 Gorman, M. Adele, Sister. Federation of Catholic Societies in the United States, 1870-1920. Notre D 1962

G175 Gorsuch, Edwin N. The Economic Problems of English Monasteries in the Early Fourteenth Century. Ohio 1967

G176 Gorvine, Harold. The New Deal in Massachusetts. Harvard 1962

G177 Gottdiener, Ruth H. Studies in the Functioning of the Royal Prerogative in the Reign of James I. NYU 1967

G178 Gottfried, Paul. Catholic Romanticism in Munich, 1826-1834. Yale 1968

G179 Gottlieb, Paul H. The Commonwealth of Nations at the United Nations. Boston U 1962

G180 Gottsacker, M. Hugh, Sister. German-American Relations, 1938-1941, and the Influence of Hans Thomsen. Georgetown 1968

G181 Gottschalk, Stephen. The Emergence of Christian Science in American Religious Life, 1885-1910. Cal, Berkeley 1969

G182 Gould, Alan B. Secretary of the Interior Walter L. Fisher and the Return to Constructive Conservation: Problems and Policies of the Conservation Movement, 1909-1913. W Va 1969

G183 Gould, John W. Italy and the United States, 1914-1918: Background to Confrontation. Yale 1969

G184 Gould, Lewis L. Willis Van Devanter in Wyoming Politics, 1884-1897. Yale 1966

G185 Gourlay, Walter E. The Kuomintang and the Rise of Chiang Kai-shek, 1920-1924. Harvard 1967

G186 Gow, June I. Military Administration in the Confederacy: The Army of Tennessee, 1862-1864. British Columbia 1970

G187 Gowaskie, Joseph M. John Mitchell: A Study in Leadership. Cath 1969

G188 Gowen, Robert J. Canada's Relations with Japan, 1895-1922: Problems of Immigration and Trade. Chicago 1966

G189 Grabill, Joseph L. Missionaries amid Conflict: Their Influence upon American Relations with the Near East, 1914-1927. Ind 1964

G190 Graebner, Alan N. The Acculturation of an Immigration Lutheran Church: The Lutheran Church-Missouri Synod, 1917-1929. Columbia 1965

G191 Graf, Christa V. The Hanoverian Reformer Johann Carl Bertram Stüve, 1798-1872. Cornell 1970

G192 Graff, Leo W. The Senatorial Career of Fred T. Dubois of Idaho, 1890-1907. Idaho 1968

G193 Graham, Edward D. American Ideas of a Special Relationship with China, 1784-1900. Harvard 1969

G194 Graham, Hugh D. Tennessee Editorial Response to Changes in the Bi-Racial System, 1954-1960. Stanford 1965

G195 Graham, James D. Changing Patterns of Wage Labor in Tanzania: A History of the Relations between African Labor and European Capitalism in Njombe District, 1931-1961. Northwestern 1968

G196 Graham, James Q., Jr. The French Radical and Radical-Socialist Party, 1906-1914. Ohio 1962

G197 Graham, Loren R. The Transformation of Russian Science and the Academy of Sciences, 1927-1932. Columbia 1964

G198 Graham, Otis L., Jr. The Old Progressive and the New Deal: A Study of the Modern Reform Tradition. Columbia 1966

G199 Graham, Thomas R. The British Impact on Brazil, 1850-1918. Tex U 1961

G200 Grame, George R. The Hamlet of Reform: The Early Political Career of Lord John Russell, 1819-1841. Case W Reserve 1969

G201 Granat, Stanley J. Chinese Participation at the Washington Conference, 1921-1922. Ind 1969

G202 Granatstein, Jack L. The Conservative Party of Canada, 1939-1945. Duke 1966

G203 Granquist, Carl R., Jr. The Diffusion of Democracy as Reflected in the Demands of the General and Parish Cahiers of 1789. Wis 1967

G204 Grant, Curtis R. The Social Gospel and Race. Stanford 1969

G205 Grant, H. Roger. Insurance Reform in the United States, 1885-1915. Mo 1970

G206 Grassman, Curtis E. Prologue to Progressivism: Senator Stephen M. White and the California Reform Impulse, 1875-1905. UCLA 1970

G207 Grathwol, Robert P. DNVP and European Reconciliation, 1924-1928: A Study of the Conflict between Party Politics and Government Foreign Policy in Weimar Germany. Chicago 1968

G208 Gravel, Jean-Yves. Le Royal 22e Régiment à Chypre. Ottawa 1968

G209 Gray, Daniel S. The Services of the King's German Legion in the Army of the Duke of Wellington, 1809-1815. Fla S 1970

G210 Gray, James. The American Civil Liberties Union of Southern California and Imperial Valley Agricultural Labor Disturbances, 1930, 1934. UCLA 1966

G211 Gray, Ralph D. A History of the Chesapeake and Delaware Canal, 1760-1960. Ill 1962

G212 Graybar, Lloyd J. Albert Shaw: Through the Progressive Years, 1857-1912. Columbia 1966

G213 Graymont, Barbara. The Border War: The Iroquois in the American Revolution. Columbia 1969

G214 Grayson, Jasper G. The Foreign Policy of Léon Blum and the Popular Front Government in France. NC 1962

G215 Grede, John F. The New Deal in the Virgin Islands, 1931-1941. Chicago 1962

G216 Gredel, Zdenka J. M. The Problem of Continuity in German History as Seen by West German Historians between 1945 and 1953. SUNY Buffalo 1969

G217 Green, Alan W. C. Legacy of Illusion: The Image of the Negro in the Pre-Civil War North, 1787-1875. Claremont 1968

G218 Green, Allen T. Hugo Preuss and the Weimar Constitution. Emory 1965

G219 Green, David E. Security and Development: The United States' Approach to Latin America, 1940-1948. Cornell 1967

G220 Green, Donald E. The Irrigation Frontier on the Texas High Plains, 1910-1960. Okla 1969

G221 Green, George N. The Far Right Wing in Texas Politics, 1930's-1960's. Fla S 1966

G222 Green, James J. The Impact of Henry George's Theories on American Catholics. Notre D 1956

G223 Green, Michael K. A History of the Public Rural Electrification Movement in Washington to 1942. Idaho 1968

G224 Green, Thomas A. Pardonable Homicide in Medieval England, 1250-1400: A Study of Legal and Social Concepts of Criminal Liability. Harvard 1970

G225 Green, William A., Jr. The Discovery and Penetration of the Niger: A Study of British Enterprise in Tropical Africa. Harvard 1962

G226 Greenbaum, Fred. Edward Prentiss Costigan: Study of a Progressive. Columbia 1962

G227 Greenberg, Allan C. Artists and the Weimar Republic: Dada and the Bauhaus, 1917-1925. Ill 1967

G228 Greenberg, Jacquelyn Janelle R. Tudor and Stuart Theories of Kingship: The Dispensing Power and the Royal Discretionary Authority in Sixteenth and Seventeenth Century England. Mich U 1970

G229 Greenberg, Louis M. Marseille, Lyon and the Paris Commune: The Search for Local Liberties, 1868-1871. Harvard 1963

G230 Greenberger, Allen J. The British Image of India, 1880-1960: A Study in the Literature of Imperialism. Mich U 1966

G231 Greenblatt, Del. The Suburban Manors of Coventry, 1279-1411. Cornell 1967

G232 Greene, Christopher M. Historical Consciousness and Historical Monuments in France after 1789. Harvard 1964

G233 Greene, Nathanael. French Socialism and the International Crisis, 1936-1939. Harvard 1964

G234 Greene, Thomas R. Henry of Rheims, 1122-1165: A Study in Ecclesiastical-Royal Relations. NYU 1967

G235 Greene, Victor R. The Attitude of Slavic Communities to the Unionization of the Anthracite Industry before 1903. Penn U 1963

G236 Greenwood, Keith M. Robert College: The American Founders. JH 1965

G237 Greer, Harold E., Jr. History of Southern Baptist Mission Work in Cuba, 1886-1916. Ala 1965

G238 Gregory, Chester W. The Problem of Labor during World War II: The Employment of Women in Defense Production. Ohio 1969

G239 Gregory, Ross M. The Ambassadorship of Walter Page. Ind 1964

G240 Greicus, Elizabeth Ann M. Efforts of the Progressive Bloc to Influence the Conduct of the War in Russia, 1915-1917. Tulane 1969

G241 Grendler, Paul F. Anton Francesco Doni: Cinquecento Critic. Wis 1964

G242 Grenier, Judson A. The Origins and Nature of Progressive Muckraking. UCLA 1965

G243 Grenquist, Peter C. The German Elections of 1912. Columbia 1963

G244 Gressley, Gene M. Wall Street to Carey Avenue: Eastern Investment in the Western Range Cattle Industry, 1870-1910. Ore 1964

G245 Greven, Helen S. Henri Estienne and Geneva, 1550-1598. Harvard 1967

G246 Greven, Philip J. Four Generations: A Study of Family Structure, Inheritance, and Mobility in Andover, Massachusetts, 1630-1750. Harvard 1965

G247 Greytak, William J. Henri Grégoire: A Study in French Church-State Relations from 1790 to 1802. Colo 1967

G247a Gribbin, William J. The War of 1812 and American Religion. Cath 1968

G248 Grieb, Kenneth J. The United States and Huerta. Ind 1966

G249 Grier, Douglas A. Confederate Emigration to Brazil, 1865-1870. Mich U 1968

G250 Griess, Thomas E. Dennis Hart Mahan: West Point Professor and Advocate of Military Professionalism, 1830-1871. Duke 1969

G251 Griffeth, Robert R. Varieties of African Resistance to the French Conquest of the Western Sudan, 1850-1900. Northwestern 1968

G252 Griffin, Edward G. The Adoption of Universal Manhood Suffrage in Japan. Columbia 1965

G253 Griffin, James D. Savannah, Georgia, during the Civil War. Ga 1963

G254 Griffin, Janet, Sister. Anticlericalism among the English Deists. St L 1969

G255 Griffin, Joseph A. The Contribution of Belgium to the Development of the Church in America, 1523-1857. Cath 1932

G256 Griffin, Martin I. J., Jr. Latitudinarianism in the Seventeenth-Century Church of England. Yale 1963

G257 Griffin, Patrick H. Fathers and Sons in Nineteenth-Century Romania: A Study of Generational Thinking. S Cal 1969

G258 Griffin, William D. John Fitzgibbon, Earl of Clare. Fordham 1962

G259 Griffith, Robert W., Jr. Joseph R. McCarthy and the United States Senate. Wis 1967

G260 Griffiths, David B. Populism in the Far West, 1890-1900. Wash U 1967

G261 Griffiths, David M. Russian Court Politics and the Question of an Expansionist Foreign Policy under Catherine II, 1762-1783. Cornell 1967

G262 Griffiths, Merwin A. The Reorganization of the Ottoman Army under Abdülhamid II, 1880-1897. UCLA 1966

G263 Griffiths, Quentin. The Counselors of Louis IX. Cal, Berkeley 1964

G264 Grimsted, David A. A Mirror for Nature: American Theater, 1800-1850. Cal, Berkeley 1963

G265 Grimsted, Patricia K. Diplomatic Spokesmen and the Tsar-Diplomat: The Russian Foreign Ministers during the Reign of Alexander I, 1801-1825. Cal, Berkeley 1964

G266 Grinnell, George J. The Darwin Case: A Computer Analysis of Scientific Creativity. Cal, Berkeley 1969

G267 Griswold, William J. Political Unrest and Rebellion in Anatolia, 1605-1609. UCLA 1966

G268 Grobovsky, Antony N. The "Chosen Council" of Ivan IV: A Reinterpretation. Yale 1968

G269 Groene, Bertram H. Ante-Bellum Tallahasee: It Was a Gay Time Then. Fla S 1967

G270 Grogin, Robert C. The French Intellectuals' Reactions to Henri Bergson, 1900-1914. NYU 1969

G271 Grollman, Catherine A. Cordell Hull and His Concept of a World Organization. NC 1965

G272 Gromada, Thaddeus V. The Slovak Question in Polish Foreign Policy, 1934-1939. Fordham 1966

G273 Groman, Richard J. British Historians and Their Views of the British Policy of Appeasement in the Foreign Policy Crises, 1931-1939. Case W Reserve 1969

G274 Gronet, Richard W. Early Latin American-United States Contacts: An Analysis of Jeremy Robinson's Communications to the Monroe Administration, 1817-1823. Cath 1970

G275 Gross, David L. Heinrich Mann: The Writer and Society, 1890-1920. A Study of Literary Politics in Germany. Wis 1969

G276 Gross, Hanns. The Debate about a German Public Law, 1600-1676: An Examination of the Declining Influence of Roman Law Principles and

Roman Imperial Traditions in the Constitutional and Political Thoughts of Lutheran Germany. Chicago 1966

G277 Gross, Jimmie F. Alabama Politics and the Negro, 1874-1901. Ga 1969

G278 Gross, Sue Ellen A. The Economic Life of the Estado do Maranhão e Grão Pará, 1686-1751. Tulane 1969

G279 Grossbach, Barry L. The Scopes Trial: A Turning Point in American Thought? Ind 1964

G280 Grosser, Edward M. The Discovery of Neptune. Stanford 1961

G281 Grossman, Ronald P. The Financing of the Crusades. Chicago 1965

G282 Grossman, Stanley. Neo-Socialism: A Study in Political Metamorphosis. Wis 1969

G283 Grozier, Richard J. The Life and Times of John Bernard Fitzpatrick: Third Roman Catholic Bishop of Boston. Boston C 1966

G284 Grubb, Charles A. The Political Biography of Duc Albert de Broglie, 1820-1901. Columbia 1969

G285 Grubbs, Donald H. The Southern Tenant Farmers' Union and the New Deal. Fla U 1963

G286 Grubbs, Frank L., Jr. The Struggle for the Mind of American Labor, 1917-1919. Va 1963

G287 Gruber, Carol S. Mars and Minerva: World War I and the American Academic Man. Columbia 1968

G288 Gruber, Helmut. The Politics of German Literature, 1914 to 1933: A Study of the Expressionist and Objectivist Movements. Columbia 1962

G289 Gruber, Ira D. Admiral, Lord Howe and the War for American Independence. Duke 1961

G290 Gruber, Robert H. Salmon P. Chase and the Politics of Reform. Md 1969

G291 Gruder, Vivian R. The Royal Provincial Intendants: A Governing Elite in Eighteenth-Century France. Harvard 1966

G292 Gruen, Erich S. Criminal Trials and Roman Politics, 149-78 B.C. Harvard 1964

G293 Gruenfelder, John K. The Use of the Royal Prerogative in Summoning and Dissolving Parliament, 1603-1642. Minn 1964

G294 Grundy, Ernest B. The Last Generation in the Perspective of Historical Criticism, 1930-1960. Denver 1969

G295 Gruver, Rebecca B. The Diplomacy of John Jay. Cal, Berkeley 1964

G296 Guarnaschelli, John S. Erasmus' Concept of the Church, 1499-1524. An Essay Concerning the Ecclesiological Conflict of the Reformation. Yale 1966

G297 Guernsey, William G. The Dictum of Kenilworth and the Exposition of the Common Law. Boston U 1969

G298 Guest, Florian F. Municipal Institutions in Spanish California, 1769-1821. S Cal 1961

G299 Guggenheim, Ann H. Calvinism and the Political Elite of Sixteenth Century Nimes. NYU 1968

G300 Guice, John D. W. The Territorial Supreme Courts of Colorado, Montana, and Wyoming, 1861-1890. Colo 1969

G301 Guida, Anthony J. Thomas F. Bayard and the Abortive Chinese Immigration Treaty of 1888. Georgetown 1962

G302 Guidorizzi, Richard P. Timothy Pickering: Opposition Politics in the Early Years of the Republic. St John's 1968

G303 Guimond, Alice A. The Honorable and Very Reverend William Herbert: Amaryllis Hybridizer and Amateur Biologist. Wis 1966

G304 Guinn, Paul S., Jr. Westerners versus Easterners: Conflicts in British Strategy, 1914-1918. Harvard 1962

G305 Guinsberg, Thomas N. Senatorial Isolationism in America, 1919-1941. Columbia 1969

G306 Gum, Ert J. The Administration of the Kingdom of Italy under Eugene Beauharnais, 1805-1814. LSU 1963

G307 Gumperz, Ellen M. English Education and Social Change in Late Nineteenth Century Bombay, 1858-1898. Cal, Berkeley 1965

G308 Gundersheimer, Werner L. Vicissitude and Variety: The Life and Works of Louis LeRoy. Harvard 1963

G309 Gunderson, Warren M. The Worlds of the Babee Rajendralal Mitra and Social and Cultural Change in Nineteenth-Century Calcutta. Chicago 1969

G310 Gurney, Ramsdell, Jr. From Recognition to Munich: Official and Historiographical Views of Soviet-American Relations, 1933-1938. SUNY, Buffalo 1969

G311 Guroff, Gregory. The State and Industrialization in Russian Economic Thought, 1909-1914. Princeton 1970

G312   Gust, Kurt.   East German Protestantism under Communist Rule, 1945-1961. Kans U 1966

G313   Gustafson, Donald R.   Mysore, 1881-1902: The Making of a Model State. Wis 1969

G314   Gustafson, Milton O.   Congress and Foreign Aid: The First Phase UNRRA, 1943-1947. Neb 1966

G315   Gutchen, Robert M.   The Genesis of the Local Government Board, 1858-1871. Columbia 1966

G316   Guth, DeLloyd J.   Exchequer Penal Law Enforcement, 1485-1509. Pitt 1967

G317   Guy, Duane F.   The Influence of Agriculture on the Tariff Act of 1930. Kans U 1964

G318   Guzman, Gregory G.   Simon of Saint-Quentin and the Dominican Mission to the Mongols, 1245-1248. Cincinnati 1968

G319   Gwin, Howell H., Jr.   The Faculty of Medicine at the University of Montpellier during the Middle Ages. Miss S 1962

H

H1   Haag, John J.   Othmar Spann and the Politics of "Totality": Corporation in Theory and Practice. Rice 1969

H2   Haas, Arthur G.   Metternich: Reorganization and Nationality, 1813-1818. Chicago 1961

H3   Haber, Samuel.   Scientific Management and the Progressive Movement, 1910-1929. Cal, Berkeley 1961

H4   Haberman, Arthur.   J. B. Bury: A Crisis of Historical and Individual Conscience. NYU 1966

H5   Habib, John S.   The Ikhwan Movement of Najd: Its Rise, Development, and Decline. Mich U 1970

H6   Habibuddin, Syed M.   Theodore Roosevelt's Attitude toward Civil Rights and Civil Liberties. Penn U 1968

H7   Hachey, Thomas E.   Neville Chamberlain and Anthony Eden: Britain's Policy of Appeasement from May 1937 to February 1938. St John's 1965

H8   Hacker, Barton C.   The Military and the Machine: An Analysis of the Controversy over Mechanization in the British Army, 1919-1939. Chicago 1968

H9   Hackett, Neil J.   The Third Sacred War. Cincinnati 1970

H10   Hackmann, William K.   English Military Expeditions to the Coast of France, 1757-1761. Mich U 1969

H11   Hackney, Francis S.   From Populism to Progressivism in Alabama, 1890-1910. Yale 1966

H12   Hadley, Robert A.   Deified Kingship and Propaganda Coinage in the Early Hellenistic Age, 323-280 B.C. Penn U 1964

H13   Haeger, John D.   Town Growth on the Western Shore of Lake Michigan, 1815-1840. Loyola 1969

H14   Hafter, Daryl M.   Critics of Mercantilism in France, 1751-1789: The Industrial Reformers. Yale 1964

H15   Hagan, Kenneth J.   Protecting American Commerce and Neutrality: The Global Gunboat Diplomacy of the Old Navy, 1877-1889. Claremont 1970

H16   Hagerman, Edward H.   The Evolution of Trench Warfare in the American Civil War. Duke 1965

H17   Hagler, Dorse H.   The Agrarian Theme in Southern History to 1860. Mo 1968

H18   Hagy, James W.   The Quebec Separatists: An American Viewpoint. Ga 1969

H19   Hahn, Roger.   The Fall of the Paris Academy of Sciences during the French Revolution. Cornell 1962

H20   Hahner, June E.   Officers and Civilians in Brazil, 1889-1898. Cornell 1966

H21   Haigh, Roger M.   Martín Güemes: A Study of the Power Structure of the Province of Salta, 1810-1821. Fla U 1963

H22   Haight, Jeffrey C.   Talleyrand and History. Rochester 1968

H23   Haines, Meredith C.   The Nonconformists and the Nonconformist Periodical Press in Mid-Nineteenth Century England. Ind 1966

H24   Hainlin, Lewis A.   Moreton Frewen: His Life. Mo 1968

H25   Hair, William I.   The Agrarian Protest in Louisiana, 1877-1900. LSU 1962

H26   Hakola, John W.   Samuel T. Hauser and the Economic Development of Montana: A Case Study in Nineteenth Century Frontier Capitalism. Ind 1961

H27   Hale, Douglas D., Jr.   The Early Career of Heinrich von Gagern, 1799-1836. Tex U 1961

H28   Hale, Nathan G.   The Origins and Foundation of the Psychoanalytic Movement in America, 1909-1914. Cal, Berkeley 1965

H29   Hall, Arthur R.   Soil Erosion and Agriculture in the Southern Piedmont: A History. Duke 1948

H30   Hall, Gwendolyn M.   Social Control in Slave Plantation Societies: A Comparison of St. Domingue and Cuba. Mich U 1970

H31   Hall, Michael M.   The Origins of Mass Immigration in Brazil, 1871-1914. Columbia 1969

H32   Hall, Thadd E.   France and the Eighteenth Century Corsican Question. Minn 1966

H33   Hall, Tom G., Jr.   Cheap Bread from Dear Wheat: Herbert Hoover, the Wilson Administration, and the Management of Wheat Prices, 1916-1920. Cal, Davis 1970

H34   Hall, Van Beck. The Commonwealth in the New Nation: Massachusetts, 1780-1790. Wis 1964

H35   Hallenbeck, Jan T. The Frankish Monarchy and the Papacy, 750-774: A Study of the Frankish-Papal Alliance in the Eighth Century. NYU 1966

H36   Haller, John S., Jr. Science and American Concepts of Race, 1859-1900. Md 1968

H37   Hallinan, Paul J. Life of Richard Gilmour, Second Bishop of Cleveland, 1872-1891. Case W Reserve 1963

H38   Halperin, Bernard S. Andrew Johnson, the Radicals, and the Negro, 1865-1866. Cal, Berkeley 1966

H39   Halpern, Irwin P. Stalin's Revolution: The Struggle to Collectivize Rural Russia, 1927-1933. Columbia 1965

H40   Halpern, Paul G. The Mediterranean Naval Situation, 1912-1914. Harvard 1966

H41   Halpern, Sidney. Caesar and the Aurelii Cottae. Penn U 1964

H42   Halpern, Stephen M. The Institute of International Education: A History. Columbia 1969

H43   Halstead, Charles R. Spain, the Powers and the Second World War. Va 1962

H44   Ham, F. Gerald. Shakerism in the Old West. Ky 1962

H45   Hamalainen, Pekka K. The Nationality Struggle between the Finns and the Swedish-Speaking Minority in Finland, 1917-1939. Ind 1966

H46   Hamby, Alonzo L. Harry S. Truman and American Liberalism, 1945-1948. Mo 1965

H47   Hamer, William S., Jr. British Army Reform in the Age of Imperialism, 1886-1906: A Study in Civil-Military Relations. Harvard 1963

H48   Hamerly, Michael T. A Social and Economic History of the City and District of Guayaquil during the Late Colonial and Independence Periods. Fla U 1970

H49   Hamilton, Albert J. The Movement for Irish Roman Catholic Relief, 1790-1793. Notre D 1967

H50   Hamilton, Charles D. Politics and Diplomacy in the Corinthian War. Cornell 1968

H51   Hamilton, James C. Parties and Voting Patterns in the Parliament of 1874-1880. Ia 1968

H52   Hamilton, Mary J. Adam of Dryburgh: Six Christmas Sermons, Introduction and Translation. Cath 1964

H53   Hamilton, Virginia Van der Veer. The Senate Career of Hugo L. Black. Ala 1968

H54   Hammersmith, Jack L. American Diplomacy and the Polish Question, 1943-1945. Va 1970

H55   Hammerton, Anthony J. A Study of Middle-Class Female Emigration from Great Britain, 1830-1914. British Columbia 1969

H56   Hammett, Hugh B. Hilary Abner Herbert: A Southerner Returns to the Union. Va 1969

H57   Hammond, William E. A Political and Economic History of the Marne-Rhine Canal, 1820-1860. Mo 1962

H58   Hampton, Harold D. Conservation and Cavalry: A Study of the Role of the United States Army in the Development of a National Park System, 1886-1917. Colo 1965

H59   Hanchett, Walter S. Moscow in the Late Nineteenth Century: A Study in Municipal Self-Government. Chicago 1964

H60   Handen, Ella F. Neutrality Legislation and Presidential Discretion: A Study of the 1930's. Rutgers 1968

H61   Handen, Ralph D., Jr. The Savoy Negotiations of the Comte de Tessé, 1693-1696. Ohio 1970

H62   Handlery, George D. General Arthur Görgey and the Hungarian Revolution of 1848-1849. Ore 1968

H63   Handy, Robert H. Johann Gustav Droysen: The Historian and German Politics in the Nineteenth Century. Georgetown 1966

H64   Haney, Herbert L. Comets: A Chapter in Science and Superstition in Three Golden Ages: The Aristotelian, the Newtonian, and the Thermonuclear. Ala 1965

H65   Haney, Richard C. A History of the Democratic Party of Wisconsin since World War Two. Wis 1970

H66   Hanft, Sheldon. Some Aspects of Puritan Opposition in the First Parliament of James I. NYU 1969

H67   Hankins, Thomas L. Jean d'Alembert: Philosopher and Scientist. Cornell 1964

H68   Hanley, Thomas O. The Impact of the American Revolution on Religion in Maryland, 1776-1800. Georgetown 1961

H69   Hanlon, Edward F. Urban-Rural Cooperation and Conflict in the Congress: The Breakdown of the New Deal Coalition, 1933-1940. Georgetown 1967

H70 Hann, John H. Brazil and the Rio de la Plata, 1808-1828. Tex U 1967

H71 Hannah, Robert W. The Origins of Indirect Rule in Northern Nigeria, 1890-1904. Mich S 1969

H72 Hannum, Sharon E. Confederate Cavaliers: The Myth in War and Defeat. Rice 1965

H73 Hanrahan, John J. The High-Cost-of-Living Controversy, 1919-1920. Fordham 1969

H74 Hansen, Erik von Stein. Hendrik de Man and the Crisis in European Socialism, 1926-1936. Cornell 1968

H75 Hansen, James E., II. Gallant, Stalwart Bennie: Elisha Benjamin Andrews (1844-1917): An Educator's Odyssey. Denver 1969

H76 Hansen, Klaus J. The Kingdom of God in Mormon Thought and Practice, 1830-1896. Wayne 1963

H77 Hanser, Albert S. Church and State in Bavaria, 1799-1806: An Absolutist Reform in the Age of Revolution. Chicago 1964

H78 Hanson, Gordon J. The French Clergy and the Development of the Capetian Dynasty in the Twelfth Century. Cal, Berkeley 1965

H79 Hanyan, Craig R. DeWitt Clinton: Years of Molding, 1769-1807. Harvard 1964

H80 Harada, Mary Ault. Family Values and Child Care during the Reformation Era: A Comparative Study of Hutterites and Some Other German Protestants. Boston U 1968

H81 Harbert, Mary E. M. The Open Door Policy: The Means of Attaining Nineteenth Century American Objectives in Japan. Ore 1967

H82 Hardcastle, David P. The Defense of Canada under Louis XIV, 1643-1701. Ohio 1970

H83 Harding, Vincent G. Lyman Beecher and the Transformation of American Protestantism, 1775- 1863. Chicago 1965

H84 Hardy, B. Carmon. The Mormon Colonies of Northern Mexico: A History, 1885-1912. Wayne 1963

H85 Hardy, Deborah W. Petr Nikitich Tkachev: A Political Biography. Wash U 1969

H86 Hardy, James D., Jr. The Parlement of Paris during the Regency, 1715-1723. Penn U 1961

H87 Hareven, Tamara K. The Social Thought of Eleanor Roosevelt. Ohio 1965

H88 Harkins, James R. The Administration of Subsistence in the Department of the Somme (1792-1795). Case W Reserve 1965

H89 Harmond, Richard P. Tradition and Change in the Gilded Age: A Political History of Massachusetts, 1878-1893. Columbia 1966

H90 Harnett, David A. Nicolas A. Berdyaev: An Intellectual Portrait. Harvard 1970

H91 Harney, Robert F. The Last Crusade: France and the Papal Army of 1860. Cal, Berkeley 1966

H92 Harper, Glenn T. German Economic Policy in Spain during the Spanish Civil War, 1936-1939. Duke 1963

H93 Harper, James E. The Cities of Gaul from the Third to the Seventh Century. Chicago 1962

H94 Harper, James W. Hugh Lenox Scott: Soldier Diplomat, 1876-1917. Va 1968

H95 Harper, Richard I. The *Kalendarium Regine* of Guillaume de St.-Cloud. Emory 1966

H96 Harper, Robert E. The Class Structure of Western Pennsylvania in the Late Eighteenth Century. Pitt 1969

H97 Harrell, David E., Jr. A Social History of the Disciples of Christ to 1866. Vanderbilt 1962

H98 Harrell, Edward J. Berlin: Rebirth, Reconstruction and Division, 1945-1948: A Study of Allied Cooperation and Conflict. Fla S 1965

H99 Harrell, Kenneth E. The Ku Klux Klan in Louisiana, 1920-1930. LSU 1966

H100 Harrington, Donald B. French Historians and the Terror: The Origins, Development, and Present-Day Fate of the *Thèse du Complot* and the *Thèse des Circonstances*. Conn 1970

H100a Harris, Alice K. The Lower Class as a Factor in Reform: New York, the Jews, and the 1890's. Rutgers 1968

H101 Harris, Anne B. The South as Seen by Travelers, 1865-1880. NC 1967

H102 Harris, Barbara R. Edward Stafford, Third Duke of Buckingham. Harvard 1968

H103 Harris, Brice, Jr. The United States and the Italo-Ethiopian Crisis. Harvard 1962

H104 Harris, Carl V. Economic Power and Politics: A Study of Birmingham, Alabama, 1890-1920. Wis 1970

H105   Harris, Charles H., III.   A Mexican Latifundio: The Economic Empire of the Sanchez Navarro Family, 1765-1821. Tex U 1968

H106   Harris, David A.   Racists and Reformers: A Study of Progressivism in Alabama, 1896-1911. NC 1967

H107   Harris, Dennis E.   The Diplomacy of the Second Front: America, Britain, Russia and the Normandy Invasion. Cal, Santa Barbara 1969

H108   Harris, Faye E.   A Frontier Community: The Economic, Social, and Political Development of Keokuk, Iowa, from 1820 to 1866. Ia 1965

H109   Harris, James F.   Eduard Lasker, 1829-1884: An Analysis of the Political Ideas of a Left-Wing Liberal. Wis 1968

H110   Harris, Joseph E.   The Kingdom of Fouta Diallon. Northwestern 1965

H111   Harris, Merne A.   The MacArthur Dismissal: A Study in Political Mail. Ia 1966

H112   Harris, Michael R.   American Critics of the Ideal of Operational Utility in Higher Education. Stanford 1966

H113   Harris, Neil.   The Artistic Enterprise in America, 1790-1860. Harvard 1965

H114   Haris, Robert C.   Austin Blair of Michigan: A Political Biography. Mich S 1969

H115   Harris, Sally Ann.   The Inter-American Conferences of the 1930's. Mo 1967

H116   Harris, William C.   Presidential Reconstruction in Mississippi: Political and Economic Aspects. Ala 1965

H117   Harrison, Benjamin T.   Chandler Anderson and American Foreign Relations (1896-1928). UCLA 1969

H118   Harrison, James P.   The Communist Treatment of Chinese Peasant Wars: A Case Study in the Reinterpretation of History According to the Theory of the Class Struggle. Columbia 1965

H119   Harrison, Marjorie D.   A National University and the National Interest, 1870-1902. Ky 1968

H120   Harrison, Sandas L.   The Role of El Salvador in the Drive for Unity in Central America. Ind 1963

H121   Harsh, Joseph L.   George Brinton McClellan and the Forgotten Alternative: An Introduction to the Conservative Strategy of the Civil War. Rice 1970

H122   Harstad, Peter T.   Health in the Upper Mississippi River Valley, 1820 to 1861. Wis 1963

H123   Hart, C. R. Desmond.   Congressmen and the Expansion of Slavery into the Territories: A Study in Attitudes, 1846-1861. Wash U 1965

H124   Hart, Clifton E.   The Minor Premise of American Nationalist Thought. Ia 1962

H125   Hart, Robert A.   The Voyage of the Great White Fleet, 1907-1909. Ind 1964

H126   Hart, Roger L.   Bourbonism and Populism in Tennessee, 1875-1896. Princeton 1970

H127   Hartdagen, Gerald E.   The Anglican Vestry in Colonial Maryland. Northwestern 1965

H128   Hartel, William C.   The French Colonial Party, 1895-1905. Ohio 1962

H129   Hartigan, Francis X.   The Foundations of Church Reform in Poitou, 900-1100. Wis 1970

H130   Hartman, Mary S.   The Liberalism of Benjamin Constant during the Bourbon Restoration. Columbia 1969

H131   Hartmann, Susan M.   President Truman and the 80th Congress. Mo 1966

H132   Hartshorne, Thomas L.   Changing Conceptions of the American Character: Alternatives to the Frontier Thesis. Wis 1965

H133   Harvey, Charles E.   Individualism and Ecumenical Thought: The Merger Controversy in Congregationalism, 1937-1961. Cal, Riverside 1968

H134   Harvey, Marvin E.   The Wesleyan Movement and the American Revolution. Wash U 1962

H135   Harvey, Richard L.   The Gospel According to the Church of England: Clergymen as Social Critics, 1681-1685. Mo 1966

H136   Hasegawa, Tsuyoshi.   The February Revolution of 1917 in Russia. Wash U 1969

H137   Haskett, Jeanne M.   The Decembrists in Siberian Exile. Ohio 1962

H138   Hassell, James E.   The Vicissitudes of Russian Administrative Reform, 1762-1801. Cornell 1967

H139   Hassett, Mary Barat, Sister.   Dupanloup and the "Roman Question." St L 1967

H140   Hastings, James R.   Historical Changes in the Vegetation of a Desert Region. Ariz 1963

H141   Hata, Donald T., Jr.   "Undesirables": Unsavory Elements among the Japanese in America prior to 1893 and Their Influence on the First Anti-Japanese Movement in California. S Cal 1970

H142 Hatch, Carl E. The First Heresy Trial of Charles Augustus Briggs: American Higher Criticism in the 1890's. SUNY, Buffalo 1964

H143 Hatch, Fred J. The British Commonwealth Air Training Plan, 1939 to 1945. Ottawa 1969

H144 Hatcher, John H. Fred Vinson, Congressman from Kentucky: A Political Biography, 1890-1938. Cincinnati 1967

H145 Hatfield, Douglas W. Schwarzenberg's German Policy, 1851-1852. Ky 1969

H146 Hatfield, Joseph T. The Public Career of William C. C. Claiborne. Emory 1962

H147 Hattaway, Herman M. Stephen Dill Lee: A Biography. LSU 1969

H148 Hauben, Paul J. Spanish Protestant Refugees in Western Europe during the Second Part of the Sixteenth Century. Princeton 1963

H149 Haugland, John C. Alexander Ramsey and the Republican Party, 1855-1875: A Study in Personal Politics. Minn 1961

H150 Haunton, Richard H. Savannah in the 1850's. Emory 1968

H151 Hause, Steven C. Théophile Delcassé's First Years at the Quai d'Orsay: French Diplomacy between Britain and Germany, 1898-1901. Wash St L 1969

H152 Hauser, Walter. The Bihar Provincial Kisan Sabha, 1929-1942: A Study of an Indian Peasant Movement. Chicago 1961

H153 Hauser, William B. Economic Institutional Change in Tokugawa Japan—The Osaka Cotton Trade. Yale 1969

H154 Havens, Thomas R. H. Nishi Amane (1829-1897) in Japanese Intellectual History. Cal, Berkeley 1965

H155 Havig, Alan R. The Poverty of Insurgency: The Movement to Progressivize the Republican Party, 1916-1924. Mo 1966

H156 Hawes, Joseph M. Society versus Its Children: Nineteenth-Century America's Response to the Challenge of Juvenile Delinquency. Tex U 1969

H157 Hawkes, James R. Stalin's Diplomatic Offensive: The Politics of the Second Front, 1941-1943. Ill 1966

H158 Hawks, Joanne V. Social Reform in the Cotton Kingdom, 1830-1860. Miss U 1970

H159 Hay, Robert P. Freedom's Jubilee: One Hundred Years of the Fourth of July, 1776-1876. Ky 1967

H160 Hayden, J. Michael. The Estates General of 1614. Loyola 1963

H161 Haydon, Anthony P. Sir Matthew Nathan: British Colonial Governor, 1899-1910. Yale 1968

H162 Hayes, Bascom B. The German *Reich* and the "Austrian Question," 1871-1914. Yale 1963

H163 Haynes, Alan E. The Federal Government and Its Policies Regarding the Frontier Era of Utah Territory, 1850-1877. Cath 1968

H164 Haynie, Kenneth E. The Constitutional Left under the July Monarchy: Orleanist Part of Opposition. Mich U 1970

H165 Hays, Garry D. The Idea of Union in Eighteenth Century Colonial America. Kans U 1964

H166 Hays, Jo N. Three London Popular Scientific Institutions, 1799-1840. Chicago 1970

H167 Haywood, Carl N. American Whalers and Africa. Boston U 1967

H168 Haywood, Richard M. The Beginnings of Railway Development in Russia in the Reign of Nicholas I, 1835-1842. Columbia 1966

H169 Hayworth, Ronald L. The Trial of Louis XVI. Emory 1968

H170 Hazard, Benjamin H., Jr. Japanese Marauding in Medieval Korea: The Wakō Impact on Late Koryō. Cal, Berkeley 1967

H170a Heacock, Roger L., Jr. Diplomatic Relations between the Austro-Hungarian Empire and the German Reich in World War I, 1916-1918: A Study Based on Documents from the Austrian State Archives. Denver 1967

H171 Head, John M. A Time to Rend: The Members of the Continental Congress and the Decision for American Independence, 1774-1776. Brown 1966

H172 Head, Marilyn C. Pope Pius II (Aeneas Silvius Piccolomini) and His Relations with England. Duke 1968

H173 Healey, Gordon D. The Reaction of the European Powers to the Franco-Soviet Pact. Tex U 1963

H174 Healy, Valentine J. John Morley, Interpreter of the French Enlightenment. St L 1961

H175 Hearn, Jana S. The Schoolmaster of Liberty: Or the Political Views of Benjamin Constant de Rebecque. Ind 1970

H176 Hearn, Walter C. Towns in Antebellum Mississippi. Miss U 1969

H177 Heath, Dale E. A Transcription and Description of Manuscript Vatican Greek 2061 (Gregory 048). Mich S 1965

H178 Heath, Frederick M. Politics and Steady Habits: Issues and Elections in Connecticut, 1894-1914. Columbia 1965

H179 Heath, Jim F. John F. Kennedy and the Business Community. Stanford 1967

H180 Heberle, Gerald C. The Predicament of the British Unionist Party, 1906-1914. Ohio 1967

H181 Hebert, Robert D. France and the United Nations, 1946-1958. Fla S 1966

H182 Hecht, Irene W. D. The Virginia Colony, 1607-1640: A Study in Frontier Growth. Wash U 1969

H183 Hecht, Robert A. Britain and America Face Japan, 1931-1933: A Study of Anglo-American Far Eastern Diplomacy during the Manchurian and Shanghai Crisis. CUNY 1970

H184 Heckart, Beverly A. From Bassermann to Bebel—The Relationships between Liberal and Social Democrats in Germany, 1905-1914. Wash St L 1968

H185 Hedtke, Charles H. Reluctant Revolutionaries: Szechwan and the Ch'ing Collapse, 1898-1911. Cal, Berkeley 1968

H186 Heffernan, Arthur J. A History of Catholic Education in Connecticut. Cath 1936

H187 Hegarty, Thomas J. Student Movements in Russian Universities, 1855-1861. Harvard 1965

H188 Heggoy, Alf A. The Colonial Policies of Gabriel Hanotaux in Africa, 1894-1898. Duke 1963

H189 Hei, Joan D. Pope Alexander III and the East. NYU 1969

H190 Heick, Welf H. Mackenzie and Macdonald: Federal Politics and Politicians in Canada, 1873-1878. Duke 1966

H191 Heidhues, Mary Frances A. S. Peranakan Chinese Politics in Indonesia. Cornell 1965

H192 Heidorn, Robert D. Urban Mass Transportation with Special Emphasis on Downstate Illinois Cities: A Study in the Formation of Public Policy. Ill 1963

H193 Heilbron, John L. A History of the Problem of Atomic Structure from the Discovery of the Electron to the Beginning of Quantum Mechanics. Cal, Berkeley 1964

H194 Heineman, John L. Constantin Freiherr von Neurath as Foreign Minister, 1932-1935: A Study of a Conservative Civil Servant and Germany's Foreign Policy. Cornell 1965

H195 Heinemann, Ronald L. Depression and New Deal in Virginia. Va 1968

H196 Heininger, Joseph F. Prussian Foreign Policy during the New Era, 1858-1862. Minn 1961

H197 Heintzen, Erich H. Wilhelm Loehe and the Missouri Synod, 1841-1853. Ill 1964

H198 Heinze, Rudolph W. Tudor Royal Proclamations, 1485-1553. Ia 1965

H199 Heiting, Thomas J. W. E. B. DuBois and the Development of Pan-Africanism, 1900-1930. Tex Tech 1969

H200 Heitman, Sidney. Nikolai Bukharin's Theory of Revolution. Columbia 1963

H201 Held, Joseph. Embattled Youth: The Independent German Youth Movements in the Twentieth Century. Rutgers 1968

H202 Heleniak, Roman J. The Election of 1936. Miss S 1964

H203 Helfrich, Ralph W., Jr. Administrative Regulation of Natural Gas Rates, 1898-1938. Ind 1962

H204 Heller, Henry. Reform and Reformers at Meaux, 1518-1525. Cornell 1969

H205 Hellie, Richard J. Muscovite Law and Society: The *Ulozhenie* of 1649 as a Reflection of the Political and Social Development of Russia since the *Sudebnik* of 1589. Chicago 1965

H206 Hellman, John W. Emmanuel Mounier and *Esprit:* Personalist Dialogue with Existentialism, Marxism and Christianity. Harvard 1969

H207 Helly, Dorothy O. British Attitudes towards Tropical Africa, 1860-1890. Radcliffe 1961

H208 Helmholz, Richard H. Marriage Litigation in Medieval England. Cal, Berkeley 1970

H209 Helmreich, Jonathan E. Belgian Diplomatic Style: A Study in Small Power Diplomacy. Princeton 1961

H210 Helmreich, Paul C. The Negotiation of the Treaty of Sèvres, January, 1919-August, 1920. Harvard 1964

H211 Helms, James M., Jr. The Early Career of Nathaniel Macon: A Study in "Pure Republicanism." Va 1962

H212 Helms, Mary Elizabeth M. The Convention Parliament of 1660. Bryn Mawr 1963

H213 Helmstadter, Richard J. Voluntaryism, 1828-1860. Columbia 1961

H214 Hemphill, John M, II. Virginia and the English Commercial System, 1689-1733: Studies in the Development and Fluctuations of a Colonial Economy under Imperial Control. Princeton 1964

H215 Henderson, Alice H. The History of the New York State Anti-Slavery Society. Mich U 1963

H216 Henderson, Bobbie G. Philip Doddridge and the Northampton Academy: Dissenting Education in England in the Eighteenth Century. Geo P 1967

H217 Henderson, Cary S. Congressman John Taber of Auburn: Politics and Federal Appropriations, 1923-1962. Duke 1964

H218 Henderson, Donald C., Jr. A Comparative Study in the Application of the Monroe Doctrine in Two Selected Instances. Mich S 1964

H219 Henderson, Dwight F. Courts for the New Nation: A History of the Inferior Federal Judiciary, 1787-1801. Tex U 1966

H220 Henderson, H. James, Jr. Political Factions in the Continental Congress, 1774-1783. Columbia 1962

H221 Henderson, John P. Sir William Paulet, the Marquess of Winchester: A Tudor Time-Server. St L 1969

H222 Henderson, Lloyd R. Earl Warren and California Politics. Cal, Berkeley 1965

H223 Henderson, Patrick C. The Public Domain in Arizona, 1863-1891. NM 1965

H224 Hendrick, Carlanna L. John Gary Evans: A Political Biography. SC 1966

H225 Hendricks, James E., Jr. Charles Thomson and the American Enlightenment. Va 1961

H226 Hendricks, William O. Guillermo Andrade and Land Development on the Mexican Colorado River Delta, 1874-1905. S Cal 1967

H227 Hendrickson, Embert J. The New Venezuelan Controversy: The Relations of the United States and Venezuela, 1904 to 1914. Minn 1964

H228 Hendrickson, James E. Joe Lane and the Disruption of the Democratic Party in Oregon, 1849-1861. Ore 1965

H229 Hendrickson, Kenneth E., Jr. The Public Career of Richard F. Pettigrew of South Dakota, 1848-1926. Okla 1962

H230 Henneman, John B., Jr. Royal Taxation in France, 1322-1348. Harvard 1966

H231 Henner, Solomon. The Career of William Tryon as Governor of the Province of New York, 1771-1780. NYU 1968

H232 Hennes, Randolph Y. The March Retreat of 1918: An Anatomy of a Battle. Wash U 1966

H233 Hennesey, James J. The Bishops of the United States at the First Vatican Council. Cath 1963

H234 Hennessy, John C. America and William Kaiser II of Germany, 1889-1918: An Inquiry into the Origin and Nature of his Image in America. UCLA 1969

H235 Hennings, Robert E. James D. Phelan and the Wilson Progressives of California. Cal, Berkeley 1961

H236 Henretta, James A. The Duke of Newcastle, English Politics, and the Administration of the American Colonies, 1724-1754. Harvard 1968

H237 Henriksen, Thomas H. The British Press and Italian Fascism, 1922-1932. Mich S 1969

H238 Henrikson, Alan K. "World Appeasement": The American Road to Munich. Harvard 1970

H239 Henriot, Peter J. One Man-One Vote, One Vote-One Value: The Theory of Equal Representation. Chicago 1967

H240 Henry, G. Seldon. Radical Republican Policy toward the Negro during Reconstruction (1862-1872). Yale 1963

H241 Henson, Curtis T., Jr. The United States Navy and China, 1839-1861. Tulane 1965

H242 Henson, Edward L., Jr. Britain, America, and the European Crisis, 1937-1938. Va 1969

H243 Hepburn, Charles M. Charles Beard and the Founding Fathers. Stanford 1966

H244 Herber, Charles J. Germany and the Papal Peace Proposal of August, 1917. Cal, Berkeley 1965

H245 Herlihy, Patricia Ann M. Russian Grain and Mediterranean Markets, 1774-1861. Penn U 1963

H246 Herman, Sondra R. Polity and Community, 1898-1921: A Study in American Internationalist Thought. Rutgers 1967

H247 Hermes, Walter G. The United States Army in the Korean War: The Last Two Years, July, 1951-July, 1953. Georgetown 1966

H248 Herrick, Walter R., Jr. General Tracy's Navy: A Study of the Development of American Sea Power, 1889-1893. Va 1962

H249   Herring, George C., Jr.   Experiment in Foreign Aid: Lend-Lease, 1941-1945. Va 1965

H250   Hertzberg, Arthur.   The Jews in France before the Revolution: Prelude to Emancipation. Columbia 1966

H251   Hertzler, James R.   The Reform of Imprisonment for Debt during the Interregnum and Later Stuart Periods. Wis 1967

H252   Herzstein, Robert E.   The Wagnerian Ethos in German History, 1848-1933: A Reinterpretation of Richard Wagner's Historical Significance. NYU 1964

H253   Hess, Gary R.   Sam Higginbottom of Allahabad: The Missionary as an Advanced Agent of American Economic and Technical Assistance in India. Va 1965

H254   Hess, James W.   George F. Hoar, 1826-1884. Harvard 1964

H255   Hess, Leland E.   The Coming of Urban Redevelopment and Urban Renewal to Oregon, 1949-1963: A Study in Democracy. Chicago 1968

H256   Hessen, Robert A.   A Biography of Charles M. Schwab, Steel Industrialist. Columbia 1969

H257   Hetmanek, Allen. Islam under the Soviets. Georgetown 1965

H258   Hett, Robert R.   John Charlton, Liberal Politician and Free Trade Advocate. Rochester 1969

H259   Heurtley, Richard W., Jr.   The Ethnogeny of Count Gobineau. Columbia 1968

H260   Hewett, David G.   Slavery in the Old South: The British Travelers' Image, 1825-1860. Fla S 1968

H261   Hewett, Robert F., Jr.   United States Civil Administration of the Ryukyu Islands, 1950-1960. Am 1966

H262   Hewsen, Robert H.   Introduction to the Study of Armenian Historical Geography: The Seventh Century Geography of Ananias of Sirak, with Translation and Commentary. Georgetown 1967

H263   Heyck, Thomas W.   English Radicals and the Irish Question, 1874-1895. Tex U 1969

H264   Heyda, Marie, Sister.   The Urban Dimension and the Midwestern Frontier: A Study of Democracy a Ypsilanti, Michigan, 1825-1858. Mich U 1966

H265   Hickin, Patricia P.   Antislavery in Virginia, 1831-1861. Va 1968

H266   Hicks, Walter E.   The 97th Bombardment Group, World War II. Ky 1961

H267   Hieronymus, Frank L.   For Now and Forever: The Chaplains of the Confederate States Army. UCLA 1964

H268   Higgins, W. Robert.   A Financial History of the American Revolution in South Carolina. Duke 1970

H269   Higonnet, Patrick L.   Social Background of Political Life in Two Villages of Central France, 1700-1962. Harvard 1964

H270   Hilden, Michele M.   The Mayors Josiah Quincy of Boston. Clark 1970

H271   Hill, Albert S.   The Radical-Socialist Party: Promise and Performance, 1900-1910. Harvard 1963

H272   Hill, Bennett D.   English Cistercian Monasteries and Their Patrons in the Twelfth Century: A Study in the Decline of an Ideal. Princeton 1963

H273   Hill, Boyd H., Jr.   The Funfbilderserie and Medieval Anatomy. NC 1963

H274   Hill, Elston J.   Buchman and Buchmanism. NC 1970

H275   Hill, Enid.   Montesquieu's *De l'Esprit des lois:* The Necessity of Relativistic Political Science to Admit Values. Chicago 1967

H276   Hill, John L.   Congress and Representative Institutions in the United Provinces, 1886-1901. Duke 1967

H277   Hill, Leonidas E.   Ernst von Weizsaecker: German Diplomat. Harvard 1963

H278   Hill, Marvin S.   The Role of Christian Primitivism in the Origin and Development of the Mormon Kingdom, 1830-1844. Chicago 1968

H279   Hill, Patricia K.   The Jacobite Bishop of Rochester. Ga 1969

H280   Hill, Peter P.   The Political and Diplomatic Career of William Vans Murray. Geo W 1966

H281   Hill, Thomas M.   The Senate Leadership and International Policy from Lodge to Vandenberg. Wash St L 1970

H282   Hiller, Harley E.   The Development of an Inter-American Peace System. Minn 1962

H283   Hillerbrand, Dieter.   Bismarck and Gorchakov: A Study in Bismarck's Russian Policy, 1852-1871. Stanford 1969

H284   Hillje, John W.   The Progressive Movement and the Graduated Income Tax, 1913-1919. Tex U 1966

H285 Hilton, Stanley E. Brazil and Great Power Trade Rivalry in South America, 1934-1939. Tex U 1969

H286 Hilty, Hiram H. North Carolina Quakers and Slavery. Duke 1969

H287 Himmelberg, Robert F. Relaxation of the Federal Anti-Trust Policy as a Goal of the Business Community during the Period 1918-1933. Penn S 1963

H288 Hinchey, Mary H. The Frustration of the New Deal Revival, 1944-1946. Mo 1965

H289 Hinckley, Theodore C., Jr. The Alaska Labors of Sheldon Jackson, 1877-1890. Ind 1961

H290 Hine, William L. The Interrelationship of Science and Religion in the Circle of Marin Mersenne. Okla 1967

H291 Hiner, Norville R., Jr. The Changing Role of History and Social Sciences in the Schools, 1892-1918. Geo P 1967

H292 Hines, Calvin W. United States Diplomacy in the Caribbean during World War II. Tex U 1968

H293 Hinger, George W. The Attitudes of *Le Correspondent* and *Le Revue des Deux Mondes* toward the Political Role of Austria-Hungary during the Years 1890-1940. Cath 1961

H294 Hingston, William R. Gifford Pinchot, 1922-1927. Penn U 1962

H295 Hinrichsen, Carl C. The History of the Diocese of Newark, 1873-1901. Cath 1963

H296 Hirsch, John L. Radical Anti-Fascism: Origins and Politics of the Italian Action Party. Wis 1965

H297 Hirshfield, Claire. The Marquis of Dufferin and Ava, Ambassador to France. Penn U 1965

H298 Hirshfield, Daniel S. The Lost Reform: A History of the Campaign for Compulsory Health Insurance in the United States from 1910 to 1943. Harvard 1967

H299 Hirst, David W. German Propaganda in the United States, 1914-1917. Northwestern 1962

H300 Hitchcock, James F. Popular Religion in Elizabethan England. Princeton 1965

H301 Hitchens, David L. Peace, World Organization and the Editorial Philosophy of Hamilton Holt and the *The Independent Magazine,* 1899-1921. Ga 1968

H302 Hitchins, Keith A. The Development of Rumanian Nationalism in Transylvania (1780-1849). Harvard 1964

H303 Hitchman, James H. Leonard Wood and the Cuban Question, 1898-1902. Cal, Berkeley 1965

H304 Hitsman, Mackay J. Defence of Canada, 1763-1871: A Study of British Strategy. Ottawa 1964

H305 Hittle, James M. The City in Muscovite and Early Imperial Russia. Harvard 1969

H306 Hixson, William B., Jr. The Last Abolitionist: A Study of Moorfield Storey, 1845-1929. Columbia 1969

H307 Hoang, Ngoc Thanh. The Social and Political Development of Vietnam as Seen through the Modern Novel. Hawaii 1968

H308 Hobbs, Joseph P. Dear General: An Analysis of the Eisenhower-Marshall Correspondence, 1942-1945. JH 1970

H309 Hodge, John E. Carlos Pellegrini, Argentine Statesman. Ill 1963

H310 Hodge, Robert W. Lining up Latin America: The United States Attempt to Bring Hemispheric Solidarity, 1939-1941. Mich S 1968

H311 Hodges, James A. The New Deal Labor Policy and the Southern Cotton Textile Industry, 1933-1941. Vanderbilt 1963

H312 Hodgins, Bruce W. The Political Career of John Sandfield Macdonald to the Fall of his Administration in March, 1864: A Study in Canadian Politics. Duke 1965

H313 Hoeben, Henry C. Frisia and the Frisians at the Time of St. Willibrord. Fordham 1967

H314 Hoermann, Alfred R. A Figure of the American Enlightenment: Cadwallader Colden. Toronto 1970

H315 Hoffecker, Carol E. President Truman's Explanation of His Foreign Policy to the American People. Harvard 1967

H316 Hoffer, Peter C. Liberty or Order: Two Views of American History from the Revolutionary Crisis to the Early Works of George Bancroft and Wendell Phillips. Harvard 1970

H317 Hoffman, Abraham. The Repatriation of Mexican Nationals from the United States during the Great Depression. UCLA 1970

H318 Hoffman, Donald S. Railways and Railway Politics in South Germany: Defensive Particularism at the State Level, 1835-1870. Del 1969

H319 Hoffman, Jerry H. The Ukrainian Adventure of the Central Powers, 1914-1918. Pitt 1967

H320 Hoffman, Nelson M. Jr. Godfrey Barnsley, 1805-1873: British Cotton Factor in the South. Kans U 1964

H321 Hoffman, Paul E. The Defense of the Indies, 1535-1574: A Study in the Modernization of the Spanish State. Fla U 1969

H322 Hoffman, Ronald. Economics, Politics, and the Revolution in Maryland. Wis 1969

H323 Hoffman, Wilson J. Mr. Secretary Thurloe: His Role in the Domestic Affairs of Oliver Cromwell's Protectorate. Case W Reserve 1963

H324 Hoffnagle, Warren M. Arthur L. Garford: A Biography of an Ohio Industrialist and Politician, 1858-1933. Ohio 1963

H325 Hogeland, Ronald W. Femininity and the Nineteenth Century Post-Puritan Mind. UCLA 1968

H326 Hohlfelder, Robert L. Ancient Coins at Indiana University: A Catalogue of Three Collections. Ind 1966

H327 Hohner, Robert A. Prohibition and Virginia Politics, 1901-1916. Duke 1965

H328 Hoidal, Oddvar K. The Road to Futility: Vidkun Quisling's Political Career in Pre-War Norway. S Cal 1970

H329 Hoing, Willard L. James Wilson as Secretary of Agriculture, 1897-1913. Wis 1964

H330 Hoisington, William A., Jr. A Businessman in Politics in France, 1935-1955: The Career of Jacques Lemaigre Dubreuil. Stanford 1968

H331 Holbo, Paul S. They Voted against War: A Study of Motivations. Chicago 1961

H332 Holbrook, Francis X. United States National Defense and Trans-Pacific Commercial Air Routes, 1933-1941. Fordham 1969

H333 Holcomb, Bob C. Senator Joe Bailey, Two Decades of Controversy. Tex Tech 1968

H334 Holcombe, Harold E. United States Arms Control and the Mexican Revolution, 1910-1924. Ala 1968

H335 Holcombe, Lee. Middle-Class Working Women in England, 1850-1914. Columbia 1962

H336 Holden, Vincent F. The Early Years of Isaac Thomas Hecker (1819-1844). Cath 1939

H337 Holder, Franklin B. André Tardieu, Politician and Statesman of the French Third Republic: A Study of His Ministries and Policies, 1929-1932. Cal, Berkeley 1962

H338 Holl, Jack M. The George Junior Republic and the Varieties of Progressive Reform. Cornell 1969

H339 Holland, Carolsue. The Foreign Contacts Made by the German Opposition to Hitler. Penn U 1967

H340 Holland, James C. The Education of Lord Acton. Cath 1968

H341 Holley, James D. The New Deal and Farm Tenancy: Rural Resettlement in Arkansas, Louisiana, and Mississippi. LSU 1969

H342 Holli, Melvin G. Hazen S. Pingree: Urban and Pre-Progressive Reformer. Mich U 1966

H343 Hollingsworth, Harold M. The Confirmation of Judicial Review under Taney and Chase. Tenn 1966

H344 Holmes, Charles F. A History of Bakwimba of Usukama, Tanzania from Earliest Times to 1945. Boston U 1969

H345 Holmes, Kenneth L. Ewing Young, Enterprising Trapper. Ore 1963

H346 Holmes, Larry E. Soviet Historical Studies of 1917 Bolshevik Activity in Petrograd. Kans U 1968

H347 Holmes, Michael S. The New Deal in Georgia: An Administrative History. Wis 1969

H348 Holmes, William F. The White Chief: James K. Vardaman in Mississippi Politics, 1890-1908. Rice 1964

H349 Holmgren, Daniel M. Edward Webster Bemis and Municipal Reform. Case W Reserve 1964

H350 Holsinger, M. Paul. Willis Van Devanter: The Early Years, 1859-1911. Denver 1964

H351 Holsten, Ned A. G. Renovation of Italy as a Nation: A Documentary Account of Allied Policy, 1940-1943. SC 1966

H352 Holt, Laurence J. Republican Insurgency in the Taft and Wilson Years. Harvard 1965

H353 Holt, Michael F. Forging a Majority: The Formation of the Republican Party in Pittsburgh, Pennsylvania, 1848-1860. JH 1967

H354 Holt, Niles R. The Social and Political Ideas of the German Monist Movement, 1871-1914. Yale 1967

H355 Holter, Howard R. A. V. Lunacharskii and the Formulation of a Policy toward the Arts in the RSFSR, 1921-1927. Wis 1967

H356 Holtzclaw, Harold W. The American War Referendum Movement, 1914-1941. Denver 1965

H357 Holub, Norman. The Liberal Movement in Brazil, 1808-1854. NYU 1968

H358 Homze, Edward L. The Administration of Nazi Germany's Foreign Labor Program, 1939 to 1945. Penn S 1963

H359 Hondros, John L. The German Occupation of Greece in World War II, 1941-1944. Vanderbilt 1969

H360 Hong, Choon Sik. The Termination of the Anglo-Japanese Alliance, 1920-1921. Ia 1965

H361 Hood, David C. Plutarch and the Persians. S Cal 1967

H362 Hood, James N. The Riots in Nîmes in 1790 and the Origins of a Popular Counterrevolutionary Movement. Princeton 1969

H363 Hooper, Robert E. The Political and Educational Ideas of David Lipscomb. Geo P 1965

H364 Hoover, Arlie J. The Gospel of Patriotism: The Nationalism of the German Protestant Clergy (1806-1815). Tex U 1965

H365 Hoover, Herbert T. History of the Republican Party in New Mexico, 1867-1952. Okla 1966

H366 Hoover, John P. Antonio José de Sucre, Grand Marshall of Ayacucho: A Review of His Public Career and Its Historical Significance. Am 1967

H367 Hopkins, George E. The Air Line Pilots Association (AFL-CIO): A Study in Elite Unionism. Tex U 1969

H368 Hooper, John E. The Purge: Franklin D. Roosevelt and the 1938 Democratic Nomination. Chicago 1966

H369 Hopwood, Robert F. Interalliance Diplomacy: Count Czernin and Germany, 1916-1918. Stanford 1965

H370 Horgan, James J. City of Flight: The History of Aviation in Saint Louis. St L 1965

H371 Hori, Kyotsu. The Mongol Invasions and the Kamakura Bakufu. Columbia 1967

H372 Horlick, Allan S. Countinghouses and Clerks: The Social Control of Young Men in New York, 1840-1860. Wis 1969

H373 Horn, Daniel. The Struggle for Constitutional Reform in Germany and Prussia, 1917-1918. Columbia 1963

H374 Horn, James J. Diplomacy by Ultimatum: Ambassador Sheffield and Mexican-American Relations, 1924-1927. SUNY, Buffalo 1969

H375 Horn, Michiel S. D. The League for Social Reconstruction: Socialism and Nationalism in Canada, 1931-1945. Toronto 1969

H376 Horn, Thomas C. R. The Empire and the Great Western Schism, 1375-1379. Cal, Berkeley 1962

H377 Horna, Hernán. Francisco Javier Cisneros: A Pioneer in Transportation and Economic Development in Colombia. Vanderbilt 1970

H378 Hornsby, Alton, Jr. Southern Negroes, 1877-1929: The Outsider's View. Tex U 1969

H379 Horowitz, Daniel. Insight into Industrialization: American Conceptions of Economic Development and Mechanization, 1865-1910. Harvard 1967

H380 Horowitz, Gary S. New Jersey Land Riots, 1745-1755. Ohio 1966

H381 Horowitz, Maryanne C. The Origin of Pierre Charron's Concept of Natural Law in Man. Wis 1970

H382 Horsnell, Margaret E. Spencer Roane: Judicial Advocate of Jeffersonian Principles. Minn 1967

H383 Horton, Albert C. Germany and the Spanish Civil War. Columbia 1966

H384 Horward, Donald D. The French Invasion of Portugal, 1810-1811. Minn 1962

H385 Hosay, Philip M. The Challenge of Urban Poverty: Charity Reformers in New York City, 1835-1890. Mich U 1969

H386 Hosford, David H. Nobles, Nottingham, and the North: Some Aspects of the Revolution of 1688. Wis 1970

H387 Hostetter, Henry G. Brandenburg's Neutrality in the Thirty Years' War, 1618-1626. Colo 1963

H388 Houdek, John T. James A. Garfield and Rutherford B. Hayes: A Study in State and National Politics. Mich S 1970

H389 Houf, Walter R. The Protestant Church in the Rural Midwestern Community, 1820-1870. Mo 1967

H390 Hough, John. Abel Stearns, 1848-1871. UCLA 1961

H391 House, Lewis. Edwin V. Morgan and Brazilian-American Diplomatic Relations, 1912-1933. NYU 1969

H392　Houseman, Philip J.　Chilean Nationalism, 1920-1952. Stanford 1961

H393　Hovannisian, Richard.　Armenia on the Road to Independence, 1918. UCLA 1966

H394　Howard, Harold C.　The Protestant Missionary and the Government Indian Policy, 1775-1850. Loyola 1965

H395　Howard, Mary K.　The French Parliament and the Italian-Roman Questions, 1859-1865. Penn U 1963

H396　Howard, Thomas C.　The Liberal Party in British Politics, 1922-1924: A Study in the Three Party System. Fla S 1965

H397　Howard, Victor B.　The Anti-Slavery Movement in the Presbyterian Church, 1835-1861. Ohio 1961

H397a　Howe, Daniel W.　The Unitarian Conscience: Harvard Moral Philosophy and the Second Great Awakening (1805-1861). Cal, Berkeley 1966

H398　Howe, John R., Jr.　The Search for Stability: An Essay in the Social Thought of John Adams. Yale 1963

H399　Howell, Sarah H. M.　Scholars of the Urban-Industrial Frontier, 1880-1889. Vanderbilt 1970

H400　Howell, Walter G.　The Origins and Results of the Anglo-Persian War of 1856-1857. Ga 1967

H401　Howes, John F.　Japan's Enigma: The Young Uchimura Kanzō. Columbia 1965

H402　Howes, Robert C.　The Testaments of the Grand Princes of Moscow. Cornell 1961

H403　Hoyt, Frederick G.　The Wood-Forbes Mission to the Philippines, 1921. Claremont 1963

H404　Hoyt, Hugh M.　The Good Roads Movement in Oregon, 1900-1920. Ore 1966

H405　Hoyt, James.　Korean Literature: The Rise of the Vernacular, 1443-1592. Cal, Berkeley 1962

H406　Hsieh, Pei-chih.　Diplomacy of the Sino-French War, 1883-1885. Penn U 1968

H407　Hu, Chang-tu.　The Yellow River Administration in the Ch'ing Dynasty. Wash U 1954

H408　Huang, Pei.　A Study of the Yung-chêng Period, 1723-1736: The Political Phase. Ind 1963

H409　Huang, Philip Chung-Chih.　A Confucian Liberal: Liang Ch'i-ch'ao in Action and Thought. Wash U 1966

H410　Huang, Ray.　The Grand Canal during the Ming Dynasty. Mich U 1965

H411　Hubbell, John T.　The Northern Democracy and the Crisis of Disunion, 1860-1861. Ill 1969

H412　Huber, Frances A.　The Progressive Career of Ben B. Lindsey, 1900-1920. Mich U 1963

H413　Huber, John P.　General Josiah Harmar's Command: Military Policy in the Old Northwest, 1784-1791. Mich U 1968

H414　Hubert, M. Gabriel, Sister.　The Role of Nelson Trusler Johnson in Sino-American Diplomatic Relations, 1930-1935. Cath 1964

H415　Huck, Eugene R.　Colombian-United States Commercial Relations, 1821-1850. Ala 1963

H416　Huddleston, Lee E.　A Study of European Concepts of the Origins of the American Indians, 1492-1729. Tex U 1966

H417　Hudson, David C.　Maupeou and the *Parlements:* A Study in Propaganda and Politics. Columbia 1967

H418　Hudson, Elizabeth K.　Matthew Parker's Contributions to the Development of Anglican Church Government. Ind 1961

H419　Hudson, Jerry E.　The United States and Latin American Independence, 1776-1812. Tulane 1965

H420　Hudson, M. Clarita, Sister.　Joseph Hodges Choate, Apostle of Good Understanding. Case W Reserve 1964

H421　Hudson, Randall O.　The Last Years of Simón Bolívar, 1828-1830: A Study in Futility. NC 1965

H422　Huebner, Lee W.　The Discovery of Propaganda: Changing Attitudes toward Public Communication in America, 1900-1930. Harvard 1968

H423　Hufbauer, Karl G.　The Formation of the German Chemical Community (1700-1795). Cal, Berkeley 1970

H424　Huff, Archie V., Jr.　Langdon Cheves: South Carolinian, 1776-1857. Duke 1970

H425　Huff, Carolyn B.　The Politics of Idealism: The Political Abolitionists of Ohio in Congress, 1840-1866. NC 1969

H426　Huff, Robert A.　Frederic C. Howe, Progressive. Rochester 1967

H427　Huggins, Koleen A. H.　The Evolution of City and Regional Planning in North Carolina, 1900-1950. Duke 1967

H428   Huggins, Nathan I. Private Charities in Boston, 1870-1900: A Social History. Harvard 1962

H429   Hughes, Arthur. Carleton J. H. Hayes: Teacher and Historian. Columbia 1970

H430   Hughes, Brady A. Owen D. Young and American Foreign Policy, 1919-1929. Wis 1969

H431   Hughes, Judith M. To the Maginot Line: The Politics of French Military Preparation in the 1920's. Harvard 1970

H431a   Hughes, Richard B. Texas Churches and Presidential Politics, 1928 and 1960. St L 1968

H432   Huhta, James K. Government by Instruction: North Carolina, 1731-1776. A Study of the Influence of the Royal Instructions on the Major Controversies between the Royal Governors and the Lower House. NC 1965

H433   Hull, Anthony F. H. Spanish and Russian Rivalry in the North Pacific Regions of the New World, 1760-1812. Ala 1966

H434   Hull, Gary W. The Prospect for Man in Early American Economic Thought, 1800-1850. Md 1969

H435   Hull, Henry L. The Holy See and Soviet Russia, 1918-1930: A Study in Full-Circle Diplomacy. Georgetown 1970

H436   Hull, Richard W. The Development of Administration in Katsina Emirate, Northern Nigeria, 1887-1944. Columbia 1968

H437   Hulse, James W. The Communist International in Its Formative Stage, 1919-1920. Stanford 1962

H438   Hume, Richard L. The "Black and Tan" Constitutional Conventions of 1867-1869 in Ten Former Confederate States: A Study of Their Membership. Wash U 1969

H439   Hummel, William W. Charles R. Buckalew: Democratic Statesman in a Republican Era. Pitt 1964

H440   Humphrey, David C. King's College in the City of New York, 1754-1776. Northwestern 1968

H441   Humphreys, Lester J. The Vorontsov Family: Russian Nobility in a Century of Change, 1725-1825. Penn U 1969

H442   Humphries, Charles W. The Political Career of Sir James P. Whitney. Toronto 1967

H443   Hundelt, M. Martine, Sister. Romolo Murri and the First Christian Democratic Movement in Italy. St L 1964

H444   Hundert, Edward J. The Conception of Work and the Worker in Early Industrial England: Studies of an Ideology in Transition. Rochester 1969

H445   Hundley, Norris C., Jr. Dividing the Waters: Mexican-American Controversies over the Waters of the Colorado River and the Rio Grande, 1880-1960. UCLA 1963

H446   Hunt, David. Methods of Childrearing and Attitudes toward Children in Seventeenth-Century France. Harvard 1969

H447   Hunt, H. Draper, III. Hannibal Hamlin of Maine: Lincoln's First Vice-President. Columbia 1968

H448   Hunt, James C. The People's Party in Württemberg and Southern Germany, 1890-1914: The Possibilities of Democratic Politics. Harvard 1970

H449   Hunt, John J. The United States Occupation of Iceland, 1941-1946. Georgetown 1966

H450   Hunt, William R. The Traveler in Ireland, 1732 to 1850. Wash U 1967

H451   Hunte, Keith D. The Ministry of Public Instruction in Quebec, 1867-1875: A Historical Study. McGill 1965

H452   Hunter, Doreen M. Richard Henry Dana, Sr.: An American Romanticist. Cal, Berkeley 1969

H453   Hunter, Robert J. The Historical Evolution of the Relationship between the United States and Puerto Rico, 1898-1963. Pitt 1963

H454   Hunter, Stephen C. Franco-Spanish Relations in the Era of Napoleon III and Isabel II. Stanford 1967

H455   Huppert, Ellen T. The Image of the City: The Paris of the Novelists from Stendhal to Zola. Cal, Berkeley 1970

H456   Huppert, George. The New History of the French Renaissance. Cal, Berkeley 1962

H457   Hurley, Alfred F. The Aeronautical Ideas of General William Mitchell. Princeton 1961

H457a   Hurt, John J. The Parlement of Brittany in the Reign of Louis XIV. NC 1970

H458   Hurwich, Judith J. Nonconformists in Warwickshire, 1660-1720. Princeton 1970

H459   Husband, Michael B. To Oregon in 1843: The Backgrounds and Organization of the "Great Migration." NM 1970

H460 Husley, Fabian V. Napoleon III and the Confederacy: A Reappraisal. Miss S 1970

H461 Hussey, Lyman A. Anglo-Canadian Relations during the Roosevelt Era, 1901-1908. Ga 1969

H462 Huston, Joseph T. Aspects of English Anti-Catholic Propaganda, 1667-1692. Mich U 1965

H463 Huston, Robert S. A. M. Simons and the American Socialist Movement. Wis 1965

H464 Hutson, James H. John Adams and the Diplomacy of the American Revolution. Yale 1964

H465 Huttenbach, Henry R. The Zemsky Sobor in Ivan IV's Reign. Wash U 1961

H466 Hutton, M. George Bernard, Sister. William M. Evarts, Secretary of State, 1877-1881. Cath 1966

H467 Hutton, Patrick H. The Boulangist Movement in Bordeaux Politics. Wis 1969

H468 Huxford, Gary L. The Old Whig Comes to America: A Study in the Transit of Ideas. Wash U 1963

H469 Huyler, David E. The Character and Personality of King Henry VI as Factors in the Lancastrian-Yorkist Struggle. Mich S 1964

H470 Hyatt, Albert M. J. The Military Career of Sir Arthur Currie. Duke 1965

H471 Hybertson, Larry D. The Contribution of Celio Calcagnini to Renaissance Astronomical Thought. Ore 1963

H472 Hyde, John M. Pierre Laval: The Illusions of a Realist, 1939-1940. Harvard 1963

H473 Hynding, Alan A. The Public Life of Eugene Semple: A Study of the Promoter-Politician on the Pacific Northwest Frontier. Wash U 1966

H474 Hynds, Ernest C. Ante-Bellum Athens and Clark County, Georgia. Ga 1961

I

I1   Iatrides, John O.   The Balkan Pact of the 1950's: A Study in Regional Security across Ideological Boundaries. Clark 1962

I2   Ignasias, C. Dennis.   Reluctant Recognition: The United States and the Recognition of Alvaro Obregón of Mexico, 1920-1924. Mich S 1967

I3   Ignatieff, Leonide.   French Émigrés in Russia, 1789-1825: The Interaction of Cultures in Time of Stress. Mich U 1963

I4   Illick, Joseph E., III.   William Penn's Relations with the British Government. Penn U 1963

I5   Imholte, John Q.   The First Minnesota Infantry Regiment, 1861-1864. Minn 1961

I6   Ingle, Homer L.   Pilgrimage to Reform: A Life of Claude Kitchin. Wis 1967

I7   Ingram, Alton E.   The Root Mission to Russia, 1917. LSU 1970

I8   Ink, Joseph W.   Lord Hastings and the Non-intervention Policy in Oudh, 1813-1816. Case W Reserve 1964

I9   Iobst, Richard W.   North Carolina Mobilizes: Nine Crucial Months, December, 1860-August, 1861. NC 1968

I10   Iorizzo, Luciano J.   Italian Immigration and the Impact of the Padrone System. Syracuse 1966

I11   Irby, James A.   Line of the Rio Grande: War and Trade on the Confederate Frontier, 1861-1865. Ga 1969

I12   Ireland, Owen S.   The Ratification of the Federal Constitution in Pennsylvania. Pitt 1966

I13   Ireland, Robert M.   The Legal Career of William Pinkney, 1764-1822. Neb 1967

I14   Iriye, Akira.   American Diplomacy and Sino-Japanese Relations, 1926-1931. Harvard 1961

I15   Irschick, Eugene F.   Politics and Social Conflict in South India: The Non-Brahmin Movement and Tamil Separatism, 1916-1929. Chicago 1964

I16   Irvin, Thomas C.   Norman H. Davis and the Quest for Arms Control, 1931-1938. Ohio 1963

I17   Isaac, Paul E.   Prohibition and Politics in Tennessee, 1885-1920. Tex U 1961

I18   Isaacman, Allen F.   The Historical Development of the Prazos da Coroa, 1750-1902. Wis 1970

I19   Isaacs, A. Joakim.   The Presidents and the Press in the Reconstruction Era. Wis 1966

I20   Isaacs, Harold.   United States-Mexican Relations during the González Administration, 1880-1884. Ala 1968

I21   Iseminger, Gordon L.   Britain's Eastern Policy and the Ottoman Christians, 1856-1877. Okla 1965

I22   Isham, Howard F., Jr.   The Idea of History: The Historical Thought of Wilhelm von Humboldt. Columbia 1962

I23   Isherwood, Robert M.   Music in the Service of the Royal Absolutism: France in the Seventeenth Century. Chicago 1964

I24   Israel, Jerome M.   Progressivism and the Open Door: America and China, 1901-1921. Rutgers 1967

I25   Israel, John W.   The Chinese Student Movement, 1927-1937. Harvard 1963

I26   Israel, Milton.   The English in India and the Passing of Empire: The Anglo-Indian in Defense of Authority, 1905-1910. Mich U 1966

I27   Israels, Elizabeth M.   The Historical Argument in French Religious Controversy, 1671-1691. UCLA 1967

I28   Isser, Natalie.   Government Sponsored Pamphlets on Foreign Policy during the Second Empire. Penn U 1962

I29   Ivanoff, Julia S.   A Study of the Bills before the House of Commons, 1621-1629. Miss S 1964

I30   Izenberg, Gerald S. N.   The Existentialist Critique of Freud: Changing Concepts of Rationality, Selfhood, and Society, 1890-1960. Harvard 1969

J

J1 Jablon, Howard. Cordell Hull, the State Department, and the Foreign Policy of the First Roosevelt Administration, 1933-1936. Rutgers 1967

J2 Jackman, Eugene T. The New Mexico Military Institute, 1891-1966: A Critical History. Miss U 1967

J3 Jackman, Francis V. America's Cuban Policy during the Period of the Machado Regime. Cath 1965

J4 Jackson, Brian J. The French Left and National Education, 1919-1938. Cath 1963

J5 Jackson, Broadus B. A History of Public Health Administration in Kentucky, 1920-1940. Ind 1963

J6 Jackson, Carl T. The Swami in America: A History of the Ramakrishna Movement in the United States, 1893-1960. UCLA 1964

J7 Jackson, Carlton L. A History of the Whig Party in Alabama, 1828-1860. Ga 1963

J8 Jackson, Charles O. Food and Drug Law Reform in the New Deal. Emory 1967

J9 Jackson, George D., Jr. The Green International and the Red Peasant International: A Study of Comintern Policy towards the Peasant Political Movement in Eastern Europe. Columbia 1961

J10 Jackson, Joy J. Municipal Problems in New Orleans, 1880-1896. Tulane 1961

J11 Jackson, Kenneth T. The Ku Klux Klan in the City, 1915-1930. Chicago 1966

J12 Jackson, Leland H. Andrés Bello: Latin American Humanist. Tex C 1968

J13 Jackson, Martin A. Richard Assheton Cross and the Artizans' Dwelling Act of 1875: A Study in Conservative Social Reform. CUNY 1970

J14 Jackson, Richard A. The Royal Coronation Ceremony in France from Charles VIII to Charles X. Minn 1967

J15 Jackson, Sherman G. Henry Dalton, Southern California Ranchero. S Cal 1970

J16 Jackson, Shirley J. The United States and Spain, 1898-1918. Fla S 1967

J17 Jackson, W. Sheldon. Ohio and Amendment Thirteen: A State Biography of the First National Reform Amendment, 1861-1865. Ohio 1969

J18 Jacob, Emerson D. Disraeli's Social Reforms, 1874-1880. Case W Reserve 1961

J19 Jacob, James R. Robert Boyle, Young Theodicean. Cornell 1969

J20 Jacob, Margaret C. The Church and the Boyle Lectures: The Social Context of the Newtonian Natural Philosophy. Cornell 1969

J21 Jacobs, Donald M. A History of the Boston Negro from the Revolution to the Civil War. Boston U 1968

J22 Jacobs, Josephine K. Sunkist Advertising. UCLA 1966

J23 Jacobson, Jon S. Germany and the West after Locarno, 1928-1929. Cal, Berkeley 1966

J24 Jaenen, Cornelius J. The Relations between Church and State in New France (1657-1684). Ottawa 1962

J25 Jaffin, David J. Eighteenth and Nineteenth Century Historical Interpretations of the Reign of James I of England. NYU 1966

J26 James, D. Clayton. Ante-Bellum Natchez. Tex U 1964

J27 Janick, Herbert F., Jr. Government for the People: The Leadership of the Progressive Party in Connecticut. Fordham 1968

J28 Jankowski, James P. The Young Egypt Party and Egyptian Nationalism, 1933-1945. Mich U 1967

J29 Jankowski, Manfred D. Prussian Policy and the Development of the Ruhr Mining Region, 1766-1865. Wis 1969

J30 Jannen, William, Jr. The Count of Waldeck in the Service of the Elector of Brandenburg, 1651-1658. Columbia 1970

J31 Jarausch, Konrad H. The Enigmatic Chancellor: A Political Biography of Theobald von Bethmann Hollweg, 1856-1921. Wis 1969

J32 Jareb, Jerome. The Adriatic Question, from June 1919 to February 1924. Columbia 1964

J33 Jarrett, H. Marshall. D'Alembert and the *Encyclopédie*. Duke 1962

J34 Jarvis, Charles A. John Greenleaf Whittier and the Anti-Slavery Movement, 1828-1860. Mo 1970

J35 Jasperson, Michael. Laval and the Nazis: A Study of Franco-German Relations. Georgetown 1967

J36 Jeanneney, John R. The Evolution of a National Forest Policy in France, 1827-1960. Columbia 1969

J37 Jegen, Mary Evelyn, Sister. Jonas of Orléans (c. 780-843): His Pastoral Writings and Their Social Significance. St L 1967

J38 Jelinek, Yeshayahu A. Hlinka's Slovak People's Party, 1939-1945. Ind 1966

J39 Jenkins, John A. To Find a Land: The Modern South and the Agrarian Tradition. Ind 1965

J40 Jenkins, William D., Jr. Robert Bulkley: Progressive Profile. Case W Reserve 1969

J41 Jenkins, William T. Ante-Bellum Macon and Bibb County, Georgia. Ga 1966

J42 Jennings, Helen L. John Mason Peck and the Impact of New England on the Old Northwest. S Cal 1961

J43 Jennings, Lawrence C. The Conduct of French Foreign Affairs in 1848: The Diplomacy of a Republic Divided within Itself. Wayne 1967

J44 Jennings, Thelma N. A Reappraisal of the Nashville Convention. Tenn 1968

J45 Jennings, Warren A. Zion is Fled: The Expulsion of the Mormons from Jackson County, Missouri. Fla U 1962

J46 Jennison, Earl W., Jr. Intrigue and Philosophy: Prussia in Mirabeau's Career and Thought. Columbia 1969

J47 Jensen, Billie B. House, Wilson, and American Neutrality, 1914-1917. Colo 1962

J48 Jensen, James M. The Development of the Central Valley Transportation Route in California to 1920. S Cal 1965

J49 Jensen, Joan M. The American Protective League, 1917-1919. UCLA 1962

J50 Jenson, Carol E. Agrarian Pioneer in Civil Liberties: The Nonpartisan League in Minnesota during World War I. Minn 1968

J51 Jessner, Sabine L. M. Edouard Herriot: Patriarch of the Republic. Columbia 1963

J52 Joffe, Ellis. Party-Army Relations in China since 1949: Professionalism and Political Control. Harvard 1967

J53 John, Douglas B. The Debate on British Military Air Policy, 1933-1939. Ky 1969

J54 Johnson, Alandus C. The Growth of Paine College: A Successful Interracial Venture, 1903-1946. Ga 1970

J55 Johnson, Andrew J., III. The Life and Constitutional Thought of Nathan Dane. Ind 1964

J56 Johnson, Bobby H. Some Aspects of Life in the "Land of the Fair God": Oklahoma Territory, 1889-1907. Okla 1967

J57 Johnson, Charles W. The Civilian Conservation Corps: The Role of the Army. Mich U 1968

J58 Johnson, Christopher H. Etienne Cabet and the Icarian Communist Movement in France, 1839-1848. Wis 1968

J59 Johnson, Dudley S. The Railroads of Florida, 1865-1900. Fla S 1965

J60 Johnson, George W., Jr. The Emergence of Modern African Politics in Senegal, 1848-1910. Columbia 1967

J61 Johnson, Harold B. The Cartulary of San Salvador de Lorenzana (Lugo). Chicago 1963

J62 Johnson, H. Thomas. Agricultural Depression in the 1920's: Economic Fact or Statistical Artifact? Wis 1969

J63 Johnson, Helene V. Alexander Hamilton and the British Orientation of American Foreign Policy, 1783-1803. S Cal 1963

J64 Johnson, Herbert A. John Jay: Colonial Lawyer. Columbia 1965

J65 Johnson, Hubert C. Politics of Discord: The Domestic Leadership of Frederick II of Prussia, 1740-1756. Cal, Berkeley 1962

J66 Johnson, James P. A "New Deal" for Soft Coal: The Attempted Revitalization of the Soft Coal Industry under the New Deal. Columbia 1968

J67 Johnson, Jerah W. From Medieval Largess to Physiocratic Economics: The Development of an Idea, the Doctrine of Spending. NC 1963

J68 Johnson, Kenneth R. The Woman Suffrage Movement in Florida. Fla S 1966

J69   Johnson, Lee R.   Aviaries and Aviculture in Ancient Rome. Md 1968

J70   Johnson, Margery R.   The Mayhew Mission to the Indians, 1643-1806. Clark 1966

J71   Johnson, Patricia C.   Sensitivity and Civil War: The Selected Diaries and Papers, 1858-1866, of Frances Adeline (Fanny) Seward. Rochester 1964

J72   Johnson, Richard R.   The Role of Parchment in Greco-Roman Antiquity. UCLA 1968

J72a   Johnson, Rita Virginia Therese, Sister. Timothy Richard's Theory of Christian Missions to the Non-Christian World. St John's 1966

J73   Johnson, Robert B.   The Punitive Expedition: A Military, Diplomatic, and Political History of Pershing's Chase after Pancho Villa, 1916-1917. S Cal 1964

J74   Johnson, Roger T.   Charles L. McNary and the Republican Party during Prosperity and Depression. Wis 1967

J75   Johnson, Ronald M.   Captain of Education: An Intellectual Biography of Andrew S. Draper, 1848-1913. Ill 1970

J77   Johnson, Warren B.   The Content of American Colonial Newspapers Relative to International Affairs, 1704-1763. Wash U 1962

J78   Johnson, William Reid.   China's 1911 Revolution in the Provinces of Yunnan and Kweichow. Wash U 1962

J79   Johnson, William Rudolph.   Farm Policy in Transition: 1932, Year of Crisis. Okla 1963

J80   Johnston, Robert H.   Continuity versus Revolution: The Russian Provisional Government and the Balkans, March-November, 1917. Yale 1966

J81   Johnston, William M.   The Formative Years of R. G. Collingwood. Harvard 1966

J82   Johnston, William R.   "Sovereignty and the Savage": A Study of British Jurisdictional Imperialism in the Late Nineteenth Century. Duke 1970

J83   Jolley, Harley E.   The Blue Ridge Parkway: Origins and Early Development. Fla S 1964

J84   Jones, Alfred H.   Roosevelt and Lincoln: The Political Uses of a Literary Image. Yale 1967

J85   Jones, Allen W.   A History of the Direct Primary in Alabama, 1840-1903. Ala 1964

J86   Jones, Alton D.   Progressivism in Georgia, 1898-1918. Emory 1963

J87   Jones, Arneta A.   The Left Opposition in the German Social Democratic Party, 1922-1933. Emory 1968

J88   Jones, Bartlett C.   The Debate over National Prohibition, 1920-1933. Emory 1961

J89   Jones, Billy M.   The Search for Health in the Development of the Southwest, 1817-1900. Tex Tech 1963

J90   Jones, Bobby F.   A Cultural Middle Passage: Slave Marriage and Family in the Ante-Bellum South. NC 1965

J91   Jones, Calvin P.   Spanish-America in Selected British Periodicals, 1800-1830. Ky 1966

J92   Jones, Charles E.   Perfectionist Persuasion: A Social Profile of the National Holiness Movement within American Methodism, 1867-1936. Wis 1968

J93   Jones, Charles T., Jr.   George Champlin Sibley: The Prairie Puritan (1782-1863). Mo 1969

J94   Jones, David N.   M. V. Lomonosov: The Formative Years, 1711-1742. NC 1969

J95   Jones, Edward B.   The Imperial Ideas of Henry Dundas and British Expansion in the East, 1783-1801. Duke 1963

J96   Jones, Eldon L.   Sir Guy Carleton and the Close of the American War of Independence, 1782-1783. Duke 1968

J97   Jones, Gene D.   The Local Political Significance of New Deal Relief Legislation in Chicago, 1933-1940. Northwestern 1970

J98   Jones, Hannah A. B.   The Struggle for Political and Cultural Unification in Liberia, 1847-1930. Northwestern 1962

J99   Jones, Hazel J.   The Meiji Government and Foreign Employees, 1868-1900. Mich U 1967

J100   Jones, Helen F.   James Lovell in the Continental Congress, 1777-1782. Columbia 1968

J101   Jones, Horace P.   Southern Opinion on the Crimean War. Miss U 1969

J102   Jones, Houston G.   The Public Archives of North Carolina, 1663-1903. Duke 1965

J103   Jones, John J.   A Historiographical Study of Jefferson Davis. Mo 1970

J104   Jones, Kenneth P.   Stresemann and the Diplomacy of the Ruhr Crisis, 1923-1924. Wis 1970

J105   Jones, Kenneth W.   The Arya Samaj in the Punjab: A Study of Social Reform and Religious Revivalism, 1877-1902. Cal, Berkeley 1966

J106   Jones, Larry E.   "The Dying Middle": Weimar Germany and the Failure of Bourgeois Unity, 1924-1930. Wis 1970

J107   Jones, Oakah L., Jr.   Pueblo Indian Auxiliaries and the Spanish Defense of New Mexico, 1692-1796. Okla 1964

J108   Jones, Philip D.   The British Army in the Age of Reform, 1830-1854. Duke 1968

J109   Jones, Robert E.   The Russian Gentry and the Provincial Reform of 1775. Cornell 1968

J110   Jones, Robert F.   The Public Career of William Duer: Rebel, Federalist Politician, Entrepreneur, and Speculator, 1775-1792. Notre D 1967

J111   Jones, Robert R.   Conservative Virginian: The Post-War Career of Governor James Lawson Kemper. Va 1964

J112   Jones, Thomas B.   Legacy of Change: The Panic of 1819 and Debtor Relief Legislation in the Western States. Cornell 1968

J113   Jonsson, Per-Olof.   The Projected Scandinavian Customs Union, 1947-1959. Fla S 1964

J114   Jordan, Daniel P., Jr.   Virginia Congressmen, 1801-1825. Va 1970

J115   Jordan, David P.   Enlightenment and Erudition in Gibbon's *Decline and Fall.* Yale 1967

J116   Jordan, David W.   The Royal Period of Colonial Maryland, 1689-1715. Princeton 1966

J117   Jordan, Donald A.   The Northern Expedition: A Military Victory. Wis 1967

J118   Jordan, James E.   Prince Napoleon Bonaparte and the Unification of Italy. Cal, Berkeley 1965

J119   Jordan, Philip H., Jr.   Connecticut Politics during the Revolution and Confederation, 1776-1789. Yale 1962

J120   Jordon, Holman D., Jr.   Ten Vermont Towns: Social and Economic Characteristics, 1850-1870. Ala 1966

J121   Josephson, Harold.   James Thomson Shotwell: Historian as Activist. Wis 1968

J122   Joyce, Davis D.   Edward Channing and the Great Work. Okla 1968

J123   Joyner, Charles W.   John Dos Passos and World War I: The Literary Use of Historical Experience. SC 1968

J124   Ju, Woo Jung.   The Rise and Fall of the Djakarta-Peking Axis, 1949-1966. Miss S 1967

J125   Juárez, Joseph R.   Conflict and Cooperation between Church and State: The Archbishopric of Guadalajara during the *Porfiriato,* 1876-1911. Tex 1967

J126   Juergens, George I.   The Birth of a Modern Newspaper: Joseph Pulitzer and the *New York World,* 1883-1885. Columbia 1965

J127   Juhnke, James C.   The Political Acculturation of the Kansas Mennonites, 1870-1940. Ind 1968

J128   Juliard, Pierre N.   Philosophies of Language in Eighteenth-Century France. Cornell 1966

J129   Juricek, John T.   English Claims in North America to 1660: A Study in Legal Constitutional History. Chicago 1970

K

K1 Kaczkowski, Conrad J. John Mackinnon Robertson: Freethinker and Radical. St L 1963

K2 Kadish, Gerald E. Early Egyptian Penetration of Nubia. Chicago 1964

K3 Kaegi, Walter E. Byzantium and the Decline of Rome: Conflicting Reactions of Byzantine Pagans and Christians. Harvard 1965

K4 Kaeuper, Richard W. The Riccardi of Lucca and English Government Finance, 1272-1294. Princeton 1967

K5 Kafker, Frank A. The Encyclopedists and the French Revolution. Columbia 1961

K6 Kagan, Richard C. The Chinese Trotskyist Movement and Ch'en Tu-hsiu: Culture, Revolution and Polity with an Appended Translation of Ch'en Tu-hsiu's Autobiography. Penn U 1969

K7 Kaganoff, Nathan M. The Traditional Jewish Sermon in the United States from Its Beginnings to the First World War. Am 1961

K8 Kahler, John K. The Genesis of the American Involvement in Indo-China, 1940-1954. Chicago 1964

K9 Kahler, Mary E. Relations between Brazil and the United States, 1815-1825, with Special Reference to the Revolutions of 1817 and 1824. Am 1968

K10 Kahn, Helen D. The Great Game of Empire: Willard D. Straight and American Far Eastern Policy. Cornell 1968

K11 Kaledin, Arthur D. The Mind of John Leverett. Harvard 1965

K12 Kalin, Berkley. Social Criticism in Twentieth Century American Poetry. St L 1967

K13 Kallina, Edmund F., Jr. A Conservative Criticism of American Foreign Policy: The Publications and Careers of Louis J. Halle, George F. Kennan, and Charles Burton Marshall. Northwestern 1970

K14 Kalnins, Anna. Liberals in the Russian Government and Constitutional Reform (1861-1881). Syracuse 1963

K15 Kamman, William. A Search for Stability: United States Diplomacy toward Nicaragua, 1925-1933. Ind 1962

K16 Kammen, Michael G. The Colonial Agents, English Politics, and the American Revolution. Harvard 1964

K17 Kanahele, George S. The Japanese Occupation of Indonesia: Prelude to Independence. Cornell 1967

K18 Kaner, Norman J. Towards a Minority of One: Vito Marcantonio and American Foreign Policy. Rutgers 1969

K19 Kang, Hi-woong. The Development of the Korean Ruling Class from Late Silla to Early Koryo. Wash U 1964

K20 Kang, Wi Jo. The Japanese Government and Religions in Korea, 1910-1945. Chicago 1967

K21 Kany, Robert H. David Hall: Printing Partner of Benjamin Franklin. Penn S 1963

K22 Kapica, Walter J. Major Socio-Political Movements and Catholicism in Partitioned Poland, 1885-1914. Cath 1968

K23 Kaplan, Edward H. Yueh Fei and the Founding of the Southern Sung. Ia 1970

K24 Kaplan, Lawrence. The Scots and English Civil War Politics, 1643-1645. Wash St L 1966

K25 Kaplan, Philip S. The Crisis in Anglo-American Relations of 1913-1914. JH 1966

K26 Kaplan, Temma E. Luís Simarro and the Development of Science and Politics in Spain, 1868-1917. Harvard 1969

K27 Kaplow, Jeffry J. The Social Structure of Elbeuf (Seine-Maritime) during the Revolutionary Period, 1770-1815. Princeton 1963

K28 Kapp, Robert A. Szechwanese Provincial Militarism and Central Power in Republican China. Yale 1970

K29 Karafiol, Emile. The Reforms of the Empress Maria Theresa in the Provincial Government of Lower Austria, 1740-1765. Cornell 1965

K30 Karanja, Josphat N. United States Attitude and Policy toward the International African Association, 1876-1886. Princeton 1962

K31 Karfunkel, Thomas. A Critical Evaluation of Hungarian Governmental Policies, 1941-1944: The Role and Policies of Horthy with Regard to German Pressures on the Hungarian Regime. NYU 1968

K32 Karges, Steven B. David Clark Everest and Marathon Paper Mills Company: A Study of a Wisconsin Entrepreneur, 1909-1931. Wis 1968

K33 Kargon, Robert H. Science and Atomism in England: From Hariot to Newton. Cornell 1964

K34 Karno, Howard L. Augusto B. Leguía: The Oligarchy and the Modernization of Peru, 1870-1930. UCLA 1970

K35 Karsten, Peter D. The Naval Aristocracy: U.S. Naval Officers from the 1840's to the 1920's: Mahan's Messmates. Wis 1968

K36 Katoke, Israel K. A History of Karagwe, Northeastern Tanzania, c. 1400-1915. Boston U 1969

K37 Katz, Irving. Investment Bankers in American Government and Politics: The Political Activities of William W. Corcoran, August Belmont, Sr., Levi P. Morton, and Henry Lee Higginson. NYU 1964

K38 Katz, Martin. Mikhail N. Katkov: A Political Biography, 1818-1887. Cal, Berkeley 1962

K39 Katz, Stanley N. An Easie Access: Anglo-American Politics in New York, 1732-1753. Harvard 1961

K40 Katzman, David M. Before the Ghetto: Black Detroit in the Nineteenth Century. Mich U 1969

K41 Katzman, Murray. News Broadcasting in the United States, 1920-1941. NYU 1968

K42 Kauffman, Christopher J. Lord Elcho (i.e., after 1883 the 10th Earl of Wemyss and March) and the Crisis of Mid-Victorian Liberalism. St L 1970

K43 Kaufman, Burton I. Henry De La Warr Flood: A Case Study of Organization Politics in an Era of Reform. Rice 1966

K44 Kaufman, Martin. Homeopathy and the American Medical Profession, 1820-1960. Tulane 1969

K45 Kavenagh, W. Keith. An Economic History of Suffolk County, New York, 1783-1812. NYU 1966

K46 Kawashima, Yasuhide. Indians and the Law in Colonial Massachusetts, 1689-1763. Cal, Santa Barbara 1967

K47 Kay, Marvin L. M. The Institutional Background to the Regulation in Colonial North Carolina. Minn 1962

K48 Kay, Miryam N. Separation of Church and State in Jeffersonian Virginia. Ky 1967

K49 Kaylani, Nabil M. British Policy toward France and Germany in the Moroccan Question, 1909-1912. Clark 1967

K50 Kaylor, Earl C., Jr. The Prohibition Movement in Pennsylvania, 1865-1920. Penn S 1963

K51 Kealey, Edward J. Roger, Bishop of Salisbury and Chief Justiciar of All England, 1100-1139. JH 1962

K52 Kearney, James R., III. Anna Eleanor Roosevelt: Years of Experiment, 1884-1940. Wis 1967

K53 Kearns, Kevin C. The History of the Acquisition, Development and Restoration of Forest Park, 1870-1910. St L 1966

K54 Keefe, Thomas M. The Response of the American Journals of Opinion to the Rise and Consolidation of National Socialism, 1930-1939. Loyola 1966

K55 Keen, Quentin B. Alexander Garden, Commissary for the Carolinas. UCLA 1961

K56 Keenan, Barry C. John Dewey in China: His Visit and the Reception of His Ideas, 1917-1927. Claremont 1969

K57 Keightley, David N. Public Work in Ancient China: A Study of Forced Labor in the Shang and Western Chou. Columbia 1969

K58 Keiser, John H. John Fitzpatrick and Progressive Unionism, 1915-1925. Northwestern 1965

K59 Keith, Henry H. Soldiers as Saviors: The Brazilian Military Revolts of 1922 and 1924 in Historical Perspective. Cal, Berkeley 1969

K60 Keith, Robert G. The Origins of the Hacienda System on the Central Peruvian Coast. Harvard 1970

K61 Kele, Max H. Nazi Appeals to the German Workers, 1919-1933. Tulane 1969

K62 Keleher, Edward P. The Historical-Political Roots of the *Anschluss*. St L 1965

K63 Keller, Clair W. Pennsylvania Government, 1710-1740: A Study of the Operation of Colonial Government. Wash U 1967

K64 Keller, Michael D. A History of the Langley Research Center, 1917-1947. Ariz 1968

K65 Keller, Ralph A. Northern Protestant Churches and the Fugitive Slave Law of 1850. Wis 1969

K66 Kelley, Brooks M. A Machine is Born: Simon Cameron and Pennsylvania, 1862-1873. Chicago 1961

K67 Kelley, Donald B. Mississippi Public Opinion in the Presidential Elections of 1928 and 1960: A Study in the Continuity of Ideas. Tulane 1965

K68 Kelley, Donald R. Historical Thought and Legal Scholarship in Sixteenth Century France. Columbia 1962

K69 Kellogg, Charles F. The National Association for the Advancement of Colored People: The New Abolition Movement Confronts the New Slavery. JH 1963

K70 Kellogg, Frederick. Rumanian Nationalism and European Diplomacy, 1866-1878. Ind 1969

K71 Kelly, Daniel K. Ultra-Royalism: Ideology and Politics under the Bourbon Restoration. Wis 1964

K72 Kelly, Dorothy A., Sister. Walter Lippmann as a Critical Observer of the American Scene, 1921-1931. Notre D 1970

K73 Kelly, Eugene T., Jr. Lord Liverpool's Government, 1822-1827. Ga 1963

K74 Kelly, Joseph M. The Parliamentary Career of Joseph Cowen. Loyola 1970

K75 Kelly, Lawrence C. The Navajos and Federal Policy, 1913-1935. NM 1961

K76 Kelly, M. Suzanne, Sister. Celestial Motors, 1543-1632. Okla 1964

K77 Kelly, Patrick J. The Naval Policy of Imperial Germany, 1900-1914. Georgetown 1970

K78 Kelly, Thomas. A History of Argos ca. 1100 to 546 B.C. Ill 1964

K79 Kelsey, Gladys H. The Political Ambiente of Peru. Wayne 1968

K80 Kelsey, Harry E., Jr. John Evans. Denver 1965

K81 Kelso, Thomas J. The German-American Vote in the Election of 1860: The Case of Indiana with Supporting Data from Ohio. Ball State 1967

K82 Kemper, Donald J. Senator Hennings and Civil Liberties. Mo 1963

K83 Kendall, John C. Blueprint Defiance of Manifest Destiny: Anti-Americanism and Anti-Republicanism in Canada West, 1858-1867. McGill 1969

K84 Kendall, Philip W. The Times and Tales of Jacob Abbott. Boston U 1968

K85 Kendall, Richard H. Edwin M. Borchard and the Defense of Traditional American Neutrality, 1931-1941. Yale 1964

K86 Kendrick, Thomas F. J. The Church-Whig Alliance: The Anti-Clericalists and the Government of Sir Robert Walpole, 1727-1737. Toronto 1961

K87 Keneally, James J. The Opposition to Woman Suffrage in Massachusetts, 1868-1920. Boston C 1963

K88 Kenez, Peter. The First Year of the Volunteer Army: Civil War in South Russia, 1918. Harvard 1967

K89 Kenkel, Joseph F. The Tariff Commission Movement: The Search for a Nonpartisan Solution of the Tariff Question. Md 1962

K90 Kennan, Elizabeth T. The *De Consideratione* of Saint Bernard of Clairvaux and the Reform of the Church in the Twelfth Century. Wash U 1966

K91 Kennedy, David M. Birth Control, Its Heroine and Its History in America: The Career of Margaret Sanger. Yale 1968

K92 Kennedy, John M. Philanthropy and Science in New York City: The American Museum of Natural History, 1868-1968. Yale 1968

K93 Kennedy, Philip W. The Concept of Racial Superiority and United States Imperialism, 1890-1910. St L 1963

K94 Kennedy, Thomas Crawford. Charles A. Beard and American Foreign Policy. Stanford 1961

K95 Kennedy, Thomas Cummins. The Hound of Conscience: A History of the No-Conscription Fellowship, 1914-1919. SC 1968

K96 Kennedy, William B. French Projects for the Invasion of Ireland, 1796-1798. Ga 1966

K97 Kennelly, Dolorosa, Sister. The Peace and Truce of God: Fact or Fiction? Cal, Berkeley 1962

K98 Kenner, Charles L. A History of New Mexican-Plains Indian Relations. Tex Tech 1966

K99 Kennett, Lee B., Jr. The French Armies in the Seven Years' War: A Study in Military Organization and Administration. Va 1962

K100 Kenney, Alice P. The Gansevoorts of Albany and Anglo-Dutch Relations in the Upper Hudson Valley, 1664-1790. Columbia 1961

K101   Kenny, Robert W.   The Political Career of Charles Howard, Earl of Nottingham, Lord Admiral of England, 1585-1618, with Special Emphasis on the Reign of Elizabeth I. Chicago 1963

K102   Kent, Herbert R., Jr.   Four Decades of Missionary Enterprise: An Institutional History of the Episcopal Church in the Pacific Northwest, 1851-1889. Tex U 1967

K103   Kent, Raymond K.   Early Kingdoms in Madagascar and the Birth of the Sakalava Empire, 1500-1700. Wis 1967

K104   Kenyon, John P. B.   High Churchmen and Politics, 1845-1865. Toronto 1967

K105   Kerber, Linda K.   The Federalist Mind: Rhetoric and Ideology in the Assessment of Jeffersonian America. Columbia 1968

K106   Kerby, Robert L.   Kirby Smith's Confederacy: The Trans-Mississippi South, 1863-1865. Columbia 1969

K107   Kern, Paul B.   The New Liberalism in Wilhelminian Germany. Chicago 1970

K108   Kern, Robert W.   Caciquismo versus Self-Government: The Problem of Liberalism and Local Government in Spain, 1858-1909. Chicago 1966

K109   Kern, Stephen.   Freud and the Emergence of Child Psychology, 1880-1910. Columbia 1970

K110   Kerr, Kathel A.   American Railroad Politics, 1914-1920. Pitt 1966

K111   Kessell, John L.   Mission Los Santos Angeles de Guevavi: Jesuits on the Pima Frontier, 1691-1767. NM 1969

K112   Kessler, Joseph A.   Turanism and Pan-Turanism in Hungary, 1890-1945. Cal, Berkeley 1967

K113   Kessler, Lawrence D.   The Apprenticeship of the K'anghsi Emperor, 1661-1684. Chicago 1969

K114   Kessler, M. Verona, Sister.   The Effects of the Laic Laws of 1901 and 1904 on the Benedictines in France. Notre D 1963

K115   Kestenbaum, Justin L.   The Question of Intervention in Mexico, 1913-1917. Northwestern 1963

K116   Ketcham, George A.   Municipal Police Reform: A Comparative Study of Law Enforcement in Cincinnati, Chicago, New Orleans, New York, and St. Louis, 1844-1877. Mo 1967

K117   Kett, Joseph F.   Regulation of the Medical Profession in America, 1780-1860. Harvard 1964

K118   Kettering, Sharon K.   Red Robes and Barricades: The Parlement of Aix-en-Provence in a Period of Popular Revolt, 1629-1649. Stanford 1969

K119   Keuchel, Edward F., Jr.   The Development of the Canning Industry in New York State to 1960. Cornell 1970

K120   Key, Jack B.   John H. Bankhead, Jr., of Alabama: Creative Conservative. JH 1964

K121   Khair, Mohammed Abul.   United States Foreign Policy in the Indo-Pakistan Subcontinent, 1940-1955. Cal, Berkeley 1962

K122   Khan, Mohammad A.   British Attitude to the Growth of Russian Influence in the Central Asian States, 1857-1878. McGill 1962

K123   Khan, Rais A.   The United States and International Arbitration, 1895-1912. Cal, Berkeley 1962

K124   Khasigian, Amos.   American Colonial Libertarianism and the Advent of the Federal Age. S Cal 1969

K125   Kieft, David O.   The Political and Diplomatic Origins of Belgium's Policy of Independence, 1936-1937. Cal, Berkeley 1966

K126   Kielman, Chester V.   The University of Texas Archives: An Analytical Guide to the Historical Manuscripts Collections in the University of Texas Library. Tex U 1966

K127   Kierstead, Raymond F., Jr.   Pomponne de Bellièvre: A Study of the Elite of High Administrators in the Age of Henry IV. Northwestern 1964

K128   Kieswetter, James K.   The Political Career of Étienne-Denis Pasquier. Colo 1968

K129   Kifer, Allen F.   The Negro under the New Deal, 1933-1941. Wis 1961

K130   Kihl, Mary R.   A Failure of Ambassadorial Diplomacy: The Case of Page and Spring Rice, 1914-1917. Penn S 1969

K131   Kilcoyne, Martin J.   The Political Influence of Rasputin. Wash U 1961

K132   Kilcup, Rodney W.   Hume and Burke: Theories of Ethics, Politics, and History. Harvard 1969

K133   Kilfoil, Jack F.   C. C. Trowbridge, Detroit Banker and Michigan Land Speculator, 1820-1845. Claremont 1969

K134 Kim, Chong Sun. The Emergence of Multi-Centered Despotism in the Silla Kingdom: A Study of the Origin of Factional Struggles in Korea. Wash U 1965

K135 Kim, Sung Bok. The Manor of Cortlandt and Its Tenants, 1697-1783. Mich S 1966

K136 Kim, Yung Chung. Great Britain and Korea, 1883-1887. Ind 1965

K137 Kimambo, Isaria N. Political History of the Pare People to 1900. Northwestern 1967

K138 Kimball, Jeffrey P. Strategy on the Northern Frontier, 1814. LSU 1969

K139 Kimball, R. Allan. The Early Political Career of Peter Lavrovich Lavrov, 1823-1873: A Study in the Liberalism and the Formation of Revolutionary Socialism in Russia. Wash U 1967

K140 Kimball, Stanley B. Czech Nationalism: A Study of the National Theatre Movement, 1845-1883. Columbia 1961

K141 Kimball, Warren F. "The Most Unsordid Act": Lend-Lease, 1941. Georgetown 1968

K142 Kincaid, Larry G. The Legislative Origins of the Military Reconstruction Act, 1865-1867. JH 1968

K143 King, Alvy L. Louis T. Wigfall: The Stormy Petrel. Tex Tech 1967

K144 King, David B. Marschall von Bieberstein and the New Course, 1890-1897. Cornell 1962

K145 King, Donald P. The Threefold Way: English Contemplatives in the Fourteenth Century. Ind 1969

K146 King, Edward B. Robert Grosseteste and the Pastoral Office. Duke 1969

K147 King, George D. The Industrialization of Indiana, 1860-1920. Ind 1963

K148 King, George W. The Civil War Career of Hugh Judson Kilpatrick. SC 1969

K149 King, Harold R. The Settlement of the Upper Connecticut River Valley to 1675. Vanderbilt 1965

K150 King, Irving H. The S.P.G. in New England, 1701-1784. Maine 1968

K151 King, James T. The War Eagle: A Life of General Eugene A. Carr. Neb 1962

K152 King, John O. Joseph Stephen Cullinan: A Study of Leadership in the Texas Petroleum Industry, 1897-1923. Vanderbilt 1966

K153 King, Patricia Ann M. A Twelfth Century Anglo-Norman Prelate: Hugh, Archbishop of Rouen, 1130-1164. Harvard 1970

K154 King, Peter J. Utilitarian Jurisprudence in America: The Influence of Bentham and Austin on American Legal Thought in the Nineteenth Century. Ill 1961

K155 King, William E. The Era of Progressive Reform in Southern Education: The Growth of Public Schools in North Carolina, 1885-1910. Duke 1970

K156 King, William J., Jr. Measurement and Natural Philosophy: A Study in the Quantification of Nature in the 17th Century. Cornell 1961

K157 Kingston, Esther R. Lenin: The Beginnings of Marxist Peasant Revolution, 1893-1917. JH 1970

K158 Kinsbruner, Jay. The Business Activities of William Wheelwright in Chile, 1829-1860. NYU 1964

K159 Kinsey, Winston L. The United States and Ghana, 1951-1966. Tex Tech 1969

K160 Kiple, Kenneth F. The Cuban Slave Trade, 1820-1862: The Demographic Implications for Comparative Studies. Fla U 1970

K161 Király, Béla K. 1790: Society in Royal Hungary. Columbia 1966

K162 Kirby, Jack T. Westmoreland Davis: A Virginia Planter, 1859-1942. Va 1965

K163 Kirk, Cooper C. A History of the Southern Presbyterian Church in Florida, 1821-1891. Fla S 1966

K164 Kirkland, John D., Jr. The Universe of the Mind: A Study of the Quest for Reality in Late Nineteenth-Century Thought. Duke 1965

K165 Kirkland, John R. Federal Troops in the South Atlantic States during Reconstruction, 1865-1877. NC 1968

K166 Kirkpatrick, Harold L. Bismarck's Insurrectionist Projects during the Austro-Prussian War, 1866. Cal, Berkeley 1962

K167 Kirschner, Don S. Conflict in the Corn Belt: Rural Responses to Urbanization, 1919-1929. Ia 1964

K168 Kirshner, Alan M. Tomás Garrido Canabal and the Mexican Red Shirt Movement. NYU 1970

K169 Kirshner, Julius. From Usury to Public Finance: The Ecclesiastical Controversy over the Public Debts of Florence, Genoa and Venice (1300-1500). Columbia 1970

K170 Kist, Eugene H. Wilhelm Sollmann: The Emergence of a Social Democratic Leader. Penn U 1969

K171 Kitchens, John W. Colombian-Chilean Relations, 1817-1845: A Diplomatic Struggle for Pacific Coast Hegemony. Vanderbilt 1969

K172 Kitchens, Joseph H., Jr. The Shearer Scandal and Its Origins: Big Navy Politics and Diplomacy in the 1920's. Ga 1968

K173 Kittelson, James M. Wolfgang Capito, Humanist and Reformer. Stanford 1969

K174 Kitzan, Laurence. The London Missionary Society in India and China, 1798-1834. Toronto 1965

K175 Klaits, Joseph A. Diplomacy and Public Opinion: Louis XIV, Colbert de Torcy and French War Propaganda, 1700-1713. Minn 1970

K176 Klang, Daniel M. Bavaria and the Age of Napoleon. Princeton 1963

K177 Klarén, Peter F. Origins of the Peruvian Aprista Party: A Study of Social and Economic Change in the Department of La Libertad, 1870-1932. UCLA 1968

K178 Klass, Bernard. John D. Black: Agricultural Economist and Policy Adviser, 1920-1942. UCLA 1969

K179 Klassen, Peter J. The Economics of Anabaptism, 1525-1560. S Cal 1962

K180 Klaustermeyer, Wiliam H. The Role of Matthew and Catherine Zell in the Strassburg Reformation. Stanford 1965

K181 Klebanow, Diana. Edwin L. Godkin and the American City. NYU 1965

K182 Kleber, John E. The Magic of His Power: Robert G. Ingersoll and His Day. Ky 1969

K183 Klein, Bernard. Hungarian Politics from Bethlen to Gömbös: The Decline of Liberal Conservatism and the Rise of Right-Radicalism. Columbia 1962

K184 Klein, George A., Jr. Sir Henry Campbell-Bannerman and the Liberal Imperialists, 1899-1903. Ohio 1969

K185 Klein, Herbert S. The Impact of the Chaco War on Bolivian Society. Chicago 1963

K186 Klein, Ira N. British Imperialism in Conflict and Alliance: Anglo-French and Anglo-Russian Relations in Asia, 1885-1914. Columbia 1968

K187 Klein, Martin A. Sine-Saloum, 1847-1914: The Traditional States and the French Conquest. Chicago 1964

K188 Klein, Maurice N. A Life of General Edward Porter Alexander. Emory 1965

K189 Kleinbaum, Abby R. Jean Jacques Dortous de Mairan (1678-1771): A Study of an Enlightenment Scientist. Columbia 1970

K190 Kleinfeld, Gerald R. Stabilization and Reconstruction in Austria: Schober and Seipel, 1921-1922. NYU 1961

K191 Kleppner, Paul J. The Politics of Change in the Midwest: The 1890's in Historical and Behavorial Perspective. Pitt 1967

K192 Kmen, Henry A. Singing and Dancing in New Orleans: A Social History of the Birth and Growth of Balls and Opera, 1791-1841. Tulane 1961

K193 Knafla, Louis A. New Model Lawyer: The Career of Sir Thomas Egerton, 1541-1616. UCLA 1964

K194 Knapp, Thomas A. Josef Wirth and the Democratic Left Wing of the German Center Party, 1918-1928. Cath 1967

K195 Knapp, Vincent J. The *Arbeiter-Zeitung,* the Mirror of Austrian Social Democracy. Rochester 1964

K196 Knauth, Lothar G. Pacific Confrontation: Japan Encounters the Spanish Overseas Empire. Harvard 1970

K197 Knautz, Harlan E. The Progressive Harvest in Colorado, 1910-1916. Denver 1969

K198 Kneer, Warren G. Great Britain and the Caribbean, 1901-1913: A Study in Anglo-American Relations. Mich S 1966

K199 Knight, Barry L. American Trade and Investment in China, 1890-1910. Mich S 1968

K200 Knight, Franklin W. C. Cuban Slave Society on the Eve of Abolition, 1838-1880. Wis 1969

K201 Knight, Isabel F. Condillac: A Study of the Geometric Spirit of the French Enlightenment. Yale 1964

K202 Knight, Tommy J. The Establishment of German Military Government in Belgium, 1940-1941. Tex U 1967

K203 Knights, Peter R. The Plain People of Boston, 1830-1860: A Demographic and Social Study. Wis 1969

K204　Knipe, John R.　The Justice of the Peace in Yorkshire, 1820-1914: A Social Study. Wis 1970

K205　Knoebel, Edgar E.　Racial Illusion and Military Necessity: A Study of SS Political and Manpower Objectives in Occupied Belgium. Colo 1965

K206　Knoll, Arthur J.　Togo under German Administration, 1884-1910. Yale 1964

K207　Knoll, Paul W.　The Foreign Policy of Casimir the Great of Poland, 1333-1370. Colo 1964

K208　Knott, Alexander W.　The Pan-American Policy of Woodrow Wilson, 1913-1921. Colo 1968

K209　Knowlton, Robert J.　The Disamortization and Nationalization of Ecclesiastical Property in Mexico, 1856-1910. Ia 1963

K210　Knox, A. J. Graham.　Race Relations in Jamaica, 1833-1958, with Special Reference to British Colonial Policy. Fla U 1962

K211　Knox, J. Wendell.　Conspiracy in American Politics, 1787-1815. NC 1965

K212　Knox, Thomas R.　Edmund Burke: Natural Law and History. Yale 1969

K213　Knudson, Jerry W.　The Jefferson Years: Response by the Press, 1801-1809. Va 1962

K214　Koblik, Steven S.　Sweden, the Neutral Victor: A Study of Anglo-American-Swedish Relations, 1917-1918. Northwestern 1970

K215　Kobrin, David R.　The Saving Remnant: Intellectual Sources of Change and Decline in Colonial Quakerism, 1690-1810. Penn U 1968

K216　Koch, Raymond L.　The Development of Public Relief Programs in Minnesota, 1929-1941. Minn 1967

K217　Koelsch, William A.　The Enlargement of a World: Harvard Students and Geographical Experience, 1840-1861. Chicago 1966

K218　Koepke, Robert L.　François Guizot and the Formation of a Conservative Party in France, 1840-1848. Stanford 1967

K219　Koesy, Sheldon F.　Continuity and Change in North Carolina, 1775-1789. Duke 1963

K220　Koginos, Emmanuel T.　The Panay Incident: Prelude to War. Am 1965

K221　Koh, Kwang I.　In Quest of National Unity and Power: Political Ideas and Practices of Syngman Rhee. Rutgers 1963

K222　Kohl, Benjamin G.　The Signoria of Francesco il Vecchio da Carrara in Padua, 1350-1388. JH 1968

K223　Kohl, James V.　The Role of the Peasant in the Bolivian Revolutionary Cycle, 1952-1964. NM 1969

K224　Kohls, Winfried A.　The State-Sponsored Russian Secondary School in the Reign of Alexander II: The First Phase: Search for a New Formula, 1855-1864. Cal, Berkeley 1967

K225　Kohn, Richard H.　The Federalists and the Army: Politics and the Birth of the Military Establishment, 1783-1795. Wis 1968

K226　Koistinen, Paul A. C.　The Hammer and the Sword: Labor, the Military and Industrial Mobilization, 1920-1945. Cal, Berkeley 1964

K227　Kolchin, Peter R.　First Freedom: The Responses of Alabama's Blacks to Emancipation and Reconstruction. JH 1970

K228　Kolinski, Charles J.　*Independencia o Muerte:* The Story of the Paraguayan War. Fla U 1963

K229　Kolko, Gabriel M.　The Federal Regulation of Railroads in the United States, 1877-1916. Harvard 1962

K230　Kolmer, Mary Arthur, Sister.　Contemporary Theories concerning Determinants of the American Character. St L 1965

K231　Kolody, Philip.　The Right in the French National Assembly, 1789-1791. Princeton 1967

K232　Kolz, Arno W.　British Foreign Policy and the Kolchak Government, November 1918-February 1920. Boston U 1965

K233　Komons, Nick A.　Chicago, 1893-1907: The Politics of Reform. Geo W 1961

K234　Koncelik, Lawrence J.　Baldwin III, King of Jerusalem, 1142-1163. NYU 1970

K235　Koonz, Claudia A.　Walther Rathenau's Vision of the Future: The Etiology of an Ideal. Rutgers 1969

K236　Kopf, David.　Orientalism and the Genesis of the Bengal Renaissance, 1800-1830. Chicago 1964

K237　Koppel, Reynold S.　Cleves-Mark in the Reign of the Great Elector (1640-1688). Wash U 1969

K238　Korgan, Julius.　Farmers Picket the Depression. Am 1961

K239　Korn, Peggy A.　The Beginnings of Mexican Nationalism: The Growth of an Ideology. Penn U 1965

K240 Kornberg, Jacques. History and Personality: The Theories of Wilhelm Dilthey. Harvard 1964

K241 Korr, Charles P. Cromwell and France, 1653-1658. UCLA 1969

K242 Kors, Alan C. The Côterie Holbachique: An Enlightenment in Paris. Harvard 1969

K243 Kos, M. Grace, Sister. California's Search for a Capital Site, 1846-1879. St L 1962

K244 Koss, Frederick M. The Boston Police Strike of 1919. Boston U 1966

K245 Koss, Stephen E. His Master's Voice: John Morley at the India Office. Columbia 1966

K246 Kosztolnyik, Zoltán J. Hungarian Cultural Policy in the Life and Writings of Gérard of Csanád. NYU 1969

K247 Kotynek, Roy A. 291: Alfred Stieglitz and the Introduction of Modern Art to America. Northwestern 1970

K248 Koumoulides, John A. Cyprus during the Struggle for Greek Independence, 1821-1829. Md 1968

K249 Kounas, Dionysios D. A. Prelude to Hegemony: Studies in Athenian Political Parties from 403 to 379 B.C. Pertaining to the Revival of Athenian Influence in Greece. Ill 1969

K250 Kovarik, Robert J. Simon de Montfort (1165-1218), His Life and Work: A Critical Study and Evaluation Based on the Sources. St L 1963

K251 Kozauer, Nikolaus J. The Carpatho Ukraine between the Two World Wars, with Special Emphasis on the German Population. Rutgers 1964

K252 Kraditor, Aileen S. The Ideas of the Woman Suffrage Movement, 1890-1920. Columbia 1962

K253 Krahn, Henry G. An Analysis of the Conflict between the Clergy of the Reformed Church and the Leaders of the Anabaptist Movement in Strasbourg, 1524-1534. Wash U 1970

K254 Kraig, Bruce Z. Deserted Medieval Villages in Yorkshire: Archaeological and Documentary Sources. Penn U 1969

K255 Kramer, Zoltan. The Road to Compromise, 1849-1867: A Study of the Habsburg-Hungarian Constitutional Struggle in Its Terminal Phase. Neb 1966

K256 Krammer, Arnold P. Soviet Bloc Relations with Israel, 1947-1953. Wis 1970

K257 Krantz, Charles K. The British Secularist Movement: A Study in Militant Dissent. Rochester 1964

K258 Kranz, Marvin W. Pioneering in Conservation: A History of the Conservation Movement in New York State, 1865-1903. Syracuse 1961

K259 Kratz, Marjorie T. The Poor Law Medical Officer and the Administration of Medical Relief in England, 1832-1842. Ore 1965

K260 Kraus, Harry. The Settlement House Movement in New York City, 1886-1914. NYU 1970

K261 Krause, Michael D. Anglo-French Military Planning, 1905-1914, before the First World War: A Study in "Military Diplomacy." Georgetown 1968

K262 Krauskopf, Robert W. French Air Power Policy, 1919-1939. Georgetown 1965

K263 Kreider, John K. Diplomatic Relations between Germany and the United States, 1906-1913. Penn S 1969

K264 Kreilkamp, Hermes D. The Origin of the Patriarchate of Constantinople and the First Roman Recognition of Its Patriarchal Jurisdiction. Cath 1964

K265 Kreindler, Isabelle. Educational Policies toward the Eastern Nationalities in Tsarist Russia: A Study of Il'Minskii's System. Columbia 1969

K266 Kreisler, Frederic F. Domesday Monachorum Re-Considered: Studies in the Genesis of Domesday Book and Its Relationship to Sources and "Satellites." Princeton 1967

K267 Kressel, Richard P. The Administration of Caffa under the Uffizio di San Giorgio. Wis 1966

K268 Kreuter, Gretchen V. The American Discussion of Genius in the Nineteenth and Twentieth Centuries. Wis 1961

K269 Kreuter, Kent K. The Literary Response to Science, Technology and Industrialism: Studies in the Thought of Hawthorne, Melville, Whitman and Twain. Wis 1963

K270 Kreutz, Barbara M. Amalfi and Salerno in the Early Middle Ages: A Regional Profile. Wis 1970

K271 Kriedman, Herbert. New York's Philip Hone: Business Man, Politician, Patron of Arts and Letters. NYU 1965

K272 Kriegel, Abraham D. The Whig Government and Ireland, 1830-1835. Duke 1965

K273 Krieger, Milton H. Studies in Civil Violence in England, 1430-1450. Toronto 1969

K274 Krishnaswamy, S. A Riot in Bombay, August 11, 1893: A Study in Hindu-Muslim Relations in Western India during the Late Nineteenth Century. Chicago 1966

K275 Krivy, Leonard P. American Organized Labor and the First World War, 1917-1918: A History of Labor Problems and the Development of a Government War Labor Program. NYU 1965

K276 Kroeker, Marvin E. William B. Hazen: A Military Career in the Frontier West, 1855-1880. Okla 1967

K277 Krosby, H. Peter. Petsamo in the Spotlight: A Case Study in Finnish-German Relations, 1940-1941. Columbia 1967

K278 Krousel, Hilda S. Translated and Annotated *Autobiografía del General José Antonio Páez,* Volume I. LSU 1970

K279 Krueger, Thomas A. The Southern Conference for Human Welfare, 1938-1948. Minn 1965

K280 Krupensky, Michael. The Secret Societies in Russia and the Decembrist Movement. Georgetown 1966

K281 Kruppa, Patricia S. Charles Hadden Spurgeon: A Preacher's Progress. Columbia 1968

K282 Kubicek, Robert V. Joseph Chamberlain and the Colonial Office: A Study in Imperial Administration. Duke 1965

K283 Kubrin, David C. Providence and the Mechanical Philosophy: The Creation and Dissolution of the World in Newtonian Thought: A Study of the Relations of Science and Religion in Seventeenth Century England. Cornell 1968

K284 Kucera, Rita C. Francesco Guicciardini: Mirror of "Cinquecento" Disillusionment. Loyola 1964

K285 Kuehl, John W. The Quest for Identity in an Age of Insecurity: The XYZ Affair and American Nationalism. Wis 1968

K286 Kuethe, Allan J. The Military Reform in the Viceroyalty of New Granada, 1773-1796. Fla U 1967

K287 Kuhn, Gary G. The History of Aeronautics in Latin America. Minn 1965

K288 Kuhn, M. Campion, Sister. The Activity of the Foreign Press Service of the NSDAP in the United States, 1937-1941. Cath 1964

K289 Kuisel, Richard F. The Career of Ernest Mercier: Politics and the Business Elite in Twentieth Century France. Cal, Berkeley 1963

K290 Kuntz, Norbert A. The Electoral Commission of 1877. Mich S 1969

K291 Kuo, Thomas C. T. Ch'en Tu-hsiu (1879-1942) and the Chinese Communist Movement. Pitt 1970

K292 Kupferman, Herbert A. The Search for Peace and Unity in Post-Westphalian Germany: The Example of the Foreign Policy of the Elector of Mainz, John Philip von Schönborn, from 1646 to 1673, with Special Attention to the Federation of the Rhine, 1656-1667. NYU 1968

K293 Kupp, Theodorus J. Fur Trade Relations, New Netherlands-New France: A Study of the Influence Exerted by the Fur Trade Interests of Holland and New Netherland on the Settlement of New France during the Years 1600-1664. Manitoba 1968

K294 Kurland, Gerald. Seth Low: A Study in the Progressive Mind. CUNY 1968

K295 Kuroda, Tadahisa. The County Court System of Virginia from the Revolution to the Civil War. Columbia 1969

K296 Kusielewicz, Eugene F. The Teschen Question at the Paris Peace Conference: A Re-examination in the Light of Materials in the Archives of the United States. Fordham 1963

K297 Kutolowski, John F. Mid-Victorian Britain and the Polish Insurrection of 1863-1864. Chicago 1966

K298 Kutzleb, Charles R. Rain Follows the Plow: The History of an Idea. Colo 1968

K299 Kuzirian, Eugene E. The Interim Republic: Domestic Affairs in England, January 30, 1648/9 to May 19, 1649. Rutgers 1969

K300 Kymlicka, Bohuslav B. National Committee in Bohemia and Moravia, 1945-1948. Columbia 1966

K301 Kynerd, Byrle A. Law Enforcement and British Liberties during the Early Reform Period, 1815-1837. Ga 1969

L

L1   Labarrère-Paulé, André. *Les instituteurs et les institutrices laiques Catholiques au Canada francais (1836-1900).* Laval 1961

L2   LaCapra, Dominick. Émile Durkheim and the Sociology of Consensus. Harvard 1970

L3   Laccetti, Silvio R. The Dissolution of the Italian Empire after World War II. Columbia 1967

L4   Lachs, Phyllis S. The Diplomatic Corps under Charles II and James II. Bryn Mawr 1963

L5   Lackner, Bede. The Eleventh-Century Background of Citeaux. Fordham 1968

L6   Lacy, Edmund E. The Conflict in Thought over the Role of Religion in American Higher Education, 1865-1910. Ill 1969

L7   Lacy, Eric R., Sr. Sectionalism in East Tennessee, 1796-1861. Ga 1968

L8   Laffey, John F. French Imperialism and the Lyon Mission to China. Cornell 1966

L9   La Forte, Robert S. The Republican Party of Kansas during the Progressive Era, 1900-1916. Kans U 1966

L10   LaGodna, Martin M. The Florida State Department of Agriculture during the Administration of Nathan Mayo, 1923-1960. Fla U 1970

L11   Lagow, Thomas K., Jr. Tensions in the Triple Entente, as Viewed from Paris and London, 1911-1914. Ga 1968

L12   LaGumina, Salvatore J. Vito Marcantonio, Labor and the New Deal (1935-1940). St John's 1966

L13   Lahiff, Bartholemew P. The Pontificate of Leo XII: A Study in Church Emancipation. Georgetown 1965

L14   Laiou-Torode, Angeliki E. The Limitations of Empire: Andronicus II, Palaeologus, and Western Europe (1282-1311). Harvard 1967

L15   Lambert, C. Roger. New Deal Experiments in Production Control: The Livestock Program, 1933-1935. Okla 1962

L16   Lambert, Walter K. New Deal Revenue Acts: The Politics of Taxation. Tex U 1970

L17   Lamberti, Marjorie E. The Rise of the Prussian Conservative Party, 1840-1858. Yale 1966

L18   Lamont, James W. The Passage, Implementation, and Amendment of the Rogers Act of 1924. Rutgers 1965

L19   Lampe, Anthony B. The Saint Louis Volunteer Fire Department, 1820-1850. St L 1966

L20   Lancaster, R. Kent. King Henry III and the Patronage of Religious Art. JH 1967

L21   Landa, Michel L. The Origin and Development of Surrealist Vision. Cal, Berkeley 1970

L22   Landen, Robert G. Modernization and Imperialism in Oman in the Late Nineteenth Century. Princeton 1961

L23   Landis, Richard B. Institutional Trends at the Whampoa Military School, 1924-1926. Wash U 1969

L24   Landon, Dale E. Church-State Relations in the Late Anglo-Saxon Period, 871-1066: A Study of Reciprocal Influence and Support. Ill 1969

L25   Landon, Michael de Laval. The Political Role of the Whig Lawyers, 1678-1689. Wis 1966

L26   Landry, Harral E. The Influence of the Caribbean in British Policy toward Spain, 1782-1793. Ala 1963

L27   Lane, Ann J. The Brownsville Affair. Columbia 1968

L28   Lane, Barbara M. Architecture and Politics in Germany, 1918-1945. Radcliffe 1962

L29   Lane, Jack C. Leonard Wood and the Shaping of American Defense Policy, 1900-1920. Ga 1963

L30   Lane, James B. Bridge to the Other Half: The Life and Urban Reform Work of Jacob A. Riis. Md 1970

L31   Lane, Roger. The Police of Boston, 1822-1885. Harvard 1963

L32   Lang, Henry J. Notions of Liberty and Freedom Presented by the Polish Delegation at the Council of Constance. Ind 1966

L33   Lange, Ruth. Three Critical Years of the National Liberal Party of Germany: 1877, 1878, 1879. NYU 1968

L34   Langley, Lester D.   The United States and Panama, 1933-1941: A Study in Strategy and Diplomacy. Kans U 1965

L35   Langley, Wendell E.   Berthier's Memoires de Trevoux (1745-1762): Fideism and the Problems of Method. St L 1960

L36   Langsam, Miriam Z.   The Nineteenth Century Wisconsin Criminal: Ideologies and Institutions. Wis 1967

L37   Langworthy, Harry W.   A History of Undi's Kingdom to 1890: Aspects of Chewa History in East Central Africa. Boston U 1969

L38   Lanier, Osmos, Jr.   Anti-Annexationists of the 1890's. Ga 1965

L39   Lankevich, George J.   The Grand Army of the Republic in New York State, 1865-1898. Columbia 1967

L40   Lankford, John E.   Protestant Stewardship and Benevolence, 1900-1941: A Study in Religious Philanthropy. Wis 1962

L41   LaPierre, Laurier J. L.   Politics, Race, and Religion in French Canada: Joseph Israel Tarte. Toronto 1962

L42   Lapomarda, Vincent A.   Maurice Joseph Tobin, 1901-1953: A Political Profile and an Edition of Selected Public Papers. Boston U 1968

L43   Lapp, John A.   The Mennonite Church in India, 1897-1962. Penn U

L44   Larew, Karl G.   The Policies of the Western Powers towards the Problem of the Turkish Straits, 1914-1923. Yale 1964

L45   Large, Stephen S.   The Labor Movement in Japan, 1912-1919: Suzuki Bunji and the Yuaikai. Mich U 1970

L46   Larkin, John A.   The Evolution of Pampangan Society: A Case Study of Social and Economic Change in the Rural Philippines. NYU 1966

L47   Larmour, Peter J. G.   The French Radical Party and the Decline of the Third Republic, 1932-1940. Columbia 1963

L48   Larmour, Ronda.   The Grocers of Paris in the Sixteenth Century: Corporations and Capitalism. Columbia 1963

L49   Larrabee, Edward C. M.   New Jersey and the Fortified Frontier System of the 1750's. Columbia 1970

L50   Larréy, Martin F.   A Viceroy and His Challengers: Supremacy Struggles during the Viceregency of Martín Enríquez, 1568-1580. Cal, Santa Barbara 1965

L51   Larsen, Lawrence H.   Glenn Frank: The Boy Wonder from Missouri. Wis 1962

L52   Larsen, William E.   Governor Andrew Jackson Montague of Virginia, 1862-1937: The Making of a Southern Progressive. Va 1961

L53   Larson, Katherine G.   Through the Looking Glass of Erich Kästner: Culture and Crisis in Germany. Stanford 1969

L54   Larson, Robert W.   Statehood for New Mexico, 1889-1912. NM 1961

L55   Lasby, Clarence.   German Scientists in America: Their Importation, Exploitation and Assimilation, 1945-1952. UCLA 1962

L56   Lasch, Christopher.   Revolution and Democracy: The Russian Revolution and the Crisis of American Liberalism, 1917-1919. Columbia 1961

L57   Lauber, Jack M.   The Merchant-Gentry Conflict in Eighteenth-Century Russia. Ia 1967

L58   Launitz-Schurer, Leopold S., Jr.   Loyal Whigs and Revolutionaries: New York Politics on the Eve of the American Revolution, 1760-1776. McGill 1970

L59   Laurens, Franklin D.   France and the Italo-Ethiopian Crisis, 1935-1936. NC 1962

L60   Laurent, Pierre H.   Conflict and Accommodation in Belgian-American Diplomatic and Commercial Relations, 1830-1846. Boston U 1964

L61   Laurenzo, Frederick E.   The Parliamentary Career of Robert Harley, 1689-1710. Ill 1969

L62   Laushey, David M.   The Bengal Terrorists and their Conversion to Marxism: Aspects of Regional Nationalism in India, 1905-1942. Va 1969

L63   Lavender, William.   Bolshevik Tactics and Propaganda in Petrograd after the February Revolution, April-November 1917. Wash U 1969

L64   Lavrin, Asunción I.   Religious Life of Mexican Women in the XVIII Century. Harvard 1963

L65   Lawless, Joseph T.   Disraeli's Concepts of English Social Classes. St L 1967

L66   Lawrence, Gerald C.   The Assimilation of Newtonian Mechanics, 1687-1736. Okla 1968

L67 Lawson, Hughie G.   Candidates and Issues in 1912: A Reexamination of the New Nationalism and the New Freedom. Tulane 1970

L68 Lawson, Richard A.   The Failure of Independent Liberalism, 1930-1941. Mich U 1966

L69 Layton, Donald L.   The Tariff of 1891 and the Debate on the Future of the Russian Economy. Ind 1965

L70 Layton, Roland V., Jr.   The *Voelkischer Beobachter,* 1925-1933: A Study of the Nazi Party Newspaper in the *Kampfzeit.* Va 1965

L71 Lazerson, Marvin F.   The Burden of Urban Education: Public Schools in Massachusetts, 1870-1915. Harvard 1970

L72 Leab, Daniel.   A Union of Individuals: The Formation of the American Newspaper Guild, 1933-1936. Columbia 1969

L73 Leach, Barry A.   German Strategic Planning for the Campaign in the East, 1939-1941. British Columbia 1968

L74 Leach, Duane M.   The Tariff and the Western Farmer, 1860-1890. Okla 1965

L75 Leach, Hamish A.   A Politico-Military Study of the Detroit River Boundary Defence during the December 1837-March 1838 Emergency. Ottawa 1963

L76 Leake, Jane C. A.   The Geats of *Beowulf:* A Study in the Geographical Mythology of the Middle Ages. Wis 1963

L77 Leamon, James S.   War, Finance, and Faction in Colonial New York: The Administration of Governor Benjamin Fletcher, 1692-1698. Brown 1961

L78 Leary, David T.   The Attitudes of Certain United States Citizens toward Mexico, 1821-1846. S Cal 1970

L79 Leary, William M., Jr.   Smith of New Jersey: A Biography of H. Alexander Smith, United States Senator from New Jersey, 1944-1959. Princeton 1966

L80 Leathers, Noel L.   France and the Balkans, 1871-1879. Okla 1963

L81 Leavell, John P., Jr.   The Ideal of the Politician in the United States, 1880-1917. Tulane 1967

L82 Leavey, William J.   Hitler's Envoy "Extraordinary," Franz von Papen: Ambassador to Austria, 1934-1938, and Turkey, 1939-1944. St John's 1968

L83 Lebedoff, Victor R.   The Development of Religious Liberty in Canada since the British Conquest. Md 1965

L84 Lebovices, Herman.   A Socialism for the German Middle Classes: The Social Conservative Response to Industrialism, 1900-1933. Yale 1965

L85 LeBreton, Marietta M.   A History of the Territory of Orleans, 1803-1812. LSU 1969

L86 Lebrun, Richard A.   Joseph de Maistre: The Relationship between His Political Thought and His Religious Thought. Minn 1963

L87 Leclerc, Jean.   *Denonville et l'alliance Anglo-Iroquoise.* Ottawa 1968

L88 Ledeen, Michael A.   *Fascismo Universale:* The Theory and Practice of the Fascist International, 1928-1936. Wis 1969

L88a Lee, Arthur O.   A History of Bemidji State College, 1913-1937. ND 1968

L89 Lee, Charles R., Jr.   The Confederate Constitutions. NC 1961

L90 Lee, Egmont.   Sixtus IV and Men of Letters. Wis 1970

L91 Lee, Loyd E.   The Civil Service of the State of Baden, 1815-1848. Cornell 1967

L92 Lee, R. Alton.   Harry S. Truman and the Taft-Hartley Act. Okla 1962

L93 Lee, Robert H. G.   Cultural Change and Political Control on the Manchurian Frontier during the Ch'ing Dynasty. Columbia 1963

L94 Lee, Ta-Ling.   T'ung-meng-Hui and the Chinese Revolution, 1905-1912. NYU 1967

L95 Lee, Won Sul.   The Impact of United States Occupation Policy on the Socio-Political Structure of South Korea, 1945-1948. Case W Reserve 1961

L96 Lee, Yur Bok.   Diplomatic Relations between Korea and the United States, 1882-1887: A Study of Foreign Services of Minister Foote and Chargé Foulk in Korea. Ga 1965

L97 Leeb, I. Leonard.   Some Political Uses of History: The Dutch Republic in the Age of Democratic Revolution. Columbia 1969

L98 Leemhuis, Roger P.   James L. Orr: The Civil War and Reconstruction Years. Wis 1970

L99 Lees, Andrew.   The German Intellectuals in the Aftermath of Revolution, 1849-1859. Harvard 1969

L100 Lees, Laurine L. H. Social Change and Social Stability among the London Irish, 1830-1870. Harvard 1969

L101 LeGacy, Arthur E. Improvers and Preservers: A History of Oak Park, Illinois, 1833-1940. Chicago 1967

L102 Legan, M. Scott. The Evolution of Public Health Services in Mississippi, 1865-1910. Miss U 1968

L103 Legassick, Martin C. The Griqua, the Sotho-Tswana, and the Missionaries, 1780-1840: The Politics of a Frontier Zone. UCLA 1969

L104 Leger, Ann Louise. Moorfield Storey: An Intellectual Biography. Ia 1968

L105 Leger, Mary Celeste, Sister. Catholic Indian Missions in Maine, 1611-1820. Cath 1929

L106 Legon, Ronald P. *Demos* and *Statis:* Studies in the Factual Politics of Classical Greece. Cornell 1966

L107 Lehman, Orin. The Early Life of Howard A. Rusk, M.D. (1901-1945). NYU 1961

L108 Lehmann, Frederick L. The Eighteenth Century Transition in India: Responses of Some Bihar Intellectuals. Wis 1967

L109 Leiding, James H. Selected Aspects of the Social Actions Programs of Muncie's United Automobile Workers Locals, 1937-1964. Ball State 1965

L110 Leighton, Albert C. Early Medieval Transport. Cal, Berkeley 1964

L111 Leith, James A. The Idea of Art as Propaganda in France, 1750-1799: A Study in the History of Ideas. Toronto 1961

L112 Leland, Earl J. The Post Office and Politics, 1876-1884: The Star Route Frauds. Chicago 1964

L113 Leland, John W. Neville Chamberlain and British Social Legislation, 1923-1929. Ohio 1970

L114 Lemons, James S. The New Woman in the New Era Woman's Movement from the Great War to the Great Depression. Mo 1967

L115 Lencyk, Wasyl. The Eastern Catholic Church and Czar Nicholas I. Fordham 1961

L116 Lengel, Leland L. The Righteous Cause: Some Religious Aspects of Kansas Populism. Ore 1968

L117 Lenk, Richard W., Jr. Hackensack, New Jersey: From Settlement to Suburb, 1686-1804. NYU 1969

L118 Leon, George B. Greece and the First Great War: From Neutrality to Intervention. Ga 1961

L118a Leonard, Glen M. Western Boundary-Making: Texas and the Mexican Cession, 1844-1850. Utah 1970

L119 Leonard, Henry B. The Open Gates: The Protest against Movement to Restrict European Immigration, 1896-1924. Northwestern 1967

L120 Leonard, Ira M. New York City Politics, 1841-1844: Nativism and Reform. NYU 1965

L121 Leonard, Janet M. A Study of the Administration of John Aylmer, Bishop of London, 1577-1594. Fordham 1970

L121a Leonard, John G. Kandukuri Viresalingam, 1848-1919: A Biography of an Indian Social Reformer. Wis 1970

L122 Leonard, Karen B. The Kayasths of Hyderabad City: Their Internal History, and Their Role in Politics and Society from 1850 to 1900. Wis 1969

L123 Leonard, Thomas M. The Commissary Issue in United States-Panamanian Relations. Am 1969

L124 Leopard, Donald D. The French Conquest and Pacification of Madagascar, 1885-1905. Ohio 1966

L125 Leotta, Louis, Jr. Abraham Epstein and the Movement for Social Security, 1920-1939. Columbia 1965

L126 Lerner, Gerda. Abolitionists from South Carolina: A Life of Sarah and Angelina Grimké. Columbia 1966

L127 Lerner, Laurence M. The Rise of the Impresario: Bernard Ullman and the Transformation of Musical Culture in Nineteenth Century America. Wis 1970

L128 Lerner, Robert E. The Heresy of the Free Spirit in the Thirteenth Century. Princeton 1964

L129 Lerner, Saul. The Concepts of History, Progress, and Perfectibility in Nineteenth Century American Transcendentalist Thought. Kans U 1966

L130 Lerner, Warren. Karl Radek on World Revolution: A Study in Revolutionary Strategy and Tactics. Columbia 1961

L131 Les Callette, Millard G. Lyman Trumbull and the Democratic Tradition. Md 1962

L132 Lesesne, Joab M., Jr. A Hundred Years of Erskine College, 1839-1939. SC 1967

L133   Lessard, Claude. *Le collège-séminaire de Nicolet,* 1863-1935. Laval 1967

L134   Levack, Brian P.   The Politics of the English Civil Lawyers, 1603-1629. Yale 1970

L135   Levenstein, Harvey A.   The United States Labor Movement and Mexico, 1910-1951. Wis 1966

L136   Leventhal, Fred M.   George Howell, 1833-1910: A Career in Radical Politics. Harvard 1968

L137   Lever, Alfred W.   The British Empire and the German Colonies, 1914-1919. Wis 1963

L138   Leverette, William E., Jr.   Science and Values: A Study of Edward L. Youmans' *Popular Science Monthly,* 1872-1887. Vanderbilt 1963

L139   Levey, Jules.   The Sorelian Syndicalists: Édouard Berth, Georges   Valois and Hubert Lagardelle. Columbia 1967

L140   Levin, Arthur A.   The Life and Work of Mikhail Osipovich Gershenzon (1869-1925): A Study in the History of the Russian Silver Age. Cal, Berkeley 1968

L141   Levin, David S.   Regulating the Securities Industry: The Evolution of a Government Policy. Columbia 1969

L142   Levine, Daniel.   Variety in Reform Thought: Social Assumptions of American Reformers, 1890-1912. Northwestern 1961

L143   Levine, David A.   Expecting the Barbarians: Race Relations and Social Control, Detroit, 1915-1925. Chicago 1970

L144   Levine, Herbert S.   The Nazis in Danzig, 1925-1939. Yale 1969

L145   Levine, Joseph M.   From Caxton to Camden: The Quest for Historical Truth in Sixteenth Century England. Columbia 1965

L146   Levine, Lawrence W.   William Jennings Bryan: The Last Decade, 1915-1925. Columbia 1962

L147   Levine, Norman.   Gerhard Ritter: His Life and Work. NYU 1965

L148   Levine, Robert M.   The Vargas Regime and the Politics of Extremism in Brazil, 1934-1938. Princeton 1967

L149   Levinson, Robert E.   The Jews in the California Gold Rush. Ore 1968

L150   Levitt, Joseph.   The Social Program of the Nationalists of Quebec (1900-1914). Toronto 1968

L151   Levy, Darline G. S.   Social Realism and the Politics of Revolt in Eighteenth Century France: An Intellectual Portrait of Simon Nicolas Henri Linguet (1736-1794). Harvard 1968

L152   Levy, David W.   The Life and Thought of Herbert Croly, 1869-1914. Wis 1967

L153   Levy, James R.   The Development and Use of the Heroic Image of José de San Martín, 1840-1900. Penn U 1964

L154   Levy, Morris.   Alfred Thayer Mahan and United States Foreign Policy. NYU 1965

L155   Levy, Richard S.   Anti-Semitic Political Parties in the German Empire. Yale 1969

L156   LeWarne, Charles P.   Communitarian Experiments in Western Washington, 1885-1915. Wash U 1970

L157   Lewinsohn, Nancy.   The National Legislature and German-Soviet Relations, 1919-1927: A Study in Legislative-Executive Cooperation. Harvard 1965

L158   Lewinson, Edwin R.   John Purroy Mitchel, Symbol of Reform. Columbia 1961

L159   Lewis, Albert L.   Los Angeles in the Civil War Decades, 1850 to 1868. S Cal 1970

L160   Lewis, Beth I.   George Grosz: Art and Politics in the Weimar Republic. Wis 1969

L161   Lewis, Charles E.   The Justiciarship of Archbishop Hubert Walter, A.D. 1194-1198. Miss S 1964

L162   Lewis, Charlton M., III.   The Opening of Hunan: Reform and Revolution in a Chinese Province, 1895-1907. Cal, Berkeley 1965

L163   Lewis, Norman.   English Missionary Interest in the Indians of North America, 1578-1700. Wash U 1968

L164   Lewis, Theodore B.   Massachusetts and the Glorious Revolution, 1660-1692. Wis 1967

L164a   Lewis, Tom T.   Franco-American Diplomatic Relations, 1898-1907. Okla 1970

L165   Lewis, Wallace L.   The Survival of the German Navy, 1917-1920: Officers, Sailors, and Politics. Ia 1969

L166   Lewis, Walter D.   Punishment and Reformation in New York, 1796-1861: A Study in Prison Reform. Cornell 1961

L167   Lewis, William F., III.   Francisco Xavier Mina: Guerrilla Warrior for Romantic Liberalism, 1789-1817. Cal, Santa Barbara 1967

L168 Leyendecker, Liston E. Bela Stevens Buell: Central City Entrepreneur (1836-1918). Denver 1966

L169 Li, Bernadette Yu-ning. A Biography of Ch'ü Ch'iu-pai: From Youth to Party Leadership (1899-1928). Columbia 1967

L170 Libourel, Jan M. Dio Cassius on the Early Roman Republic. UCLA 1968

L171 Liddle, William. A Patriot King, or None: American Public Attitude towards George III and the British Monarchy, 1754-1776. Claremont 1970

L172 Lidtke, Vernon L. The Politics of German Social Democracy, 1878-1890. Cal, Berkeley 1962

L173 Lieberstein, Samuel. Leninism: A Study in the Sociology of Political Alienation. Cal, Berkeley 1967

L174 Liedel, Donald E. The Antislavery Novel, 1836-1861. Mich U 1961

L175 Lightner, David L. Labor on the Illinois Central Railroad, 1852-1900. Cornell 1969

L176 Liguori, Mary, Sister. The Impact of a Century of Irish Catholic Immigration in Nova Scotia (1750-1850). Ottawa 1961

L177 Lilley, William, III. The Early Career of Francis G. Newlands, 1848-1897. Yale 1965

L178 Limbaugh, Ronald H. The Idaho Spoilsmen: Federal Administrators and Idaho Territorial Politics, 1863-1890. Idaho 1967

L179 Limoli, Donald A. F. Crispi, A Study in Italian Foreign Policy. Princeton 1961

L180 Lin, Han-sheng. Wang Ching-wei and the Japanese Peace Efforts. Penn U 1967

L181 Linabury, George. British-Sa'udi Arab Relations, 1902-1927. Columbia 1970

L182 Lincoln, William B. Nikolai Alekseevich Milyutin and Problems of State Reform in Nicholaeven Russia. Chicago 1966

L183 Linden, Allen B. Politics and Higher Education in China: The Kuomintang and the University Community, 1927-1937. Columbia 1969

L184 Linden, Glenn M. Congressmen, "Radicalism" and Economic Issues, 1861 to 1873. Wash U 1963

L185 Linder, Doris H. The Reaction of Norway to American Foreign Policy, 1918-1939. Minn 1961

L186 Linder, Robert D. The Political Ideas of Pierre Viret. Ia 1963

L187 Lindley, Christopher. Franklin D. Roosevelt and the Politics of Isolationism, 1932-1936. Cornell 1963

L188 Lindsay, James E. The Failure of Liberal Opposition to British Entry into World War I. Columbia 1969

L189 Lindsay, Robert O. Antoine Lefèvre de la Boderie's Mission to England: A Study of French-English Relations, 1606-1611. Ore 1966

L190 Linick, Anthony. A History of the American Literary *Avant-garde* since World War II. UCLA 1965

L191 Linker, Ronald W. Philip Pusey, Esquire: Country Gentleman, 1799-1855. JH 1961

L192 Lipschitz, Joseph W. The Little Loaf and Free Trade: Failure of the Attack on Free Trade, 1895-1906. Case W Reserve 1970

L193 Lipscomb, Oscar H. The Administration of Michael Portier, Vicar Apostolic of Alabama and the Floridas, 1825-1829, and the First Bishop of Mobile, 1829-1859. Cath 1963

L194 Lipsey, Richard C. The Impact of the Evangelicals and the Humanitarians on the Political Situation in South Africa. Md 1968

L195 Lischka, Johannes R. Ludwig Mond and the British Alkali Industry: A Study in the Interrelations of Science, Engineering, Education, Industry, and Government. Duke 1970

L196 Lisenby, William F. An Administrative History of Public Programs for Dependent Children in North Carolina, Virginia, Tennessee, and Kentucky, 1900-1942. Vanderbilt 1962

L197 Lisio, Donald J. Investing in Pittsburgh's Progress: The History of the Buhl Foundation. Wis 1965

L198 Liss, Sheldon B. The Chamizal Conflict, 1864-1964. Am 1965

L199 Litchfield, Robert B. The Expansion of the French Revolution in Tuscany, 1790-1801. Princeton 1965

L200 Little, Dwayne L. The Political Leadership of Speaker Sam Rayburn, 1940-1961. Cincinnati 1970

L201 Little, George F. G. Fazenda Cambuhy: A Case History of Social and Economic Development in the Interior of São Paulo, Brasil. Fla U 1960

L202 Little, John E. John Adams and American Foreign Affairs, 1775-1780. Princeton 1966

L203 Little, Lester K., II. Frater Ludovicus: A Study of Saint Louis' Involvement in Evangelical Christianity. Princeton 1962

L204 Liu, Tai. Saints in Power: A Study of the Barebones Parliament. Ind 1969

L205 Livesay, Harold C. The Changing Distribution System in American Manufacturing, 1815-1860. JH 1970

L206 Livingston, John C. Clarence Darrow: Sentimental Rebel. Wis 1965

L207 Livingston, John M. *Infamia* in the Decretists from Rufinus to Johannes Teutonicus. Wis 1962

L208 Livingston-Little, Dallas E. An Economic History of North Idaho from 1800 to 1900. S Cal 1961

L209 Locke, Bobby R. The Legitimists: A Study in Social Mentality: The Royalist Right in the French National Assembly of 1871. UCLA 1965

L210 Lockhart, James M. Spanish Peru, 1532-1560: A Portrait of Peruvian Colonial Society at Its Origin. Wis 1967

L211 Lockridge, Kenneth A. Dedham, 1636-1736: The Anatomy of a Puritan Utopia. Princeton 1965

L212 Lodge, Martin E. The Great Awakening in the Middle Colonies. Cal, Berkeley 1964

L213 Loengard, Janet. The Assizes of Novel Dissein and Nuisance in the King's Courts before the Statute of Merton (1236). Columbia 1969

L214 Loewen, Alice L. A Survey of the Correspondence of the Early Tudor Nobility, 1492-1537. Miss S 1967

L215 Loewenberg, Peter J. Walther Rathenau and German Society. Cal, Berkeley 1966

L216 Lofgren, Charles A. Congress and the Korean Conflict. Stanford 1966

L217 Logsdon, Joseph A. Horace White: Nineteenth Century Liberal. Wis 1966

L218 Logue, William H. The Career of Léon Blum to 1914. Chicago 1964

L219 Lohrenz, Otto. The Virginia Clergy and the American Revolution, 1774-1799. Kans U 1970

L220 Lombardi, John V. The Decline and Abolition of Negro Slavery in Venezuela, 1820-1854. Columbia 1968

L221 Lommel, Anne W. The United States Efforts to Foster Peace and Stability in Central America, 1923-1954. Minn 1967

L222 Long, Everett L. Jefferson and Congress: A Study of the Jeffersonian Legislative System, 1801-1809. Mo 1966

L223 Long, James W. The Economics of the Franco-Russian Alliance, 1904-1906. Wis 1968

L224 Long, Robert E. Thomas Amlie: A Political Biography. Wis 1969

L225 Long, Ronald B. The Role of American Diplomats in the Fall of China, 1941-1949. St John's 1961

L226 Long, Ronald W. Religious Revivalism in the Carolinas and Georgia, 1740-1805. Ga 1968

L227 Longaker, John H., Jr. Lord Clarendon's Pre-Crimean War Diplomacy, 1853-1854. Penn U 1970

L228 Longton, William H. Some Aspects of Intellectual Activity in Ante-Bellum South Carolina, 1830-1860: An Introductory Study. NC 1969

L229 Lonsdale, David L. The Movement for an Eight-Hour Law in Colorado, 1893-1913. Colo 1963

L230 Looks, Bernard J. National Renaissance and Educational Reform in France, 1863-1914: *Normaliens,* Political Change, and the Schools. Columbia 1968

L231 Looney, John F. The King's Representative: Benning Wentworth, Colonial Governor, 1741-1767. Lehigh 1961

L232 Loosbrock, Richard J. The History of the Kansas Department of the American Legion, 1919-1968. Kans U 1968

L233 Lora, Ronald G. Conservatism in American Thought, 1930-1950. Ohio 1967

L234 Lorantas, Raymond M. Lord Cowley's Mission to Paris, 1852-1856. Penn U 1963

L235 Lord, Charles A. The West Virginia Education Association, 1865-1961. W Va 1963

L236 Lord, Donald C. In His Steps: A Biography of Dan Beach Bradley, Medical Missionary to Thailand, 1835-1873. Case W Reserve 1964

L237 Lorence, James J. The American Asiatic Association, 1898-1925: Organized Business and the Myth of the China Market. Wis 1970

L238   Lorentz, M. René, Sister. Henrik Shipstead: Minnesota Independent, 1923-1946. Cath 1963

L239   Lorimer, M. Madeline, Sister. America's Response to Europe's Displaced Persons, 1945-1952: A Preliminary Report. St L 1964

L240   Loss, Carol M. *Status in Statu:* The Concept of Estate in the Organization of German Political Life, 1750-1825. Cornell 1970

L241   Losty, James A. The Soldiers and Sailors Insurance Act. Cath 1921

L242   Lotchin, Roger W. A History of San Francisco, 1846-1856. Chicago 1969

L243   Lothrop, Gloria R. Father Gregory Mengarini, an Italian Jesuit Missionary in the Transmontane West: His Life and Memoirs. S Cal 1970

L244   Lou, Dennis W. Fall Committee: An Investigation of Mexican Affairs. Ind 1963

L245   Loughran, Miriam E. The Historical Development of Child Labor Legislation in the United States. Cath 1921

L246   Louis, James P. Woman Suffrage and Progressive Reform: The Fight for the Nineteenth Amendment, 1913-1920. Harvard 1968

L247   Love, Joseph L., Jr. Rio Grande do Sul as a Source of Political Instability in Brazil's Old Republic, 1909-1932. Columbia 1967

L248   Loveland, Anne C. Lafayette and America: The Image of Lafayette as a Reflection of the American Mind. Cornell 1968

L249   Lovett, Clara M. P. Carlo Cattaneo and the Politics of the *Risorgimento,* 1820-1860. Tex U 1970

L250   Lovin, Clifford R. German Agricultural Policy, 1933-1936. NC 1965

L251   Lovin, Hugh T. The American Communist Party and the Spanish Civil War, 1936-1939. Wash U 1963

L252   Low, Marian A. László Németh: A Study in Hungarian Populism. Harvard 1966

L253   Low, Myron J. The Objectives of German Foreign Policy at the London Conference, 1912-1913. Tex U 1968

L254   Low, Victor N. The Border States: A Political History of Three Northeast Nigerian Emirates, ca. 1800-1902. UCLA 1967

L255   Lowe, Donald M. The Idea of China in Marx, Lenin, and Mao: A Study in Marxist Ideological Persistence and Transformation. Cal, Berkeley 1963

L256   Lowe, Richard G. Republicans, Rebellion, and Reconstruction: The Republican Party in Virginia, 1856-1870. Va 1968

L257   Lowe, Robert A. Racial Segregation in Indiana, 1920-1950. Ball State 1965

L258   Lowenfish, Lee E. American Radicals and Soviet Russia, 1917-1940. Wis 1968

L259   Lowenthal, William. The Expansion and Modernization of Argentina: Society, Economy and Politics, 1880-1916. Georgetown 1966

L260   Lower, Richard C. Hiram Johnson and the Progressive Denouement, 1910-1920. Cal, Berkeley 1969

L261   Lowerre, Nan K. J. Warren G. Harding and American Foreign Affairs, 1915-1923. Stanford 1968

L262   Lowery, Charles D. James Barbour, A Politician and Planter of Ante-Bellum Virginia. Va 1966

L263   Lowry, Francis B. The Generals, the Armistice, and the Treaty of Versailles, 1919. Duke 1963

L264   Lowther, Lawrence L. Rhode Island Colonial Government, 1732. Wash U 1964

L265   Loy, Jane M. Modernization and Educational Reform in Colombia, 1863-1886. Wis 1969

L266   Lubachko, Ivan. Belorussia under Soviet Rule, 1917-1939. Ind 1964

L267   Lubek, M. Evangela, Sister. An Inquiry into United States-Czechoslovakian Relations between 1918 and 1948 with Special Reference to the Munich Crisis and the Slovak Question. Georgetown 1969

L268   Lubenow, William C. The Politics of Government Growth: Early Victorian Attitudes toward State Intervention, 1833-1848. Ia 1968

L269   Lubot, Eugene S. Ts'ai Yuan-p'ei from Confucian Scholar to Chancellor of Peking University, 1868-1923: The Evolution of a Patient Reformer. Ohio 1970

L270   Lucas, Marion B. The Burning of Columbia. SC 1965

L271   Lucas, Paul A. Essays in the Margin of Blackstone's *Commentaries.* Princeton 1963

L272   Lucas, Paul R. Valley of Discord: The Struggle for Power in the Puritan Churches of the Connecticut Valley, 1636-1720. Minn 1970

L273 Lucas, Robert H. The *Livre du corps de policie* of Christine de Pisan, a Critical Edition. Columbia 1966

L274 Luckingham, Bradford F. Associational Life of the Urban Frontier: San Francisco, 1848-1856. Cal, Davis 1968

L275 Luebke, Frederick C. The Political Behavior of an Immigrant Group: The Germans of Nebraska, 1880-1900. Neb 1966

L276 Luehrs, Robert B. Franz Overbeck. Stanford 1969

L277 Luetkemeyer, Alexander J. Don Luigi Sturzo and the Italian Popular Party. St L 1962

L278 Luidens, John P. The Americanization of the Dutch Reformed Church. Okla 1969

L279 Lukas, Richard C. Air Force Aspects of American Aid to the Soviet Union: The Crucial Years, 1941-1942. Fla S 1963

L280 Lukashevich, Stephen. Ivan Aksakov: A Study in Russian Thought and Politics, 1823-1886. Cal, Berkeley 1961

L281 Lukowitz, David C. The Defence Policy of the British Labour Party, 1933-1939. Ia 1968

L282 Luman, Richard G. Influences of the Conciliar Theories of Henry of Langenstein and Conrad of Gelnhausen. Ia 1965

L283 Lunde, Erik S. The Idea of American Nationalism: A Study in Presidential Campaign Literature, 1860-1876. Md 1970

L284 Lundeen, Thomas B. The Bench of Bishops: A Study of the Secular Activities of Bishops of the Church of England and of Ireland, 1801-1871. Ia 1963

L285 Lunenfeld, Marvin. The Council of the Santa Hermandad of Ferdinand and Isabella (1476-1498): A Study of Castilian Centralization and Urban Independence. NYU 1968

L286 Lunn, Eugene. Gustav Landauer: The Development of a Romantic Socialist. Cal, Berkeley 1968

L287 Lunt, Richard D. The High Ministry of Government: The Political Career of Frank Murphy. NM 1962

L288 Lurie, Jonathan. The Chicago Board of Trade, 1874-1905, and the Development of Certain Rules and Regulations Governing Its Operation: A Study in the Effectiveness of Internal Regulation. Wis 1970

L289 Luscombe, Irving F. WNYC, 1922-1940: The Early History of a Twentieth Century Urban Service. NYU 1968

L290 Luther, Michael M. The Birth of the Soviet Ukraine. Columbia 1962

L291 Lutter, Martin H. Oklahoma and the World War, 1914-1917: A Study in Public Opinion. Okla 1961

L292 Lutzker, Michael A. The "Practical" Peace Advocates: An Interpretation of the American Peace Movement, 1898-1917. Rutgers 1969

L293 Lye, William F. The Sotho Wars in the Interior of South Africa, 1822-1837. UCLA 1969

L294 Lynd, Staughton C. The Revolution and the Common Man: Farm Tenants and Artisans in New York Politics, 1777-1788. Columbia 1962

L295 Lyne, Stephen R. The French Socialist Party and the Indochina War, 1944-1954. Stanford 1965

L296 Lyon, John J. The Reaction of English Catholics to Developments in the Earth and Life Sciences, 1825-1864. Pitt 1966

L297 Lyon, Thomas E. Evangelical Protestant Missionary Activities in Mormon Dominated Areas, 1865-1900. Utah 1962

L298 Lyons, Michael J. The Liberal Reconsideration of Property: The Debate over the Irish Land Act of 1881. Minn 1969

L299 Lysiak, Arthur W. T. H. S. Escott, Victorian Journalist. Loyola 1970

L300 Lythgoe, Dennis L. The Changing Image of Mormonism in Periodical Literature. Utah 1969

M

M1   Mabon, David W.   The West Coast Waterfront and Sympathy Strikes of 1934. Cal, Berkeley 1966

M2   McAdams, Donald R.   Politicians and the Electorate in the Late Eighteenth Century. Duke 1967

M3   McAfee, Ward M.   Local Interests and Railroad Regulation in Nineteenth Century California. Stanford 1965

M4   McAhren, Robert W.   Making the Nation Safe for Childhood: A History of the Movement for Federal Regulation of Child Labor, 1900-1938. Tex U 1967

M5   McAllister, Frances A. E.   The Lakota Sioux: Their Ceremonies and Recreation. St L 1968

M6   McAree, James G.   The Passage of the Government of India Bill of 1858. Minn 1961

M7   McArthur, Gilbert H.   The Novikov Circle in Moscow, 1779-1792. Rochester 1968

M7a   Macaulay, Neill W., Jr.   Sandino and the Marines: Guerrilla Warfare in Nicaragua, 1927-1933. Tex U 1965

M8   McAvoy, Muriel G.   Boston Sugar Merchants before the Civil War. Boston U 1967

M9   McCagg, William O.   Communism and Hungary, 1944-1946. Columbia 1965

M10   McCain, Johnny M.   Contract Labor as a Factor in United States-Mexican Relations, 1942-1947. Tex U 1970

M11   McCann, Francis D.   Brazil and the United States and the Coming of World War II, 1937-1942. Ind 1967

M12   McCann, Mary Agnes, Sister.   Archbishop Purcell and the Archdiocese of Cincinnati: A Study Based on Original Sources. Cath 1918

M13   McCarthy, Albert J. P.   The Oswego River: A Study in Historical Geography. St L 1965

M14   McCarthy, G. Michael.   Colorado Confronts the Conservation Impulse, 1891-1907. Denver 1969

M15   McCarthy, John P.   Hilaire Belloc: Critic of the New Liberalism. Columbia 1969

M16   McCarthy, Mary Barbara, Sister.   The Widening Scope of the American Constitutions. Cath 1928

M17   McCarthy, Michael P.   Businessmen and Professionals in Municipal Reform: The Chicago Experience, 1887-1920. Northwestern 1970

M18   McCarty, Kenneth G., Jr.   Stanley K. Hornbeck and the Far East, 1931-1941. Duke 1970

M19   McCash, William B.   Thomas R. R. Cobb: A Biography. Ga 1968

M20   McCaughey, Robert A. P.   Josiah Quincy, 1772-1864: The Last of the Boston Federalists. Harvard 1970

M22   McCauley, M. Janet, Sister.   The Fate of the Catholic Schools in the Third Reich: A Case Study. St L 1966

M24   McClellan, Robert F., Jr.   The American Image of China, 1890-1905. Mich S 1964

M25   McClellan, Woodford D.   Svetozar Markovíc and the Origins of Balkan Socialism. Cal, Berkeley 1963

M25a   McClelland, Charles E., III.   The German Historians and England: A Study of Nineteenth Century Views. Yale 1967

M26   McClelland, Charles W.   The Chemical Experiments and Theories of Joseph Priestley, 1794-1804. Stanford 1962

M27   McClure, Arthur F., II.   The Truman Administration and Labor Relations, 1945-1948. Kans U 1966

M28   McComb, David G.   Houston, the Bayou City. Tex U 1968

M29   McConville, Mary Patrick, Sister. Political Nativism in the State of Maryland, 1830-1860. Cath 1928

M30   McCord, James N.   Lord Holland and the Politics of the Whig Aristocracy (1807-1827): A Study in Aristocratic Liberalism. JH 1968

M31   McCorkle, James L., Jr.   The Mississippi Vegetable Industry: A History. Miss U 1966

M32   McCorkle, William L.   Nelson's *Star* and Kansas City, 1880-1898. Tex U 1968

M33   MacCormack, John R.   The Long Parliament House of Commons, 1643-1648. Toronto 1960

M34   McCoy, Alexandra.   Political Affiliations of American Economic Elites: Wayne County,

Michigan, 1844-1860, as a Test Case. Wayne 1965

M35   McCraw, Thomas K.   TVA and the Power Fight, 1933-1939. Wis 1970

M36   McCreary, Eugene C.   Essen, 1869-1914: A Case Study of the Impact of Industrialization on German Community Life. Yale 1964

M37   McCue, Robert J.   The Ambassadorial Career of Sir Edward Stafford, Elizabethan Ambassador to France, 1583-1590. Brigham Young 1970

M38   McCully, George E., Jr.   Juan Luis Vives (1493-1540) and the Problem of Evil in His Time. Columbia 1967

M39   McCusker, John J.   The Rum Trade and the Balance of Payments of the Thirteen Continental Colonies. Pitt 1970

M40   McDaniel, Robert A.   The Shuster Mission and the Culmination of the Persian Revolution of 1905-1911. Ill 1966

M41   McDean, Harry C.   M. L. Wilson and Agricultural Reform in the Twentieth Century. UCLA 1969

M42   McDonald, Archie P.   The Journal of Jedediah Hotchkiss, 1861-1865. LSU 1965

M43   MacDonald, Donald R. H.   Russian Interest in Korea, to 1895. Harvard 1966

M44   MacDonald, John F.   Camille Barrère and the Conduct of Delcassian Diplomacy, 1898-1902. UCLA 1969

M45   MacDonald, Mary J.   The Lewis and Clark Expedition: The Return Trip. St L 1970

M46   McDonald, Michael J.   Napoleon III and His Ideas of Italian Confederacy, 1856-1860. Penn U 1968

M47   McDonald, Timothy G.   Sourthern Democratic Congressmen and the First World War, August 1914-April 1917: The Public Record of Their Support for or Opposition to Wilson's Policies. Wash U 1962

M48   McDonald, William S.   The Union Traction Company of Indiana. Ball State 1969

M49   MacDonald, William W.   The Early Parliamentary Career of John Pym. NYU 1965

M50   McDonnell, James R.   The Rise of the CIO in Buffalo, New York, 1936-1942. Wis 1970

M51   McDonough, James L.   The Civil War Career of John M. Schofield. Fla S 1966

M52   McDougall, Elizabeth A.   The Presbyterian Church in Western Lower Canada, 1815-1842. McGill 1969

M53   McDowell, James G.   The Captive Government: A Study of the Flensburg Enclave and the German Surrender in World War II, April-May 1945. JH 1964

M54   McErlean, John M. P.   The Formative Years of a Russian Diplomat: Charles Andre Pozzo di Borgo in Corsica, 1789-1796. Wash U 1967

M55   McEwen, William C.   Working Class Politics in Gothenburg, Sweden, 1919-1934: A Study of a Social Democratic Party in an Industrial and Urban Setting. Case W Reserve 1970

M56   McFadden, Joseph M.   From Invention to Monopoly: The History of the Consolidation of the Barbed Wire Industry, 1873-1899. N Ill 1968

M57   McFarland, Charles K.   Coalition of Convenience: The Roosevelt-Lewis Courtship, 1933-1941. Ariz 1965

M58   McFarland, Gerald W.   Politics, Morals, and the Mugwump Reformers. Columbia 1965

M59   McFarland, Keith D.   Secretary of War Harry H. Woodring and the Problems of Readiness, Rearmament and Neutrality, 1936-1940. Ohio 1969

M60   McFarlane, Larry A.   Missouri Land and Live Stock Company, Limited, of Scotland: Foreign Investment on the Missouri Farming Frontier, 1882-1908. Mo 1963

M61   McFaul, John M.   The Politics of Jacksonian Finance. Cal, Berkeley 1963

M62   McGarry, Patrick S.   Ambassador Abroad: The Career and Correspondence of Sir Thomas Roe at the Courts of the Mogul and Ottoman Empires, 1614-1628: A Chapter in Jacobean Diplomacy. Columbia 1963

M63   McGee, Patricia E.   Issues and Factions: New York State Politics from the Panic of 1837 to the Election of 1848. St John's 1970

M64   McGeoch, Lyle A.   The Role of Lord Lansdowne in the Diplomatic Negotiations Connected with the Anglo-French Agreement of 8 April 1904. Penn U 1964

M65   McGill, William J., Jr.   The Political Education of Wenzel Anton von Kaunitz-Rittberg. Harvard 1961

M66   MacGillivray, Royce C.   Restoration Historians and Their Interpretations of the English Civil War. Harvard 1965

M67 McGinnis, David P. Labor Supply to Rural Industry: A Regional Study, Picardy, 1750 to 1850. Cal, Berkeley 1968

M68 McGinnis, Patrick E. Republican Party Resurgence in Congress, 1936-1946. Tulane 1967

M69 McGovern, John F. The Language of the Genoese Notaries at the Beginning of the Thirteenth Century. Wis 1967

M70 McGrath, James W. The Catholicism of Orestes A. Brownson. NM 1961

M71 McGrath, William J. Wagnerianism in Austria: The Regeneration of Culture through the Spirit of Music. Cal, Berkeley 1965

M72 Machado, Manuel A., Jr. An Industry in Crisis: Mexican-United States Cooperation in the Control of Foot-and-Mouth Disease. Cal, Santa Barbara 1964

M73 McHale, James M. The New Deal and the Origins of Public Lending for Foreign Economic Development, 1933-1945. Wis 1970

M74 Macías, Anna. The Genesis of Constitutional Government in Mexico, 1808-1820. Columbia 1965

M75 McIlvenna, Don E. Prelude to D-Day: American Strategy and the Second Front Issue. Stanford 1966

M76 McIntosh, Marjorie K. The Cooke Family of Gidea Hall, Essex, 1460-1661. Harvard 1967

M77 MacIntyre, Donald J. Constantine Dimitrievich Kavelin (1818-1885): A Study of His Life and Thought. Ia 1966

M78 MacIsaac, David. The United States Strategic Bombing Survey, 1944-1947. Duke 1970

M79 McJimsey, George T. The Life of Manton Marble. Wis 1968

M80 McJimsey, Robert D. The Englishman's Choice: English Opinion and the War of King William III, 1689-1697. Wis 1968

M81 McKale, Donald M. The Nazi Party Courts: Instruments for Establishing Discipline and Unity, 1926/1934. Kent 1970

M82 McKay, Ernest A. Henry Wilson: Practical Radical. NYU 1969

M83 McKay, John P. Foreign Entrepreneurs and Russian Industrialization, 1885-1913. Cal, Berkeley 1968

M84 McKee, James W., Jr. William Barksdale: The Intrepid Mississippian. Miss S 1966

M85 McKee, William F. The Social Gospel and the New Social Order, 1919-1929. Wis 1961

M86 McKelvey, Elaine B. Thomas Stanley, First Earl of Derby, 1435-1504. Penn S 1966

M87 McKelvey, James L. Lord Bute and George III: The Leicester House Years. Northwestern 1965

M87a McKenna, M. Berard, Sister. Samuel N. Wood: Chronic Agitator. St L 1968

M88 McKenna, Stephen J. Paganism and Pagan Survivals in Spain up to the Fall of the Visigothic Kingdom. Cath 1938

M89 McKennan, Theodora, Sister. Santander and the Vogue of Benthamism in Colombia and New Granada. Loyola 1970

M90 MacKenzie, David. Serbian-Russian Relations, 1875-1878. Columbia 1962

M91 MacKenzie, John M. African Labour in South Central Africa, 1890-1914, and Nineteenth Century Colonial Labour Theory. British Columbia 1969

M92 McKeon, Peter R. The Revival of the Papacy and the Transformation of the General Council. Chicago 1965

M93 Mackey, Philip E. Anti-Gallows Activity in New York State, 1776-1861. Penn U 1969

M94 McKey, Richard H., Jr. Elias Hasket Derby: Merchant of Salem, Massachusetts, 1739-1799. Clark 1961

M95 Mackey, Richard W. The Zabern Affair, 1913-1914. UCLA 1967

M96 Mackie, William E. The Conscription Controversy and the End of Liberal Power in England, 1905-1916. NC 1966

M97 McKiernan, F. Mark. The Voice of One Crying in the Wilderness: Sidney Rigdon, Religious Reformer, 1793-1876. Kans U 1968

M98 McKinley, Blaine. "The Stranger in the Gates": Employer Reactions toward Domestic Servants in America, 1825-1875. Mich S 1969

M99 McKinney, Henry L. Alfred Russel Wallace and the Discovery of Natural Selection. Cornell 1967

M100 Mackinnon, Clarence S. The Imperial Fortresses in Canada: Halifax and Esquimalt, 1871-1906. Toronto 1965

M101 McKinnon, Peter A. Geoffrey Dawson, *The Times* and the Formation of the British Appeasement Policy to 1936. Mich S 1966

M102 McKinzie, Kathleen H. Writers on Relief, 1935-1942. Ind 1970

M103 McKinzie, Richard D. The New Deal for Artists. Ind 1969

M104 McKirdy, Charles R. Lawyers in Crisis: The Massachusetts Legal Profession, 1760-1790. Northwestern 1969

M105 McKnight, James L. Admiral Ushakov and the Ionian Republic: The Genesis of Russia's First Balkan Satellite. Wis 1965

M106 McLachan, James S. The Education of the Rich: The Origin and Development of the Private Prep School, 1778-1916. Columbia 1966

M107 MacLachlan, Colin M. The Tribunal of the Acordada: A Study of Criminal Justice in Eighteenth Century Mexico. UCLA 1969

M108 MacLachlan, Patricia P. Scientific Professionals in the Seventeenth Century. Yale 1968

M109 McLaughlin, Andrew C. Satire as a Weapon against Prohibition, 1920-1928: Expression of a Cultural Conflict. Stanford 1970

M110 McLaughlin, Eleanor C. The Heresy of the Free Spirit: A Study in Medieval Religious Life. Harvard 1968

M111 McLaughlin, Virginia Y. Like the Fingers of the Hand: The Family and Community Life of First-Generation Italian-Americans in Buffalo, New York, 1880-1930. SUNY, Buffalo 1970

M112 McLaurin, Melton A. The Southern Cotton Textile Operative and Organized Labor, 1880-1905. SC 1967

M113 MacLean, Raymond A. Joseph Howe and British-American Union. Toronto 1966

M114 MacLeod, Murdo J. Bolivia and Its Social Literature before and after the Chaco War: A Historical Study of Social and Literary Revolution. Fla U 1962

M115 McLeod, William R. Parliamentary Elections in the Home Counties, 1713-1715: A Comparative Study. Md 1970

M115a McMahan, Russell S., Jr. The Protestant Churches during World War I: The Home Front, 1917, 1918. St L 1968

M116 McMahon, Adrian M. The Concept of Freedom and the Radical Abolitionists, 1860-1870. Tex U 1970

M117 McMahon, John L. Recent Changes in the Recognition Policy of the United States. Cath 1933

M118 MacMaster, Richard K. The United States, Great Britain and the Suppression of the Cuban Slave Trade, 1835-1860. Georgetown 1968

M119 MacMichael, David C. The United States and the Dominican Republic, 1871-1940: A Cycle in Caribbean Diplomacy. Ore 1964

M120 McMillan, Cynthia Ann. The Concept of the Mathematical Infinite in French Thought, 1670-1760. Va 1970

M121 McMillen, Neil R. The Citizen's Council: A History of Organized Southern White Resistance to the Second Reconstruction. Vanderbilt 1969

M122 McMullan, Alasdair M. The Minor Diplomatic Missions of the American Revolution. St John's 1965

M123 McMurchy, Donald J. A. David Mills: Nineteenth Century Canadian Liberal. Rochester 1969

M124 McMurry, Richard M. The Atlanta Campaign, December 23, 1863, to July 18, 1864. Emory 1967

M125 McNally, James R. Rafael Altamira y Crevea, Historian: The Man and His Influence. NYU 1967

M126 McNamara, Jo Ann K. Giles Aycelin: A Councillor of Philip the Fair. Columbia 1967

M127 McNamara, William M. The Catholic Church on the Northern Indiana Frontier, 1789-1844. Cath 1931

M128 MacNaughton, John G. Democratic Hostility to the Navigation and Commerce of the Great Lakes as a Neglected Factor in the Rise of the Republican Party. SUNY, Buffalo 1961

M129 McNeally, Douglass H. Constitutional Monarchy in France, 1814-1848. Northwestern 1963

M130 McNulty, John W. Chief Justice Sidney Breese and the Illinois Supreme Court: A Study of Law and Politics in the Old West. Harvard 1962

M131 Macoll, John D. The New Muckraking, 1920-1929. Ind 1967

M132 McPherson, James M. Abolitionists and the Negro in the Civil War and Reconstruction. JH 1963

M133 Macpherson, Joseph T., Jr. Democratic Progressivism in Tennessee: The Administrations of Governor Austin Peay, 1923-1927. Vanderbilt 1969

M134 McPherson, Milton M. Federal Taxes on Cotton, 1862-1868. Ala 1970

M135 McSeveney, Samuel T. The Politics of Depression: Voting Behavior in Connecticut, New York, and New Jersey, 1893-1896. Ia 1965

M136 McVaugh, Michael R. The Mediaeval Theory of Compound Medicines. Princeton 1965

M137 Madaras, Lawrence H. The Public Career of Theodore Roosevelt, Jr. NYU 1964

M138 Madden, M. James Eugene, Sister. The English Cistercians: Taxation by King and Pope, 1216-1377. Fordham 1961

M139 Maddex, Jack P., Jr. The Virginia Conservatives: A Study in "Bourbon" Redemption, 1869-1879. NC 1966

M140 Maddox, Robert J. William E. Borah and American Foreign Policy, 1907-1929. Rutgers 1964

M141 Maddux, Thomas R. American Relations with the Soviet Union, 1933-1941. Mich U 1969

M142 Madison, Kenneth G. The Wydevilles, 1086-1491: The Background and Rise of a Family in Medieval English Politics. Ill 1968

M143 Maganzin, Louis. Economic Depression in Maryland and Virginia, 1783-1787. Georgetown 1967

M144 Magden, Ronald E. Attitudes of the American Religious Press toward Soviet Russia, 1939-1941. Wash U 1964

M145 Mage, Lily D. Public Spirit and Public Opinion in Auvergne before and during the French Revolution to 1791. Columbia 1963

M146 Maginnis, Paul. The Social Philosophy of Frederick Jackson Turner. Ariz 1968

M147 Magnuson, Norris A. Salvation in the Slums: Evangelical Social Welfare Work, 1865-1920. Minn 1968

M148 Magoulias, Harry J. The Lives of the Saints as Sources of Data for Sixth and Seventh Century Byzantine Social and Economic History. Harvard 1962

M149 Magruder, Nathaniel F. The Administration of Governor Cameron Morrison of North Carolina, 1921-1925. NC 1968

M150 Mahan, Joseph B. Identification of the Tsoyaha Waeno, Builders of Temple Mounds. NC 1970

M151 Mahar, Franklyn D. Douglas McKay and the Issues of Power Development in Oregon, 1953-1956. Ore 1968

M152 Mahoney, Joseph F. New Jersey Politics after Wilson: Progressivism in Decline. Columbia 1964

M153 Mahoney, Leonard P. The Genesis, Proceedings, and Aftermath of the Trial of the Polignac Ministry of Charles X before the Court of Peers. Georgetown 1963

M154 Mahoney, Margaret H. A Study in Sumerian Administrative History of the Third Ur Dynasty. Minn 1965

M155 Maier, Charles S. The Strategies of Bourgeois Defense, 1918-1924: A Study of Conservative Politics and Economics in France, Germany, and Italy. Harvard 1967

M156 Maier, Pauline R. From Resistance to Revolution: American Radicals and the Development of Intercolonial Opposition to Britain, 1765-1776. Harvard 1968

M157 Maingot, Anthony P. Colombia: Civil-Military Relations in a Political Culture of Conflict. Fla U 1967

M158 Majeska, George P. The Journey of Ignatius of Smolensk to Constantinople (1389-92). Ind 1968

M159 Majors, William R. Gordon Browning and Tennessee Politics. Ga 1967

M160 Malament, Barbara C. British Politics and the Crisis of 1931. Yale 1969

M161 Malefakis, Edward E. Land Tenure, Agrarian Reform and Peasant Revolution in Twentieth Century Spain. Columbia 1965

M162 Malik, Salah-ud D. Mutiny, Revolution or Muslim Rebellion? British Public Reactions towards the Indian Crisis of 1857. McGill 1966

M163 Malloy, James A., Jr. The Zemstvo Reform of 1864: Its Historical Background and Significance in Tsarist Russia. Ohio 1965

M164 Malone, Billy C. A History of Commercial Country Music in the United States, 1920-1964. Tex U 1965

M165 Malone, Preston S. The Political Career of Charles Frederick Crisp. Ga 1962

M166 Malone, Thomas E. The California Irrigation Crisis of 186: Origins of the Wright Act. Stanford 1965

M167 Maloney, Joan M. States Rights Theory in Massachusetts, 1850-1857. Georgetown 1961

M168 Malpass, Elizabeth D. Sir John Simon and British Diplomacy during the Sino-Japanese Crisis, 1931-1933. Tex C 1969

M169 Maltby, William S. The Black Legend in England, 1558-1660. Duke 1967

M170 Malyshev, Alexey N. Russia's Early Relations with China, 1619-1792. Colo 1967

M171 Mammitzsch, Ulrich H. Wei Chung-Hsien (1568-1628): A Reappraisal of the Eunuch and the Factional Strife at the Late Ming Court. Hawaii 1968

M172 Manarin, Louis H. Lee in Command: Strategical and Tactical Policies. Duke 1965

M173 Mandelbaum, Seymour J. Community and Politics: New York City in the Eighteen Seventies. Princeton 1962

M174 Mandell, Richard D. Politicians, Intellectuals, and the Universal Exposition of 1900 in Paris. Cal, Berkeley 1965

M174a Manley, Jeanne F. Disraeli's Tory Democracy: A Parliamentary Study. St L 1968

M175 Manley, Robert N. Nebraskans and the Federal Government, 1854-1916. Neb 1962

M176 Mann, Harold W. The Life and Times of Atticus Greene Haygood. Duke 1962

M177 Mann, Ralph E., II. The Social and Political Structure of Two California Gold Towns. Stanford 1970

M178 Manning, Eugene A. Old Bob La Follette: Champion of the People. Wis 1966

M179 Manning, Patrick. An Economic History of Southern Dahomey, 180-1914. Wis 1969

M180 Manning, Roger B. The Episcopate of Richard Curteys, Bishop of Chichester, 1570-1582: An Aspect of the Enforcement of the Elizabethan Religious Settlement in Sussex. Georgetown 1961

M181 Mannock, James H. C. Anglo-American Relations, 1921-1928. Princeton 1962

M182 Mansfield, Stephen S. Thomas Roderick Dew: Defender of the Southern Faith. Va 1968

M183 Mansur, Abed Al-Hafiz. Anglo-French Rivalry in the Levant and the Question of Syrio-Lebanese Independence, 1939-1943. Ore 1964

M184 Mantell, Martin E. The Election of 1868: The Response to Congressional Reconstruction. Columbia 1969

M185 Marcello, Ronald E. The North Carolina Works Progress Administration and the Politics of Relief. Duke 1969

M186 March, George P. The Cossacks of Zaporozhe. Georgetown 1965

M187 Marcopoulos, George J. The Role of the Monarchy in Greek Foreign Affairs during the Reign of King George I, 1863-1913. Harvard 1966

M188 Marcum, Richard T. Fort Brown, Texas: The History of the Border Post. Tex Tech 1964

M189 Marcus, Harold G. Britain and Ethiopia, 1896 to 1914: A Study in Diplomatic Relations. Boston U 1964

M190 Marcus, Irwin M. The Knights of Labor: Reform Aspects. Lehigh 1965

M191 Marcus, Richard H. The Militia of Colonial Connecticut, 1639-1775: An Institutional Study. Colo 1965

M192 Marcus, Robert D. Republican National Party Organization, 1880-1896. Northwestern 1967

M193 Marcy, Peter T. A Chapter in the History of the "Bristol Hogs": A Social and Economic History of Bristol, 1740-1780. Claremont 1965

M194 Mariboe, William H. The Life of William Franklin, 1730(1)-1813: "Pro Rege et Patria." Penn U 1962

M195 Marietta, Jack D. Ecclesiastical Discipline in the Society of Friends, 1682-1776. Stanford 1969

M196 Marina, William F. Opponents of Empire: An Interpretation of American Anti-Imperialism, 1898-1921. Denver 1968

M197 Marinelli, Lawrence A. Liberia: A Current Historical Survey. St John's 1965

M198 Marino, Carl W. General Alfred Howe Terry: Soldier from Connecticut. NYU 1968

M199 Marion, Carol J. Ministers in Moscow. Ind 1970

M200 Mariz, George E. The Life and Work of L. T. Hobhouse: A Study in the History of Ideas. Mo 1970

M201 Markoff, Robert A. Opposition to the War in France, 1914-1918. Penn U 1962

M202 Marks, Frederick W., III. The Impact of Foreign Affairs on the United States Constitution, 1783-178. Mich U 1968

M202a Marley, Bert W. Alaska: Its Transition to Statehood. Utah 1970

M203 Marlow, Holt C. The Ideology of the Woman's Movement, 1750-1860. Okla 1966

M204 Marr, David G. Viet-Nam's Anti-Colonial Movements: The Early Years (1885-1925). Cal, Berkeley 1968

M205 Marrin, Albert. The Church of England in the First World War. Columbia 1968

M206 Marrus, Michael R. The Politics of Assimilation: A Study of the French Jewish Community at the Time of the Dreyfus Affair. Cal, Berkeley 1968

M207 Marsala, Vincent J. Sir John Peter Grant, Governor of Jamaica, 1866-1874: An Administrative History. LSU 1967

M208 Marschall, John Peter. Francis Patrick Kenrick, 1851-1863: The Baltimore Years. Cath 1965

M209 Marshall, Byron K. Ideology and Industrialization in Japan, 1868-1941: The Creed of the Prewar Business Elite. Stanford 1966

M210 Marshall, Caroline T. Gertrude Bell: Her Work and Influence in the Near East, 1914-1926. Va 1968

M211 Marshall, Hugh. Orestes Brownson and the American Civil War. Cath 1963

M212 Marshall, Lynn L. The Early Career of Amos Kendall: The Making of a Jacksonian. Cal, Berkeley 1962

M213 Marshall, Philip C. The Social Ideas of American Historians, 1815-1865. Rutgers 1963

M214 Marshall, Philip R. France and the Congress of Berlin. Penn U 1969

M215 Marszalek, John F. W. T. Sherman and the Press, 1861-1865. Notre D 1968

M216 Marthaler, Bernard L. Two Studies in the Greek Imperial Coinage of Asia Minor. Minn 1968

M217 Marti, Donald B. Agrarian Thought and Agricultural Progress: The Endeavor for Agricultural Improvement in New England and New York, 1815-1840. Wis 1966

M218 Martin, Albro. Enterprise Denied: American Railroads in the Progressive Era, 1897-1970. Columbia 1970

M219 Martin, Douglas D. Indian-White Relations on the Pacific Slope, 1850-1890. Wash U 1969

M220 Martin, James K. Political Elites and the Outbreak of the American Revolution: A Quantitative Profile in Continuity, Turnover, and Change, 1774-1777. Wis 1969

M221 Martin, Jane J. The Dual Legacy: Government Authority and Mission Influence among the Glebo of Eastern Liberia, 1834-1910. Boston U 1968

M222 Martin, Kenneth R. British and French Diplomacy and the Sardinian War, 1848-1849. Penn U 1965

M223 Martin, Luis. The College of San Pablo in Lima, 1568-1767: History of a Colonial Institution. Columbia 1966

M224 Martin, Neil A. Khrushchev and the Non-Russians: A Study of Soviet Nationality Policy since the Death of Stalin. Georgetown 1968

M225 Martin, Walter R. Ideas in the Political Life of England, 1760-1783. Mo 1966

M226 Marty, Myron A. Missouri Synod Lutherans and Roman Catholicism: Opposition and Reappraisal, 1917-1963. St L 1967

M227 Marzahl, Peter G. The Cabildo of Popayán in the Seventeenth Century: The Emergence of a Creole Elite. Wis 1970

M228 Marzio, Peter C. The Art Crusade: A Study of American Drawing Books and Lithographs, 1830-1860. Chicago 1969

M229 Masek, Rosemary. The English Episcopate in the Reign of Henry VII. Ill 1965

M230 Mason, Joyce E. The Use of Indian Scouts in the Apache Wars, 1870-1886. Ind 1970

M231 Mason, Paul T., Jr. Industrial Technology in the *Encyclopédie*. St L 1964

M232 Massey, Robert K., Jr. The State Politics of Massachusetts Democracy, 1928-1938. Duke 1968

M233 Massmann, John C. German Immigration to Minnesota, 1850-1890. Minn 1966

M234 Mast, Herman W., III. An Intellectual Biography of Tai Chi-t'ao from 1891 to 1928. Ill 1970

M235 Mastny, Catherine L. Durand of Champagne and the "Mirror of the Queen": A Study in Medieval Didactic Literature. Columbia 1969

M236 Mastny, Vojtech. The Czechs under Nazi Rule, 1939-1942: A Study in a Failure of National Resistance. Columbia 1968

M237   Mate, Mavis E. H.   The Monetary Policy of Edward I, 1272-1307. Ohio 1967

M238   Mather, Richard S.   Cardinal Matthew of Acquasparta in the Roman Curia. Cal, Berkeley 1961

M239   Mathes, William L.   The Struggle for University Autonomy in the Russian Empire during the First Decade of the Reign of Alexander II (1855-1866). Columbia 1966

M240   Mathes, William M.   Sebastián Vizcaíno and Spanish Exploration in the Pacific Ocean, 1580 to 1630. NM 1966

M241   Mathews, Alice E.   Pre-College Education in the Southern Colonies. Cal, Berkeley 1968

M242   Mathews, Donald G.   Antislavery, Piety, and Institutionalism: The Slavery Controversies in the Methodist Episcopal Church, 1780-1844. Duke 1962

M243   Mathews, Jane D.   Art, Relief and Politics: The Federal Theatre, 1935-1939. Duke 1966

M244   Mathews, Naiven F.   The Public View of Military Policy, 1945-1950. Mo 1964

M245   Mathias, Frank F.   The Turbulent Years of Kentucky Politics, 1820-1850. Ky 1966

M246   Mathieu, Donald R.   The Role of Russia in French Foreign Policy, 1908-1914. Stanford 1969

M247   Mathis, Gerald R.   Walter B. Hill: Chancellor, the University of Georgia, 1899-1905. Ga 1967

M248   Mathis, Robert N.   Gazaway Bugg Lamar: A Southern Entrepreneur. Ga 1968

M249   Matré, Richard A.   The Chicago Press and Imperialism, 1899-1902. Northwestern 1961

M250   Matsuda, Mitsugu.   The Government of the Kingdom of Ryukyu, 1609-1872. Hawaii 1967

M251   Mattheisen, Donald J.   The Prussian National Assembly of 1848. Minn 1966

M252   Matthew, Virgil L., Jr.   Joseph Simon Gallieni (1849-1916): Marshal of France. UCLA 1967

M253   Matthews, John M.   Studies in the Race Relations in Georgia, 1890-1930. Duke 1970

M254   Matthews, Kenneth D., Jr.   Cicero and the Age of Marius. Penn U 1961

M255   Matthews, Roy T.   The British Reaction to the Accession of the National Socialists to Power in Germany. NC 1966

M256   Matthias, Ronald F.   The Know Nothing Movement in Iowa. Chicago 1965

M257   Mattingly, Paul H.   Professional Strategies and New England Educators, 1825-1860. Wis 1968

M258   Mattson, J. Stanley.   Charles Grandison Finney and the Emerging Tradition of "New Measure" Revivalism. NC 1970

M259   Mattsson-Bozé, Martin H.   James McHenry, Secretary of War, 1796-1800. Minn 1965

M260   Matusow, Allen J.   Food and Farm Policies of the First Truman Administration, 1945-1948. Harvard 1963

M260a   Maughan, Scott J.   Francisco Garcés and New Spain's Northwestern Frontier, 1768-1781. Utah 1968

M261   Maurer, David J.   Public Relief Programs and Policies in Ohio, 1929-1939. Ohio 1962

M262   Mauskopf, Seymour H.   Molecular Structure and Composition: The Interaction of Crystallography, Chemistry and Optics in the Early Nineteenth Century. Princeton 1966

M263   Maxwell, C. Mervyn.   Chrysostom's Homilies against the Jews: An English Translation. Chicago 1966

M264   Maxwell, John A.   Social Democracy in a Divided Germany: Kurt Schumacher and the German Question, 1945-1952. W Va 1969

M265   Maxwell, Kenneth R.   Conflicts and Conspiracies: Brazil and Portugal, 1750-1807. Princeton 1969

M266   May, Anita M. R.   The Challenge of French Catholic Press to Episcopal Authority, 1842 to 1860: A Crisis of Modernization. Pitt 1970

M267   May, Joseph T.   John Foster Dulles and the European Defense Community. Kent 1969

M268   May, Robert E.   The Southern Dream of a Caribbean Empire, 1854-1861. Wis 1969

M269   Mayer, Robert S.   The Influence of Frank A. Vanderlip and the National City Bank on American Commerce and Foreign Policy, 1910-1920. Rutgers 1968

M270   Mayo, Edward L.   The *National Intelligencer* and Jacksonian Democracy: A Whig Persuasion. Claremont 1970

M271   Mayo, Marlene J.   The Iwakura Embassy and the Unequal Treaties, 1871-1873. Columbia 1961

M272 Mazaraki, George A. The Public Career of Andrew Haswell Green. NYU 1966

M273 Mazuzan, George T. Warren R. Austin: A Republican Internationalist and United States Foreign Policy. Kent 1969

M274 Mazzaferri, Anthony J. Public Health and Social Revolution in Mexico, 1877-1930. Kent 1968

M275 Mazzaoui, Maureen F. The Organization of the Fine Wool Industry of Bologna in the Thirteenth Century. Bryn Mawr 1966

M276 Meacham, Standish, Jr. Henry Thornton of Clapham, 1760-1815. Harvard 1961

M277 Meade, Carroll W. American Assyriology: Its Growth and Development. Tex U 1969

M278 Meador, John A., Jr. Florida Political Parties, 1865-1877. Fla U 1964

M279 Meaker, Gerald H. Spanish Anarcho-Syndicalism and the Russian Revolution, 1917-1922. S Cal 1967

M280 Mears, John A. Count Raimondo Montecuccoli: Practical Soldier and Military Theoretician. Chicago 1964

M281 Medzini, Meron. French Policy in Japan during the Closing Years of the Tokugawa Regime. Harvard 1964

M282 Meehan, Brenda M. The Russian Generalitet of 1730: Towards a Definition of Aristocracy. Rochester 1970

M283 Meerse, David E. James Buchanan, the Patronage and the Northern Democratic Party, 1857-1858. Ill 1969

M284 Megargee, Richard. The Diplomacy of John Bassett Moore: Realism in American Foreign Policy. Northwestern 1963

M285 Megrian, Leon D. Tiflis during the Russian Revolution of 1905. Cal, Berkeley 1968

M286 Mehl, Joseph M., Jr. Intelligence Reporting by American Observers from the European Neutrals, 1917-1919: Select Cases. Am 1962

M287 Mehlinger, Howard D. Count Sergei Iu. Witte and the Problems of Constitutionalism in Russia, 1905-1906. Kans U 1964

M288 Meiklejohn, Norman A. The Observance of Negro Slave Legislation in Colonial Nueva Granada. Columbia 1968

M289 Meisner, Maurice J. Li Ta-chao and the Origins of Chinese Marxism. Chicago 1962

M290 Meister, Richard J. A History of Gary, Indiana, 1930-1940. Notre D 1967

M291 Mejia, Arthur, Jr. The Upper Class in Late Victorian and Edwardian England: A Study of the Formation and Perpetuation of Class Bias. Stanford 1968

M292 Melka, Robert L. The Axis and the Arab Middle East, 1930-1945. Minn 1966

M293 Mellander, Gustavo A. The United States in Panamanian Politics, 1903-1908. Geo W 1966

M294 Melton, Frank T. London and Parliament: An Analysis of a Constituency, 1661-1702. Wis 1969

M295 Melton, George E. Admiral Darlan and the Diplomacy of Vichy, 1940-1942. NC 1966

M296 Menashe, Louis. Alexander Guchkov and the Origins of the Octobrist Party: The Russian Bourgeoisie in Politics, 1905. NYU 1966

M297 Mendel, Clarence H. Imperial Finance Reform and the Politics of German Agrarian Conservatism, 1906-1909. Cal, Berkeley 1966

M298 Mendelson, Ezra. The Jewish Labor Movement in Czarist Russia, from Its Origin to 1905. Columbia 1966

M299 Méndez, J. Ignacio. Panama: Public Administration and the *Censo* in the Early Nineteenth Century. Cal, Berkeley 1970

M300 Menig, Paul H. Public Opinion in Massachusetts Relative to Anglo-French Relations, 1748-1756. Wash U 1962

M301 Menn, Joseph K. The Large Slaveholders of the Deep South, 1860. Tex U 1964

M302 Mennard, Michael. Bishop Strossmayer, the Serbs, and the Croats in the Second Half of the Nineteenth Century. Georgetown 1964

M303 Mennel, Robert M. Attitudes and Policies toward Juvenile Delinquency in the United States, 1825-1935. Ohio 1969

M304 Mennell, James E. William T. Stead: Social Politics and the New Journalism. Ia 1967

M305 Mensing, Raymond C., Jr. Attitudes on Religious Toleration as Expressed in English Parliamentary Debates, 1660-1719. Emory 1970

M306 Menze, Ernest A. Lujo Brentano and *Brentanismus:* A Study in Bourgeois Reformism. Columbia 1966

M307 Meredith, Howard L. A History of the Socialist Party in Oklahoma. Okla 1970

M308 Merikangas, Robert J. Vernon L. Parrington's Method of Intellectual History. Cath 1966

M309 Merino, James A. A Great City and Its Suburbs: Attempts to Integrate Metropolitan Boston, 1865-1920. Tex U 1968

M310 Merkley, Paul C. Reinhold Niebuhr, the Decisive Years, 1916-1941: A Study of the Interaction of Religious Faith and Political Commitment in an American Intellectual. Toronto 1966

M311 Merli, Frank J. Great Britain and the Confederate Navy, 1861-1865. Ind 1964

M312 Merriam, George H. Israel Williams, Monarch of New Hampshire, 1709-1788. Clark 1961

M313 Merritt, Raymond H. Engineering and American Culture, 1850-1875. Minn 1968

M314 Mershart, Ronald V. S. -N. -H. Linguet: The Regretful Prophet. Chicago 1969

M315 Mertz, Richard R. The Diplomats and the Dictator: A Study of Western Diplomatic Reactions to the Rise of Hitler, September 1930-November 1933. Geo W 1963

M316 Merwick, Donna J., Sister. Changing Thought Patterns of Three Generations of Catholic Clergymen of the Boston Archdiocese from 1850 to 1910. Wis 1968

M317 Metcalfe, William C. The Public Career of Thomas Howard, First Earl of Suffolk, 1603-1618. Minn 1967

M318 Metzgar, Joseph V. Thomas Paine: A Study in Social and Intellectual History. NM 1965

M319 Metzger, Fraser K. The Political Role of the Prince of Condé during the Fronde. Rutgers 1966

M320 Meyer, Dolores J. Excursion Steamboating on the Mississippi with Streckfus Steamers, Inc. St L 1967

M321 Meyer, Donald H. The American Moralists: Academic Moral Philosophy in the United States, 1835-1880. Cal, Berkeley 1967

M322 Meyer, Luciana R.-W. German-American Migration and the Bancroft Naturalization Treaties, 1868-1910. CUNY 1970

M323 Meyer, Lysle E., Jr. Henry Shelton Sanford and the Congo. Ohio 1967

M324 Meyer, Michael C. The Career of Pascual Orozco, Jr.: A Case Study of a Mexican Revolutionist. NM 1963

M325 Meyer, Richard E. Colonial Values and the Development of the American Nation as Expressed in Almanacs, 1700-1970. Kans U 1970

M326 Meza, Pedro T. The Controversy in Convocation, 1701-1717: A Study of the Church and Politics in Early Eighteenth Century England. NYU 1967

M327 Micarelli, William F. The Rhode Island Supreme Court and Social Change, 1865-1900. Cath 1969

M328 Michaels, Albert L. Mexican Politics and Nationalism from Calles to Cárdenas. Penn U 1966

M329 Mickel, Ronald E. Patterns of Agrarian Self-Consciousness in the 1920's. Wayne 1961

M330 Middlekauff, Robert L. Ancients and Axioms: A History of Secondary Education in Eighteenth Century New England. Yale 1961

M331 Middleton, Charles R. The Administration of British Foreign Policy, 1782-1846. Duke 1969

M332 Middleton, James R. The Embassy of Wilhelm Mayer: A Case Study in Weimar Diplomacy. Columbia 1969

M333 Middleton, Robert N. French Policy and Prussia after the Peace of Aix-la-Chapelle, 1749-1753: A Study of the Pre-History of the Diplomatic Revolution of 1756. Columbia 1968

M334 Midelfort, H. C. Erik. The Social and Intellectual Foundations of Witch Hunting in Southwestern Germany, 1562-1684. Yale 1970

M335 Mikkelson, Dwight L. *Kentucky Gazette*, 1787-1848: "The Herald of a Noisy World." Ky 1963

M336 Mikulak, Maxim W. Relativity Theory and Soviet Communist Philosophy, 1922-1960. Columbia 1965

M337 Millar, David R. The Militia, the Army, and Independency in Colonial Massachusetts. Cornell 1967

M338 Miller, Barbara R. S. Creative Man in a Dynamic World: Renaissance Themes in the Thought of Charles de Bouelles. Mo 1970

M339 Miller, Daniel A. Sir Joseph Yorke and Anglo-Dutch Relations, 1774-1780. Mich U 1964

M340 Miller, David B. The Literary Activities of Metropolitan Macarius: A Study of Muscovite Political Ideology in the Time of Ivan IV. Columbia 1967

M341 Miller, David H. Pope Paul I and the Roman Revolution of the Eighth Century. Mich S 1967

M342 Miller, Dean A. Studies in Byzantine Diplomacy: Sixth to Tenth Centuries. Rutgers 1962

M343 Miller, Douglas T. The Rise of Aristocracy in the State of New York, 1830-1860. Mich S 1965

M344 Miller, Edward A., Jr. The Founding of the Air Force Academy: An Administrative and Legislative History. Denver 1969

M345 Miller, Forrestt A. Dmitrii Miliutin and the Reform Era in Russia, 1861-1881. Cal, Berkeley 1963

M346 Miller, Frederick G. Sir Norman Angell: Peace, Politics and the Press, 1919-1924. Ball State 1969

M347 Miller, Gene R. A History of the North Mississippi Conference of the Methodist Church, 1820-1900. Miss S 1964

M348 Miller, Howard S. A Bounty for Research: The Philanthropic Support of Scientific Investigation in America, 1838-1902. Wis 1964

M349 Miller, Hubert J. The Church and State Question in Guatemala, 1871-1885. Loyola 1965

M350 Miller, James M., Jr. The Concert of Europe in the First Balkan War, 1912-1913. Clark 1969

M351 Miller, Joyce L. Henry de Jouvenel and the Syrian Mandate. Bryn Mawr 1970

M352 Miller, Larry C. Dimensions of Mugwump Thought, 1880-1920: Sons of Massachusetts Abolitionists as Professional Pioneers. Northwestern 1969

M353 Miller, Lillian B. Art and Nationality: The Encouragement of the Fine Arts in the United States, 1790-1860. Columbia 1962

M354 Miller, Louise W. Henry III of France and the Revolt of the Netherlands to 1579. Cal, Berkeley 1961

M355 Miller, Marion S. Europe and the Sardinian Annexations of the Duchies, Tuscany, and the Romagna, 1859-1860. Penn U 1965

M356 Miller, Martin A. The Formative Years of P. A. Kropotkin, 1842-1876: A Study of the Origins and Development of Populist Attitudes in Russia. Chicago 1967

M357 Miller, Mary E. The Delaware Oyster Industry, Past and Present. Boston U 1962

M358 Miller, Mietzel. Factors Affecting Government Sanction of the Performing Arts. Ball State 1966

M359 Miller, Orlando W. The Frontier in Alaska and the Matanuska Colony. Columbia 1966

M360 Miller, Richard C. Otis and his *Times:* The Career of Harrison Gray Otis of Los Angeles. Cal, Berkeley 1961

M361 Miller, Sally M. Victor L. Berger and the Promise of Constructive Socialism, 1910-1920. Toronto 1966

M362 Miller, William J. European Reaction to Hitler's First Moves against Austria (January 1933-July 1934). Cal, Berkeley 1968

M363 Miller, Zane L. Boss Cox and the Municipal Reformers: Cincinnati Progressivism, 1880-1914. Chicago 1966

M364 Millet, Donald J. The Economic Development of Southwest Louisiana, 1865-1900. LSU 1964

M365 Millett, Allan R. The Politics of Intervention: The Military Occupation of Cuba, 1906-1909. Ohio 1966

M366 Millett, Richard L. The History of the *Guardia Nacional de Nicaragua,* 1925-1965. NM 1966

M367 Milligan, John D. The Federal Fresh-Water Navy and the Opening of the Mississippi River: Its Organization, Construction and Operations through the Fall of Vicksburg. Mich U 1961

M368 Millinger, James F. Ch'i Chi-kuang, Chinese Military Official: A Study of Civil-Military Roles and Relations in the Career of a Sixteenth Century Warrior, Reformer, and Hero. Yale 1968

M369 Millman, Richard. British Foreign Policy and the Coming of the Franco-Prussian War. Penn U 1963

M370 Millon, Robert P. Vicente Lombardo Toledano: An Intellectual Biography of a Mexican Marxist. NC 1963

M371 Mills, Frederick V. Anglican Resistance to an American Episcopate, 1761-1789. Penn U 1967

M372 Mills, James C. Dmitrii Tolstoi as Minister of Education in Russia, 1866-1880. Ind 1967

M373 Milone, Pauline D. Queen City of the East: The Metamorphosis of a Colonial Capital. Cal, Berkeley 1966

M374 Miner, H. Craig. The Thirty-Fifth Parallel Project: The Formation of a St. Louis-San

Francisco Railway System, 1853-1890. Colo 1970

M375 Minge, Ward A. Frontier Problems in New Mexico Preceding the Mexican War, 1840-1846. NM 1965

M376 Mirak, Robert. The Armenians in the United States, 1890-1915. Harvard 1965

M377 Mirsky, Jonathan. Rebellion in Ho-pei: The Successful Rising of the T'ang Provincial Governors. Penn U 1967

M378 Misbach, Henry L. Genoese Trade and the Flow of Gold, 1154-1253. Wis 1968

M379 Misse, Frederick B., Jr. The Loss of Eastern Europe, 1938-1946. Ill 1964

M380 Mitchell, Franklin D. Embattled Democracy: Missouri Democratic Politics, 1918-1932. Mo 1964

M381 Mitchell, J. Paul. Progressivism in Denver: The Municipal Reform Movement, 1904-1916. Denver 1966

M382 Mitchell, Kell F., Jr. Frank L. Polk and the Paris Peace Conference, 1919. Ga 1966

M383 Mitchell, Norma T. The Political Career of Governor David Campbell of Virginia. Duke 1967

M384 Mitchell, Otis C., Jr. An Institutional History of the National Socialist SA: A Study of the SA as a Functioning Organization within the Party Structure (1931-1934). Kans U 1964

M385 Mitchell, Peter M. Wei-Yüan (1794-1857) and the Early Modernization Movement in China and Japan. Ind 1970

M386 Mitchell, Peter McQuilkin. Loyalist Property and the Revolution in Virginia. Colo 1965

M387 Mitchell, Richard E. Rome's Southern Expansion and the Introduction of Coinage. Cincinnati 1965

M388 Mitchell, Richard H. The Korean Minority in Japan, 1910-1963. Wis 1963

M389 Mitchell, Robert A. Kurt Eisner and the Question of Soviet Government in Bavaria, 1918-1919. Harvard 1961

M390 Mitchell, Robert G. Loyalist Georgia. Tulane 1964

M391 Mitchell, Robert M. The Weber Thesis as Tested by the Writings of John Calvin and the English Puritans of the Sixteenth and Seventeenth Centuries. Mich S 1969

M392 Miwa, Kimitada I. Crossroads of Patriotism in Imperial Japan: Shiga Shigetaka (1863-1927), Uchimura Kanzō (1861-1930), and Nitobe Inazō (1862-1933). Princeton 1967

M393 Miyoshi, Setsuko, Mother. The Role of Kokugaku and Yogaku during the Tokugawa Period. Georgetown 1965

M394 Modell, John. The Japanese of Los Angeles: A Study in Growth and Accommodation, 1900-1946. Columbia 1969

M395 Moeller, Beverley B. Phil Swing in Washington: The Boulder Canyon Project Legislation. UCLA 1968

M396 Moeller, Walter O. The Woolen Industry at Pompeii. Md 1962

M397 Moffat, Edward S. Trinity School, New York City, 1709-1959. Columbia 1963

M398 Moffett, William A. Pitt's Friends: The Fortunes of a Political Party, 1801-1807. Duke 1968

M399 Mohl, Raymond A., Jr. Poverty, Public Relief, and Private Charity in New York City, 1784-1825. NYU 1967

M400 Mohr, James C. Civil and Institutional Reform in New York State, 1864-1868: A Radical Reconstruction at Home. Stanford 1969

M401 Molho, Anthony. The Florentine Oligarchy of the Late Trecento, 1393-1402. Case W Reserve 1965

M402 Molyneaux, John L. Clientage Groups in the English Parliaments of the 1620's. Va 1968

M403 Monahan, Forrest D., Jr. Trade Goods on the Prairie: The Kiowa Tribe and White Trade Goods, 1794-1875. Okla 1965

M404 Monet, Jacques. The Last Cannon Shot: A Study of French-Canadian Nationalism, 1837-1850. Toronto 1964

M405 Monroe, Haskell M. The Presbyterian Church in the Confederate States of America. Rice 1961

M406 Monter, E. William. The Government of Geneva, 1536-1605. Princeton 1963

M407 Montgomery, David. Labor and the Radical Republicans: A Study of the Revival of the American Labor Movement, 1864-1868. Minn 1962

M408 Montgomery, Martha D. Eleanor of Provence, Queen of England (1223-1291). Miss S 1965

M409 Moodie, Thomas. The *Parti ouvrier français*, 1879-1893: The Formation of a Political Sect. Columbia 1966

M410 Moody, Jesse C. The Steel Industry in the National Recovery Administration: An Experiment in Industrial Self-Government. Okla 1965

M411 Moon, Shirley B. The Reconciliation of Science and Religion in Symbolo-Fideism. Wayne 1968

M412 Mooney, Anne L. Dexter Perkins: A Study in American Diplomatic Philosophy. St L 1965

M413 Moore, Anne T. France and the Schuman Plan, 1948-1953. NC 1964

M414 Moore, George E. Kozaki Hiromichi and the Kumamoto Band: A Study in Samurai Reaction to the West. Cal, Berkeley 1966

M415 Moore, Jamie W. The Logic of Isolation and Neutrality: American Foreign Policy 1933-1935. NC 1970

M416 Moore, John H. America Looks at Turkey, 1876-1909. Va 1961

M417 Moore, John R. Josiah W. Bailey of North Carolina and the New Deal, 1931-1941. Duke 1962

M418 Moore, Michael A. The A. F. of L. and the Anti-Trust Laws, 1890-1932. Case W Reserve 1964

M419 Moore, Ray A. Samurai Social Mobility in Tokugawa, Japan. Mich U 1968

M420 Moore, Richard R. The Impact of the Oil Industry in West Texas. Tex Tech 1965

M421 Moore, Robert J. Historians' Interpretation of the Reconstruction Period in American History. Boston U 1961

M422 Moore, Robert L. European Socialists and the American Promised Land, 1880-1917. Yale 1968

M423 Moore, Waddy W. Territorial Arkansas, 1819-1836. NC 1963

M424 Moorman, Donald R. A Political Biography of Holm O. Bursum, 1899-1924. NM 1962

M425 Moosa, Matti I. *Kitab al-Lu'lu' al-Manthur fi Tarikh al-Ulum wa al-Adab al-Suryaniyya* [by Ignatius Aphram Barsoum]. Columbia 1965

M426 Moran, Robert E. The History of Child Welfare in Louisiana, 1850-1960. Ohio 1968

M427 Morchain, Janet K. Anti-Americanism in Canada, 1871-1891. Rochester 1967

M428 Moreau, John A. Bourne, A Biography. Va 1964

M429 Moreno, José A. Sociological Aspects of the Dominican Revolution. Cornell 1967

M430 Morgan, David T., Jr. The Great Awakening in the Carolinas and Georgia, 1740-1775. NC 1968

M431 Morgan, Edward J. D. Sources of Capital for Railroads in the Old Northwest before the Civil War. Wis 1964

M432 Morgan, George T., Jr. The Fight against Fire: Development of Cooperative Forestry in the Pacific Northwest, 1900-1950. Ore 1964

M433 Morgan, Thomas S., Jr. A Step toward Altruism: Relief and Welfare in North Carolina, 1930-1938. NC 1969

M434 Morgan, William C., III. The Church and Feudal Society in Tenth-Century France. Mich S 1966

M435 Morgan, William G. Presidential Nominations in the Federal Era, 1788-1828. S Cal 1969

M436 Moriarty, Thomas F. The Harcourt Viceroyalty in Ireland, 1772-1777. Notre D 1964

M437 Mork, Gordon R. The National Liberal Party in the German Reichstag and the Prussian Landtag, 1866-1874. Minn 1966

M438 Morrill, Dan L. The Independent Social Democratic Party of Germany and the Communist International, March 1919-October 1920. Emory 1966

M439 Morrill, James R., III. North Carolina Public Finance, 1783-1789: The Problem of Minimal Government in an Underdeveloped Land. NC 1967

M440 Morris, Herman P. A History of British Historiography of the Munich Crisis. Okla 1967

M441 Morris, James M. The Road to Trade Unionism: Organized Labor in Cincinnati to 1893. Cincinnati 1969

M442 Morris, John D. The New York State Whigs, 1834-1842: A Study of Political Organization. Rochester 1970

M443 Morris, John R. Davis Hanson Waite: The Ideology of a Western Populist. Colo 1965

M444 Morris, Richard A. Joseph Rey of Grenoble, 1779-1855: Revolutionary, Educator, Humanitarian. Ia 1966

M445 Morris, Robert J., Jr. Eighteenth-Century Theories of the Nature of Heat. Okla 1965

M446   Morris, Robert L.   The Wheeling *Daily Intelligencer* and the Civil War. W Va 1965

M447   Morris, Ronald L.   The Labour Party and the General Strike of 1926. S Cal 1969

M448   Morris, Thomas D.   The Personal Liberty Laws, 1780-1861: Constitutional and Legal Aspects. Wash U 1969

M449   Morrison, Barrie M.   The Property-Transfer Inscriptions of Bengal from the Fifth to the Thirteenth Century. Chicago 1966

M450   Morrison, Chaplain W.   The Wilmot Proviso and the Democratic Party, 1846-1848. NC 1963

M451   Morrison, Jack G.   The Intransigents: Alsace-Lorrainers against the Annexation, 1900-1914. Ia 1970

M452   Morrison, James L., Jr.   The United States Military Academy, 1833-1866: Years of Progress and Turmoil. Columbia 1970

M453   Morrison, Joseph L.   Josephus Daniels as "Tar Heel Editor," 1894-1913. Duke 1961

M454   Morrison, Karl F.   Dualism in Frankish Political Thought, 814-887. Cornell 1961

M455   Morse, Darrell P.   Soldiers in Politics during the First French Republic, 1795-1799. Cal, Berkeley 1962

M456   Morton, Joseph C.   Stephen Bordley of Colonial Annapolis. Md 1964

M457   Morton, William F.   The Tanaka Cabinet's China Policy, 1927-1929. Columbia 1969

M458   Moseley, Clement C.   Invisible Empire: A History of the Ku Klux Klan in Twentieth Century Georgia, 1915-1965. Ga 1968

M459   Moseley, Edward H.   The Public Career of Santiago Vidaurri, 1855-1858. Ala 1963

M460   Moseley, Thomas R.   A History of the New York Manumission Society, 1785-1849. NYU 1963

M461   Moseley, Thomas V.   Evolution of the American Civil War Infantry Tactics. NC 1967

M462   Mosher, Paul H.   The Abbey of Cava in the Eleventh and Twelfth Centuries: Cava, the Normans, and the Greeks in Southern Italy. Cal, Berkeley 1969

M463   Moss, Jean-Kathleen D.   The Family of Love in England. W Va 1969

M464   Mothershead, Harmon R.   The Swan Land and Cattle Company, Limited. Colo 1969

M465   Mottahedeh, Roy P.   Administration in the Buyid Kingdom of Rayy. Harvard 1970

M466   Moulton, Harland B.   American Strategic Power: Two Decades of Nuclear Strategy and Weapon Systems, 1945-1965. Minn 1969

M467   Mount, Graeme S.   American Imperialism in Panama. Toronto 1969

M468   Mouratides, Anastasio I.   Byzantine Immunity System. McGill 1965

M469   Moyer, Laurence V.   The *Kraft durch Freude* Movement in Nazi Germany, 1933-1939. Northwestern 1967

M470   Muccigrosso, Robert H.   Richard W. G. Welling: A Reformer's Life. Columbia 1966

M471   Mueller, Reinhold C.   The Procuratori di San Marco and the Venetian Credit Market: A Study of the Development of Credit and Banking in the Trecento. JH 1970

M472   Mugridge, Ian.   The Old West in Anglo-American Relations, 1783-1803. Cal, Santa Barbara 1969

M473   Muldoon, James M.   The Medieval Origins of the State: The Contribution of the Canonists from Gratian to Hostiensis. Cornell 1965

M474   Mulhollan, Paige E.   Philander C. Knox and Dollar Diplomacy, 1909-1913. Tex U 1966

M475   Mulholland, Daniel M.   The Crisis of NEP. Harvard 1969

M476   Mulkeen, Thomas A.   Evolution of Ireland's Role among the Emerging Nations in the United Nations. St John's 1967

M477   Mulkern, John R.   The Know-Nothing Party in Massachusetts. Boston U 1963

M478   Mullay, M. Camilla, Sister.   John Brophy, Militant Labor Leader and Reformer: The CIO Years. Cath 1966

M479   Mullen, Pierce C.   The Preconditions and Reception of Darwinian Biology in Germany, 1800-1870. Cal, Berkeley 1964

M480   Mullen, Walter F.   Rhode Island and the Imperial Reorganization of 1763-1766. Fordham 1965

M481   Muller, H. N., III.   The Commercial History of the Lake Champlain-Richelieu River Route, 1760-1815. Rochester 1969

M482   Mullin, Gerald W.   Patterns of Slave Behavior in Eighteenth Century Virginia. Cal, Berkeley 1968

M483 Mullins, Jack S. The Sugar Trust: Henry O. Havemeyer and the American Sugar Refining Company. SC 1964

M484 Mullins, Patrick J., Sister. The Spiritual Life According to St. Isidore of Seville. Cath 1940

M485 Mulvihill, Peggy M. The United States and the Russo-Finnish War. Chicago 1964

M486 Mumford, Richard L. Constitutional Development in the State of Delaware, 1776-1897. Del 1968

M487 Mumper, James A. The Jefferson Image in the Federalist Mind, 1801-1809: Jefferson's Administration from the Federalist Point of View. Va 1966

M488 Muncie, John G. The Struggle to Obtain Federal Aid for Elementary and Secondary Schools, 1940-1965. Kent 1969

M489 Munholland, John K. The Emergence of the Colonial Military in France, 1880-1905. Princeton 1964

M490 Munro, John F. S. The Machakos Kamba under British Rule, 1889-1939: A Study of Colonial Contact in Kenya. Wis 1968

M491 Munro, John H. A. Wool, Cloth, and Gold: Bullionism in Anglo-Burgundian Commercial Relations, 1384-1478. Yale 1965

M492 Munsell, F. Darrel. Peelite Opinions and Political Activities, 1846-1859. Kans U 1967

M493 Munson, Vivian L. American Merchants of Capital in China: The Second Chinese Banking Consortium. Wis 1968

M494 Muraskin, Jack D. Missouri Politics during the Progressive Era, 1896-1916. Cal, Berkeley 1969

M495 Murphy, Donald J. Professors, Publicists, and Pan Americanism, 1905-1917: A Study in the Origins of the Use of "Experts" in Shaping American Foreign Policy. Wis 1970

M496 Murphy, Frederick I. The American Christian Press and Pre-War Hitler's Germany, 1933-1939. Fla U 1970

M497 Murphy, Harry J., Jr. The British Image of Man in the Eighteenth Century. Mo 1969

M498 Murphy, James B. L. Q. C. Lamar: Pragmatic Patriot. LSU 1968

M499 Murphy, James M. Positivism in England: The Reception of Comte's Doctrines, 1840-1870. Columbia 1968

M500 Murphy, James M. The Pitt Administration and the Irish Roman Catholics, 1791-1801. Fordham 1968

M501 Murphy, James T., Jr. A History of American Diplomacy at the Paris Peace Conference of 1898. Am 1965

M502 Murphy, John F. Cutter Captain: The Life and Times of John C. Cantwell. Conn 1968

M503 Murphy, Joseph F. Potawotomi Indians of the West: Origins of the Citizen Band. Okla 1961

M504 Murphy, Lawrence R. Crusader in the West: The Life of W. F. M. Arny, 1813-1881. Tex C 1968

M505 Murray, Bruce K. The People's Budget. Kans U 1967

M506 Murray, Lawrence L, III. Andrew W. Mellon, Secretary of the Treasury, 1921-1932: A Study in Policy. Mich S 1970

M507 Murray, Stanley N. An Agricultural History in the Valley of the Red River of the North, 1812 to 1920. Wis 1963

M508 Murrin, John M. Anglicizing an American Colony: The Transformation of Provincial Massachusetts. Yale 1966

M509 Murtha, Ronin J. The Life of the Most Reverend Ambrose Maréchal, Third Archbishop of Baltimore, 1768-1828. Cath 1965

M510 Murzyn, John S. Principles and Politics in Pre-Revolutionary Pennsylvania, 1756-1776. NYU 1969

M511 Musselman, Lloyd K. Rocky Mountain National Park, 1915-1965: An Administrative History. Denver 1969

M512 Muth, Edwin A. Elihu Root: His Role and Concepts Pertaining to United States Policies of Intervention. Georgetown 1966

M513 Muth, Philip A. The Ashursts: Friends of New England. Boston U 1967

M514 Myers, Charles B. Public Secondary Schools in Pennsylvania during the American Revolutionary Era, 1760-1800. Geo P 1968

M515 Myers, Duane P. Germany and the Question of Austrian *Anschluss*, 1918-1922. Yale 1968

M516 Myers, Ellen H. The Mexican Liberal Party, 1903-1910. Va 1970

M517 Myers, John L. The Agency System of the Anti-Slavery Movement, 1832-1837, and Its Antecedents in Other Benevolent and Reform Societies. Mich U 1961

M518 Myres, Sandra Lynn S. The Development of the Ranch as a Frontier Institution in the Spanish Province of Texas, 1691-1800. Tex C 1967

N

N1   Nadelhaft, Jerome J.   The Revolutionary Era in South Carolina, 1775-1788. Wis 1965

N2   Naff, Thomas.   Ottoman Diplomacy and the Great European Powers, 1789-1802. Cal, Berkeley 1961

N3   Nagasawa, Arthur.   The Governance of Hawaii from Annexation to 1908: Major Problems and Developments. Denver 1968

N4   Nagazumi, Akira.   The Origin and the Earlier Years of the Budi Utomo, 1908-1918. Cornell 1967

N5   Nagle, Dermot B.   A Historiographic Study of Plutarch's *Tiberius Gracchus.* S Cal 1968

N6   Nahm, Andrew C.   Kim Ok-kyun and the Korean Progressive Movement, 1882-1884. Stanford 1961

N7   Najita, Tetsuo.   The Seiyūkai in the Politics of Compromise, 1905-1915. Harvard 1965

N8   Nall, Charles T.   The Role of the Swiss in France in the Revolution, 1789-1799. Ky 1966

N9   Nammack, Georgiana C.   A Century of Conflict: Politics and Rivalries over Indian Lands in Colonial New York. Cal, Santa Barbara 1963

N10   Náñez Falcón, Guilliermo.   Erwin Paul Dieseldorff, German Entrepreneur in the Alta Verapaz of Guatemala, 1889-1937. Tulane 1970

N11   Nash, Gary B.   Economics and Politics in Colonial Pennsylvania, 1681-1701. Princeton 1964

N12   Nash, Lee M.   Refining a Frontier: The Cultural Interests and Activities of Harvey W. Scott. Ore 1961

N13   Nash, Roderick W.   Wilderness and the American Mind. Wis 1965

N14   Nass, David L.   Public Power and Politics in New York State, 1918-1958. Syracuse 1970

N15   Nathan, Meyer J.   The Presidential Election of 1916 in the Middle West. Princeton 1966

N16   Nathans, Sydney H.   Daniel Webster and the Whig Party, 1828-1844. JH 1969

N17   Nauen, Franz G.   Revolution, Idealism, and Human Freedom: Schelling, Hölderlin and Hegel and the Crisis of Early German Idealism. Harvard 1969

N18   Navarrete, George.   The Latin American Policy of Charles Evans Hughes, 1921-1925. Cal, Berkeley 1964

N19   Naylor, John F.   British Labour's International Policy, 1931-1939. Harvard 1964

N20   Nazzaro, John.   The Triple Entente: The July Crisis of 1914. Laval 1967

N21   Neat, Donald R.   The Parliamentary Career of Sir James Mackintosh. Ky 1965

N22   Necheles, Ruth F.   The Abbé Grégoire and the Constitutional Church. Chicago 1963

N23   Nedava, Joseph.   Trotsky and the Jewish Question. Penn U 1970

N24   Needham, David C.   William Howard Taft, the Negro, and the White South, 1908-1912. Ga 1970

N25   Neel, Joanne L.   His Britannic Majesty's Consul General, Phineas Bond, esq. Bryn Mawr 1963

N26   Neff, Robert R.   The Early Career and Governorship of Paul V. McNutt. Ind 1964

N27   Neil, Robert E.   The Nazi Revolution: The First Stages. Harvard 1963

N28   Neilson, Peter R.   Financial History of the United States, 1811-1816. Cath 1926

N29   Nelles, Henry V.   The Politics of Development: Forests, Mines and Hydro-Electric Power in Ontario, 1890-1939. Toronto 1970

N30   Nelli, Humbert S.   The Role of the "Colonial" Press in the Italian-American Community of Chicago, 1886-1921. Chicago 1965

N31   Nelson, Carolyn A.   Regionalism in Visigothic Spain. Kans U 1970

N32   Nelson, Charles A.   A History of the Forest Products Laboratory. Wis 1964

N33   Nelson, Clyde K.   The Social Ideas of Russell H. Conwell. Penn U 1968

N34   Nelson, Daniel M.   The Development of Unemployment Insurance in the United States, 1915-1935. Wis 1967

N35   Nelson, David P.   A Study of the Inter-Institutional Coordination of Public Higher Education in Colorado, 1937 to 1965. Denver 1969

N36 Nelson, H. Viscount, Jr. Race and Class Consciousness of Philadelphia Negroes with Special Emphasis on the Years between 1927 and 1940. Penn U 1969

N37 Nelson, John K. Anglican Missions in America, 1701-1725: A Study of the Society for the Propagation of the Gospel in Foreign Parts. Northwestern 1962

N38 Nelson, Keith L. The First American Military Occupation in Germany, 1918-1923. Cal, Berkeley 1965

N39 Nelson, Kenneth R. United States Occupation Policy and the Establishment of a Democratic Newspaper Press in Bavaria, 1945-1949. Va 1966

N40 Nelson, Lynn H. The Normans in South Wales, 1070-1171. Tex U 1963

N41 Nelson, Otto M. The German Social Democratic Party and France, 1918-1933. Ohio 1968

N42 Nelson, Paul D. Horatio Gates: Republican Soldier of the American Revolution, 1728-1806. Duke 1970

N43 Nelson, Ronald R. The Home Office, 1782-1801. Duke 1967

N44 Nelson, Ronald Roy. The Life and Thought of William Robertson Smith, 1846-1894. Mich U 1969

N45 Nelson, Russell S., Jr. Backcountry Pennsylvania, 1709 to 1744: The Ideals of William Penn in Practice. Wis 1968

N46 Nelson, Walter D. British Rational Secularism: Unbelief from Bradlaugh to the Mid-Twentieth Century. Wash U 1963

N47 Nelson, Wilbur K. Educational Goals in China with Emphasis on the Relationship of Public and Private Schools on Taiwan during the Period 1949-1962. Claremont 1963

N48 Nethers, John L. Simeon D. Fess: Educator and Politician. Ohio 1964

N49 Netting, Anthony G. Russian Liberalism: The Years of Promise, 1842-1855. Columbia 1967

N50 Neu, Charles E. The Far Eastern Policy of Theodore Roosevelt, 1906-1909. Harvard 1964

N51 Neuman, Mark D. Aspects of Poverty and Poor Law Administration in Berkshire, 1782-1834. Cal, Berkeley 1967

N52 Neuringer, Sheldon M. American Jewry and United States Immigration Policy, 1881-1953. Wis 1969

N53 Neustadt, Maxine F. Proprietary Purposes in the Anglo-American Colonies: Problems in the Transplantation of English Patterns of Social Organization. Wis 1968

N54 New, John F. H. Anglican and Puritan: The Basis of Their Opposition Reconsidered. Toronto 1962

N55 Newbold, Catharine. The Antislavery Background of the Principal State Department Appointees in the Lincoln Administration. Mich U 1962

N56 Newcomb, Benjamin H. The Political Partnership of Benjamin Franklin and Joseph Galloway, 1755-1775. Penn U 1964

N57 Newhall, David S. Georges Clemenceau, 1902-1906: "An Old Beginner." Harvard 1963

N58 Newman, Edgar L. Republicanism during the Bourbon Restoration in France, 1814-1830. Chicago 1969

N59 Newquist, Gloria W. James A. Farley and the Politics of Victory, 1928-1936. S Cal 1966

N60 Newton, Craig A. Southern Writers of National History, 1785-1816. Case W Reserve 1964

N61 Newton, Ronald C. A Theoretical Approach to the Study of Spanish American Institutionalized Functional Groups. Fla U 1963

N62 Newton, Wesley P. Aviation in the Relations of the United States and Latin America, 1916-1929. Ala 1964

N63 Nicholas, David M., Jr. Town and Countryside: Social and Economic Tensions in the County of Flanders, 1280-1384. Brown 1967

N64 Nicholls, Robert L. The Prescriptive Guardian: Parliament and Public Morality, 1830-1880. Md 1970

N65 Nichols, Glenn O. The Earl of Danby's Administration of the Treasury, 1673-1679. Ill 1966

N66 Nichols, Roger L. General Henry Atkinson: Frontier Soldier, 1782-1842. Wis 1964

N67 Nichols, William G. The Course and Development of Spanish-Imperial Relations, 1618-1637. Ala 1970

N68 Nicoll, G. Douglas. Russian Participation in the Second International, 1889-1914. Boston U 1961

N69 Nicolson, John A. New England Idealism in the Civil War: The Military Career of Joseph Roswell Hawley. Claremont 1970

N70 Niehaus, Earl F. The Irish in New Orleans, 1803-1862. Tulane 1961

N71 Nielson, George R. The Indispensable Institution: The Congressional Party during the Era of Good Feelings. Ia 1968

N72 Niemeyer, Glenn A. The Automotive Career of Ransom E. Olds. Mich S 1962

N73 Niewyk, Donald L. German Social Democracy Confronts the Problem of Anti-Semitism, 1918-1933. Tulane 1968

N74 Nimocks, Walter B. Lord Milner's "Kindergarten" and the Origins of the Round Table Movement. Vanderbilt 1965

N75 Nish, Cameron. The Canadian Bourgeoisie, 1729-1748: Character, Composition and Functions. Laval 1967

N76 Nissenbaum, Stephen W. Careful Love: Sylvester Graham and the Emergence of Victorian Sexual Theory in America, 1830-1840. Wis 1968

N77 Nodyac, Kenneth R. The Role of De Witt Clinton and the Municipal Government in the Development of Cultural Organizations in New York City, 1803 to 1817. NYU 1969

N78 Noel, Charles C. Campomanes and the Secular Clergy in Spain, 1760-1780: Enlightenment vs Tradition. Princeton 1970

N79 Noel, Francis R. A History of the Bankruptcy Clause of the Constitution of the United States. Cath 1918

N80 Nohl, Lessing H., Jr. Bad Hand: The Military Career of Ranald Slidell MacKenzie, 1871-1889. NM 1962

N81 Nolen, Claude H. Aftermath of Slavery: Southern Attitudes toward Negroes, 1865-1900. Tex U 1963

N82 Nomikos, Eugenia V. The International Position of Greece during the Crimean War. Stanford 1962

N83 Noonan, Thomas S. The Dnieper Trade Route in Kievan Russia, 900-1240 A.D. Ind 1965

N84 Nordhauser, Norman E. The Quest for Stability: Domestic Oil Policy, 1919-1935. Stanford 1970

N85 Nordin, Dennis S. Mainstreams of Grangerism: A Revisionist View of the Order of Patrons of Husbandry, 1867-1900. Miss S 1969

N86 Nordquist, Philip A. The Ecology of Religious Denominational Preference in the United States, 1850. Wash U 1964

N87 Norman, Mary Paul, Sister. The Reform Thought of Edwin Lawrence Godkin. St L 1967

N88 Norris, James D. The Maramec Iron Works, 1826-1876: The History of a Pioneer Iron Works in Missouri. Mo 1961

N89 Norris, Marjorie M. Nonviolent Reform in the United States, 1860-1886. Md 1970

N90 Norris, Parthenia E. United States and Liberia: The Slavery Crisis, 1929-1935. Ind 1961

N91 Norse, Clifford C. *The Southern Cultivator*, 1843-1861. Fla S 1969

N92 Norton, Donald H. Karl Haushofer and His Influence on Nazi Idealogy and German Foreign Policy, 1919-1945. Clark 1965

N93 Norton, Mary B. The British-Americans: The Loyalist Exiles in England, 1774-1789. Harvard 1969

N94 Norton, Nile B. Frank R. McCoy and American Diplomacy, 1929-1932. Denver 1966

N95 Notaro, Carmen A. Franklin D. Roosevelt and the American Communists: Peacetime Relations, 1932-1941. SUNY, Buffalo 1969

N96 Notehelfer, Frederick G. Kōtoku Shūsui: Portrait of a Japanese Radical. Princeton 1968

N97 Nott, John W. The Artisan as Agitator: Richard Carlile, 1816-1843. Wis 1970

N98 Novak, Bogdan C. The Ethnic and Political Struggle in Trieste, 1943-1954. Chicago 1961

N99 Novick, Joel R. Bainbridge Colby: Profile in Progressivism. NYU 1970

N100 Novick, Peter. The Purge in Liberated France, 1944-1946. Columbia 1965

N101 Noyes, William R. Influenza Epidemic, 1918-1919: A Misplaced Chapter in United States Social and Institutional History. UCLA 1968

N102 Nugent, Donald G. The Colloquy of Poissy: A Study in Sixteenth Century Ecumenism. Ia 1965

N103 Nugent, Walter T. K. Populism and Nativism in Kansas, 188-1900. Chicago 1961

N104 Numbers, Ronald L. The Nebular Hypothesis in American Thought. Cal, Berkeley 1969

N105   Nunn, Frederick M.   Civil-Military Relations in Chile, 1891-1938. NM 1963

N106   Nutsch, James G.   Bolshevik Agrarian Policies, 1917-1921. Kans U 1968

N107   Nuttall, Donald A.   Pedro Fages and the Advance of the Northern Frontier of New Spain, 1767-1782. S Cal 1964

N108   Nutter, Glen L.   Education and Politics in the *New Republic* Magazine, 1914-1928. Geo P 1969

N109   Nwabara, Samuel N.   Ibo Land: A Study in British Penetration and the Problem of Administration, 1860-1930. Northwestern 1965

N110   Nye, Robert A.   An Intellectual Portrait of Gustave LeBon: A Study of the Development and Impact of a Social Scientist in His Historical Setting. Wis 1969

N111   Nye, Roger H.   The United States Military Academy in an Era of Educational Reform, 1900-1925. Columbia 1968

O

O1   Oard, Ronald J.   Bancroft and Hildreth: A Critical Evaluation. St L 1961

O2   Oates, Stephen B.   The Bloody Pilgrimage of John Brown. Tex U 1969

O3   Obendorf, Donald L.   Samuel P. Langley: Solar Scientist, 1867-1891. Cal, Berkeley 1969

O4   O'Brien, Albert C.   *L'Osservatore Romano* and Fascism, 1919-1929: Study of Journalistic Opinion. Notre D 1968

O5   O'Brien, Charles H.   Ideas of Religious Toleration at the Time of Joseph II. Columbia 1967

O6   O'Brien, David J.   American Catholic Social Thought in the 1930's. Rochester 1965

O7   O'Brien, Gerard F. J.   James A. Seddon, Statesman of the Old South. Md 1963

O8   O'Brien, Gregory C.   The Life of Robert Dollar, 1844-1932. Claremont 1969

O9   O'Brien, John M.   Fulk of Neuilly. S Cal 1965

O10   O'Brien, M. Carita, Sister.   *Koinonia* from Classical to Christian Times. Loyola 1966

O11   O'Brien, M. Philomena, Sister.   Executive Agreements: Extent and Influence in Domestic and Foreign Affairs. St John's 1964

O12   O'Brien, Patrick G.   A Study of Political and Sectional Voting Alignments in the United States Senate, 1921-1929. Wayne 1968

O13   O'Connell, Brian T.   Croatian Politics and Political Parties, 1905-1910. Wash U 1969

O14   O'Connell, James R.   The Spanish Parliament and the Clerical Question, 1868-1936. Columbia 1966

O15   O'Connell, Maurice R.   The Irish Free Trade Crisis, 1777-1780: A Study of the Political Awakening of the Middle Classes. Penn U 1962

O16   O'Connor, John T.   William Egon von Fürstenberg and French Diplomacy in the Rhineland Prior to the Outbreak of the War of the League of Augsburg in 1688. Minn 1965

O17   O'Connor, Joseph E.   Laurence A. Steinhardt and American Policy toward the Soviet Union, 1939-1941. Va 1968

O18   Odom, Edwin D.   Louisiana Railroads, 1830-1880: A Study of State and Local Aid. Tulane 1961

O19   Odom, James L.   Viceroy Abascal versus the *Cortés* of Cádiz. Ga 1968

O19a   O'Donnell, J. Dean, Jr.   Charles Cardinal Lavigerie and the Establishment of the 1881 French Protectorate in Tunisia. Rutgers 1970

O20   O'Donnell, James H., III.   The Southern Indians in the War of Independence, 1775-1783. Duke 1963

O21   O'Donnell, James J.   Thomas Cushing: A Reluctant Rebel. Boston U 1962

O22   O'Donnell, John H.   The Catholic Hierarchy of the United States, 1790-1922. Cath 1922

O23   O'Donnell, Mary De LaSalle, Sister.   Wessel Gansfort: A Study of the Christological Aspects of His Humanism and Spirituality. Boston C 1963

O24   Oehling, Richard A.   Late Elizabethan Governmental Treatment of Religious Nonconformity, 1589-1603. Rutgers 1969

O25   Oerter, Herbert L.   The Florence of Corso Donati. Colo 1965

O26   Oeste, George I.   The Diplomatic Career of John Randolph Clay. Penn U 1961

O27   O'Farrell, Brian.   Politician, Patron, Poet: William Herbert, Third Earl of Pembroke, 1580-1630. UCLA 1966

O28   Offenberg, Richard S.   The Political Career of Thomas Brackett Reed. NYU 1963

O29   Offner, Arnold A.   American Diplomacy and Germany, 1933-1938. Ind 1964

O30   O'Flaherty, Patrick D.   The History of the Sixty-Ninth Regiment of the New York State Militia, 1851-1861. Fordham 1963

O31   Ogelsby, John C. M.   War at Sea in the West Indies, 1739-1748. Wash U 1963

O32   Oggins, Robin S.   The English Kings and Their Hawks: Falconry in Medieval England to the Time of Edward I. Chicago 1967

O33   Ogilvie, Charles F.   Academic Freedom in the Colleges of Three Major Southern Denominations, 1865-1965. SC 1966

O34   Ogilvie, Leon P.   The Development of the Southeast Missouri Lowlands. Mo 1966

O35 Oglesby, Richard E. Vision of Empire: Manuel Lisa and the Opening of the Missouri Fur Trade. Northwestern 1962

O36 O'Grady, Joseph P. Irish-Americans and Anglo-American Relations, 1880-1888. Penn U 1965

O37 Oh, Wonyung Hyun. Opinions of Continental American Leaders on International Relations, 1763-1775. Wash U 1963

O38 O'Hare, Aloysius. The Birth of the Sudanese Republic. St John's 1961

O39 Ohline, Howard A. Politics and Slavery: The Issue of Slavery in National Politics, 1787-1815. Mo 1969

O40 Ojala, Jeanne A. The Military Career of Auguste Colbert, 1793-1809. Fla S 1969

O41 O'Keefe, Thomas E. Liu Shao-ch'i: A Political Biography. St John's 1968

O42 O'Keefe, Timothy J. British Attitudes toward India and the Dependent Empire, 1857-1874. Notre D 1968

O43 Okoye, Felix N. C. The American Image of Africa: Myth and Reality. UCLA 1969

O44 Olaniyan, Richard A. The Anglo-Portuguese Dispute over Bulama: A Study in British Colonial Policy, 1860-1870. Georgetown 1970

O45 Oldani, John L. The Woman as Reformer: A Facet of the American Character. St L 1967

O46 Oldson, William O. The Historical and Nationalistic Thought of Nicolae Iorga. Ind 1970

O47 Olin, Spencer C. Hiram W. Johnson: The California Years, 1911-1917. Claremont 1965

O48 Oliva, Leo E. Soldiers on the Santa Fe Trail, 1829-1880. Denver 1964

O49 Oliver, James M., III. The *Corps des Ponts et Chaussées*, 1830-1848. Mo 1967

O50 Oliver, Peter N. The Making of a Provincial Premier: Howard Ferguson and Ontario Politics, 1870-1923. Toronto 1969

O51 Olkhovsky, George A. Vladimir Stasov and His Quest for Russian National Music. Georgetown 1968

O51a Olsen, Barton C. Lawlessness and Vigilantes in America: An Historical Analysis Emphasizing California and Montana. Utah 1968

O52 Olsen, Glenn W. The Legal Definition of the Ecclesiastical Benefice during the Period of the Appearance of Papal Provisioning (1140-1230). Wis 1965

O53 Olson, Audrey L. St. Louis Germans, 1850-1920: The Nature of an Immigrant Community and Its Relation to the Assimilation Process. Kans U 1970

O54 Olson, Charles W. Decolonization in French Politics (1950-1956): Indo-China, Tunisia, Morocco. N Ill 1966

O55 Olson, Gary D. Between Independence and Constitution: The Articles of Confederation, 1783-1787. Neb 1968

O56 Olson, Keith W. Franklin K. Lane: A Biography. Wis 1964

O57 Olson, Richard A. Studies in the Coinage of the Arsacid Rulers of Parthia from Mithradates I to Artavasdes. Minn 1968

O58 Olson, Robert C. Advocate of Reform: A Biography of Wayne MacVeagh. Penn S 1970

O59 Olssen, Erik N. Dissent from Normalcy: Progressives in Congress, 1918-1929. Duke 1970

O60 Olton, Charles S. Philadelphia Artisans and the American Revolution. Cal, Berkeley 1967

O61 Olusanya, Gabriel O. The Impact of the Second World War on Nigeria's Political Evolution. Toronto 1964

O62 O'Malley, John W. Giles of Viterbo: The Structure of His Thought on Church and Reform. Harvard 1966

O63 O'Neil, Daniel J. The United States Navy in the Californias, 1840-1850. S Cal 1969

O64 O'Neill, James E. Health and the State in Great Britain, 1865-1909: A Study in the Origins of the Welfare State. Chicago 1961

O65 O'Neill, James N. Queen Elizabeth I as a Patron of the Arts: The Relationship between Royal Patronage, Society, and Culture in Renaissance England. Va 1966

O66 O'Neill, William L. The Divorce Crisis of the Progressive Era. Cal, Berkeley 1963

O67 O'Neill, Ynez V. A Consideration of Theories on Speech from Earliest Times through the Sixteenth Century. UCLA 1964

O68 Onwumelu, John A. Congo Paternalism: An Isolationist Colonial Policy. Chicago 1966

O69 Oppel, Bernard F. Russo-German Relations, 1904-1906. Duke 1966

O70 O'Quinn, Ann E. British Interests in Argentina and Paraguay during the First Gladstone Administration. Ga 1965

O71 Orbach, Laurence F. "Homes for Heroes": A Study in the Politics of British Social Reform, 1915-1921. Columbia 1967

O72 Orchard, George E. Economic and Social Conditions in Muscovy during the Reign of Ivan III. McGill 1967

O73 Ord, Edmund B. H. State Sacrifices in the Former Han Dynasty according to the Official Histories. Cal, Berkeley 1967

O74 O'Reilly, Donald F. Rondon: Biography of a Brazilian Republican Army Commander. NYU 1969

O75 Orlando, Francis P. The Policy of Catholic Abstention from Italian Parliamentary Affairs, 1861-1919. Notre D 1970

O76 Orlow, Dietrich O. A Study of the Nazi Südosteuropa-Gesellschaft. Mich U 1962

O77 O'Rourke, M. Martinice, Sister. The Diplomacy of William H. Seward during the Civil War: His Policies as Related to International Law. Cal, Berkeley 1963

O78 O'Rourke, Paul A. Liberal Journals and the New Deal. Notre D 1969

O79 Orr, Richard B. In Durance Vile: Attitudes towards Imprisonment in England during the Du Cane Regime, 1877-1895. Wis 1968

O80 Orr, William J. *Anschluss:* Austro-German Relations, 1933-1938. Mich U 1961

O81 Ortquist, Richard T. Depression Politics in Michigan, 1929-1933. Mich U 1968

O82 Osborn, George K., III. Sino-Indian Border Conflicts: Historical Background and Recent Developments. Stanford 1963

O83 Osborn, Wayne S. A Community of Metztit-lán, New Spain, 1520-1810. Ia 1970

O84 Osborne, John W. William Cobbett and His England: A Study in Social and Political Ideas. Rutgers 1961

O85 Osburn, J. Douglas. Lloyd Jones, Labour Journalist, 1871-1878: A Study in British Working-Class Thought. Okla 1969

O86 Osen, James L. The Revival of the French Reformed Church, 1830-1852. Wis 1966

O87 Osofsky, Gilbert. Harlem, the Making of a Ghetto: A History of Negro New York, 1900-1920. Columbia 1963

O88 Oster, Donald B. Community Image in the History of Saint Louis and Kansas City. Mo 1969

O89 Ostrower, Gary B. The United States, the League of Nations, and Collective Security, 1931-1934. Rochester 1970

O90 Otte, James K. Alfred of Sareshel's Commentary on the *Metheora* of Aristotle. S Cal 1969

O91 Ouellet, Fernand. *Histoire économique et sociale du Québec, 1760-1850: Structures et conjonctures.* Laval 1965

O92 Overfield, James H. Humanism and Scholasticism in Germany, 1450-1520. Princeton 1968

O93 Overfield, Richard A. The Loyalists of Maryland during the American Revolution. Md 1968

O94 Overy, David H. Robert Lewis Dabney: Apostle of the Old South. Wis 1967

O95 Owens, Gary L. Norfolk, 1620-41: Local Government and Central Authority in an East Anglican County. Wis 1970

O96 Owens, Harry P. Apalachicola before 1861. Fla S 1966

O97 Owings, William A. Socialism in South Slav Lands before 1914: Antecedents of the Communist Party of Yugoslavia. Fla S 1965

O98 Oxnam, Robert B. Policies and Factionalism in the Oboi Regency, 1661-1669. Yale 1969

P

P1   Packard, Hyland B., Jr.   Critic as Witness: Francis Hackett and His America, 1883-1914. LSU 1970

P2   Packer, James E.   The *Insulae* of Imperial Ostia. Cal, Berkeley 1964

P3   Padberg, John W.   The Jesuit Colleges in France between the Falloux Law and the Ferry Decrees, 1850-1880. Harvard 1965

P4   Padgug, Robert A.   Polybios and the Population of Greece in the Third and Second Centuries B.C. Harvard 1970

P5   Page, Leroy E.   The Rise of the Diluvial Theory in British Geological Thought. Okla 1963

P6   Page, Oscar C.   Critique of the *Courrier d'Avignon, 1734-1774.* Ky 1967

P7   Painter, Borden W., Jr.   The Anglican Vestry in Colonial America. Yale 1965

P8   Painter, William E.   Baptista Mantuanus, Carmelite Humanist. Mo 1960

P9   Palecek, Marvin A.   The United Defense Fund: A Study of the Coordination of Voluntary Welfare Services during Wartime. Minn 1969

P10   Palmegiano, Eugenia M.   Henry Broadhurst and Working Class Politics, 1869-1880. Rutgers 1966

P11   Palmer, Colin A.   Negro Slavery in Mexico, 1570-1650. Wis 1970

P12   Palmer, John A.   Some Antecedents of Progressivism: Buffalo in the 1890's. SUNY, Buffalo 1967

P13   Palmer, Spencer J.   Protestant Christianity in China and Korea: The Problem of Identification with Tradition. Cal, Berkeley 1964

P14   Paludan, Phillip S.   Law and Equal Rights: The Civil War Encounter: A Study of Legal Minds in the Civil War Era. Ill 1968

P15   Pang, Eul Soo.   The Politics of *Coronelismo* in Brazil: The Case of Bahia, 1889-1930. Cal, Berkeley 1970

P16   Panzella, Emmett E.   The Atlantic Union Committee: A Study of a Pressure Group in Foreign Policy. Kent 1969

P17   Papachristou, Judith R.   American-Soviet Relations and United States Policy in the Pacific, 1933-1941. Colo 1968

P18   Papadakis, Aristeides.   Iconoclasm: A Study of the Hagiographical Evidence. Fordham 1968

P19   Papalas, Anthony J.   Studies in Roman Athens, 29 B.C. to A.D. 180. Chicago 1969

P20   Papayanis, Nicholas C.   Alphonse Merrheim and Revolutionary Syndicalism, 1871-1917. Wis 1969

P21   Papazian, Dennis.   Nicholas Ivanovich Kostomarov: Russian Historian, Ukrainian Nationalist, Slavic Federalist. Mich U 1966

P22   Papp, Nicholas G.   The Anglo-German Naval Agreement of 1935. Conn 1969

P23   Parham, Paul M.   Malcolm Glenn Wyer, Western Librarian: A Study in Leadership and Innovation. Denver 1964

P24   Parker, Keith A.   The Staple Industries and Economic Development, Canada, 1841-1867. Md 1966

P25   Parker, Russell D.   "Higher Law": Its Development and Application to the American Antislavery Controversy. Tenn 1966

P26   Parker, Watson.   The Black Hills Gold Rush, 1874-1879. Okla 1965

P27   Parkinson, Russell J.   Politics, Patents and Planes: Military Aeronautics in the United States, 1863-1907. Duke 1963

P28   Parkman, Aubrey L.   David Jayne Hill. Rochester 1961

P29   Parks, Gordon E.   Martin Van Buren and the Re-organization of the Democratic Party, 1841-1844. Wis 1965

P30   Parks, Robert J.   The Democracy's Railroads: Internal Improvements in Michigan, 1825-1846. Mich S 1967

P31   Parks, Roger N.   The Roads of New England, 1790-1840. Mich S 1966

P32   Parman, Donald L.   The Indian Civilian Conservation Corps. Okla 1967

P33   Parmet, Robert D.   The Know-Nothings in Connecticut. Columbia 1966

P34   Parramore, Thomas C.   Anson's Voyage and the Dawn of Scientific Navigation. NC 1965

P35   Parrini, Carl P.   American Empire and Creating a Community of Interest: Economic Diplomacy, 1916-1922. Wis 1963

P36   Parrish, Michael E.   Securities Regulation and the New Deal. Yale 1968

P37   Parrish, Noel F.   Behind the Sheltering Bomb: Military Indecision from Alamogordo to Korea. Rice 1968

P38   Parsons, Lynn H.   The Hamiltonian Tradition in the United States, 1804-1912. JH 1967

P39   Parsons, Stanley B., Jr.   The Populist Context: Nebraska Farmers and Their Antagonists, 1882-1895. Ia 1964

P40   Parsons, William H.   Soviet Historians and "Bourgeois" Interpretations of the Russian Revolution. Ind 1966

P41   Partin, Malcolm O.   The Politics of Anticlericalism: Waldeck-Rousseau, Combes, and the Church, 1899-1905. Duke 1967

P42   Paschal, George H., Jr. The History of the U.S.A. Presbyterian Church in Texas and Louisiana, 1868-1920. LSU 1967

P43   Paschal, Herbert R., Jr.   Proprietary North Carolina: A Study in Colonial Government. NC 1961

P44   Pascoe, Louis B.   Jean Gerson: Principles of Church Reform. UCLA 1970

P45   Pastor, Leslie P.   The Young Széchenyi: The Shaping of a Conservative Reformer, 1791-1832. Columbia 1967

P46   Pastor, Peter.   The Hungarian Revolution of 1918 and the Allies: A Study of International Relations. NYU 1969

P47   Pate, James P.   The Chickamauga: A Forgotten Segment of Indian Resistance on the Southern Frontier. Miss S 1969

P48   Paterno, Robert M.   The Yangtze Valley Anti-Missionary Riots of 1891. Harvard 1968

P49   Paterson, Thomas G.   The Economic Cold War: American Business and Economic Foreign Policy, 1945-1950. Cal, Berkeley 1968

P50   Pathak, Sushil M.   American Protestant Missionaries in India: A Study of Their Activities and Influence, 1813-1910 (as Drawn Chiefly from Missionary Sources). Hawaii 1964

P51   Patrucco, Armand I.   The Critics of the Italian Parliamentary System, 1860-1915. Columbia 1969

P52   Patsouras, Louis.   Jean Grave: French Intellectual and Anarchist, 1854-1939. Ohio 1966

P53   Patterson, David S.   The Travail of the American Peace Movement, 1887-1914. Cal, Berkeley 1969

P54   Patterson, E. Palmer, II.   Andrew Paull and Canadian Indian Resurgence. Wash U 1962

P55   Patterson, Graeme H.   Studies in Elections and Public Opinion in Upper Canada. Toronto 1970

P56   Patterson, James T.   The Conservative Coalition in Congress, 1933-1939. Harvard 1964

P57   Patterson, Robert B.   Robert Fitz Roy, Earl of Gloucester: A Study of a Baron, c. 1093-1147. JH 1962

P58   Patterson, Stephen E.   A History of Political Parties in Revolutionary Massachusetts, 1770-1780. Wis 1968

P59   Pattison, Dale P.   C. E. M. Joad's Search for Meaning in the Twentieth Century. Chicago 1970

P60   Paul, Charles B.   Rameau's Musical Theories and the Age of Reason. Cal, Berkeley 1966

P61   Paul, George H.   The Religious Frontier in Oklahoma: Dan T. Muse and the Pentecostal Holiness Church. Okla 1965

P62   Paul, Harry W.   The Second Ralliement: Church-State Relations in France, 1919-1928. Columbia 1962

P63   Paul, Justus F.   The Political Career of Senator Hugh Butler, 1940-1954. Neb 1966

P64   Paul, Norma A.   The History of Catholic Education in Illinois. Loyola 1940

P65   Pauley, Bruce F.   Hahnenschwanz and Swastika: The Styrian Heimatschutz and Austrian National Socialism, 1918-1934. Rochester 1967

P66   Paulson, Ross E.   The Vrooman Brothers and the American Reform Tradition. Harvard 1962

P67   Pauw, Alan D.   The Historical Background Relating to Access Rights to Berlin. S Cal 1965

P68   Paxton, Robert O.   Army Officers in Vichy France: "The Armistice Army, 1940-1942." Harvard 1963

P69 Paxton, Roger V. Russia and the First Serbian Revolution: A Diplomatic and Political Study, the Initial Phase, 1804-1807. Stanford 1969

P70 Payne, David S. The Foreign Policy of Georges Clemenceau, 1917-1920. Duke 1970

P71 Pearl, Jonathan L. Guise and Provence: Political Conflict in the Epoch of Richelieu. Northwestern 1968

P72 Pearson, Alden B. The American Christian Press and the Sino-Japanese Crisis of 1931-1933: An Aspect of Public Response to the Breakdown of World Peace. Duke 1968

P73 Pearson, Fred L., Jr. Spanish-Indian Relations in Florida: A Study of Two *Visitas,* 1657-1678. Ala 1968

P74 Pearson, Ralph L. Charles S. Johnson: The Urban League Years, a Study of Race Leadership. JH 1970

P75 Pease, Jane H. The Freshness of Fanaticism: Abby Kelley Foster, an Essay in Reform. Rochester 1969

P76 Peck, Warren G. The Military and Political Career of John Dudley, Duke of Northumberland. Ala 1964

P77 Pedersen, Lyman C., Jr. History of Fort Douglas, Utah. Brigham Young 1967

P78 Peek, Ralph L. Lawlessness and the Restoration of Order in Florida, 1868-1871. Fla U 1964

P79 Peeples, Dale H. The Senate Debate on the Philippine Legislation of 1902. Ga 1964

P80 Pelenski, Jaroslaw. Muscovite Imperial Claims to the Kazan' Khanate: A Case Study in the Emergence of Imperial Ideology. Columbia 1968

P81 Pells, Richard H. Intellectuals and the Depression: American Thought in the 1930's. Harvard 1969

P82 Peloso, Vincent. The Politics of Federation in Central America, 1885-1921. Ariz 1969

P83 Peltier, David P. Border State Democracy: A History of Voting in Delaware, 1682-1897. Del 1967

P84 Pendleton, Lawson A. James Buchanan's Attitude toward Slavery. NC 1964

P85 Penick, James L. The Ballinger-Pinchot Controversy. Cal, Berkeley 1962

P86 Pennanen, Gary A. The Foreign Policy of William Maxwell Evarts. Wis 1969

P87 Pennington, Loren E. The Origins of English Promotional Literature for America, 1553-1625. Mich U 1962

P88 Penton, Marvin J. Mexico's Reformation: A History of Mexican Protestantism from Its Inception to the Present. Ia 1965

P89 Perceval Maxwell, Michael B. E. The Migration of Scots to Ulster during the Reign of James I. McGill 1967

P90 Percy, William A., Jr. The Revenues of the Kingdom of Sicily under Charles I of Anjou, 1266-1285, and Their Relationship to the Vespers. Princeton 1964

P91 Pereyra, Lillian A. James Lusk Alcorn: A Biography. UCLA 1962

P92 Perinbam, B. Marie. Trade and Politics on the Senegal and Upper Niger, 1854-1900: African Reaction to French Penetration. Georgetown 1969

P93 Perkins, Charles A. French Catholic Opinion and Imperial Expansion, 1880-1886. Harvard 1965

P94 Perkins, Robert C. Independence for Kenya: A Study in the Development of British Colonial Policy, 1955-1963. SC 1968

P95 Perkins, Van L. Crisis in Agriculture: The Agricultural Adjustment Administration from Its Inception to the Peek Resignation. Harvard 1966

P96 Perlinski, Jerome J. A Stem of Man: Theory of History in Teilhard de Chardin. St L 1968

P97 Perman, John M. Southern Politics and American Reunion, 1865-1914. Chicago 1969

P98 Permenter, Hannelore R. The Personality and Cultural Interests of the Empress Catherine II as Revealed in Her Correspondence with Friedrich Melchoir Grimm. Tex U 1969

P99 Permenter, Wayne E. The Academy of Science at Toulouse in the Eighteenth Century. Tex U 1964

P100 Pernoud, Mary A. Tradition and Innovation in Ockham's Theory of Divine Omnipotence: A Study of Possibility and Singularity. St L 1969

P101 Perrin, John W. *Legatus* in Roman Law and the Legists. Wis 1964

P102   Perry, John A.   A History of the East Indian Indentured Worker in Trinidad, 1845-1917. LSU 1969

P103   Perry, John C.   Great Britain and the Imperial Japanese Navy, 1858-1905. Harvard 1962

P104   Perry, Lewis C.   Antislavery and Anarchy: A Study of the Ideas of Abolitionism before the Civil War. Cornell 1967

P105   Perry, Percival.   The Naval Stores Industry in the Ante-Bellum South, 1789-1861. Duke 1947

P106   Persell, Stuart M.   The French Colonial Lobby, 1899-1914. Stanford 1969

P107   Pertzoff, Margaret H.   "Lady in Red": A Study of the Early Career of Alexandra Mikhailovna Kollontai. Va 1968

P108   Perzel, Edward S.   The First Generation of Settlement in Colonial Ipswich, Massachusetts, 1633-1660. Rutgers 1967

P108a   Pescatello, Ann M.   Both Ends of the Journey: An Historical Study of Migration and Change in Brazil and Portugal, 1889-1914. UCLA 1970

P108b   Pešek, Thomas G.   Karel Havlíček and the Origins of Czech Political Life. Ind 1970

P109   Peskin, Allan J.   James A. Garfield, 1831-1863. Case W Reserve 1965

P110   Petersen, Eric F.   Prelude to Progressivism: California Election Reform, 1870-1909. UCLA 1969

P110a   Petersen, Neal H.   Nor Call Too Loud on Freedom: The Department of State, General de Gaulle, and the Levant Crisis of 1945. Georgetown 1970

P111   Petersen, Richard J.   Scottish Common Sense in America, 1768-1850: An Evaluation of Its Influence. Am 1963

P112   Peterson, Charles A.   The Autonomy of the Northeastern Provinces in the Period following the An Lu-shan Rebellion. Wash U 1966

P113   Peterson, Charles S.   Settlement on the Little Colorado, 1873-1900: A Study of the Processes and Institutions of Mormon Expansion. Utah 1967

P114   Peterson, Dale A.   Lumbering on the Chippewa: The Eau Claire Area, 1845-1885. Minn 1970

P115   Peterson, Dale W.   The Diplomatic and Commercial Relations between the United States and Peru from 1883 to 1918. Minn 1969

P116   Peterson, John E.   Freetown: A Study of the Dynamics of Liberated African Society, 1807-1870. Northwestern 1963

P117   Peterson, Jon A.   The Origins of the Comprehensive City Planning Ideal in the United States, 1840-1911. Harvard 1967

P119   Peterson, Raymond G., Jr.   George Washington, Capitalistic Farmer: A Documentary Study of Washington's Business Activities and the Sources of His Wealth. Ohio 1970

P120   Petroelje, Marvin J.   Levi Lincoln, Sr., Jeffersonian Republican of Massachusetts. Mich S 1969

P121   Petropulos, John A.   Political Parties, Statecraft, and the Politics of Absolutism in the Kingdom of Greece (1833-1843). Harvard 1963

P122   Petrowski, William R.   The Kansas Pacific: A Study in Railroad Promotion. Wis 1966

P123   Petrowsky, Clarence L.   Kansas Agriculture before 1900. Okla 1968

P124   Petschauer, Peter.   The Education and Development of an Enlightened Absolutist: The Youth of Catherine the Great, 1729-1762. NYU 1969

P125   Pettit, Arthur G.   Mark Twain, Southerner, and His Attitude toward the Negro. Cal, Berkeley 1970

P126   Phelan, Doris A.   Boosterism in Saint Louis, 1810-1860. St L 1970

P127   Philipp, Kurt D.   The Independent Socialist's Attempt to Govern Germany, November-December, 1918. Kans U 1969

P128   Philips, R. Craig.   The Life and Political Thought of Simonde de Sismondi. Chicago 1968

P129   Phillips, Earl H.   The Church Missionary Society, the Imperial Factor, and Yoruba Politics, 1842-1873. S Cal 1966

P130   Phillips, Howard J.   The U. S. Diplomatic Establishment in the Critical Period, 1783-1789. Notre D 1968

P131   Phillips, John D.   The Politics of State School Support: California as a Case Study, 1919-1960. Stanford 1965

P132   Phillips, Kim T.   William Duane, Revolutionary Editor. Cal, Berkeley 1968

P133   Phillips, Paul D.   A History of the Freedmen's Bureau in Tennessee. Vanderbilt 1964

P134 Phillips, Thomas D. The Black Regulars: Negro Soldiers in the United States Army, 1866-1891. Wis 1970

P135 Philp, Kenneth R. John Collier and the American Indian, 1920-1945. Mich S 1968

P136 Phinney, Edward S. Alfred B. Meacham, Promoter of Indian Reform. Ore 1963

P137 Piazza, Richard M. Ludendorff: The Totalitarian and *Voelkisch* Politics of a Military Specialist. Northwestern 1969

P138 Pickard, Mary H. Symon Patrick, 1626-1707, Bishop of Ely: Divine, Theologian, Ecclesiastical Statesman. Wis 1961

P139 Pickens, Donald K. American Eugenists: Conservative Naturalists as Progressives. Tex U 1964

P140 Pickering, James D. The Legend of Hereward the Saxon: An Investigation of *De Gestis Herwardi Saxonis,* Its Historical Basis, Its Debt to Saga and Early Romance, Its Place in English Literary History. Columbia 1964

P141 Picó, Fernando A. The Bishops of France in the Reign of Louis IX (1226-1270). JH 1970

P142 Pidhaini, Oleg O. The Formation of the Ukrainian Republic in the First World War, 1917-1918. McGill 1965

P143 Pierard, Richard V. The German Colonial Society, 1882-1914. Ia 1964

P144 Pierce, Gerald S. The Army of the Texas Republic, 1836-1845. Miss U 1963

P145 Pierson, Peter O. The Seventh Duke of Medina Sidonia and the Defense Establishment in Andalusia, 1575-1598. UCLA 1967

P146 Pietraszek, Bernadine F. San Martín and Free Trade: Theory and Fact, 1812-1822. Loyola 1966

P147 Pilapil, Vincente R. Spain in the European State-System, 1898-1913. Cath 1964

P148 Pilcher, George W. Preacher of the New Light: Samuel Davies, 1724-1761. Ill 1963

P149 Pilgrim, Donald G. The Uses and Limitations of French Naval Power in the Reign of Louis XIV: The Administration of the Marquis de Seignelay, 1683-1690. Brown 1969

P150 Pililis, George. The Beginnings of Christian Monachism. Fordham 1969

P151 Pinchuk, Ben-Cion. The Octobrists in the Third Duma, 1907-1912. Wash U 1970

P152 Pinckney, Paul J. A Cromwellian Parliament: The Elections and Personnel of 1656. Vanderbilt 1962

P153 Pine, Martin. Pietro Pomponazzi and the Immortality Controversy, 1516-1524. Columbia 1965

P154 Pintner, Walter M. Count Kankrin's Administration, 1823-1844. Harvard 1962

P155 Piper, Linda J. A History of Sparta, 323-146 B.C. Ohio 1966

P156 Pitchford, Louis C., Jr. The Diplomatic Representatives from the United States to Mexico from 1836 to 1848. Colo 1965

P157 Pittman, Walter E. Richmond P. Hobson, Crusader. Ga 1969

P158 Pitzer, Donald E. Professional Revivalism in Nineteenth-Century Ohio. Ohio 1966

P159 Pivar, David J. The New Abolitionism: The Quest for Social Purity, 1876-1900. Penn U 1965

P160 Place, Frank R. French Policy and the Turkish War, 1679-1688. Minn 1963

P161 Plakans, Andrejs. The National Awakening in Latvia, 1850-1900. Harvard 1969

P162 Platt, Franklin D. The English Parliamentary Radicals—Their Collective Character, Their Failure to Find a Leader: A Study in the Psycho-sociological Sources of Radical Behavior, 1833-1841. Wash St L 1969

P163 Platt, Herman N. K. The Political Reminiscences of Charles Perrin Smith, New Jersey Republican. Rutgers 1963

P164 Platt, Wilfred C., Jr. Egypt on the Eve of the Great War. Ga 1966

P165 Plavchan, Ronald J. A History of Anheuser-Busch, 1852-1933. St L 1969

P166 Plough, James H. Catholic Colleges and the Catholic Educational Association: The Foundation and Early Years of the CEA, 1899-1919. Notre D 1967

P167 Pluth, Edward J. The Administration and Operation of German Prisoner of War Camps in the United States during World War II. Ball State 1970

P168 Poe, William A. The Suppression of the Academies during the French Revolution. Ala 1968

P169   Poen, Monte M.   The Truman Administration and National Health Insurance. Mo 1967

P170   Pohl, James W.   The General Staff and American Military Policy: The Formative Period, 1898-1917. Tex U 1967

P171   Poindexter, Harry E.   From Copy Desk to Congress: The Pre-Congressional Career of Carter Glass. Va 1966

P172   Poinsatte, Charles R.   Fort Wayne, Indiana during the Canal Era, 1828-1855: A Study of a Western Community during the Middle Period of American History. Notre D 1964

P173   Pois, Robert A.   Friedrich Meinecke and German Politics in the Twentieth Century. Wis 1965

P174   Poivan, James H.   The British Labour Party and International Sanctions, 1918-1935. Rutgers 1968

P175   Polakoff, Keith I.   The Disorganized Democracy: An Institutional Study of the Democratic Party, 1872-1880. Northwestern 1968

P176   Polenberg, Richard.   Franklin D. Roosevelt and the Reorganization Controversy, 1936-1939. Columbia 1964

P177   Polich, John L.   Foreign Maritime Intrusion on Spain's Pacific Coast, 1786-1810. NM 1968

P178   Polinski, Gerald R.   Benjamin Franklin: Scientist-Inventor. St L 1968

P179   Polishook, Irwin H.   Rhode Island and the Union, 1774-1790: A Study in State History during the Confederation Era. Northwestern 1961

P180   Polka, Leon B.   The Religious Thought of Lorenzo Valla. Harvard 1964

P181   Pollard, Alan P.   Consciousness and Crisis: The Self-Image of the Russian Intelligentsia, 1855-1882. Cal, Berkeley 1968

P182   Pollitt, Ronald L.   The Elizabethan Navy Board: A Study in Administrative Evolution. Northwestern 1968

P183   Pollock, Norman H.   The English Game Laws in the Nineteenth Century. JH 1968

P184   Pompa, Edward M.   Canadian Foreign Policy during the Suez Crisis of 1956. St John's 1969

P185   Pomper, Philip.   Peter Lavrov: His Life and Thought. Chicago 1965

P186   Poole, Richard S.   The Indian Problem in the Third Provincial Council of Mexico (1585). St L 1961

P187   Poole, Walter S.   The Quest for a Republican Foreign Policy, 1941-1951. Penn U 1968

P188   Poor, Harold L.   Kurt Tucholsky: A Leftist Intellectual Views the Weimar Republic. Columbia 1965

P189   Poor, Matile R.   A Study of the Political Ideas of Denis Diderot. Columbia 1969

P190   Popofsky, Linda S.   The Lawyers and the Crown: The Political Leadership of the Barristers in the Parliament of 1628-1629. Cal, Berkeley 1970

P191   Porten, Bezalel.   The Elephantine Jewish Community: Studies in the Life and Society of an Ancient Military Colony. Columbia 1964

P192   Porter, Dale H.   The Defense of the British Slave Trade, 1784-1807. Ore 1967

P193   Porter, Earl W.   A History of Trinity College, 1892-1924: Foundations of Duke University. Duke 1961

P194   Porter, Henry P., Jr.   Strategy, Speculation, and Capitulation: The Background to British East Africa, 1873-1890. Duke 1965

P195   Porter, Jack W.   Bernhard Rothmann, 1495-1535, Royal Orator of the Münster Anabaptist Kingdom. Wis 1964

P196   Porter, Lorle A.   Social Status at the Court of Alfonso VIII of Castile. NM 1965

P197   Porter, Patrick G.   The Changing Distribution System in American Manufacturing, 1870-1900. JH 1970

P198   Porterfield, Charles E.   A Rhetorical-Historical Analysis of the Third Party Movement in Alabama, 1890-1894. LSU 1965

P199   Portuondo, Emma.   The Impact of Bishop Charles Henry Brent upon American Colonial and Foreign Policy, 1901-1917. Cath 1969

P200   Posey, John P.   David Hunter Miller at the Paris Peace Conference, November 1918-May 1919. Ga 1962

P201   Post, Ernest H., Jr.   A Century of Ecumenical and Unionist Tendencies in the Reformed Church in America, 1850-1950. Mich S 1966

P202   Post, Gaines, Jr.   German Foreign Policy and Military Planning: The Polish Question, 1924-1929. Stanford 1969

P203   Post, John D.   The Economic Crisis of 1816-1817 and Its Social and Political Consequences. Boston U 1969

P204   Poster, Mark S.   The Utopian Thought of Restif de la Bretonne. NYU 1968

P205   Postma, Johannes.   The Dutch Participation in the African Slave Trade: Slaving on the Guinea Coast, 1675-1795. Mich S 1970

P206   Potter, Raymond J.   Royal Samuel Copeland, 1868-1938: A Physician in Politics. Case W Reserve 1967

P207   Pottinger, Evelyn A.   Napoleon III and the German Crisis, 1865-1866. Radcliffe 1962

P208   Potts, Louis W.   Arthur Lee: American Revolutionary. Duke 1970

P209   Powell, Benjamin.   Coal, Philadelphia, and the Schuylkill. Lehigh 1968

P210   Powell, David O.   The Union Party of 1936. Ohio 1962

P211   Powell, Milton B.   The Abolitionist Controversy in the Methodist Episcopal Church, 1840-1864. Ia 1963

P212   Powers, James F.   The Municipal Armies of León and Castile from the Early Reconquest to 1252: A Study in the Expansion of the Medieval Iberian Frontier. Va 1966

P213   Powers, Stephen T.   The Decline and Extinction of American Naval Power, 1781-1787. Notre D 1965

P214   Powles, Cyril H.   Victorian Missionaries in Meiji Japan: The Shiba Sect, 1873-1900. British Columbia 1968

P215   Prasad, Sajja A.   Country of the Soul: Some Japanese Varieties of Patriotic Experience, 1600-1700. A Descriptive Essay. Harvard 1970

P216   Pratt, William C.   The Reading Socialist Experience: A Study of Working Class Politics. Emory 1969

P217   Predergast, Patricia A.   History of the London Missionary Society in British New Guinea, 1871-1901. Hawaii 1968

P218   Prescott, Gerald L.   Yeomen, Entrepreneurs, and Gentry: A Comparative Study of Three Wisconsin Agricultural Organizations, 1873-1893. Wis 1968

P219   Preston, Joseph H.   English Ecclesiastical Historiography: From Foxe to Lingard. Mo 1966

P220   Preston, Robert M.   Toward a Better World: The Christian Moralist as Scientific Reformer. Cath 1969

P222   Price, Don C.   The Chinese Intelligentsia's Image of Russia, 1896-1911. Harvard 1968

P223   Price, Glenn W.   The Origins of the War with Mexico: The Polk-Stockton Intrigue. S Cal 1966

P224   Price, Jack D.   Behemoth Unborn: The Idea of a Continental Coalition against Great Britain, 1899-1900. SC 1966

P225   Price, Joedd.   Ecuadorian Opinions of the United States in the Nineteenth Century: An Attitudinal Study. NC 1968

P226   Prince, Carl E.   New Jersey's Democratic Republicans, 1790-1817: A Study of Early Party Machinery. Rutgers 1963

P227   Prince, Vinton M., Jr.   Major-General Thomas Harrison in Politics, 1648-1653. Va 1969

P228   Pringle, James W.   The Committee for Compounding with Delinquents, 1643-1654: A Study of Parliamentary Finance during the English Civil Wars. Ill 1961

P229   Pringle, Robert M.   The Ibans of Sarawak under Brooke Rule, 1841-1941. Cornell 1967

P230   Prinz, Andrew K.   Sir William Gooch in Virginia: The King's Good Servant. Northwestern 1963

P231   Prisco, Salvatore, III.   John Barrett, Exponent of Commercial Expansion: A Study of a Progressive Era Diplomat, 1887-1920. Rutgers 1969

P232   Pritchard, Robert L.   Southern Politics in the Truman Administration: Georgia as a Test Case. UCLA 1970

P233   Procko, Bohdan P.   The Byzantine Catholic Province of Philadelphia: A History of the Ukrainian Catholic Church in the U.S.A. Ottawa 1963

P234   Procter, Ben H.   John H. Reagan. Harvard 1961

P235   Proctor Donald J.   From Insurrection to Independence: The Continental Congress and the Military Launching of the American Revolution. S Cal 1965

P236   Proctor, Raymond L.   The "Blue Division": An Episode in German-Spanish Wartime Relations. Ore 1966

P237   Provan, James G.   The Political Career of Sidney Herbert, 1845-1860. Case W Reserve 1969

P238   Prowe, Diethelm M.   City between Crises: The International Relations of West Berlin from the

End of the Berlin Blockade in 1949 to the Khrushchev Ultimatum of 1958. Stanford 1967

P238a   Pruessen, Ronald W.   Toward the Threshold: John Foster Dulles, 1888-1939. Penn U 1968

P239   Pryce, Donald B.   German Government Policies towards the Radical Left, 1918-1923. Stanford 1970

P240   Pryke, Kenneth G.   Nova Scotia and Confederation, 1864-1870. Duke 1962

P241   Pugach, Noel H.   Progress, Prosperity and the Open Door: The Ideas and Career of Paul S. Reinsch. Wis 1967

P242   Pugh, Evelyn L.   John Stuart Mill in America: The Early Impact, 1843-1873. Am 1966

P243   Pullapilly, Cyriak K.   Caesar Baronius: Counter Reformation Historian. Chicago 1969

P244   Pulley, Judith P.   Thomas Jefferson at the Court of Versailles: An American *Philosophe* and the Coming of the French Revolution. Va 1966

P245   Pulley, Raymond H.   Old Virginia Restored: An Interpretation of the Progressive Impulse. Va 1966

P246   Pulliam, William E.   Political Propaganda in the Secondary School History Program of National Socialist Germany, 1933-1945. Ill 1968

P247   Pulman, Michael B.   The Elizabethan Privy Council, 1568-1582. Cal, Berkeley 1964

P248   Purcell, David C.   Japanese Expansion in the South Pacific, 1890-1935. Penn U 1967

P249   Purcell, Edward A., Jr.   The Crisis of Democratic Theory: American Thought between the Wars, 1919-1941. Wis 1968

P250   Purdy, Virginia C.   Portrait of a Know-Nothing Legislature: The Massachusetts General Court of 1855. Geo W 1970

P251   Purifoy, Lewis M., Jr.   The Methodist Episcopal Church, South, and Slavery, 1844-1865. NC 1965

P252   Pursell, Carroll W.   Stationary Steam Engines in America before the Civil War. Cal, Berkeley 1962

P253   Pursinger, Marvin G.   Oregon's Japanese in World War II: A History of Compulsory Relocation. S Cal 1961

P254   Pusateri, Cosmo J.   A Businessman in Politics: David R. Francis, Missouri Democrat. St L 1965

P255   Putnam, George F.   The Russian Non-Revolutionary Intelligentsia Evaluates Its Relation to the Russian Folk (1900-1910). Harvard 1962

P256   Putnam, Jackson K.   The Influence of the Older Age Groups on California Politics, 1920-1940. Stanford 1964

P257   Pyle, Kenneth B.   The New Generation: Young Japanese in Search of National Identity, 1887-1895. JH 1965

P258   Pyle, Norman R.   A Study of United States' Propaganda Efforts and Pro-Allied Sentiments in Argentina during World War II. Georgetown 1968

Q

Q1   Qanungo, Bhupen.   Lord Canning's Administration and the Modernization of India, 1856-1862. Ind 1962

Q1a   Quandt, Jean B.   From the Small Town to the Great Community: The Idea of Community in the Progressive Period. Rutgers 1969

Q2   Quay, William L.   Philadelphia Democrats, 1880-1910. Lehigh 1969

Q3   Quealey, Francis M.   The Administration of Sir Peregrine Maitland, Lieutenant-Governor of Upper Canada, 1818-1828. Toronto 1968

Q4   Quebbeman, Frances E.   Medicine in Territorial Arizona. Ariz 1966

Q5   Quiason, Serafin D.   English Trade Relations with the Philippines, 1644-1765. Penn U 1962

Q6   Quigley, Robert E.   American Catholic Opinions of Mexican Anticlericalism, 1910-1936. Penn U 1965

Q7   Quinn, Charlotte A.   Traditionalism, Islam and European Expansion: The Gambia, 1850-1890. UCLA 1967

Q8   Quinn, Joseph R.   The U.S.-USSR Exchange Agreements in Public Health, 1958-1967. Georgetown 1968

Q9   Quinn, Larry D.   Politicians in Business: A History of the Montana State Liquor Control System, 1933-1968. Mont 1970

Q10   Quinn, Maria Margaret, Sister.   William Henry Harrison Miller, Attorney General of the United States, 1889-1893. Cath 1965

Q11   Quinney, Valerie Y.   The Committee on Colonies of the French Constituent Assembly, 1789-1791. Wis 1967

Q12   Quitt, Martin H.   Virginia House of Burgesses, 1660-1706: The Social, Educational and Economic Bases of Political Power. Wash St L 1970

R

R1   Raat, William D.   Positivism in Díaz Mexico, 1876-1910: An Essay in Intellectual History. Utah 1967

R2   Rabb, Theodore K.   The Early Life of Sir Edwin Sandys and Jacobean London. Princeton 1961

R3   Rabe, Valentin H.   The American Protestant Foreign Mission Movement, 1880-1920. Harvard 1965

R4   Rabinowitch, Alexander.   The Petrograd Bolsheviks and the June and July Demonstrations of 1917. Ind 1965

R5   Rachum, Ilan.   Nationalism and Revolution in Brazil, 1922-1930: A Study of Intellectual, Military and Political Protesters and of the Assault on the Old Republic. Columbia 1970

R6   Racine, Philip N.   Atlanta's Schools: A History of the Public School System, 1869-1955. Emory 1969

R7   Radabaugh, Jack S.   The Military System of Colonial Massachusetts, 1690-1740. S Cal 1965

R8   Radcliffe, David J.   Education and Cultural Change among the Malays, 1900-1940. Wis 1970

R9   Rader, Benjamin G.   The Professor as a Reformer: Richard T. Ely, 1854-1943. Md 1964

R10   Rader, Ronald R.   Decline of the Afghan Problem as a Crisis Factor in Russian Foreign Policy, 1892-1907. Syracuse 1965

R11   Raditsa, Leo F.   A Historical Commentary to Sallust's *Letter of Mithridates.* Columbia 1969

R12   Radosh, Ronald.   The Development of the Corporate Ideology of American Labor Leaders, 1914-1933. Wis 1967

R13   Radvany, Egon.   Metternich's Projects for Reform in Austria. CUNY 1969

R14   Rady, Donald E.   Brazil's Volta Redonda Steel Center: A Quarter Century of Progress, 1941-1966. Cal, Berkeley 1967

R15   Ragan, Fred D.   *The New Republic:* Red Hysteria and Civil Liberties. Ga 1965

R16   Ragsdale, Hugh A., Jr.   Russian Diplomacy in the Age of Napoleon: The Franco-Russian Rapprochement of 1800-1801. Va 1964

R17   Rainbolt, John C.   The Virginia Vision: A Political History of the Efforts to Diversify the Economy of the Old Dominion, 1650-1706. Wis 1966

R18   Rainey, Thomas B., Jr.   The Union of 17 October: An Experiment in Moderate Constitutionalism (1905-1906). Ill 1966

R19   Rainsford, George N.   Federal Assistance to Higher Education in the Nineteenth Century. Stanford 1968

R20   Ralston, David B.   The Army and the Republic: The Place of the Military in the Political and Constitutional Evolution of France, 1871-1914. Columbia 1964

R21   Ramage, Jean H.   The English Woolen Industry and Parliament, 1750-1830: A Study in Economic Attitudes and Political Pressure. Yale 1970

R22   Ramage, Thomas W.   Augustus Owsley Stanley: Early Twentieth Century Kentucky Democrat. Ky 1968

R23   Rammelkamp, Julian S.   Pulitzer's *Post Dispatch:* Its Formative Years, 1878-1883. Harvard 1961

R24   Ramsdell, Daniel B.   Japan's China Policy (1929-1931): A Fateful Failure. Wis 1961

R25   Ramsey, Robert W.   Carolina Cradle: Settlement of the Northwest Carolina Frontier, 1747-1762. NC 1964

R26   Ramusack, Barbara N.   Indian Princes as Imperial Politicians, 1914-1939. Mich U 1969

R27   Randall, Francis B.   The Major Prophets of Russian Peasant Socialism: A Study in the Social Thought of N. K. Mikhailovskii and V. M. Chernov. Columbia 1961

R28   Randall, Henry C.   Public Disorder in England and Wales, 1765-1775. NC 1963

R29   Randall, Robert W.   Anatomy of a Failure: The British Real del Monte Mining Company in Mexico, 1824-1849. Harvard 1965

R30   Randolph, J. Ralph.   British Travelers among the Southern Indians, 1660-1763. NM 1970

R31   Rankin, Mary Louise B.   Student Revolutionaries in Shanghai and Chekiang, 1902-1907. Harvard 1966

R32 Ranlett, John. Railway Members of the House of Commons, 1841-1847: A Cross-Section of the Political Nation. Harvard 1967

R33 Ransel, David L. Nikita Panin's Role in Russian Court Politics of the Seventeen Sixties: A Critique of the Gentry Opposition Thesis. Yale 1969

R33a Ransome, Joyce O. Cotton Mather and the Catholic Spirit. Cal, Berkeley 1966

R34 Rappaport, Rhoda. Guettard, Lavoisie, and Monnet: Geologists in the Service of the French Monarchy. Cornell 1964

R35 Rappe, Marion L. The Austrian Christian Social Movement, 1885-1897. Cal, Berkeley 1960

R36 Rapson, Richard L. The British Traveler in America, 1860-1935. Columbia 1966

R37 Rasmussen, John P. The American Imperialist Elite: A Study in the Concept of National Efficiency. Stanford 1962

R38 Rasporich, Anthony W. The Development of Political and Social Ideas in the Province of Canada, 1848-1858. Manitoba 1970

R39 Rassekh, Nosratollah. Lord Bryce and the American Commonwealth: An Analysis of His Works and His Views. Stanford 1962

R40 Ratner, Lorman A. Northern Opposition to the Anti-Slavery Movement, 1831-1840. Cornell 1961

R41 Rattan, Sumitra. The Four-Power Treaty of 1921 and the American National Interest. Am 1967

R42 Ratté, John E. The Kingdom of Heaven and the Church of the Future: The Modernist Religious Philosophies of Alfred Firmin Loisy, George Tyrrell, and William Laurence Sullivan. Harvard 1962

R43 Rauch, Rufus W., Jr. Politics and Beliefs in Modern France: Emmanuel Mounier and the Christian Democratic Movement, 1932-1950. Columbia 1964

R44 Raucher, Alan R. The Emergence of Public Relations in Business, 1900-1929. Penn U 1964

R45 Raun, Toivo U. The Revolution of 1905 and the Movement for Estonian National Autonomy, 1896-1907. Princeton 1969

R46 Ravitch, Norman. Government and Episcopate in the Age of Aristocracy: France and England in the 18th Century. Princeton 1962

R47 Rawlyk, George A. New England and Louisbourg, 1744-1745. Rochester 1966

R48 Rawson, Donald M. Party Politics in Mississippi, 1850-1860. Vanderbilt 1964

R49 Rayfield, Jo Ann. Daniel Florencio O'Leary: From Bolivarian General to British Diplomat, 1834-1854. Vanderbilt 1969

R50 Read, Ira B. The Origin and Development of the Idea of the Levée en masse in the French Revolution. Emory 1965

R51 Ready, Milton L. An Economic History of Colonial Georgia, 1732-1754. Ga 1970

R52 Reagan, Hugh D. The Presidential Campaign of 1928 in Alabama. Tex U 1961

R53 Reardon, Michael F. Providence and Tradition in the Writings of Bonald, de Maistre, Ballanche and Buchez, 1793-1848. Ind 1965

R54 Rearick, Charles W. Historians and Folklore in Nineteenth-Century France. Harvard 1968

R55 Rebane, Peep P. Denmark and the Baltic Crusade, 1150-1227. Mich S 1969

R56 Reed, Gerard A. The Ross-Watie Conflict: Factionalism in the Cherokee Nation, 1839-1865. Okla 1967

R57 Reed, Germaine M. David Boyd: Southern Educator. LSU 1970

R58 Reed, John J. American Diplomatic Relations with Australia during the Second World War. S Cal 1970

R59 Reed, Nathaniel. The Role of the Connecticut State Government in the Development of Inland Transportation Facilities from 1784 to 1821. Yale 1964

R60 Reed, Richard B. Sir Robert Cecil and the Diplomacy of the Anglo-Spanish Peace, 1603-1604. Wis 1970

R60a Reeder, Clarence A. The History of Utah's Railroads, 1869-1883. Utah 1970

R61 Reeder, Ray M. The Mormon Trail: A History of the Salt Lake to Los Angeles Route to 1869. Brigham Young 1966

R62 Reedy, William T. The Itinerant Royal Judicature in England in the Reign of Henry I, 1100-1135. JH 1963

R63 Reel, Jerome V. The Parliament of 1316. Emory 1967

R64 Reese, Calvin L. The United States Army and the Indian: Low Plains Area, 1815-1854. S Cal 1964

R65 Reese, James V. The Worker in Texas, 1821-1876. Tex U 1964

R66 Reeves, A. Compton. The Welch Marcher Lordship of Newport, 1317-1536. Emory 1967

R67 Reeves, Thomas C. The Fund for the Republic, 1951-1957: An Unusual Chapter in the History of American Philanthropy. Cal, Santa Barbara 1966

R68 Reeves, William D. The Politics of Public Works, 1933-1935. Tulane 1968

R69 Regehr, Theodore D. The Canadian Northern Railway: Agent of Growth, 1896-1911. Alberta 1967

R70 Reid, Bill G. Proposed American Plans for Soldier Settlement during the World War I Period. Okla 1963

R71 Reid, Jasper B., Jr. "The Mephistopheles of Southern Politics": A Critical Analysis of Some of the Political Thought of Alexander Hamilton Stephens, Vice-President of the Confederacy. Mich U 1966

R72 Reid, Robert L. The Professionalization of Public School Teachers: The Chicago Experience, 1895-1920. Northwestern 1968

R73 Reiger, John F. George Bird Grinnell and the Development of American Conservation, 1870-1901. Northwestern 1970

R74 Reill, Peter H. The Rise of the Historical Consciousness during the Enlightenment at the University of Göttingen, 1735-1780. Northwestern 1969

R75 Reilly, Bernard F. The Nature of Church Reform at Santiago de Compostela during the Episcopate of Don Diego Gelmirez, 1100-1140 A.D. Bryn Mawr 1966

R76 Reilly, Mary Lonan, Sister. A History of the Catholic Press Association, 1911-1968. Notre D 1970

R77 Reimers, David M. Protestant Churches and the Negro: A Study of Several Major Protestant Denominations and the Negro from World War One to 1954. Wis 1961

R78 Reinerman, Alan J. The Papacy and the Restoration of Europe: The Diplomacy of Cardinal Consalvi, 1814-1823. Loyola 1964

R79 Reinhardt, William W. The Legislative Council of the Punjab, 1897-1912. Duke 1969

R80 Reinitz, Richard M. Symbolism and Freedom: The Use of Biblical Typology as an Argument for Religious Toleration in Seventeenth Century England and America. Rochester 1967

R81 Reitman, Renee L. A. Pierre Charron: The Crisis in Morality and Thought at the End of the Sixteenth Century in France. Mich U 1969

R82 Remington, Rodger A. The Function of the "Conspiracy Theory" in American Intellectual History. St L 1965

R83 Remmey, Paul B. British Diplomacy and the Far East, 1892-1898. Harvard 1965

R84 Renaldo, John J. M. Daniello Bartoli: Historian. Chicago 1967

R86 Renkiewicz, Frank A. The Polish Settlement of St. Joseph County, Indiana, 1855-1935. Notre D 1967

R87 Renna, Thomas J. Royalist Political Thought in France, 1285-1303. Brown 1970

R88 Rennie, Ian S. Evangelicalism and English Public Life, 1823-1850. Toronto 1963

R89 Renzi, William A., Jr. In the Shadow of the Sword: Italy's Neutrality and Entrance into the Great War, 1914-1915. Md 1968

R90 Renzulli, Libero M., Jr. Maryland Federalism, 1787-1819. Va 1962

R91 Repczuk, Helma J. Nicholas Mordvinov (1754-1845): Russia's Would-be Reformer. Columbia 1962

R92 Resch, John P. Anglo-American Efforts in Prison Reform, 1850-1900: The Work of Thomas Barwick Lloyd Baker. Ohio 1969

R93 Resh, Richard W. Tutors to Society: Five American Intellectuals and War, 1917-1945. Wis 1966

R94 Resis, Albert. The Profintern: Origins to 1923. Columbia 1964

R95 Resnick, Daniel P. The White Terror and the Political Reaction of 1815-1816 in France. Harvard 1962

R95a Resnick, Enoch F. The Council of State and Spanish America, 1814-1820. Am 1970

R96 Resovich, Thomas. France in Transition: Pre-Vichy Diplomatic and Political Realignments, May 10-June 25, 1940. Wis 1966

R97   Reuter, William C.   Anglophobia in American Politics, 1865-1900. Cal, Berkeley 1966

R98   Reynolds, Clark G.   History and Development of the Fast Carrier Task Forces, 1943-1945. Duke 1964

R99   Reynolds, Donald E.   Southern Newspapers in the Secession Crisis, 1860-1861. Tulane 1966

R100   Reynolds, Michael C.   Paul Painlevé and the Parliamentary Crisis in France in 1917. Northwestern 1966

R101   Reynolds, Robert L.   Benevolence on the Home Front in Massachusetts during the Civil War. Boston U 1970

R102   Rheault, Michel.   La Noblesse au Canada (1636-1686). Ottawa 1967

R103   Rhoads, James B.   The Campaign of the Socialist Party in the Election of 1920. Am 1965

R104   Rhodes, Benjamin D.   The United States and the War Debt Question, 1917-1934. Colo 1965

R105   Rhyne, George N.   The Constitutional Democratic Party from Its Origins through the First State Duma. NC 1968

R106   Rice, Lawrence D.   The Negro in Texas, 1874-1900. Tex Tech 1967

R107   Rice, Mary C.   Holmes and Laski on Natural Law. Boston U 1962

R108   Rich, Myra L.   The Experimental Years: Virginia, 1781-1789. Yale 1965

R109   Richard, Alfred C., Jr.   The Panama Canal in American National Consciousness, 1870-1922. Boston U 1969

R110   Richards, Carolyn H.   Chilean Attitudes toward the United States, 1860-1867. Stanford 1970

R111   Richards, Ira D.   The Urban Frontier: Little Rock in the Nineteenth Century. Tulane 1964

R112   Richards, James O.   English Parliamentary Elections and Party Propaganda in the Early Eighteenth Century. Ill 1962

R113   Richards, Kent D.   Growth and Development of Government in the Far West: The Oregon Provisional Government, Jefferson Territory, Provisional and Territorial Nevada. Wis 1966

R114   Richards, Leonard L.   Gentlemen of Property and Standing: A Study of Northern Anti-Abolition Mobs. Cal, Davis 1968

R115   Richards, Michael D.   Reform or Revolution: Rosa Luxemburg and the Marxist Movement, 1893-1919. Duke 1969

R116   Richards, Noel J.   The Political and Social Impact of British Nonconformity in the Late Nineteenth Century, 1870-1902. Wis 1968

R117   Richardson, Charles O.   The Ideas of Napoleon III on the Principle of Self-Determination of Nationalities and Their Influence on His Foreign Policies. Georgetown 1963

R118   Richardson, James F.   The History of Police Protection in New York City, 1800-1870. NYU 1961

R119   Richardson, Joe M.   The Negro in the Reconstruction of Florida. Fla S 1963

R120   Richardson, Ralph D.   Comintern Army: The International Brigades in the Spanish Civil War. Md 1969

R121   Richardson, William J.   Alexander Campbell's Use of History in His Apologetical Theology. Ore 1962

R122   Richman, Irwin.   The Brightest Ornament: A Biography of Nathaniel Chapman, M.D., 1780-1853. Penn U 1965

R123   Richter, Donald C.   Public Order and Popular Disturbances in Great Britain, 1865-1914. Md 1965

R124   Ricketson, William F., Jr.   A Puritan Approach to Manifest Destiny: Case Studies from Artillery Election Sermons. Ga 1965

R125   Rickey, Roger M.   Southeast Asia, Crossroads of Civilization: A Comparative Study of Conflicting Influences and Early European Explorations. Denver 1966

R126   Riddle, John M.   Amber and Ambergris in Materia Medica during Antiquity and the Middle Ages. NC 1964

R127   Ridgley, Ronald H.   Railroads and the Development of the Dakotas, 1872-1914. Ind 1967

R127a   Ridley, Jack B.   Marshal Bugeaud, the July Monarchy and the Question of Algeria, 1841-1847: A Study in Civil-Military Relations. Okla 1970

R128   Riedlsperger, Max E.   The Third-Party Movement in Post-World War II Austria: Right-Wing Extremism or *Dritte Kraft?* Colo 1969

R129   Rienstra, Miller H.   Giovanni Battista della Porta and Renaissance Science. Mich U 1963

R130   Riesterer, Berthold P.   Karl Löwith's View of History: A Humanist Alternative to Historicism. Wayne 1966

R131 Rietveld, Ronald D. The Moral Issue of Slavery in American Politics, 1854-1860. Ill 1967

R132 Rife, John M., Jr. The Political Career of Louis Barthou, 1889-1913. Ohio 1964

R133 Riggs, Alvin R. Arthur Lee and the Radical Whigs, 1768-1776. Yale 1967

R134 Riggs, Charles H., Jr. A History of Criminal Asylum in England from Ine to James I: A Study of the Medieval Institution of Temporary Asylum with Special Emphasis on the Custom of *Abjuratio Regni* from 1202 to 1279. Columbia 1962

R135 Righter, Robert W. Theodore Henry Hittell: A Biographical Study of a 19th Century California Historian and Intellectual. Cal, Santa Barbara 1968

R136 Riha, Thomas. Paul Miliukov's Parliamentary Career, 1907-1917. Harvard 1962

R137 Riley, G. Michael. The Estate of Fernando Cortés in the Cuernavaca Area of Mexico, 1522-1547. NM 1965

R138 Riley, Glenda L. G. From Chattel to Challenger: The Changing Image of the American Woman, 1828-1848. Ohio 1967

R139 Ringenbach, Paul T. Tramps and Reformers, 1873-1916: The Discovery of Unemployment in New York. Conn 1970

R140 Ringenberg, William C. The Protestant College on the Michigan Frontier. Mich S 1970

R141 Ringer, Fritz F. K. The German Universities and the Crisis of Learning, 1918-1932. Harvard 1961

R142 Ringrose, David R. Land Transportation in Eighteenth-Century Castile. Wis 1966

R143 Ripper, M. Marcella, Sister. The German Center Party from the November Revolution 1918 to the Adoption of the Weimar Constitution. Loyola 1967

R144 Rissler, Herbert J. Charles Warren Fairbanks: Conservative Hoosier. Ind 1961

R145 Ristuben, Peter J. Minnesota and the Competition for Immigrants. Okla 1964

R146 Ritchie, Galen B. The Asiatic Department during the Reign of Alexander II, 1855-1881. Columbia 1970

R147 Ritsch, Frederick F., Jr. The French Political Parties of the Left and European Integration, 1947-1949. Va 1962

R148 Ritter, Harry R., Jr. Hermann Neubacher and the German Occupation of the Balkans, 1940-1945. Va 1969

R149 Rizopoulos, Nicholas X. Greece at the Paris Peace Conference, 1919. Yale 1964

R150 Roach, Elmo E. Alexander I and the Unofficial Committee. Ohio 1968

R151 Robbert, George S. Matthias Flacius Illyricus' Treatment of Frederick Barbarossa in the *Magdeburg Centuries*. Ind 1964

R152 Robbins, David E., Jr. The Congressional Career of William Ralls Morrison. Ill 1963

R153 Robbins, Donald C. Joseph Story: The Early Years, 1779-1811. Ky 1965

R154 Robbins, James H. Voting Behavior in Massachusetts, 1800-1820: A Case Study. Northwestern 1970

R155 Robbins, John B. Confederate Nationalism: Politics and Government in the Confederate South, 1861-1865. Rice 1964

R156 Robbins, William G. The Far Western Frontier: Economic Opportunity and Social Democracy in Early Roseburg, Oregon. Ore 1969

R157 Roberson, Jere W. Construction Proposals for a Pacific Railroad, 1845-1860. Ga 1966

R158 Roberts, Andrew D. A Political History of the Bemba (North-Eastern Zambia), to 1900. Wis 1966

R159 Roberts, Warren E. Morality and the Social Classes in Eighteenth-Century French Literature and Painting. Cal, Berkeley 1966

R160 Robertson, James O. The Progressives in National Republican Politics, 1916 to 1921. Harvard 1964

R161 Robertson, John B. Lincoln and Congress. Wis 1966

R162 Robertson, Joseph R. The English Administration of Gascony, 1372-1390. Emory 1963

R163 Robinson, Edward F. Continental Treasury Administration, 1775-1781: A Study in the Financial History of the American Revolution. Wis 1969

R164 Robinson, James F. The History of Soccer in the City of Saint Louis. St L 1966

R165 Robinson, Lewis M. A History of the Half-Way Covenant. Ill 1963

R166 Robinson, Paul A. The Freudian Left: Wilhelm Reich, Géza Róheim, Herbert Marcuse. Harvard 1968

R167 Robinson, Peter E. The United States and the World Court, 1930-1946. Miss S 1964

R168 Robinson, Robert L. British Colonial Policy and Trade on the Windward Coast of Africa, 1812-1832. Duke 1966

R169 Roche, George C., III. Public Opinion and the China Policy of the United States, 1941-1951. Colo 1965

R170 Rock, Kenneth W. Reaction Triumphant: The Diplomacy of Felix Schwarzenberg and Nicholas I in Mastering the Hungarian Insurrection, 1848-1850. A Study in Dynastic Power, Principles, and Politics in Revolutionary Times. Stanford 1969

R171 Rockaway, Robert A. From Americanization to Jewish Americanism: The Jews of Detroit, 1850-1914. Mich U 1970

R172 Rodden, Brian W. Anatomy of the 1886 Schism in the British Liberal Party: A Study of the Ninety-Four Liberal Members of Parliament Who Voted against the First Home Rule Bill. Rutgers 1969

R173 Roddy, Edward G., Jr. The Catholic Newspaper Press and the Quest for Social Justice, 1912-1920. Georgetown 1961

R174 Rodechko, James P. Patrick Ford and His Search for America: A Case Study of Irish-American Journalism, 1870- 1913. Conn 1967

R175 Rodemann, H. William. Tanganyika, 1890-1914: Selected Aspects of German Administration. Chicago 1961

R176 Rodgers, Hugh I. The Search for Security in the Baltic: Dilemmas of Latvian Diplomacy, 1919-1934. Tex U 1968

R177 Rodis, Themistocles C. Morals: Marriage, Divorce, and Illegitimacy during the French Revolution, 1789-1795. Case W Reserve 1968

R178 Rodney, Joel M. Henry Frederick, Prince of Wales, and His Circle: A Study of Early Stuart Political Parties. Cornell 1965

R179 Rodnitzky, Jerome L. A History of Public Relations at the University of Illinois, 1904-1930. Ill 1967

R180 Rodríguez O, Jaime E. Vicente Rocafuerte and Mexico, 1820-1832. Tex U 1970

R181 Roe, Alfred L. Banking and Politics in the New Era. Minn 1968

R182 Roemer, Beatrice B. Jesuit Beginnings in the Viceroyalty of Peru. Loyola 1946

R183 Roethler, Michael D. Negro Slavery among the Cherokee Indians, 1540-1866. Fordham 1964

R184 Rogan, Francis E. Military History of New Mexico Territory during the Civil War. Utah 1961

R185 Rogel, Carole. The Slovenes and the Southern Slav Question, 1889-1914. Columbia 1966

R186 Rogers, Alfred H. Racial and Cultural Values of Three Victorian Explorers in Africa. Mo 1970

R187 Rogers, Howard A. The Fall of the Old Representative System in the Leeward and Windward Islands, 1854-1877. S Cal 1970

R188 Rogers, James A. Northern Colonial Opposition to British Imperial Authority during the French and Indian War. Cal, Santa Barbara 1968

R189 Rogosin, Boris I. The Politics of Mikhail P. Dragomanov: Ukrainian Federalism and the Question of Political Freedom in Russia. Harvard 1967

R190 Rogozinski, Jan. Lawyers of Lower Languedoc: A Study of the Social Origins, Training, Career Patterns, and Wealth of the Professionally Trained Lawyers and Judges Resident in the Sénéchaussée of Beaucaire and Nîmes and the Baronnie of Montpellier between *circa* 1270 and *circa* 1345. Princeton 1967

R191 Rohfeld, Rae W. James Harvey Robinson and the New History. Case W Reserve 1965

R192 Rohne, Carl F. The Origins and Development of the Catalan Consulados Ultramarinos from the Thirteenth to the Fifteenth Centuries. S Cal 1966

R193 Rohrbough, Malcolm J. The General Land Office, 1812-1826: An Administrative Study. Wis 1963

R194 Roider, Karl A., Jr. A Case Study in Eighteenth Century War and Diplomacy: Austria's Policy in the Austro-Russian-Turkish War of 1737-1739. Stanford 1970

R195 Rolak, Bruno J. European Military Thought in the 1930's. Ind 1968

R196 Roland, Joan G. The Alliance Israélite Universelle and French Policy in North Africa, 1860-1918. Columbia 1969

R197 Roley, Paul L. In Search of an Accommodation: Anglo-Soviet Relations, 1919-1921. Ill 1966

R198 Roller, David C. The Republican Party of North Carolina, 1900-1916. Duke 1965

R199 Rollins, Patrick J. Russia's Ethiopian Adventure, 1888-1905. Syracuse 1967

R200 Romanek, Carl L. John Reynell, Quaker Merchant of Colonial Philadelphia. Penn S 1969

R201 Romaniuk, Gertrud U. Re-examination of Karl Marx's and Friedrich Engels' Views on Polish Independence. Loyola 1970

R202 Romanofsky, Peter. The Early History of Adoption Practices, 1870-1930. Mo 1969

R203 Romasco, Albert U. American Institutions in the Great Depression: The Hoover Years. Chicago 1961

R204 Romer, Kinsley G., Jr. Parliament and the Death Penalty during the Age of Reform, 1815-1868. Ga 1970

R205 Rommel, John G., Jr. Richard Varick: New York Aristocrat. Columbia 1966

R206 Romney, Joseph B. American Interests in Mexico: Development and Impact during the Rule of Porfirio Diaz, 1876-1911. Utah 1969

R207 Ronda, James P. Robert Quary in America: A Study of Colonial and Imperial Factional Politics, 1684-1712. Neb 1970

R208 Roosa, Ruth A. The Association of Industry and Trade, 1906-1918: An Examination of the Economic Views of Organized Industrialists in Prerevolutionary Russia. Columbia 1967

R209 Roosen, William J. The Ambassador's Craft: A Study of the Functioning of French Ambassadors under Louis XIV. S Cal 1967

R210 Roper, Donald M. Mr. Justice Thompson and the Constitution. Ind 1963

R211 Rose, Klaras B. Napoleon III and the Austro-Sardinian War of 1859. Tex U 1963

R212 Rose, Linda C. Britain in the Middle East, 1914-1918: Design or Accident? Columbia 1969

R213 Rose, Lisle A. Prologue to Democracy: The Federalists in the South, 1789-1800. Cal, Berkeley 1966

R214 Rose, Willie Lee N. Rehearsal for Reconstruction: The Port Royal Experiment. JH 1962

R215 Rosen, Marvin S. Authorship in the Days of Coleridge and Wordsworth. Cal, Berkeley 1965

R216 Rosen, Richard B. The National Heritage Opposition to the New Culture and Literary Movements of China in the 1920's. Cal, Berkeley 1969

R217 Rosenbaum, Kurt. The Brockdorff-Rantzau Period: German-Russian Diplomatic Relations, 1922-1928. Syracuse 1961

R218 Rosenberg, Arnold S. John Adams Kingsbury and the Struggle for Social Justice in New York City, 1906-1918. NYU 1968

R219 Rosenberg, Carroll S. Evangelicalism and the New City: A History of the City Mission Movement in New York, 1812 to 1870. Columbia 1968

R220 Rosenberg, Charles E. The Cholera Years: The United States in 1832, 1849, and 1866. Columbia 1961

R221 Rosenberg, William G. Constitutional Democracy and the Russian Civil War. Harvard 1967

R222 Rosenblatt, Nancy Ann K. The Moderado Party in Spain, 1820-1854. Cal, Berkeley 1965

R223 Rosenkrantz, Barbara G. Men against Filth and Corruption: Changing Views of Public Health and the State, Massachusetts, 1842-1936. Clark 1970

R224 Rosenstock, Morton. Louis Marshall and the Defense of Jewish Rights in the United States. Columbia 1963

R225 Rosenstone, Robert A. The Men of the Abraham Lincoln Battalion: Soldiers and Veterans, 1937-1965. UCLA 1965

R226 Rosenthal, Bernice G. The Artist as Prophet and Revolutionary: Dmitri Sergeevich Merezhkovsky and the "Silver Age." Cal, Berkeley 1970

R227 Rosenthal, Harry K. German-Polish Relations in the Caprivi Era. Columbia 1967

R228 Rosenthal, Joel T. Estates and Finances of Richard, Duke of York, 1411-1460. Chicago 1963

R229 Ross, Barbara J. J. E. Spingarn and the Rise of the National Association for the Advancement of Colored People, 1911-1939. Am 1969

R230 Ross, Carl A., Jr. Chile and Its Relations with the United States during the Ministry of Thomas Henry Nelson, 1861-1866. Ga 1966

R231   Ross, Davis R. B.   Preparing for Ulysses: The Federal Government and Nondisabled World War II Veterans, 1940-1946. Columbia 1967

R232   Ross, Delmer G.   The Construction of the Railroads of Central America. Cal, Santa Barbara 1970

R233   Ross, Dorothy.   G. Stanley Hall, 1844-1895: Aspects of Science and Culture in the Nineteenth Century. Columbia 1965

R234   Ross, Gordon D.   The Crowninshield Family in Business and Politics, 1790-1830. Claremont 1965

R235   Ross, John R.   "Pork Barrels" and the General Welfare: Problems in Conservation, 1900-1920. Duke 1969

R236   Ross, Marc.   John Swinton, Journalist and Reformer: The Active Years, 1857-1887. NYU 1969

R237   Ross, Maude E. C. H.   Moral Values of the American Woman as Presented in Three Major American Authors. Tex U 1964

R238   Ross, Nelson P.   Prelude to Conflict: The Movement for Church Patronage Reform in Scotland (1824-1834). Ore 1968

R239   Ross, Steven T.   The War of the Second Coalition. Princeton 1963

R240   Ross, W. Braxton.   A Study of the Latin Letters at the Court of Avignon in the Time of Clement V and John XXII, 1309-1334. Colo 1964

R241   Rossabi, Morris.   Ming China's Relations with Hami and Central Asia, 1404-1513: A Reexamination of Traditional Chinese Foreign Policy. Columbia 1970

R242   Rossi, John P.   The Transformation of the British Liberal Party: Defeat and Revival, 1873-1876. Penn U 1965

R243   Rossie, Jonathan G.   The Politics of Command: The Continental Congress and Its Generals. Wis 1966

R244   Rothaus, Barry.   The Emergence of Legislative Control over Foreign Policy in the Constituent Assembly, 1789-1791. Wis 1968

R245   Rothblatt, Sheldon.   Cambridge University and Society in the Nineteenth Century. Cal, Berkeley 1965

R246   Rothfeder, Herbert P.   A Study of Alfred Rosenberg's Organization for National Socialist Ideology. Mich U 1963

R247   Rothkrug, Lionel N.   Government and Reform in France, 1660-1700. Cal, Berkeley 1963

R248   Rothman, David J.   Party, Power and the United States Senate, 1869-1901. Harvard 1964

R249   Rothney, John A. M.   The Resurgence and Eclipse of Bonapartism, 1870-1879. Harvard 1964

R250   Rotz, Rhiman A., Jr.   Urban Uprisings in Fourteenth-Century Germany: A Comparative Study of Brunswick (1374-1380) and Hamburg (1376). Princeton 1970

R251   Rouse, Richard H.   *Catalogus de Libris Autenticis et Apocrifis:* A Critical Edition. Cornell 1963

R252   Rout, Leslie B., Jr.   The Chaco War: A Study in Inter-American Diplomacy. Minn 1966

R253   Rowan, Steven W.   The Guilds of Freiburg im Breisgau in the Later Middle Ages as Social and Political Entities. Harvard 1970

R254   Rowe, Gail S.   Power, Politics, and Public Service: The Life of Thomas McKean, 1734-1817. Stanford 1969

R255   Rowe, John A.   Revolution in Buganda, 1856-1900: Part One: The Reign of Kabaka Mukabya Mutesa, 1856-1884. Wis 1966

R256   Rowley, William D.   Wheat and Politics: The Growth of a National Agricultural Program. Neb 1966

R257   Rowney, Don K.   "The Generation of October": The Politics of Twentieth Century Social Revolution in the View of L. D. Trotsky. Ind 1965

R258   Roy, Patricia E.   The British Columbia Electric Railway Company, 1897-1928: A British Company in British Columbia. British Columbia 1970

R259   Roy, Reginald H.   The British Columbia Dragoons and Its Predecessors. Wash U 1965

R260   Royal, Leslie J. Popular Diversions in Sixteenth-Century Mexico. Cal, Berkeley 1966

R261   Ruark, Lawrence B.   Admiration for Mussolini among German Intellectuals, 1922-1932. Boston U 1970

R262   Rubin, Israel I.   New York State and the Long Embargo. NYU 1961

R263   Rubinstein, Jonathan B.   Society and Politics in Southwest Germany, 1760-1819. Harvard 1969

R264 Rudoff, Robin M. The Influence of the German Navy on the British Search for Naval Arms Control, 1928-1935. Tulane 1964

R265 Rudolph, Richard L. The Role of Financial Institutions in the Industrialization of the Czech Crownlands, 1880-1914. Wis 1968

R266 Ruedy, John D. The Origins of the Rural Public Domain in French Algeria, 1830-1851. UCLA 1965

R267 Ruestow, Edward G. Physics at Seventeenth-Century Leiden: The Scientific Revolution and the University. Ind 1970

R268 Ruetten, Richard T. Burton K. Wheeler of Montana: A Progressive between the Wars. Ore 1961

R269 Ruigh, Robert E. The Parliament of 1624: Foreign Policy, Prerogative and Politics. Harvard 1966

R270 Rumbarger, John J. The Social Origins and Function of the Political Temperance Movement in the Reconstruction of American Society, 1825-1917. Penn U 1968

R271 Russell, Frederick H. The Medieval Theories of the Just War according to the Romanists and Canonists of the Twelfth and Thirteenth Centuries. JH 1969

R272 Russell, James M. Business and the Sherman Act, 1890-1914. Ia 1966

R273 Russett, Cynthia M. E. Equilibrium in American Social Thought. Yale 1964

R274 Russo, David J. The Southern Republicans and American Political Nationalism, 1815-1825. Yale 1966

R275 Russo, Severino A. Unpublished Letters of Jules, Cardinal Mazarin, Written during the Fronde, 1649-1650. Penn U 1967

R276 Rutman, Herbert S. Defense and Development: A History of Minneapolis Jewry, 1930-1950. Minn 1970

R277 Ruud, Charles A. The Russian Censorship, 1855-1865: A Study in the Formation of Policy. Cal, Berkeley 1965

R278 Ruyter, Nancy. Reformers and Visionaries: The Americanization of the Art of Dance. Claremont 1970

R279 Ryan, Carl W. Modern Scott: A History of Scott Air Force Base. St L 1969

R280 Ryan, Carmelita S. The Carlisle Indian Industrial School. Georgetown 1962

R281 Ryan, Garry D. War Department Topographical Bureau, 1831-1863: An Administrative History. Am 1968

R282 Ryan, Guy A. The Acton Circle, 1864-1871: *The Chronicle* and the *North British Review.* Notre D 1969

R283 Ryan, Howard. Selected Aspects of American Activity in Mexico, 1876-1910. Chicago 1964

R284 Ryan, John W. The Emergence of the Republic of Guinea, 1946-1962. St John's 1965

R285 Ryan, Joseph F. Abraham Lincoln and New York City, 1861-1865: War and Politics. St John's 1969

R286 Ryan, Stephen. Pétain and French Military Planning, 1900-1940. Columbia 1961

R287 Ryan, William F. *La Croix* and the Development of Rightist Nationalism in France: 1883-1889. Conn 1970

R288 Ryant, Carl G. Garet Garrett's America. Wis 1968

R289 Ryerson, Ellen G. Between Justice and Compassion: The Rise and Fall of the Juvenile Court. Yale 1970

R290 Ryland, Robert S. The Making of the Government of India Act, 1919. Duke 1970

R291 Ryle, J. Martin. International Red Aid, 1922-1928: The Founding of a Comintern Front Organization. Emory 1967

R292 Ryon, Roderick N. Roberts Vaux: A Biography of a Reformer. Penn S 1966

R293 Ryu, In-Ho Lee. Freemasonry under Catherine the Great: A Reinterpretation. Harvard 1967

S

S1   Saadallah, Belkacem. The Rise of Algerian Nationalism, 1900-1930. Minn 1965

S2   Saalberg, John J. Roosevelt, Fechner and the CCC: A Study in Executive Leadership. Cornell 1962

S3   Sabean, David W. The Social Background to the Peasants' War of 1525 in Southern Upper Swabia. Wis 1969

S4   Sablinsky, Walter. The Road to Bloody Sunday: Father Gapon, His Labor Organization, and the Massacre of Bloody Sunday. Cal, Berkeley 1968

S5   Sadât, Deena R. Urban Notables in the Ottoman Empire: The Ayan. Rutgers 1969

S6   Sadler, Richard W. The Impact of the Slavery Question on the Whig Party in Congress, 1843-1854. Utah 1969

S7   Saeger, James S. The Role of José de Antequera in the Rebellion of Paraguay, 1717-1735. Ohio 1969

S8   Saffell, John E. The Ashanti Wars of 1873-1874. Case W Reserve 1965

S9   Safford, Frank R. Commerce and Enterprise in Central Colombia, 1821-1870. Columbia 1965

S10   Safford, Jeffrey J. The United States Merchant Marine and American Commercial Expansion, 1860-1920. Rutgers 1968

S11   Saffron, Morris H. Maurus of Salerno: Commentary on the Prognostics of Hippocrates. Columbia 1968

S12   St. Clair, Charles S. The Classification of Minerals: Some Representative Mineral Systems from Agricola to Werner. Okla 1965

S13   St. Jacques, Ernest H. A History of the Guidance-Personnel Movement in the United States from 1946 to 1961. Geo P 1963

S14   St. John, Jacqueline D. John F. Stevens: American Assistance to Russian and Siberian Railroads, 1917-1922. Okla 1969

S15   Saladino, Gaspare J. The Economic Revolution in Late Eighteenth Century Connecticut. Wis 1964

S16   Salisbury, Richard V. Costa Rican Relations with Central America, 1920-1936. Kans U 1969

S17   Sallis, William C. The Color Line in Mississippi Politics, 1865-1915. Ky 1967

S18   Salmond, John A. "Roosevelt's Tree Army": A History of the Civilian Conservation Corps, 1933-1942. Duke 1964

S19   Salomon, Hilel B. China's Policy toward Outer Mongolia, 1912-1920. Columbia 1969

S20   Salomon, Laurence. Socio-Economic Aspects of South African History, 1870-1962. Boston U 1962

S21   Salsbury, Stephen M. Private Enterprise in Massachusetts: The Beginnings of the Boston and Albany Railroad, 1825-1842. Harvard 1961

S22   Saltvig, Robert D. The Progressive Movement in Washington. Wash U 1966

S23   Samarrai, Alauddin I. Europe in the Medieval Arabic Sources. Wis 1966

S24   Samkange, Stanlake J. T. The Establishment of African Reserves in Matebeleland, 1893-1898. Ind 1968

S25   Sampson, Charles S. The Formative Years of the Soviet Press: An Institutional History, 1917-1924. Mass 1970

S26   Sanchez, José M. Church and State during the Second Spanish Republic, 1931-1936. NM 1961

S27   Sandels, Robert L. Silvestre Terrazas, the Press, and the Origins of the Mexican Revolution in Chihuahua. Ore 1967

S28   Sanders, Frank J. Proposals for Monarchy in Mexico, 1823-1860. Ariz 1966

S29   Sandiford, Keith A. P. Great Britain and the Schleswig-Holstein Question: A Study in Diplomacy, Politics, and Public Opinion. Toronto 1966

S30   Sandquist, Thayron A. English Coronations, 1377-1483. Toronto 1963

S31   Sanford, Paul L. The Origins and Development of Higher Education for Negroes in South Carolina to 1920. NM 1965

S32   Sansing, David G. The Role of the Scalawag in Mississippi Reconstruction. S Miss 1969

S33   Santoni, Wayne D. P. N. Durnovo as Minister of Internal Affairs in the Witte Cabinet: A Study of Suppression. Kans U 1968

S34   Santoro, Carmela E.   United States and Mexican Relations during World War II. Syracuse 1967

S35   Sapio, Victor A.   Pennsylvania: Protagonist of the War of 1812. Ohio 1965

S36   Sarafian, Winston L.   Russian-American Company Employee Policies and Practices, 1799-1867. UCLA 1970

S37   Sar Desai, Damodar Ramaji.   India's Relations with Vietnam, Laos and Cambodia, 1954-1961. UCLA 1965

S38   Sargent, Charles W.   Virginia and the West Indies Trade, 1740-1765. NM 1964

S39   Sarti, Roland.   The General Confederation of Italian Industry under Fascism: A Study in the Social and Economic Conflicts of Fascist Italy. Rutgers 1967

S40   Sater, William F.   Arturo Prat: Secular Saint. UCLA 1968

S41   Satre, Lowell J.   The Unionists and Army Reform, 1900-1903: The Abortive Proposals of St. John Brodrick. SC 1968

S42   Satterfield, Robert B.   Andrew Jackson Donelson: A Moderate Nationalist Jacksonian. JH 1961

S43   Saucier, Roger.   L'hygiène Privée et Publique au Canada sous le Régime Français. Ottawa 1969

S44   Saul, Norman E.   Russia and the Mediterranean, 1797-1807. Columbia 1965

S45   Saum, Lewis O.   Fur Trade Attitudes toward the American Indian. Mo 1962

S46   Saunders, John H.   Diplomacy under Difficulties: United States Relations with Paraguay during the War of the Triple Alliance. Ga 1966

S47   Saunders, Judith P.   The People's Party in Massachusetts during the Civil War. Boston U 1970

S48   Saunders, Richard F., Jr.   The Origin and Early History of the Society of the Cincinnati: The Oldest Hereditary and Patriotic Association in the United States. Ga 1970

S49   Saunders, Robert M.   The Ideology of Southern Populists, 1892-1895. Va 1967

S50   Savage, David W.   The Irish Question in British Politics, 1914-1916. Princeton 1963

S51   Savage, Hugh J.   Political Independents of the Hoover Era: The Progressive Insurgents of the Senate. Ill 1961

S52   Savage, William R., Jr.   The Image of Jaurès, 1914-1930. Chicago 1962

S53   Savard, Pierre.   *La France et les Etats-Unis dans la vie et dans l'oeuvre de Jules-Paul Tardivel (1851-1905).* Laval 1964

S54   Saville, Allison W.   The Development of the German U-Boat Arm. Wash U 1963

S54a   Sawczuk, Konstantyn.   The Ukraine in the United Nations Organization: A Study in Soviet Foreign Policy, 1944-1950. Columbia 1969

S55   Sawyer, Richard J.   The Failure of the Irish Parliamentary Movement for Home Rule, 1910-1918. Columbia 1966

S56   Saxton, Alexander P.   The Indispensable Enemy: A Study of the Anti-Chinese Movement in California. Cal, Berkeley 1967

S57   Saywell, William G. G.   The Thought of Tai Chi-t'ao, 1912-1928. Toronto 1969

S58   Scally, Robert J.   The Sources of the National Coalition of 1916: A Political History of British Social-Imperialism. Princeton 1966

S59   Scanlon, James E.   A Life of Robert Hunter, 1666-1734. Va 1969

S60   Scarborough, John S.   The Theory and Practice of Medicine in the Early Roman Empire. Ill 1967

S61   Scarborough, William K.   Plantation Management in the Ante-Bellum South: The Overseer. NC 1962

S62   Scavone, Daniel C.   The Historical and Religious Views of the Pagan Historian Zosimus. Loyola 1969

S63   Schaar, Stuart H.   Conflict and Change in Nineteenth Century Morocco. Princeton 1966

S64   Schaeffer, Mary E.   The Political Policies of P. A. Stolypin. Ind 1964

S65   Schaffer, Alan L.   Caucus in a Phone Booth: The Congressional Career of Vito Marcantonio, 1934-1950. Va 1962

S66   Schalk, David L.   The Novels of Roger Martin du Gard: A Case Study in the Attainment of Historical Consciousness. Harvard 1964

S67   Schalk, Ellery S.   Changing Conceptions of Nobility in France during the Wars of Religion. Cal, Berkeley 1970

S68   Schantz, Mrs. Roy Neil.   The Image of China in the Age of Discovery. NYU 1968

S69 Schapsmeier, Edward L. Henry A. Wallace: The Origins and Development of His Political Philosophy, the Agrarian Years, 1920-1940. S Cal 1965

S70 Schapsmeier, Frederick H. The Political Philosophy of Walter Lippmann: A Half Century of Thought and Commentary. S Cal 1965

S71 Scharnau, Ralph W. Thomas J. Morgan and the Chicago Socialist Movement, 1876-1901. N Ill 1969

S72 Schatz, Arthur W. Cordell Hull and the Struggle for the Reciprocal Trade Agreements Program, 1932-1940. Ore 1965

S73 Scheck, John F. Transplanting a Tradition: Thomas Lamb Eliot and the Unitarian Conscience in the Pacific Northwest, 1865-1905. Ore 1969

S74 Scheiber, Harry N. Internal Improvements and Economic Change in Ohio, 1820-1860. Cornell 1962

S75 Scheidenhelm, Richard J. The Legal and Political Rhetoric of William Henry Seward. Wis 1970

S76 Scheinberg, Stephen J. The Development of Corporation Labor Policy, 1900-1940. Wis 1966

S77 Scheiner, Irwin. The Beginning of Modern Social Criticism in Japan: A Study of the Samurai and Christian Values, 1867-1891. Mich U 1966

S78 Scheiner, Seth M. The Negro in New York City, 1865-1910. NYU 1962

S79 Scheips, Paul J. Albert James Myer, Founder of the Army Signal Corps: A Biographical Study. Am 1966

S80 Schelbert, Leo. Swiss Migration to America: The Swiss Mennonites. Columbia 1966

S81 Schellhase, Kenneth C. Tacitus in Renaissance Political Thought. Chicago 1969

S82 Scherer, John L. The Myth of the "Alienated" Russian Intellectual: Michael Rakunin, Aleksei Khomyakov, Vissarion Belinsky, Nikolai Stankevich, Alexander Herzen. Ind 1968

S83 Scherer, Paul H. British Policy with Respect to the Unification of Germany, 1848-1871. Wis 1964

S84 Scherer, Stephen P. The Life and Thought of Russia's First Lay Theologian, Grigorij Savvič Skovoroda (1722-94). Ohio 1969

S85 Schiller, Edward H. The Development and the Influence of Ghanian Ideology in Emergent Africa, 1957-1963. St John's 1964

S86 Schilling, William A. H., Jr. The Central Government and the Municipal Corporations in England, 1642-1663. Vanderbilt 1970

S87 Schimmel, Barbara B. The Judicial Policy of Mr. Justice McReynolds. Yale 1964

S88 Schlabach, Theron F. Edwin E. Witte: Cautious Reformer. Wis 1966

S89 Schleich, Rudolf J. Melchoir Khlesl and the Habsburg Bruderzwist, 1605-1612. Fordham 1968

S90 Schlereth, Thomas J. The Cosmopolitan Ideal in Enlightenment Thought: Its Form and Function in the Ideas of Franklin, Hume, and Voltaire, 1694-1790. Ia 1969

S91 Schlesinger, Mildred S. The French Radical Party: Its Organization and Parliamentary Politics, 1914-1932. Yale 1961

S92 Schlesinger, Roger. The Influence of Italian Renaissance Civilization in Fifteenth Century Spain: A Study in Cultural Transmission. Ill 1970

S93 Schleunes, Karl A. Nazi Policy toward German Jews, 1933-1938. Minn 1966

S94 Schlight, John. Medieval Mercenaries: Their Importance to Eleventh- and Twelfth-Century English Kings. Princeton 1965

S95 Schlobohm, Dietrich H. The Declaration of Independence and Negro Slavery, 1776-1876. Mich S 1970

S96 Schlossberg, Herbert. Pierre Bayle and the Politics of the Huguenot Diaspora. Minn 1965

S97 Schmauch, Fred H. Oliver Wolcott: His Political Role and Thought between 1789 and 1800. St John's 1969

S98 Schmeller, Kurt R. Ambassadorial Conferences and the Problem of International Co-operation in the Nineteenth Century. Princeton 1962

S99 Schmid, Gregory C. The Politics of Financial Instability: France, 1924-1926. Columbia 1968

S100 Schmidt, Hans R., Jr. United States Occupation of Haiti, 1915-1934. Rutgers 1968

S101 Schmidt, Martin E. The Diplomacy of Alexandre Ribot, 1890-1893. Penn U 1966

S102 Schmidt, William J. The North Carolina Delegates in the Continental Congress, 1774-1781. NC 1968

S103   Schmidtlein, Eugene F.   Truman the Senator. Mo 1962

S104   Schmiel, Eugene D. The Career of Jacob Dolson Cox, 1828-1900: Soldier, Scholar, Statesman. Ohio 1969

S105   Schmier, Louis E.   Martin Bormann and the Nazi Party, 1941-1945. NC 1969

S106   Schmitt, Carl B. An Introduction to the Study of Heredity and Election in the Merovingian and Carolingian Kingship. Harvard 1966

S107   Schmokel, Wolfe W.   Dream of Empire: A Study of Colonial Agitation and Planning in Germany, 1919-1945. Yale 1962

S108   Schmutz, Richard A.   The Foundations of Medieval Papal Representation. S Cal 1966

S109   Schneider, Donald O.   Education in Colonial American Colleges, 1750-1770, and the Occupation and Political Offices of Their Alumni. Geo P 1965

S110   Schneider, Laurence A.   Reorganizing the Nation's Past: Ku Chieh-kang and China's New History. Cal, Berkeley 1968

S111   Schneider, Susan C. The General Company of the Cultivation of the Vine of the Upper Douro, 1756-1777: A Case Study of the Marquis of Pombal's Economic Reform Program. Tex U 1970

S111a   Schneiderman, Jeremiah.   The Tsarist Government and the Labor Movement, 1898-1903: The *Zubatovshchina.* Cal, Berkeley 1966

S112   Schoenberg, Wallace K.   The Young Men's Association, 1833-1876: The History of a Social-Cultural Organization. NYU 1962

S113   Schoenfeld, Maxwell P.   The Restored House of Lords. Cornell 1962

S114   Schoenhals, Kai Peter.   The Russian Policy of Count Friedrich Ferdinand von Beust, 1866-1871. Rochester 1964

S115   Schoenl, William J.   The Intellectual Crisis in English Catholicism, 1890-1907: Liberals, Modernists, and the Vatican. Columbia 1968

S116   Schofer, Lawrence.   The Formation of a Modern Industrial Labor Force: The Case of Upper Silesia, 1865-1914. Cal, Berkeley 1970

S117   Schofield, Kent M.   The Figure of Herbert Hoover in the 1928 Campaign. Cal, Riverside 1966

S118   Scholz, Robert F.   "The Reverend Elders": Faith, Fellowship and Politics in the Ministerial Community of Massachusetts Bay, 1630-1710. Minn 1966

S119   Schonberger, Howard B.   Transportation to the Seaboard: A Study in the "Communication Revolution" and American Foreign Policy, 1860-1900. Wis 1968

S120   Schorsch, Ismar.   Organized Jewish Reactions to German Anti-Semitism, 1870-1914. Columbia 1969

S121   Schott, Matthew J.   John M. Parker of Louisiana and the Varieties of American Progressivism. Vanderbilt 1969

S122   Schottenstein, Isaac M.   The Russian Conquest of Kamchatka, 1697-1731. Wis 1969

S123   Schrack, Vivian B.   A Search for the Half-Breeds. Penn S 1968

S124   Schriver, Edward O.   The Antislavery Impulse in Maine, 1833-1855. Maine 1967

S125   Schruben, Francis W.   Kansas during the Great Depression, 1930-1936. UCLA 1961

S126   Schuchman, John S.   The Use of History in the Reapportionment Cases. Ind 1969

S127   Schuker, Stephen A.   The French Financial Crisis and the Adoption of the Dawes Plan, 1924. Harvard 1969

S128   Schulenburg, Jane Alice T.   Savigny in the Lyonnais, *ca.* 825-1138: An Analysis of a Rural Society. Wis 1969

S129   Schult, Frederick C., Jr.   The Extension of Suffrage and the Movement for Admission of New States into the Union, 1777-1803. NYU 1962

S130   Schulte, Josephine H.   Gabino Barreda and the Positivist Reforms in Mexican Education: The Law of Public Instruction, 1867, and Its Reform, 1869. Loyola 1969

S131   Schultejann, Mary Annunciata, Sister.   Henry L. Stimson's Latin American Policy, 1929-1933. Georgetown 1967

S132   Schultz, Charles R.   Hayne's Magnificent Dream: Factors Which Influenced Efforts to Join Cincinnati and Charleston by Railroad, 1835-1860. Ohio 1966

S133   Schultz, George A.   An Indian Canaan: Isaac McCoy, Baptist Missions, and Indian Reform. Ia 1963

S134   Schultz, Stanley K.   The Education of Urban Americans: Boston, 1789-1860. Chicago 1970

S135 Schumacher, John N. The Filipino Nationalists' Propaganda Campaign in Europe, 1880-1895. Georgetown 1965

S136 Schuster, Alice. The Struggle between Clericals and Anticlericals for Control of French Schools (1789-1879). Columbia 1967

S137 Schutte, Anne C. J. Pier Paolo Vergerio: The Making of an Italian Reformer. Stanford 1969

S138 Schuyler, Michael W. Agricultural Relief Activities of the Federal Government in the Middle West, 1933-1936. Kans U 1969

S140 Schwartz, Donald R. An Analysis of the Anglo-American Rift over the Suez Canal Crisis, 1956. Ind 1967

S141 Schwartz, Stuart B. The High Court of Bahia: A Study in Hapsburg Brazil, 1580-1630. Columbia 1968

S142 Schwarz, Jordan A. The Politics of Fear: Congress and the Depression during the Hoover Administration. Columbia 1967

S143 Schwarz, Marc L. The Religious Thought of the Protestant Laity in England, 1590-1640. UCLA 1965

S144 Schwarz, Richard W. John Harvey Kellogg: American Health Reformer. Mich U 1964

S145 Schwarzman, Richard C. The Pinal Dome Oil Company: An Adventure in Business—1901-1917. UCLA 1967

S146 Schwemmer, Ora-Westley. The Belgian Colonization Company, 1840-1858. Tulane 1966

S147 Scionti, Joseph N., Jr. Sylvester Prierias and His Opposition to Martin Luther. Brown 1967

S148 Scobie, Ingrid W. Jack B. Tenney: Molder of Anti-Communist Legislation in California, 1940-1949. Wis 1970

S149 Scontras, Charles A. Two Decades of Organized Labor and Labor Politics in Maine, 1880-1900. Maine 1968

S150 Scott, Clifford H. American Images of Sub-Sahara Africa, 1900-1939. Ia 1968

S151 Scott, Donald M. Watchmen on the Walls of Zion: Evangelicals and American Society, 1800-1860. Wis 1968

S152 Scott, Ivan C. The Powers and the French Occupation of Rome, 1859-1865. Penn U 1964

S153 Scott, Jack A. A Critical Edition of John Witherspoon's *Lectures on Moral Philosophy*. Claremont 1970

S154 Scott, Joan W. Les Verriers de Carmaux, 1850-1914. Wis 1969

S155 Scott, Samuel F. The French Revolution and the Line Army, 1787-1793. Wis 1968

S156 Scoufopoulos, Niki. Mycenaean Citadels on Mainland Greece. Yale 1965

S157 Scovel, Raleigh D. Orthodoxy in Princeton: A Social and Intellectual History of Princeton Theological Seminary, 1812-1860. Cal, Berkeley 1970

S158 Seabold, Richard. *Normalien* Alumni of the *Facultés* and *Lycées* of France from 1871 to 1910 *Promotions* 1831 to 1869. UCLA 1970

S159 Seager, Frederic H. The Boulanger Affair: Political Crossroad of France, 1886-1889. Columbia 1965

S160 Seale, William, Jr. Margaret Lea Houston, 1819-1867: The First Lady of Texas. Duke 1965

S161 Searle, C. Stanley. William Laud and the System of "Thorough." Columbia 1969

S162 Seaver, Paul S. The Puritan Lectureships in London: A Study in Institutional Development and Ecclesiastical Politics, 1560-1662. Harvard 1965

S163 Seavoy, Ronald E. The Origin of the American Business Corporation, 1784-1855: New York, the National Model. Mich U 1969

S164 Sedgwick, Alexander. The *Ralliement* in French Politics, 1890-1898. Harvard 1963

S165 Sedgwick, Charlene M. The Politics of the *Cour des Aides* of Paris, 1750-1771. Harvard 1969

S166 Seeger, Martin L., III. A Study of Four Problems of Real Hacienda of New Spain in the Sixteenth Century. Cal, Santa Barbara 1966

S167 Sefton, James E. The United States Army and Reconstruction, 1865-1877. UCLA 1965

S168 Segal, Lester A. Nicolas Lenglet du Fresnoy (1674-1755): A Study of Historical Criticism and Methodology in Early Eighteenth-Century France. Columbia 1968

S169 Segel, Edward B. Sir John Simon and British Foreign Policy: The Diplomacy of Disarmament in the Early 1930's. Cal, Berkeley 1969

S170 Segré, Claudio G. *Quarta Sponda:* The Italian Demographic Colonization of Libya, 1922-1942. Cal, Berkeley 1970

S171 Seguin, Robert-Lionel. *L'habitant aux XVIIe et XVIIIe siècles.* Laval 1963

S172 Sehlinger, Peter, Jr. The Educational Thought and Influence of Valentin Letelier. Ky 1969

S173 Seigel, Jerrold E. Rhetoric and Philosophy in Renaissance Humanism from Petrarch to Valla. Princeton 1963

S174 Selden, Mark. Yenan Communism: Revolution in the Shensi-Kansu-Ninghsia Border Region, 1927-1945. Yale 1967

S175 Seligman, Gustav L., Jr. The Political Career of Senator Bronson M. Cutting. Ariz 1967

S176 Selinger, Suzanne T. Winckelmann, Möser, and Savigny: A Study in the Development of German Historicism. Yale 1965

S177 Seller, Maxine S. Isaac Leeser, Architect of the American Jewish Community. Penn U 1965

S178 Sellers, John R. The Virginia Continental Line, 1775-1780. Tulane 1968

S179 Sellmeyer, Francis Marie, Sister. The Southern Province of the School Sisters of Notre Dame, 1925-1965. St L 1967

S180 Selo, Peter A. John Tillotson, Archbishop of Canterbury, 1630-1694: A Study in Anglican Ideology. Del 1970

S181 Semonche, John E. Progressive Journalist: Ray Stannard Baker, 1870-1914. Northwestern 1962

S182 Senese, Donald J. The Development of Legal Thought in South Carolina, 1800-1860. SC 1970

S183 Senese, Donald L. Kravchinski and the London Emigration. Harvard 1970

S184 Senning, Calvin F. The Gondomar Embassy: Religious Aspects, 1613-1614. Ala 1968

S185 Sessions, Kyle C. Luther's Hymns in the Spread of the Reformation. Ohio 1963

S186 Settle, Thomas B. Galilean Science: Essays in the Mechanics and Dynamics of the *Discorsi.* Cornell 1966

S187 Sewell, Richard H. John P. Hale: Anti-Slavery Advocate, 1806-1861. Harvard 1962

S188 Sexter, Dorothy A. The Belgian Coal Mines in the European Coal and Steel Community. Cal, Davis 1969

S189 Seymour, Mary Elizabeth, Sister. Agricultural Credit and Banking in the Philippines, 1913-1917: An Administrative Study. Chicago 1962

S190 Shade, William G. The Politics of Free Banking in the Old Northwest, 1837-1863. Wayne 1966

S191 Shadel, Gerald L. The Anglican Mind in the 1690's. Md 1963

S192 Shadgett, Olive H. A History of the Republican Party in Georgia from Reconstruction through 1900. Ga 1962

S193 Shaeffer, John N. Constitutional Change in the Unicameral States, 1776-1793. Wis 1968

S194 Shaffer, Arthur H. The Shaping of a National Tradition: Historical Writing in America, 1783-1820. UCLA 1966

S195 Shaffer, Dallas B. Mr. Lincoln and West Virginia. W Va 1966

S196 Shaffer, Ralph E. Radicalism in California, 1869-1929. Cal, Berkeley 1962

S197 Shalhope, Robert E. Sterling Price: Portrait of a Southerner. Mo 1967

S198 Shaloff, Stanley. The American Presbyterian Congo Mission: A Study in Conflict, 1890-1921. Northwestern 1967

S199 Shanahan, Robert J. The Catholic Hospital Association: Its First Twenty-Five Years (1915-1940). St L 1961

S200 Shand, James D. Internationalism and the German Revolution, 1918-1919. Loyola 1967

S201 Shanks, Alexander G. Sam Rayburn and the New Deal, 1933-1936. NC 1965

S202 Shapiro, Barbara J. John Wilkins, 1614-1672. Harvard 1966

S203 Shapiro, Edward S. The American Distributists and the New Deal. Harvard 1968

S204 Shapiro, Henry D. A Strange Land and Peculiar People: The Discovery of Appalachia, 1870-1920. Rutgers 1966

S205 Shapiro, Herbert. Lincoln Steffens: The Evolution of an American Radical. Rochester 1964

S206 Shapiro, Seymour. Capital and the Cotton Industry in the Industrial Revolution. Columbia 1965

S207 Shapiro, Sheldon. The Relations between Louis XIV and Leopold of Austria from the Treaty of Nymegen to the Truce of Ratisbon. UCLA 1966

S208 Shapiro, Stanley. Hand and Brain: The Farmer-Labor Party of 1920. Cal, Berkeley 1967

S209　Shapiro, Stephen R.　The Big Sell: Attitudes of Advertising Writers about Their Craft in the 1920's and 1930's. Wis 1969

S210　Sharp, James R.　Banking and Politics in the States: The Democratic Party after the Panic of 1837. Cal, Berkeley 1966

S211　Sharp, William F.　Forsaken but for Gold: An Economic Study of Slavery and Mining in the Colombian Chocó, 1680-1810. NC 1970

S212　Sharrow, Walter G.　William Henry Seward: A Study in Nineteenth Century Politics and Nationalism, 1855-1861. Rochester 1965

S213　Shashko, Philip.　Unity and Dissent among the Russian Westerners. Mich U 1969

S214　Shatz, Marshall S.　Jan Waclaw Machajski and "Makhaevshchina," 1866-1926: Anti-Intellectualism and the Russian Intelligentsia. Columbia 1968

S215　Shay, Ralph S.　Italy's Loyalty to the Triple Alliance, 1900-1902. Penn U 1962

S216　Shea, M. Margretta, Sister.　Patrick Cardinal Hayes and the Catholic Charities in New York City. NYU 1966

S217　Shearer, Donald C.　Pontifica Americana: A Documentary History of the Catholic Church in the United States, 1784-1884. Cath 1933

S218　Sheehan, Bernard W.　Civilization and the American Indian in the Thought of the Jeffersonian Era. Va 1965

S219　Sheehan, James J.　Lujo Brentano, German Intellectual, 1866-1918. Cal, Berkeley 1964

S220　Shefftz, Melvin C.　British Labour, the General Strike, and the Constitution, 1910-1927. Harvard 1962

S221　Sheifer, Isobel C.　Ida M. Tarbell and Morality in Big Business: An Analysis of a Progressive Mind. NYU 1967

S222　Shelby, Lonnie R.　The Technical Supervision of Masonry Construction in Medieval England. NC 1962

S223　Sheldon, Richard.　Richmond Pearson Hobson: The Military Hero as Reformer during the Progressive Era. Ariz 1970

S224　Sheldon, William F.　The Intellectual Development of Justus Möser: The Growth of a German Patriot. Minn 1967

S225　Shelton, Brenda K.　Social Reform and Social Control in Buffalo, 1890-1900. SUNY, Buffalo 1970

S226　Shelton, William G.　Sir James Hudson and the Unification of Italy, 1858-1861. Penn U 1961

S227　Shenton, Robert.　The Chartered Company, 1889-1898: A Financial and Political History of the British South Africa Company. Harvard 1962

S228　Shepard, Carl E.　Germany and the Hague Conferences, 1929-1930. Ind 1964

S229　Shepard, Michael D.　Adrian Molin, Study of a Swedish Right-Wing Radical. Northwestern 1969

S230　Shepardson, Donald E.　The *Daily Telegraph* Affair: A Case Study in the Politics of the Second German Empire. Ill 1970

S231　Sheppard, Thomas F.　A Provincial Village in Eighteenth-Century France: Lourmarin, 1685-1800. JH 1969

S232　Sheppard, William F., Jr.　The Mid-19th Century Foundation for 20th Century Reforms in the British and American Foreign Services. Ga 1970

S233　Sherburne, James C.　Ruskin, or the Ambiguities of Abundance: A Study in Victorian Social Romanticism. Harvard 1970

S233a　Sherer, Robert G.　Let Us Make Man: Negro Education in Nineteenth Century Alabama. NC 1970

S234　Sheridan, James E.　The Early Career of Feng Yü-hsiang. Cal, Berkeley 1961

S235　Sheridan, Mary Quentin, Sister.　John Stuart Mill's Concept of Class. St L 1967

S236　Sherman, Jacqueline G.　The Oklahomans in California during the Depression Decade, 1931-1941. UCLA 1970

S237　Sherman, Richard M.　The Ghents: A Flemish Family in Norman England. Penn U 1969

S238　Sherman, William L.　Indian Slavery in Spanish Guatemala, 1524-1550. NM 1967

S239　Sherr, Merrill F.　Bishop Bonner: Bulwark against Heresy. NYU 1969

S240　Sherrill, Anne H.　John Hay: Shield of Union. Cal, Berkeley 1966

S241　Sherter, Sidney R.　The Soviet System and the Historian: E. V. Tarle (1875-1955) as a Case Study. Wayne 1968

S242　Sherwood, John M.　The Life of Georges Mandel: A Study in French Politics from Clemenceau to Pétain. Columbia 1967

S243 Sherwood, Morgan B. American Scientific Exploration of Alaska, 1865-1900. Cal, Berkeley 1962

S244 Shewchuk, Serge M. The Russo-Polish War of 1920. Md 1966

S245 Shewmaker, Kenneth E. Persuading Encounter: American Reporters and Chinese Communists, 1927-1945. Northwestern 1966

S246 Shields, Robert A. M. The Quest for Empire Unity: The Imperial Federationists and Their Cause, 1869-1893. Penn U 1961

S247 Shiman, Lilian L. Crusade against Drink in Victorian England. Wis 1970

S247a Shin, Linda P. China in Transition: The Role of Wu T'ing-fang (1842-1922). UCLA 1970

S248 Shinkawa, Kensaburo. The Emergence of American "State Capitalism," 1913-1940. Md 1968

S249 Shipe, Scott H., Jr. The American Legation in Bolivia, 1848-1879. St L 1967

S250 Shipkey, Robert C. Robert Peel's Irish Policy, 1812-1846. Harvard 1962

S251 Shipley, Neal R. Thomas Sutton, Tudor-Stuart Moneylender and Philanthropist. Harvard 1967

S252 Shipps, Jo Ann B. The Mormons in Politics: The First Hundred Years. Colo 1965

S253 Shirigian, John. Lucius Lyon: His Place in Michigan History. Mich U 1961

S254 Shirk, Albert E., Jr. The Problem of the Communist International for French and German Socialism, 1919-1920. Harvard 1968

S255 Shirley, James R. Political Conflict in the Kuomintang: The Career of Wang Ching-wei to 1932. Cal, Berkeley 1962

S256 Shiroya, Okete E. J. The Impact of World War II on Kenya: The Role of Ex-Servicemen in Kenyan Nationalism. Mich S 1968

S257 Shively, Charles A. A History of the Conception of Death in America, 1650-1860. Harvard 1969

S258 Shiverick, Nathan C. Virginia and the Western Land Problems, 1776-1880. Harvard 1965

S259 Shoalmire, Jimmy G. Carpetbagger Extraordinary: Marshall Harvey Twitchell, 1840-1905. Miss S 1969

S260 Shofner, Jerrell H. Florida's Political Reconstruction and the Presidential Election of 1876. Fla S 1963

S261 Shorrock, William I. France in Syria and Lebanon, 1901-1914: Pre-War Origins of the Mandate. Wis 1968

S262 Short, Audrey S. The Great Exhibition of 1851. Cincinnati 1968

S263 Shorter, Edward L. Social Change and Social Policy in Bavaria, 1800-1860. Harvard 1968

S264 Shover, Kenneth B. The Life of Benjamin F. Wade. Cal, Berkeley 1962

S265 Showalter, Dennis E. Railroads and Rifles: The Influence of Technological Development on German Military Thought and Practice, 1815-1966. Minn 1969

S266 Showan, Daniel P. United States Policy regarding League of Nations Social and Humanitarian Activities. Penn S 1969

S267 Shumway, Floyd M. Early New Haven and Its Leadership. Columbia 1968

S268 Shumway, Gary L. A History of the Uranium Industry on the Colorado Plateau. S Cal 1970

S269 Shy, John W. The British Army in North America, 1760-1775. Princeton 1961

S270 Sibley, Marilyn M. Travelers in Texas, 1761-1860. Rice 1965

S271 Sicher, Erwin. Leopold I of Austria: A Reappraisal. S Cal 1970

S272 Sicherman, Barbara. The Quest for Mental Health in America, 1880-1917. Columbia 1967

S273 Sider, Earl M. Dissent and the Religious Issue in British Politics, 1840-1868. SUNY, Buffalo 1966

S274 Sider, Ronald J. The Life and Thought of Andreas Bodenstein von Karlstadt through 1524. Yale 1969

S275 Sides, Sudie D. Women and Slaves: An Interpretation Based on the Writings of Southern Women. NC 1969

S276 Siegel, Martin. Science and the Historical Imagination: Patterns in French Historiographical Thought, 1866-1914. Columbia 1965

S277 Sievers, Sharon L. Kōtoku Shūsui, *The Essence of Socialism:* A Translation and Biographical Essay. Stanford 1969

S278 Siff, Paul. Views of Business in the American Business Press, 1840-1860. Rochester 1969

S279 Sigler, Phil S. The Attitudes of Free Blacks towards Emigration to Liberia. Boston U 1969

S280   Sigmund, Elwin W.   Federal Laws concerning Railroad Labor Disputes: A Legislative and Legal History, 1877-1934. Ill 1961

S281   Silberstein, Gerard E.   German-Austrian Relations, 1914-1916. Harvard 1963

S282   Silbert, Edward M.   Support for Reform among Congressional Democrats, 1897-1913. Fla U 1966

S283   Silbey, Joel H.   Congressional Voting Behavior and the Southern-Western Alliance, 1841-1852. Ia 1963

S284   Silver, Paul L.   Wilsonians and the New Deal. Penn U 1964

S285   Silvera, Alan D.   Daniel Halévy and His Times: A Gentleman-Commoner in the Third Republic. Harvard 1963

S286   Silverglate, Jesse J.   The Role of the Conspiracy Doctrine in the Nuremberg War Crimes Trials. Wis 1969

S287   Silveri, Louis D.   The Political Education of Alfred E. Smith: The Assembly Years, 1904-1915. St John's 1964

S288   Silverman, Dan P.   German Policy in Alsace-Lorraine, 1871-1885. Yale 1963

S289   Silverman, Lawrence F.   N. I. Turgenev, His Life and Works from 1789 to 1824. Harvard 1967

S290   Silverman, Sheldon A.   At the Water's Edge: Arthur Vandenberg and the Foundation of American Bipartisan Foreign Policy. UCLA 1967

S291   Silvestri, Gino D.   Paul Reynaud and the Fall of France. Syracuse 1969

S292   Simmonds, George W.   The Congress of Representatives of the Nobles' Associations, 1906-1916: A Case Study of Russian Conservatism. Columbia 1964

S293   Simmons, Marc S.   Spanish Government in New Mexico at the End of the Colonial Period. NM 1965

S294   Simmons, Richard C.   Studies in the Massachusetts Franchise, 1631-1691. Cal, Berkeley 1965

S295   Simms, Lyman M., Jr.   Philip Alexander Bruce: His Life and Works. Va 1966

S296   Simon, John Y.   Congress under Lincoln, 1861-1863. Harvard 1961

S296a   Simon, Paul L.   Frank Walker, New Dealer. Notre D 1965

S297   Simons, Thomas W., Jr.   Sebastian Brunner of the *Biedermeier* Day in Vienna. Harvard 1963

S298   Simonson, David F.   The History of the Department of Health of Chicago, 1947-1956. Chicago 1962

S299   Simpson, Alexander J., Jr.   Boniface of Canterbury, 1241-1270. Miss S 1969

S300   Simpson, Harold B.   The History of Hood's Texas Brigade, 1861-1865. Tex C 1969

S301   Sims, Harold D.   The Expulsion of the Spaniards from Mexico, 1827-1829. Fla U 1968

S302   Sinel, Allen A.   Count Dmitrii Tolstoi and the Russian Ministry of Education, 1866-1880. Harvard 1966

S303   Singer, David F.   The Acculturation of Ludwig Lewisohn: An Intellectual Portrait. Brown 1968

S304   Singh, Bawa S.   Gulab Singh of Jammu Ladakh, and Kashmir, 1792-1846. Wis 1966

S305   Singh, Diwakar P.   American Official Attitudes towards the Indian Nationalist Movement, 1905-1929. Hawaii 1964

S306   Sinton, John W.   The Instructions from Kazan *Guberniia* at the Legislative Commission of 1767. Ind 1968

S307   Sippel, Cornelius, III.   The *Noblesse de la Robe* in Early Seventeenth-Century France: A Study in Social Mobility. Mich U 1963

S308   Sippel, Donald V.   Rhodes and the Nesiotic League. Cincinnati 1966

S309   Siraisi, Nancy G.   Arts and Sciences in the *Studium* (University) of Padua in the Thirteenth and First Half of the Fourteenth Century. CUNY 1970

S310   Skaggs, David C.   Democracy in Colonial Maryland, 1753-1776. Georgetown 1966

S311   Skates, John R., Jr.   A Southern Editor Views the National Scene: Frederick Sullens and the Jackson, Mississippi, *Daily News.* Miss S 1965

S312   Skau, George H.   Woodrow Wilson and the American Presidency: Theory and Practice. St John's 1969

S313   Skeen, Carl E.   John Armstrong and the Role of the Secretary of War in the War of 1812. Ohio 1966

S314   Skelton, William B.   The United States Army, 1821-1837: An Institutional History. Northwestern 1968

S315 Skidmore, Thomas E. The Chancellorship of Caprivi: A Constitutional Study. Harvard 1961

S316 Sklar, Kathryn K. Household Divinity: A Life of Catharine Beecher. Mich U 1969

S317 Skolnik, Richard S. The Crystallization of Reform in New York City, 1890-1917. Yale 1964

S318 Skop, Arthur L. The British Left and the German Revolution, 1918-1920. Cath 1969

S319 Skotheim, Robert A. American Historians and American Ideas: Histories of Ideas between the 1870s and the 1950s. Wash U 1963

S320 Slagle, Robert O. The Von Lossberg Regiment: A Chronicle of Hessian Participation in the American Revolution. Am 1965

S321 Slavenas, Julius P. The Klaipeda-Memel Controversy, 1919-1939. Chicago 1970

S322 Slavens, George E. A History of the Missouri Negro Press. Mo 1969

S323 Slavin, Arthur J. Sir Ralph Sadler, 1507-1547. NC 1962

S324 Slavin, Morris. Left of the Mountain: The Enragés and the French Revolution. Case W Reserve 1961

S325 Sloan, David A. The Paxton Riots. Cal, Santa Barbara 1969

S326 Sloan, Edward W., III. Steam for the Union Navy: Benjamin F. Isherwood as Engineer-in-Chief, 1861-1869. Harvard 1962

S327 Sloan, Henry S. The German Social Democrats in the Reichstag Elections, 1871-1912. NYU 1962

S328 Slusser, Robert M. The Moscow Soviet of Workers' Deputies of 1905: Origin, Structure, and Policies. Columbia 1963

S329 Smail, John R. W. Bandung in the Early Revolution, 1945-1946. Cornell 1964

S330 Smaldone, Joseph P. Historical and Sociological Aspects of Warfare in the Sokoto Caliphate. Northwestern 1970

S331 Small, Melvin. The American Image of Germany, 1906-1914. Mich U 1965

S332 Smallwood, Johnny B., Jr. George W. Norris and the Conception of a Planned Region. NC 1963

S333 Smart, James G. Whitelaw Reid: A Biographical Study. Md 1964

S334 Smart, Terry L. French Intervention in the Ukraine, 1918-1919. Kans U 1968

S335 Smelser, Ronald M. Volkstumspolitik and the Formulation of Nazi Foreign Policy: The Sudeten Problem, 1933-1938. Wis 1970

S336 Smemo, Irwin K. Progressive Judge: The Public Career of Charles Fremont Amidon. Minn 1967

S337 Smetherman, Robert M. U.S. Aid to Latin America, 1945-1960. Claremont 1967

S338 Smethurst, Richard J. The Social Basis for Japanese Militarism: The Case of the Imperial Military Reserve Association. Mich U 1968

S339 Smith, Agnes M. The First Historians of the French Revolution. Case W Reserve 1966

S340 Smith, Alan M. Virginia Lawyers, 1680-1776: The Birth of an American Profession. JH 1967

S341 Smith, Arthur G. London and the Crown, 1681-1685. Wis 1967

S342 Smith, Bernard S. The Life and Work of Rupert of Deutz. Harvard 1965

S343 Smith, Carlton B. The United States War Department, 1815-1842. Va 1967

S344 Smith, Charles D., Jr. Muhammad Husayn Haykal: An Intellectual and Political Biography. Mich U 1968

S345 Smith, Charles W. S. S. General Karl Wolff and the Surrender of the German Troops in Italy, 1945. S Miss 1970

S346 Smith, Cortland V. Church Organization as an Agency of Social Control: Church Discipline in North Carolina, 1800-1860. NC 1967

S347 Smith, David C. A History of Lumbering in Maine, 1860-1930. Cornell 1965

S348 Smith, Don A. Cabinet and Constitution in the Age of Peel and Palmerston. Yale 1966

S349 Smith, Duane A. Mining Camps and the Settlement of the Trans-Mississippi Frontier, 1860-1890. Colo 1964

S350 Smith, Edward O. Thomas Penn, Chief Proprietor of Pennsylvania: A Study of His Public Governmental Activities from 1763 to 1775. Lehigh 1966

S351 Smith, Geoffrey S. A Social and Diplomatic History of American Extremism, 1933-1941. Cal, Santa Barbara 1969

S352 Smith, Glenn H. Senator William Langer: A Study of Isolationism. Ia 1968

S353 Smith, Howard W. The Early Public Career of Stephen A. Douglas. Ind 1963

S354 Smith, Irving H. The Political Ideas of Daniel Defoe. McGill 1963

S355 Smith, James H. Honorable Beggars: The Middlemen of American Philanthropy. Wis 1968

S356 Smith, John M., Jr. A History of the Sarbadarid Dynasty, 1336-1381 A.D., and Its Sources. Columbia 1964

S357 Smith, John S. Organized Labor and Government in the Wilson Era, 1913-1921: Some Conclusions. Cath 1962

S358 Smith, Julia H. The Plantation Belt in Middle Florida, 1850-1860. Fla S 1964

S359 Smith, Kenneth A. California: The Wheat Decades. S Cal 1969

S360 Smith, Kent C. Ch'ing Policy and the Development of Southwest China: Aspects of Ortai's Governor-Generalship, 1726-1731. Yale 1970

S361 Smith, Leonard S. Otto Hintze's Comparative Constitutional History of the West. Wash St L 1967

S362 Smith, Loren E. The Library List of 1783. Claremont 1969

S363 Smith, Mary Avila, Sister. L'Ere nouvelle: Organ of Catholic Political and Social Thought, 1848-1849. St L 1965

S364 Smith, Michael J. J. Henry L. Stimson and the Philippines. Ind 1970

S365 Smith, Norman W. A History of Commercial Banking in New Hampshire, 1792-1843. Wis 1967

S366 Smith, Paul H. American Loyalists in British Military Policy, 1775-1781. Mich U 1962

S367 Smith, Peter Damian, Sister. Politique: A Current of French Christian Democracy. Cath 1967

S368 Smith, Peter H. The Politics of Argentine Beef, 1900-1946. Columbia 1966

S369 Smith, Peter S. Petroleum in Brazil: A Study in Economic Nationalism. NM 1969

S370 Smith, Philbrook W. A Study in the Lists of Military and Parliamentary Summons in the Reign of Edward I: The Families of Lists and Their Significance. Ia 1967

S371 Smith, Ralph C. Charles Godfrey Leland: The American Years, 1824-1869. NM 1961

S372 Smith, Ray T. The "Liberals" in the Indian Nationalist Movement, 1918-1947: Their Role as Intermediaries. Cal, Berkeley 1964

S373 Smith, Richard C. Hellenistic Attitudes toward War. Ill 1961

S374 Smith, Richard K. The Airships Akron and Macon: Flying Aircraft Carriers of the United States Navy. Chicago 1966

S375 Smith, Robert J. The École Normale Supérieure in the Third Republic: A Study of the Classes of 1890-1904. Penn U 1967

S375a Smith, Robert R. Radicalism in the Province of San Juan: The Saga of Federico Cantoni (1916-1934). UCLA 1970

S375b Smith, Robert T. Alone in China: Patrick J. Hurley's Attempt to Unify China, 1944-1945. Okla 1966

S376 Smith, Ronald D. French Interests in Louisiana: From Choiseul to Napoleon. S Cal 1964

S377 Smith, Samuel B. Joseph Buckner Killebrew and the New South Movement in Tennessee. Vanderbilt 1962

S378 Smith, Selden K. Ellison Durant Smith: A Southern Progressive, 1909-1929. SC 1970

S379 Smith, Thomas H. The Senatorial Career of Atlee Pomerene of Ohio, 1911-1923. Kent 1966

S380 Smith, W. Wayne. The Whig Party in Maryland, 1826-1856. Md 1967

S381 Smith, Wilfred I. The Origins and Early Development of the Office of High Commissioner. Minn 1968

S382 Smith, William A. Anglo-Colonial Society and the Mob, 1740-1775. Claremont 1965

S383 Smith, William B. The Attitudes of American Catholics toward Italian Fascism between the Two World Wars. Cath 1969

S384 Smoot, Joseph G. Freedom's Early Ring: The Northwest Ordinance and the American Union. Ky 1964

S385 Smyrl, Frank H. Tom Connally and the New Deal. Okla 1968

S386 Smythe, Donald W. The Early Career of General John J. Pershing, 1860-1903. Georgetown 1961

S387 Snapp, Harry F. The Interregnum Bishops of the Anglican Church and the Ideas of Church and State in Caroline England. Tulane 1963

S388 Snetsinger, John G. Truman and the Creation of Israel. Stanford 1970

S389 Sniffen, Barbara G. The Secretaries-General of the Dutch Civil Service, 1940-1945: A Study in Conflicting Loyalties. Tulane 1969

S390 Snow, Lewis F., Jr. The Páez Years: Venezuelan Economic Legislation, 1830-1846. NC 1970

S391 Snow, William R. Britain and Morocco, 1900-1906. Cal, Berkeley 1970

S392 Snyder, Henry L. Charles Spencer, Third Earl of Sunderland, as Secretary of State, 1706-1710: A Study in Cabinet Government and Party Politics in the Reign of Queen Anne. Cal, Berkeley 1963

S393 Snyder, John R. Edward P. Costigan and the U.S. Tariff Commission. Colo 1966

S394 Snyder, Lee D. Wessel Gansfort and the Art of Meditation. Harvard 1966

S395 Sobel, May L. An Experiment in Perfectionism: The Religious Life of the Putney and Oneida Communities. Boston U 1968

S396 Sobiesk, Norman M. The Crisis of 1051: A Study on English Political History. Wis 1970

S397 Socarrás, Cayetano J. Alfonso X of Castile and the Idea of Empire. NYU 1969

S398 Sochen, June. "Now Let Us Begin": Feminism in Greenwich Village, 1910-1920. Northwestern 1967

S399 Soder, John P., Jr. The Impact of the Tacna-Arica Dispute on the Pan-American Movement. Georgetown 1970

S400 Soderland, Arthur E. Charles A. Beard and the Social Studies. Ia 1961

S401 Sofchalk, Donald G. The Little Steel Strike of 1937. Ohio 1961

S402 Soffer, Reba. Liberalism and the Liberal Attitude in Early Twentieth Century England. Radcliffe 1962

Sohn, Pow-key. *See* Son, Po-gi

S403 Solberg, Carl E. The Response to Immigration in Argentina and Chile, 1890-1914. Stanford 1967

S404 Solberg, Curtis B. As Others Saw Us: Travelers in America during the Age of the American Revolution. Cal, Santa Barbara 1968

S405 Soldon, Norbert C. Laissez-Faire on the Defensive: The Story of the Liberty and Property Defence League, 1882-1914. Del 1969

S406 Soldwedel, Eileen K. The Immediate Origins of the Constitution of the Year III. Fordham 1968

S407 Soliday, Gerald L. The Social Structure of Frankfurt am Main in the Seventeenth and Early Eighteenth Century. Harvard 1969

S408 Solomon, Howard M. The Innocent Inventions of Théophraste Renaudot: Public Welfare, Science and Propaganda in 17th Century France. Northwestern 1969

S409 Solon, Paul D. Charles VII and the *Compagnies d'Ordonnance,* 1445-1461: A Study in Medieval Reform. Brown 1970

S410 Solvick, Stanley D. William Howard Taft and the Progressive Movement: A Study in Conservative Thought and Politics. Mich U 1963

S411 Soman, Alfred. Book Censorship in France (1599-1607) with Emphasis upon Diplomatic Relations between Paris and Rome. Harvard 1968

S412 Somers, Dale A. The Rise of Sports in New Orleans, 1850-1900. Tulane 1966

S413 Somerville, James K. Patriot Moralist: An Intellectual Portrait of Samuel Adams. Case W Reserve 1965

S414 Somkin, Fred. Unquiet Eagle: Memory and Desire in the Idea of American Freedom, 1815-1860. Cornell 1967

S415 Sommers, Lawrence E. Lawyers and Progressive Reform: A Study of Attitudes and Activities in Illinois (1890-1920). Northwestern 1967

S416 Sommers, Richard J. Grant's Fifth Offensive at Petersburg: A Study in Strategy, Tactics and Generalship: The Battle of Chaffin's Bluff, the Battle of Poplar Spring Church, the First Battle of the Darbytown Road, the Second Battle of Squirrel Level Road, the Second Battle of the Darbytown Road. Rice 1970

S417 Sommerville, Charles J. Popular Religious Literature in England, 1660-1711: A Content Analysis. Ia 1970

S418 Son, Po-gi. Social History of the Early Yi Dynasty, 1392-1592: With Emphasis on the Functional Aspects of Governmental Structure. Cal, Berkeley 1963

S419 Sonderegger, Richard P. The Southern Frontier from the Founding of Georgia to the End of King George's War. Mich U 1964

S420 Songy, Benedict G. Alexis de Tocqueville and Slavery: Judgments and Predictions. St L 1969

S421 Sonnino, Paul M. Louis XIV's Correspondence, *Memoires*, and His Views of the Papacy (1661-1667). UCLA 1964

S422 Sontag, John P. Russian Diplomacy, the Balkans and Europe, 1908-1912. Harvard 1967

S423 Soremekun, Fola. A History of the American Board Missions in Angola, 1880-1940. Northwestern 1965

S424 Sorin, Gerald S. The Historical Theory of Political Radicalism: New York State Abolitionist Leaders as a Test Case. Columbia 1969

S425 Soucy, Robert J. The Image of the Hero in the Works of Maurice Barrès and Pierre Drieu La Rochelle. Wis 1963

S426 South, Oron P. Systematics in American Historiography since 1900. Vanderbilt 1967

S427 Soviak, Eugene. Baba Tatsui: A Study of Intellectual Acculturation in the Early Meiji Period. Mich U 1962

S428 Sowle, Patrick M. The Conciliatory Republicans during the Winter of Secession. Duke 1963

S429 Spain, Rufus B. Attitudes and Reactions of Southern Baptists to Certain Problems of Society, 1865-1900. Vanderbilt 1961

S430 Spalding, Billups P. Georgia and South Carolina during the Oglethorpe Period, 1732-1743. NC 1963

S431 Spalding, Hobart A., Jr. Aspects of Change in Argentina, 1890-1914. Cal, Berkeley 1965

S432 Spalding, Karen W. Indian Rural Society in Colonial Peru: The Example of Huarochirí. Cal, Berkeley 1967

S433 Spalding, Robert V. The Boston Mercantile Community and the Promotion of the Textile Industry in Northern New England, 1810-1860. Yale 1963

S434 Spangenberg, Bradford B. Status and Policy: The Character of the Covenanted Civil Service of India and Its Ramifications for British Administration and Policy in the Late Nineteenth Century. Duke 1967

S435 Spaniolo, Charles V. Charles Anderson Dana: His Early Life and Civil War Career. Mich S 1965

S436 Spaulding, James E. The Mint-Cities of Visigothic Spain: Leovigild to Achila II. Duke 1970

S437 Spaulding, Robert M., Jr. Imperial Japan's "Higher Examinations." Mich U 1965

S438 Spear, Allan H. Black Chicago, 1900-1920: The Making of a Negro Ghetto. Yale 1965

S439 Speck, William A. The Role of the Christian Historian in the Twentieth Century as Seen in the Writing of Kenneth Scott Latourette, Christopher Dawson, and Herbert Butterfield. Fla S 1965

S440 Spector, Robert M. W. Cameron Forbes and the Hoover Commissions to Haiti. Boston U 1961

S441 Spector, Ronald H. "Professors of War": The Naval War College and the Modern American Navy. Yale 1967

S442 Spector, Stanley. Li Hung-chang and the Huai-chun. Wash U 1953

S443 Spector, Stephen D. United States Attempts at Regional Security and the Extension of the Good Neighbor Policy in Latin America, 1945-1952. NYU 1970

S444 Speidel, William M. Liu Ming-ch'uan in Taiwan, 1884-1891. Yale 1967

S445 Speizman, Milton D. Attitudes toward Charity in American Thought, 1865-1901. Tulane 1962

S446 Spence, Jonathan D. Ts'ao Yin and the Chinese Bondservants: Imperial Bureaucracy in the Early Ch'ing Period. Yale 1965

S447 Spence, Vernon G. Colonel Morgan Jones, 1839-1926: Grand Old Man of Texas Railroading. Colo 1968

S448 Spencer, Elaine G. West German Coal, Iron and Steel Industrialists as Employers, 1896-1914. Cal, Berkeley 1969

S449 Spencer, George W. Royal Leadership and Imperial Conquest in Medieval South India: The Naval Expedition of Rajendra Chola I, c. 1025 A.D. Cal, Berkeley 1967

S450 Sperry, James R. Organized Labor and Its Fight against Military and Industrial Conscription, 1917-1945. Ariz 1968

S451 Spetter, Allan B. Harrison and Blaine: Foreign Policy, 1889-1893. Rutgers 1967

S452 Spielvogel, Jackson J. Willibald Pirckheimer and the Nuernberg City Council. Ohio 1967

S453 Spiese, John G. John Ruskin as a Writer of History. Penn S 1969

S454 Spindler, Frank M. The Political Thought of Juan Montalvo. Am 1966

S455 Spinner, Thomas J., Jr. George Joachim Goschen, 1831-1907: British Statesman and Politician. Rochester 1964

S456 Spira, Thomas. The Growth of Magyar National Awareness under Francis I, 1792-1835. McGill 1970

S457 Spitz, Douglas R. The Marquis of Argyll, 1618-1644. Neb 1964

S458 Spitzer, Anne L. The *Summa de Legibus* of Gilbert of Thornton. Harvard 1966

S459 Spitzer, Leo. Sierra Leone Creole Reactions to Westernization, 1870-1925. Wis 1969

S460 Sponholtz, Lloyd L. Progressivism in Microcosm: An Analysis of the Political Forces at Work in the Ohio Constitutional Convention of 1912. Pitt 1969

S461 Springer, William H. The Military Apprenticeship of Arthur Wellesley in India, 1797-1805. Yale 1966

S462 Sprunger, Keith L. The Learned Doctor Ames. Ill 1963

S463 Spurgeon, Jonathan W. London during the Commonwealth, 1649-1653. Wis 1963

S464 Spurk, John H. Catholicism and Protestantism: Their Contributions and Responses to the Movement toward Western European Integration, 1945-1965. Boston U 1968

S465 Spyridakis, Stylianos. Itanos: A Ptolemaic Possession in Crete. UCLA 1966

S466 Stabler, Carey V. The History of the Alabama Public Health System. Duke 1945

S467 Stachowski, Floyd J. The Political Career of Daniel Webster Hoan. Northwestern 1966

S468 Stackman, Ralph R. Laurence A. Steinhardt: New Deal Diplomat, 1933-1945. Mich S 1967

S469 Stadelman, Bonnie S. S. The Amusements of the American Soldiers during the Revolution. Tulane 1969

S470 Stagakis, George J. Institutional Aspects of the Hetairos Relationship. Wis 1962

S471 Stalnaker, John C. The Emergence of the Protestant Clergy in Central Germany: The Case of Hesse. Cal, Berkeley 1970

S472 Standard, Diffee W. *DeBow's Review*, 1846-1880: A Magazine of Southern Opinion. NC 1970

S473 Stanley, Judith M. The Congressional Democrats, 1918-1928. Cal, Berkeley 1969

S474 Stanley, Peter W. A Nation in the Making: The Philippines and the United States, 1899-1921. Harvard 1970

S475 Stansky, Peter D. L. The Leadership of the Liberal Party, 1894-1899. Harvard 1961

S476 Starbuck, James C. Oakland, Michigan: A Statistical History of a Detroit Suburban County. Chicago 1968

S477 Stark, Bruce P. Lebanon, Connecticut: A Study of Society and Politics in the Eighteenth Century. Conn 1970

S478 Stark, John D. William Watts Ball: A Study in Conservatism. Duke 1961

S479 Starkey, Armstrong M., III. The Diplomatic Career of Alexander Campbell, Lord Polwarth, 1716-1725. Ill 1968

S480 Starkey, John B. The Inquisition and Its American Interpretations (1800-1900). St John's 1966

S481 Starn, Randolph R. Donati Iannocti *Aliorumque Epistolae (Biblioteca Universitaria Alessandrina,* Rome, MS 107): A Critical Edition with Introduction and Commentary. Harvard 1967

S482 Starobin, Robert S. Industrial Slavery in the Old South, 1790-1861: A Study in Political Economy. Cal, Berkeley 1968

S483 Starr, Daniel P. Nelson Trusler Johnson: The United States and the Rise of Nationalist China, 1925-1937. Rutgers 1967

S484 Starr, Raymond G. Conservative Revolution: South Carolina Public Affairs, 1775-1790. Tex U 1964

S485 Starr, S. Frederick. Decentralization and Self-Government in Russia, 1855-1865. Princeton 1968

S486 Startt, James D. American Editorial Opinion of Woodrow Wilson and the Main Problems of Peacemaking in 1919. Md 1965

S487 Staude, John R. Max Scheler: Philosopher, Sociologist, and Critic of German Culture (1912-1928). Cal, Berkeley 1964

S488 Stave, Bruce M. The New Deal and the Building of an Urban Political Machine: Pittsburgh, a Case Study. Pitt 1966

S489 Stavrou, Theofanis G. The Russian Imperial Orthodox Palestine Society, 1882-1914. Ind 1961

S490 Stayer, James M. The Doctrine of the Sword in the First Decade of Anabaptism. Cornell 1964

S491 Stea, Patricia Ellen W. Exiles and Citizens: Spanish Republican Refugees in Mexico. Stanford 1970

S492 Stearns, Owen P. James Bryce and American Democracy, 1870-1922. Rochester 1965

S493 Stearns, Peter N. Employer and Worker in France, 1820-1848: A Study of Attitudes. Harvard 1963

S494 Stearns, Robert A. The Morgan-Guggenheim Syndicate and the Development of Alaska, 1906-1915. Cal, Santa Barbara 1967

S495 Stearns, Stephen J. The Caroline Military System, 1625-1627: The Expeditions to Cadiz and Ré. Cal, Berkeley 1967

S496 Stebbins, Phillip E. A History of the Role of the United States Supreme Court in Foreign Policy. Ohio 1966

S497 Stebbins, Robert E. French Reactions to Darwin, 1859-1882. Minn 1965

S498 Steckler, Gerard G. Charles John Seghers, Missionary Bishop in the American Northwest. Wash U 1963

S499 Steckling, Ronald A. Jean Lemoine as Canonist and Political Thinker. Wis 1964

S500 Steele, Hollins M., Jr. European Settlement vs. Muslim Property: The Foundation of Colonial Algeria, 1830-1880. Columbia 1965

S501 Steele, Richard W. Roosevelt, Marshall, and the First Offensive: The Politics of Strategy Making, 1941-1942. JH 1969

S502 Steen, Charlie R., III. A Survey of the Notion of Christendom, Principally in France, 1580-1690. UCLA 1970

S503 Steen, Ivan D. The British Traveler and the American City, 1850-1860. NYU 1962

S504 Steeples, Douglas W. Five Troubled Years: A History of the Depression of 1893-1897. NC 1961

S505 Steffel, Richard V. Housing for the Working Classes in the East End of London, 1890-1907. Ohio 1969

S506 Steffens, Henry J. James Prescott Joule and the Development of the Principle of the Conservation of Energy. Cornell 1968

S507 Stehlin, Stewart A. Bismarck and the Guelph Problem, 1866-1890. Yale 1965

S508 Steidle, Barbara C. Conservative Progressives: A Study of the Attitudes and Role of Bar and Bench, 1905-1912. Rutgers 1969

S509 Steiman, Lionel B. Stefan Zweig: The Education of an Aesthete and His Response to War and Politics. Penn U 1970

S510 Stein, George H. The Waffen SS: A Political Army at War, 1939-1945. Columbia 1964

S511 Stein, Harry H. Lincoln Steffens: An Intellectual Portrait. Minn 1965

S512 Stein, Leon. The Revival of German Patriotic Humanism in the Age of the Thirty Years War, c. 1630-1670. NYU 1966

S513 Stein, Walter J. California and the "Dust Bowl" Migration. Cal, Berkeley 1969

S514 Steinberg, David J. The Philippines during World War Two: A Study in Political Collaboration. Harvard 1964

S515 Steinel, James H. The Political Thought of Jaime Balmes. St L 1963

S516 Steiner, Bruce E. Samuel Seabury and the Forging of the High Church Tradition: A Study in the Evolution of New England Churchmanship, 1722-1796. Va 1962

S517 Steinmeyer, George W. Disposition of Surplus War Property: An Administrative History, 1944-1949. Okla 1969

S518 Stelter, Gilbert A. The Urban Frontier: A Western Case Study, Cheyenne, Wyoming, 1867-1887. Alberta 1968

S519 Stembridge, Stanley R. British Attitudes towards Empire, 1846-1880. Harvard 1962

S520 Steneck, Nicholas H. The Problem of the Internal Senses in the 14th Century. Wis 1970

S521 Stenger, Wilbur J., Jr. Walther Rathenau and the Policy of Fulfillment: The Reparations Issue in German Foreign Policy, 1919-1922. Georgetown 1965

S522 Stephens, Alva R. A History of the Taft Ranch and Its Role in the Development of the South Texas Plains. Tex U 1962

S523 Stern, Howard N. Political Crime and Justice in the Weimar Republic. JH 1966

S524   Stern, Sheldon M.   The American Perception of the Emergence of Adolf Hitler and the Nazis, 1923-1934. Harvard 1970

S525   Sterns, Indrikis.   The Statutes of the Teutonic Knights: A Study of Religious Chivalry. Penn U 1969

S526   Sternstein, Jerome L.   Nelson W. Aldrich: The Making of the "General Manager of the United States," 1841-1886. Brown 1968

S527   Stevens, Donald G.   The United States and the League of Nations during the Manchurian Crisis, September-December, 1931. St John's 1967

S528   Stevens, John K.   Franco-Russian Relations, 1856-1863. Ill 1962

S529   Stevens, L. Tomlin.   Carter Braxton: Signer of the Declaration of Independence. Ohio 1969

S530   Stevens, Paul D.   Laurier and the Liberal Party in Ontario, 1887-1911. Toronto 1966

S531   Stevens, Robert C.   Mexico's Forgotten Frontier: A History of Sonora, 1821-1846. Cal, Berkeley 1963

S532   Stevens, Wesley M.   Hrabanus Maurus on Reckoning. Emory 1968

S533   Stevenson, Thomas H.   The Early Maturity of Jean, Bastard of Orléans: A Consideration of Roles and Allegiances (1430-1449). Chicago 1964

S534   Steward, Dick H.   In Search of Markets: The New Deal, Latin America, and Reciprocal Trade. Mo 1969

S535   Stewart, Barbara M.   United States Government Policy on Refugees from Nazism, 1933-1940. Columbia 1969

S536   Stewart, James B.   Joshua R. Giddings and the Tactics of Radical Politics, 1795-1864. Case W Reserve 1968

S537   Stewart, Paul J., Jr.   The Army of the Catholic Kings: Spanish Military Organization and Administration in the Reign of Ferdinand and Isabella, 1474-1516. Ill 1961

S538   Stewart, Peter C.   The Commercial History of Hampton Roads, Virginia, 1815-1860. Va 1967

S539   Still, William N., Jr.   The Construction and Fitting Out of Ironclad Vessels-of-War within the Confederacy. Ala 1964

S540   Stinchcombe, William C.   The French-American Alliance in American Politics, 1778-1783. Mich U 1967

S541   Stites, Francis N.   The Dartmouth College Case, 1819. Ind 1968

S542   Stites, Richard T.   The Question of the Emancipation of Women in Nineteenth Century Russia. Harvard 1968

S543   Stoan, Stephen K., Jr.   Pablo Morillo and Venezuela, 1815-1820. Duke 1970

S544   Stock, Leo F.   The British Parliament in Early Colonial Administration as Shown by Its Proceedings Relating to America, 1572-1625. Cath 1920

S545   Stock, Phyllis H.   New Quarrel of Ancients and Moderns: The French University and Its Opponents, 1899-1914. Yale 1965

S546   Stocker, Christopher W.   Offices and Officers in the Parlement of Paris, 1483-1515. Cornell 1965

S547   Stockton, Constant N.   Hume's *Constitutional History of England*. Claremont 1968

S548   Stoddart, Jessie L.   Constitutional Crisis and the House of Lords, 1621-1629. Cal, Berkeley 1966

S549   Stoesen, Alexander R.   The Senatorial Career of Claude D. Pepper. NC 1965

S550   Stokes, Dewey A., Jr.   Public Affairs in Arkansas, 1836-1850. Tex U 1966

S551   Stokes, Durward T.   The Clergy of the Carolinas and the American Revolution. NC 1968

S552   Stokesbury, James L.   British Concepts and Practices of Amphibious Warfare, 1867-1916. Duke 1968

S553   Stolfi, Russel H.   Reality and Myth: French and German Preparations for War, 1933-1940. Stanford 1966

S554   Stone, Bernard B.   Nationalist and Internationalist Currents in Polish Socialism: The PPS and SDKPiL, 1893-1921. Chicago 1965

S555   Stone, Ralph A.   The Irreconcilables and the Fight against the League of Nations. Ill 1961

S556   Stonehouse, Merlin.   Lincoln's Carpetbagger, J. W. North. UCLA 1961

S557   Stoneman, William E.   A History of the Economic Analysis of the Great Depression in America. Harvard 1970

S558   Stonesifer, Roy P., Jr.   The Forts Henry-Heiman and Fort Donelson Campaigns: A Study of Confederate Command. Penn S 1965

S559   Storch, Neil T.   Congressional Politics and Diplomacy, 1775-1783. Wis 1969

S560   Storch, Rudolph H.   Tropaea on the Coinage of Ancient Rome. Ohio 1967

S561   Storey, Brit A.   William Jackson Palmer: A Biography. Ky 1968

S562   Storey, John W.   The Negro in Southern Baptist Thought, 1865-1900. Ky 1968

S563   Stout, Neil R.   The Royal Navy in American Waters, 1760-1775. Wis 1962

S564   Stowe, Noel J.   The *Tumulto* of 1624: Turmoil at Mexico City. S Cal 1970

S565   Strain, Jacqueline.   Feminism and Political Radicalism in the German Social Democratic Movement, 1890-1914. Cal, Berkeley 1964

S566   Strait, Paul W.   The Urban Community of Cologne in the Twelfth Century. Princeton 1970

S567   Straka, Waclaw W.   The Scottish Industrial Labourer during the Age of Reform, 1792-1832. McGill 1963

S568   Strand, Wilson E.   The Canadianism of Sir Wilfrid Laurier: A Study of His Liberalism and Nationalism from 1871-1911. Geo P 1967

S569   Strassmaier, James F.   Karl Grün: The Confrontation with Marx, 1844-1848. Loyola 1970

S570   Stratton, Porter A.   The Territorial Press of New Mexico, 1834-1912. Tex Tech 1967

S571   Strausberg, Stephen, F.   The Administration and Sale of Public Land in Indiana, 1800-1860. Cornell 1970

S572   Strauss, David.   Anti-Americanism and the Defense of France: An Analysis of French Travel Reports, 1917-1960. Columbia 1968

S573   Strauss, Sylvia.   H. G. Wells and America. Rutgers 1968

S574   Strawbridge, George, Jr.   Militarism and Nationalism in Chile, 1920-1932. Penn U 1968

S575   Strebel, George L.   Irrigation as a Factor in Western History, 1847-1890. Cal, Berkeley 1965

S576   Stremski, Richard.   Britain's China Policy, 1920-1928. Wis 1968

S577   Strickland, Arvarh E.   The Chicago Urban League, 1915-1956. Ill 1962

S578   Stricklen, Charles G., Jr.   The Emergence of Modern Liberal Constitutionalism in France, 1770-1789. Yale 1966

S579   Stricklin, Thomas E.   The Privilege of Freedom from Arrest and Molestation in the House of Commons, 1604-1629. Miss S 1968

S580   Stroik, Raymond J.   Ideas of Individualism: A Twentieth Century Social Critique. Wis 1968

S581   Strong, George V.   Nationalism and Socialism: A Study in the Attitudes of the German-Austrian Social Democratic Party to the Nationality Question, 1907-1918, with Special Attention to the Czechs and South Slavs. NC 1969

S582   Strong, John W.   Russian Relations with Khiva, Bukhara, and Kokand, 1800-1858. Harvard 1964

S583   Struever, Nancie S.   Rhetoric and Historical Consciousness in Italian Humanism: Rhetorical and Historical Modes in Coluccio Salutati, Leonardo Bruni, and Poggio Bracciolini. Rochester 1966

S584   Struve, Walter C.   Elite *versus* Democracy: The Conflict of Elite Theories with the Ideals of Political Democracy in Germany, 1918-1933. Yale 1963

S585   Stuart, Charles H.   The Lower Congo and the American Baptist Mission to 1910. Boston U 1969

S586   Stuart, Frank C.   The British Nation and India, 1906-1914. NM 1964

S587   Stuart, Jack M.   William English Walling: A Study in Politics and Ideas. Columbia 1968

S588   Studley, Elizabeth N.   Shaping of a New Era: The Politics of Georgia Reconstruction, 1865-1872. JH 1966

S589   Stukes, Joseph T.   The American Nation in 1876. SC 1962

S590   Stults, Taylor.   Imperial Russia through American Eyes, 1894-1904: A Study in Public Opinion. Mo 1970

S591   Stump, William D.   The English View Negro Slavery, 1660-1780. Mo 1962

S592   Stumpf, Vernon O.   Colonel Eleazer Oswald: Politician and Editor. Duke 1968

S593   Stunkel, Kenneth R.   Indian Ideas and Western Thought during the Romantic Age: A Critical Study. Md 1966

S594   Sturgill, Claude C.   Marshall Villars in the War of the Spanish Succession. Ky 1963

S595 Sturm, James L. Investing in the United States, 1798-1893: Upper Wealth-Holders in a Market Economy. Wis 1969

S596 Suchlicki, Jaime. University of Havana Students and Politics, 1920-1966. Tex C 1967

S597 Suggs, George G., Jr. Colorado Conservatives versus Organized Labor: A Study of the James Hamilton Peabody Administration, 1903-1905. Colo 1964

S598 Suhler, Samuel A. Significant Questions Relating to the History of Austin, Texas, to 1900. Tex U 1966

S599 Sullivan, Donald D. Nicholas of Cusa and Church Reform in the German Empire. Colo 1967

S600 Sullivan, James P. Louisville and Her Southern Alliance, 1865-1890. Ky 1965

S601 Sullivan, M. Carol, Sister. The Concept of Man in the Twelfth-Century Humanism of Chartres. Loyola 1967

S602 Sullivan, Margaret J. L. Hyphenism in Saint Louis, 1900-1921: The View from the Outside. St L 1968

S603 Sullivan, Richard. Some Dynastic Answers to the Armenian Question: A Study in East Anatolian Prosopography. UCLA 1970

S604 Sumler, David E. Polarization in French Politics, 1909-1914. Princeton 1969

S605 Sumners, Mary F. Edgar Stewart Wilson: The Mississippi Eagle, Journalist of the New South. Miss S 1962

S606 Suny, Ronald G. The Baku Commune, 1917-1918: Political Strategy in a Social Revolution. Columbia 1968

S607 Suplick, Stanley M., Jr. The United States Invalid Corps/Veteran Reserve Corps. Minn 1969

S608 Susskind, Jacob L. A Critical Edition of the Scientific Sections of Samuel Miller's *A Brief Retrospect of the Eighteenth Century*. Geo P 1969

S609 Sussman, Stanley A. Anglo-Byzantine Relations during the Middle Ages. Penn U 1966

S610 Sutch, Victor D. The Career of Gilbert Sheldon. Colo 1962

S611 Sutherland, Jon N. Liudprand of Cremona: Bishop, Diplomat, Historian: Three Studies of the Man and His Age. UCLA 1969

S612 Sutherland, Keith A. Congress and Crisis: A Study in the Legislative Process, 1860. Cornell 1966

S613 Sutton, Robert P. The Virginia Constitutional Convention of 1829-1830: A Profile Analysis of Late-Jeffersonian Virginia. Va 1967

S614 Sutton, Walter A. The Command of Gold: Progressive Republican Senators and Foreign Policy, 1912-1917. Tex U 1964

S615 Suval, Stanley. The *Anschluss* Problem in the Stresemann Era (1923-1929). NC 1964

S616 Svensson, Eric H. F. The Military Occupation of Japan: The First Years: Planning, Policy Formulation, and Reforms. Denver 1966

S617 Swain, Donald C. The Role of the Federal Government in the Conservation of Natural Resources, 1921-1933. Cal, Berkeley 1961

S618 Swainson, Donald W. The Personnel of Politics: A Study of the Ontario Members of the Second Federal Parliament. Toronto 1969

S619 Swank, Scott T. The Unfettered Conscience: A Study of Sectarianism, Spiritualism, and Social Reform in the New Jerusalem Church, 1840-1870. Penn U 1970

S620 Swann, Leonard A., Jr. John Roach, Maritime Entrepreneur. Harvard 1963

S621 Swanson, Glen W. Mahmud Şevet Paşa and the Defense of the Ottoman Empire: A Study of War and Revolution during the Young Turk Period. Ind 1970

S622 Swanson, James M. The Bolshevization of Scientific Societies in the Soviet Union: An Historical Analysis of the Character, Function, and Legal Position of Scientific and Scientific-Technical Societies in the USSR, 1929-1936. Ind 1968

S623 Swanson, Maynard W. The Rise of Multiracial Durban: Urban History and Race Policy in South Africa, 1830-1930. Harvard 1965

S624 Swanson, Richard A. Edmund J. James, 1855-1925: A "Conservative Progressive" in American Higher Education. Ill 1966

S625 Swartz, Marvin. The Union of Democratic Control in British Politics during World War I. Yale 1969

S626 Sweeney, David. The Life of John Lancaster Spalding, First Bishop of Peoria, 1840-1916. Cath 1963

S627 Sweeney, Ernest S. Catholic and Protestant Missionaries in Argentina, 1938-1962. Tex U 1970

S628 Sweeney, Eugene T. The Ideal of the Good Citizen, 1920-1940, as Seen by Selected Major Groups. Chicago 1961

S629 Swenson, Loyd S., Jr. The Etheral Aether: A Descriptive History of the Michelson-Morley Aether-Drift Experiments, 1880-1930. Claremont 1962

S630 Swidler, Leonard J. The History of the Una Sancta Movement in Germany. Wis 1961

S631 Swierenga, Robert P. Pioneers and Profits: Land Speculation on the Iowa Frontier. Ia 1965

S632 Swietochowski, Tadeusz A. Modernizing Trends and the Growth of National Awareness in the 19th Century Russian Azerbaidjan. NYU 1968

S633 Swift, Donald C. The Ohio Republicans, 1866-1880. Del 1967

S634 Swinney, Everette. Suppressing the Ku Klux Klan: The Enforcement of the Reconstruction Amendments, 1870-1874. Tex U 1966

S635 Sylvester, John A. Arthur Bliss Lane: American Career Diplomat. Wis 1967

S636 Sylvester, Lorna L. Oliver P. Morton and Hoosier Politics during the Civil War. Ind 1968

S637 Sylwester, Harold J. American Public Reaction to Communist Expansion: From Yalta to NATO. Kans U 1970

S638 Symcox, Geoffrey W. Louis XIV and the War in Ireland, 1689-1691. UCLA 1967

S639 Syme, Eric D. Seventh-Day Adventist Concepts on Church and State. Am 1969

S640 Synan, Harold V. The Pentecostal Movement in the United States. Ga 1967

S641 Sypher, G. Wylie. La Popelinière: Historian and Historiographer. Cornell 1961

S642 Sypher, Sallie S. Mary of Lorraine and the End of the Old Alliance. Cornell 1965

S643 Szaluta, Jacques. Marshall Petain between Two Wars, 1918-1940: The Interplay of Personality and Circumstances. Columbia 1969

S644 Szasz, Ferenc M. Three Fundamentalist Leaders: The Roles of William Bell Riley, John Roach Straton, and William Jennings Bryan in the Fundamentalist-Modernist Controversy. Rochester 1969

S645 Szporluk, Roman. M. N. Pokrovsky's Interpretation of Russian History. Stanford 1965

T

T1 Tager, Jack. The Search for Freedom: Brand Whitlock and Urban Reform. Rochester 1965

T2 Tague, James A. Public Opinion in Ohio toward the Acquisition of Oregon. Case W Reserve 1963

T3 Takaki, Ronald T. A Pro-Slavery Crusade: The Movement to Reopen the African Slave Trade. Cal, Berkeley 1967

T4 Talbott, John E. Politics and Educational Reform in Interwar France, 1919-1939. Stanford 1966

T5 Tambs, Lewis A. March to the West: Seven Centuries of Luso-Brazilian Expansion, Origins to 1808. Cal, Santa Barbara 1967

T6 Tan, Antonio S. The Emergence of Philippine Chinese National and Political Consciousness, 1880-1935. Cal, Berkeley 1969

T7 Tanenbaum, Jan K. The Radical Republican General: A Political and Military Study of General Sarrail, 1900-1917. Cal, Berkeley 1969

T8 Tanner, Helen H. Vincente Manuel de Zéspedes and the Restoration of Spanish Rule of East Florida, 1784-1790. Mich U 1961

T9 Tanner, Ralph M. James Thomas Heflin: United States Senator, 1920-1931. Ala 1967

T10 Tao, Jing-shen. The Jurched in Twelfth-Century China: A Study of Sinification. Ind 1967

T11 Tapia, Francisco X. The Existence and Development of the Town Meeting *(Cabildo Abierto)* in Spanish Colonial America. Georgetown 1963

T12 Tarnovecky, Joseph. The Purchase of Alaska: Background and Reactions. McGill 1968

T13 Tarpey, Marie V., Sister. The Role of Joseph McGarrity in the Struggle for Irish Independence. St John's 1970

T14 Tarr, Curtis W. Unification of America's Armed Forces: A Century and a Half of Conflict, 1798-1947. Stanford 1962

T15 Tarr, Joel A. William Lorimer of Illinois: A Study in Boss Politics. Northwestern 1963

T16 Tatnall, Edith C. Church and State according to John Wyclyf. Colo 1964

T17 Tatsios, Theodore G. The Cretan Problem and the Eastern Question: A Study of Greek Irredentism, 1866-1898. Georgetown 1967

T18 Tatum, Elbert L. The Changed Political Thought of the Negroes of the United States, 1915-1940. Loyola 1946

T19 Taylor, Arnold H. The United States and the International Movement to Control the Traffic in Narcotic Drugs, 1900-1939. Cath 1963

T20 Taylor, James S. Poverty in Rural Devon, 1780-1840. Stanford 1966

T21 Taylor, Mary Christine, Sister. A History of the Foundations of Catholicism in Northern New York. St L 1967

T22 Taylor, Mary Eustace, Sister. William J. Mickle (1734-1788): A Critical Study. Cath 1938

T23 Taylor, Patrick R. The Trans-Siberian Railroad and the Russian Revolution of 1905. Tenn 1969

T24 Taylor, Paul C. The Entrance of Women into Party Politics: The 1920's. Harvard 1967

T25 Taylor, Paul F. Coal and Conflict: The UMWA in Harlan County, 1931-1939. Ky 1969

T26 Taylor, Robert R. "The Word in Stone": The Role of Architecture in the National Socialist Ideology. Stanford 1970

T27 Taylor, William B. The Valley of Oaxaca: A Study of Colonial Land Distribution. Mich U 1969

T28 Taylor, William L. A Productive Monopoly: The Effect of Railroad Control on the New England Coastal Steamship Lines, 1871-1916. Brown 1968

T29 Teagarden, Ernest M. The Haldane Army Reforms, 1905-1912. Case W Reserve 1962

T30 Tedesco, Paul. Patriotism, Protection, and Prosperity: James Moore Swank, the American Iron and Steel Association, and the Tariff, 1873-1913. Boston U 1970

T31 Teffeteller, Gordon L. The Role of General Sir Rowland Hill in the Peninsular War, 1808-1814. Fla S 1969

T32 Telesca, William J. Commendatory Abbeys and the Order of Citeaux: A Study of Papal-Gallican Rivalry from 1438 to 1516. Fordham 1969

T33 Temu, Arnold J. The British Protestant Missions on the Kenya Coast and Highlands, 1873-1929. Alberta 1967

T34 Teng, Yuan-chung. Americans and the Taiping Tien Kuo: A Case of Cultural Confrontation. Georgetown 1961

T35 Tentler, Thomas N. The Problem of Anxiety and Preparation for Death in Luther, Calvin, and Erasmus. Harvard 1961

T36 Terrill, Tom E. The Tariff and Foreign Policy, 1880-1892. Wis 1966

T36a Terry, Robert L. J. Waties Waring, Spokesman for Racial Justice in the New South. Utah 1970

T37 Teruya, Yoshihiko. Bernard J. Bettelheim and Okinawa: A Study of the First Protestant Missionary to the Island Kingdom, 1845-1854. Colo 1969

T38 Têtu, Michel. *Les premiers syndicats catholiques canadiens* (1900-1921). Laval 1961

T39 Tevebaugh, John L. Merchant on the Western Frontier: William Morrison of Kaskaskia, 1790-1837. Ill 1962

T40 Texada, David K. The Administration of Alejandro O'Reilly as Governor of Louisiana, 1769-1770. LSU 1968

T41 Thacker, Jack W., Jr. The Partition of Samoa. SC 1966

T42 Thacker, Joseph A. James B. Finley: A Biography. Ky 1967

T43 Thavenet, Dennis. William Alexander Richardson, 1811-1875. Neb 1967

T44 Thayer, John A. Italy: The Post-Risorgimento and the "Great War." Wis 1961

T45 Thelen, David P. The Social and Political Origins of Wisconsin Progressivism, 1885-1900. Wis 1967

T46 Theoharis, Athan G. The Yalta Myths: An Issue in American Politics, 1945-1955. Chicago 1965

T47 Therry, James R. The Life of General Robert Cumming Schenck. Georgetown 1968

T48 Thomaidis, Speros T. The Political Theory of Philip Melanchthon. Columbia 1965

T49 Thomas, David N. Early History of the North Carolina Furniture Industry, 1880-1921. NC 1964

T50 Thomas, Emory M. The Confederate State of Richmond: A Biography of the Capital. Rice 1966

T51 Thomas, Jack R. Marmaduke Grove: A Political Biography. Ohio 1962

T52 Thomas, John L. Isaiah to the Nation: The Life of William Lloyd Garrison. Brown 1961

T53 Thomas, Nathan G. The Second Coming in the Third New England (The Millennial Impulse in Michigan, 1830-1860). Mich S 1967

T54 Thomas, Phillip D. The "Icocedron" of Walter of Odington. NM 1965

T55 Thomas, Richard H. Jenkin Lloyd Jones: Lincoln's Soldier of Civic Righteousness. Rutgers 1967

T56 Thomas, Richard J. Caleb Blood Smith: Whig Orator and Politician, Lincoln's Secretary of Interior. Ind 1969

T57 Thomas, Samuel B. The Doctrine and Strategy of the Chinese Communist Party: Domestic Aspects, 1945-1956. Columbia 1964

T58 Thomason, Michael V. R. The Colonial Government and Economic Development in Kenya, 1900-1912. Duke 1969

T59 Thompson, George H. Leadership in Arkansas Reconstruction. Columbia 1968

T60 Thompson, James H. Great Britain and the World Disarmament Conference, 1932-1934. NC 1961

T61 Thompson, Joe A. British Conservatives and Collective Security, 1918-1928. Stanford 1966

T62 Thompson, John N. The Anti-Appeasers: Backbench Conservative Critics of the National Government's Foreign Policy, 1931-1940. Princeton 1967

T63 Thompson, Larry V. Nazi Administrative Conflict: The Struggle for Executive Power in the General Government of Poland, 1939-1943. Wis 1967

T64 Thompson, Margaret Regina, Sister. The Jews and the Minorities Treaties, 1918-1929. Cath 1966

T65 Thompson, Paul S. The Summer Campaign in the Lower Valley, 1864. Va 1966

T66 Thompson, Richard H. Lothar Franz von Schönborn and the Diplomacy of the Electorate of Mainz from the Treaty of Ryswick to the Outbreak of the War of the Spanish Succession. Ind 1970

T67 Thompson, Robert A. Defense of the Northern Frontier in Ming China: Especially the Chi-Chou Area Northeast of Peking, 1569-1583. Chicago 1962

T68 Thompson, Thomas G. The Cultural History of Colorado Mining Towns, 1859-1920. Mo 1966

T69 Thomson, George. The History of Penal Institutions in the Rocky Mountain West, 1846-1900. Colo 1965

T70 Thomson, James C., Jr. Americans as Reformers in Kuomintang China, 1928-1937. Harvard 1961

T71 Thorburn, Neil A. Brand Whitlock: An Intellectual Biography. Northwestern 1965

T72 Thorn, William H., III. Russia and the British Periodical Press, 1856-1903: A Study of Attitudes toward Russian Internal Affairs. Rochester 1968

T73 Thorning, Joseph F. Religious Liberty in Transition. Cath 1931

T74 Thornton, Richard C. The Comintern and the Chinese Communists, 1928-1931. Wash U 1966

T75 Thoroughman, Thomas V. Some Political Aspects of Anglo-French Relations, 1610-1619. NC 1968

T76 Thurman, Michael E. The Naval Department of San Blas, 1768-1797. S Cal 1963

T77 Thurner, Arthur W. The Impact of Ethnic Groups on the Democratic Party in Chicago, 1920-1928. Chicago 1966

T78 Tice, Nancy Jo. The Territorial Delegate, 1794-1820. Wis 1967

T79 Tillman, Elvena B. The Rights of Childhood: The National Child Welfare Movement, 1890-1919. Wis 1968

T80 Tilman, Lee R. The American Business Community and the Death of the New Deal. Ariz 1966

T81 Timberlake, Charles E. The Birth of Zemstvo Liberalism in Russia: Ivan Il'ich Petrunkevich in Chernigov. Wash U 1968

T82 Tipton, Charles L. The English *Langue* of the Knights Hospitallers during the Great Schism. S Cal 1965

T83 Tiryakian, Josefina C. The *Mercurio Peruano:* Herald of the Modernization of Peru in the Eighteenth Century. Harvard 1969

T84 Tishler, Hace S. Self-Reliance and Social Security, 1870-1917. Columbia 1969

T85 Tobey, Ronald C. The New Sciences and Democratic Society: The American Ideology of National Science, 1919-1930. Cornell 1969

T86 Tobias, Norman. Basil I (867-886), the Founder of the Macedonian Dynasty: A Study of the Political and Military History of the Byzantine Empire in the Ninth Century. Rutgers 1969

T87 Tobler, Douglas F. German Historians and the Weimar Republic. Kans U 1967

T88 Toborg, Alfred. Frederick II of Prussia and His Relations with Great Britain during the American Revolution. Columbia 1965

T89 Todd, Albert C., Jr. The Romantic Resurrection: Origins of Berdyaev's Philosophy of History. Georgetown 1968

T90 Todd, James E. Charles de Gaulle: His Role in the Military Controversies of the 1930's and in the Formation of the Free French Movement in the Summer of 1940. Colo 1964

T91 Todd, Joan M. Persian *Paedia* and Greek *Historia:* An Interpretation of the *Cyropaedia* of Xenophon, Book One. Pitt 1968

T92 Todd, Richard A. Popular Violence and Internal Security in Hellenistic Alexandria. Cal, Berkeley 1963

T93 Todd, Willie G. The Slavery Issue and the Organization of a Southern Baptist Convention. NC 1964

T94 Toews, John A. Sebastian Franck: Friend and Critic of Early Anabaptism. Minn 1964

T95 Toews, John B. Emperor Frederick III and His Relations with the Papacy from 1440 to 1493. Colo 1962

T96 Toft, Daniel J. Shadows of Kings: The Political Thought of David Pareus, 1548-1622. Wis 1970

T97 Tolis, Peter. Elihu Burritt, Crusader for Brotherhood. Columbia 1965

T98   Tolles, Bryant F.   College Architecture in Northern New England before 1860: A Social and Cultural History. Boston U 1970

T99   Tolmie, Murray M.   General and Particular Baptists in the Puritan Revolution. Harvard 1961

T100   Tolson, Arthur L.   The Negro in Oklahoma Territory, 1889-1907: A Study in Racial Discrimination. Okla 1966

T101   Tomberlin, Joseph A.   The Negro and Florida's System of Education: The Aftermath of the *Brown* Case. Fla S 1967

T102   Tompkins, Clinton D.   Senator Arthur H. Vandenburg, 1884-1945. Mich U 1966

T103   Tompson, Richard S.   Classics and Charity: The English Grammar School in the 18th Century. Mich U 1967

T104   Tomsich, John M.   The Genteel Tradition in America, 1850-1910. Wis 1963

T105   Ton, Paul.   Henry Miller Porter, Merchant, Private Banker and Cattleman, 1858-1917: The Education and Basic Vocations of a Western Entrepreneur. Denver 1969

T105a   Toplin, Robert B.   The Movement for the Abolition of Slavery in Brazil, 1880-1888. Rutgers 1968

T106   Torodash, Martin.   Woodrow Wilson and the Tariff Question: The Importance of the Underwood Act in His Reform Program. NYU 1966

T107   Totman, Conrad D.   Politics in the Tokugawa Bakufu. Harvard 1964

T108   Touhill, Blanche V.   *The Nation:* A Study of Nationalism. St L 1962

T109   Toussaint, Willard I.   Biography of an Iowa Businessman: Charles Mason, 1804-1882. Ia 1963

T110   Towle, Edward L.   Science, Commerce and the Navy on the Seafaring Frontier, (1842-1861): The Role of Lieutenant M. F. Maury and the U.S. Naval Hydrographic Office in Naval Exploration, Commercial Expansion and Oceanography before the Civil War. Rochester 1966

T111   Townsend, Charles R.   The Thought of Samuel Adams. Wis 1968

T112   Toy, Eckard V., Jr.   Ideology and Conflict in American Ultraconservatism, 1945-1960. Ore 1965

T113   Tracey, Donald R.   Thuringia under the Early Weimar Republic, 1919-1924: A Study in Reform and Reaction. Md 1967

T114   Tracy, Edward.   A History of the Socio-Economic Status of the Public School Teacher of Northampton County, 1930-1960. Lehigh 1966

T115   Tracy, James D.   Erasmus: The Growth of a Mind. Princeton 1967

T116   Traer, James F.   Marriage and the Family in French Law and Social Criticism from the End of the *Ancien Régime* to the Civil Code. Mich U 1970

T117   Traina, Michael J.   Lenin, Religion, and the Russian Orthodox Church: An Analysis of Theory and Practice. Kent 1970

T118   Traina, Richard P.   American Diplomacy and the Spanish Civil War, 1936-1939. Cal, Berkeley 1964

T119   Trainer, Edwin H.   The Dilemma of the Center: The *Mouvement Républicain Populaire* and the Radical Socialists Face the *Rassemblement du Peuple Français,* 1947-1951. Emory 1964

T120   Trani, Eugene P.   The Treaty of Portsmouth: An Adventure in Rooseveltian Diplomacy. Ind 1966

T121   Trattner, Walter I.   Social Statesman: Homer Folks, 1867-1947. Wis 1964

T122   Traylor, Idris R., Jr.   The Double-Eagle and the Fox: The Dual Monarchy and Bulgaria, 1911-1913. Duke 1965

T123   Treacy, Mildred F.   Nathanael Greene and the Southern Campaign, August, 1780-April, 1781. Utah 1962

T124   Treat, Victor H.   Migration into Louisiana, 1834-1880. Tex U 1967

T125   Tredway, Gilbert R.   Indiana against the Administration, 1861-1865. Ind 1962

T126   Trennert, Robert A.   The Far Western Indian Frontier and the Beginnings of the Reservation System, 1846-1851. Cal, Santa Barbara 1969

T127   Treon, John A.   *Martin v Hunter's Lessee:* A Case History. Va 1970

T128   Trevathan, Norman E.   The Toynbee Vogue in the United States, 1947-1957. Geo P 1968

T129   Tricamo, John E.   Tennessee Politics, 1845-1861. Columbia 1965

T130 Trigg, Hugh L. The Impact of a Pessimist: The Reception of Oswald Spengler in America, 1919-1939. Geo P 1968

T131 Tripathi, Dwijendra. United States and India: Economic Links, 1860-1900. Wis 1963

T132 Troen, Selwyn K. Schools for the City: The Growth of Public Education in St. Louis, 1838-1880. Chicago 1970

T133 Trotter, Agnes Anne. The Development of the Merchants of Death Theory of American Intervention in the First World War, 1914-1937. Duke 1966

T134 Trout, Andrew P. The Jurisdiction and the Role of the Municipality of Paris during the Colbert Ministry: A Study Based on *Registres des Délibérations du Bureau de la Ville.* Notre D 1968

T135 Trow, Clifford W. Senator Albert B. Fall and Mexican Affairs, 1912-1921. Colo 1966

T136 Troxler, George W. The Home Front in Revolutionary North Carolina. NC 1970

T137 True, Marshall M. Revolutionaries in Exile: The Cuban Revolutionary Party, 1891-1898. Va 1965

T138 Trusty, Norman L. Massachusetts Public Opinion and the Annexation of Texas, 1835-1845. Boston U 1964

T139 Tryon, Warren S. The Singing Shepherd: The Life of James T. Fields, Publisher to the Victorian Age, 1817-1881. Harvard 1961

T140 Tsai, Shih-shan Henry. Reaction to Exclusion: Ch'ing Attitudes toward Overseas Chinese in the United States, 1848-1906. Ore 1970

T141 Tsao, Kai-fu. The Rebellion of the Three Feudatories against the Manchu Throne in China, 1673-1681: Its Setting and Significance. Columbia 1965

T142 Tselos, George D. The Minneapolis Labor Movement in the 1930s. Minn 1970

T143 Tucker, Arthur W., Jr. Matthew Parker and Cecil. Ohio 1964

T144 Tucker, Clara J. The Foreign Policy of Tsar Paul I. Syracuse 1965

T145 Tucker, David M. The Mugwumps and the Money Question, 1865-1900. Ia 1965

T146 Tucker, Louis L. Thomas Clap, First President of Yale College: A Biography. Wash U 1957

T147 Tucker, M. Timothy. Political Leadership in the Illinois-Missouri German Community, 1836-1872. Ill 1968

T148 Tucker, Melvin J. The Life of Thomas Howard, Earl of Surrey and Second Duke of Norfolk, 1443-1524. Northwestern 1962

T149 Tucker, Richard P. M. G. Ranade and the Moderate Tradition in India, 1842-1901. Harvard 1966

T150 Tucker, Spencer C. The Fourth Republic and Algeria. NC 1966

T151 Tulchin, Joseph S. Dollar Diplomacy and Non-Intervention: The Latin American Policy of the United States, 1919-1924. Harvard 1965

T152 Tuleja, Thaddeus V. United States Naval Policy in the Pacific, 1930-1941. Fordham 1961

T153 Tulga, Louis C. Imperial Regulation of Morals and Conduct in the Early Principate. Ohio 1967

T154 Tull, Charles J. Father Coughlin, the New Deal, and the Election of 1936. Notre D 1962

T155 Turbow, Gerald D. Wagnerism in France, 1839-1870: A Measure of a Social and Political Trend. UCLA 1965

T156 Turner, Albert B. The Origins and Development of the War Relocation Authority. Duke 1967

T157 Turner, George D. The Aristocratic Widow in Law and Society according to the Canon Law and Customary Law of France during the Twelfth and Thirteenth Centuries. Mich U 1969

T158 Turner, John J., Jr. New York in Presidential Politics, 1789-1804. Columbia 1968

T159 Turner, Ralph V. The Role of the King in the English Royal Courts of Justice, 1199-1240. JH 1962

T160 Turney, Alfred W. Field Marshall Fedor von Bock and the German Campaigns in Russia, 1941-1942. NM 1968

T161 Tusa, Jacqueline B. Power, Priorities, and Political Insurgency: The Liberal Republican Movement, 1869-1872. Penn S 1970

T162 Tutorow, Norman E. Whigs of the Old Northwest and the Mexican War. Stanford 1968

T163 Tuttle, William M., Jr. James B. Conant, Pressure Groups, and the National Defense, 1933-1945. Wis 1967

T164 Tuve, Jeanette E. The Role of Foreign Trade and Foreign Capital in the Development of the USSR to 1927. Case W Reserve 1969

T165 Tway, Duane C. The Influence of the Hudson's Bay Company upon Canada, 1870-1889. UCLA 1963

T166 Twenter, R. Frederick. Radical Parliamentary Democrats in Prussia, 1848-1849. Conn 1970

T167 Tweton, Donald J. The Attitudes and Policies of the Theodore Roosevelt Administration toward American Agriculture. Okla 1964

T168 Twining, Charles E. Orrin Ingram: Wisconsin Lumberman. Wis 1970

T169 Twombly, Robert C. Architect: The Life and Ideas of Frank Lloyd Wright. Wis 1968

T170 Tyler, Lyon G. Civil Defense: The Impact of the Planning Years, 1945-1950. Duke 1967

T171 Tyler, Ronnie C. The Age of Cotton: Santiago Vidaurri and the Confederacy, 1861-1864. Tex C 1968

T172 Tyler, Warwick P. N. Sir Frederic Rogers, Permanent Undersecretary at the Colonial Office, 1860-1871. Duke 1963

T173 Tyrrell, Joseph M. A History of the Estates of Poitou. Emory 1961

U

U1   Udo, Edet A.   The Methodist Contribution to Education in Eastern Nigeria, 1893-1960. Boston U 1965

U2   Uhalley, Stephen, Jr.   The Foreign Relations of the Taiping Revolution. Cal, Berkeley 1967

U3   Ulibarri, Richard O.   American Interest in the Spanish-Mexican Southwest, 1803-1848. Utah 1963

U4   Ullmann, Walter.   The Quebec Bishops and Confederation. Rochester 1961

U5   Underhill, Frances A.   Papal Legates to England in the Reign of Henry III, 1216-1272. Ind 1965

U6   Underwood, Mary E.   Angus Milton McLean, Governor of North Carolina, 1925-1929. NC 1962

U7   Unger, Robert W.   Lewis Cass: Indian Superintendent of the Michigan Territory, 1813-1831: A Survey of Public Opinion as Reported by the Newspapers of the Old Northwest Territory. Ball State 1967

U8   Unrau, William E.   The Role of the Indian Agent in the Settlement of the South-Central Plains, 1861-1868. Colo 1963

U9   Unruh, Fred P.   A Historical Study of Robert Vaughan and His Views on Politics, Education, Religion and History as Reflected in the *British Quarterly Review.* Mo 1962

U10   Updike, Jon E.   The Special Commission and the Danubian Elections of 1857. Penn U 1968

U11   Upson, Helen R.   Order and System: Charles Francis Adams, Jr., and the Railroad Problem. Ia 1969

U12   Urban, William L.   The Baltic Crusade of the Thirteenth Century. Tex U 1967

U13   Urbansky, Andrew B.   Hungary, the Balkans and Byzantium during the Period of the Comneni. NYU 1964

U14   Urgo, Louis A.   British Newspaper Reaction to the Rise of Mussolini, August 1922-August 1923. Georgetown 1967

U15   Urofsky, Melvin I.   Big Steel and the Wilson Administration: A Study in Business-Government Relations. Columbia 1968

U16   Ursul, George R.   The Greek Church in the English Travel Literature of the Nineteenth Century. Harvard 1966

U17   Usher, Jean E.   William Duncan of Metlakatla: A Victorian Missionary in British Columbia. British Columbia 1969

U18   Utley, Jonathan G.   The Department of State and the Far East, 1937-1941: A Study of the Ideas behind Its Diplomacy. Ill 1970

U19   Uya, Okon E.   From Servitude to Service: Robert Smalls, 1839-1915. Wis 1969

U20   Uz-Zaman, Waheed.   Major Currents of Muslim Politics in India, 1928-1940. Toronto 1961

V

V1 Vadney, Thomas E. Donald Richberg and American Liberalism. Wis 1968

V2 Vahle, Cornelius W., Jr. Congress, the President, and Overseas Expansion, 1897-1901. Georgetown 1967

V3 Valaik, John D. American Catholics and the Spanish Civil War, 1931-1939. Rochester 1964

V4 Vallely, Lois M. George Stephens and the Saar Basin Governing Commission. McGill 1965

V5 Valone, James S. The Huguenots and the War of the Spanish Marriages. Mich U 1965

V6 Vandenplas, Jacques E. The Social and Economic Policies of the First Blum Government, 1936-1937. Cal, Davis 1967

V7 Vanderheyden, Mark A. The Reactions of the Press in Ghent to the Social Revolt of March 1886. Cath 1968

V8 Vander Hill, C. Warren. Gerrit J. Diekema: A Michigan Dutch-American Political Leader, 1859-1930. Denver 1967

V9 Vander Molen, Ronald J. Richard Cox (1499-1581), Bishop of Ely: An Intellectual Biography of a Renaissance and Reformation Administrator. Mich S 1969

V10 Vanderwood, Paul J. The Rurales: Mexico's Rural Police Force, 1861-1914. Tex U 1970

V11 Van Deventer, Carroll F. The Free Soil Party in the Northwest in the Elections of 1848. Ill 1968

V12 Van Deventer, David E. The Emergence of Provincial New Hampshire, 1628-1741. Case W Reserve 1969

V13 Vanek, Wilda M. Piero Gobetti as Critic of Italian Life, 1918-1926. Harvard 1963

V14 Van Horn, Harold E. Humanist as Educator: The Public Life of Henry Merritt Wriston. Denver 1968

V15 Van Hove, Peter J. Working-Class Crowds and Political Change in Buenos Aires, 1919-1945. NM 1970

V16 Van Kley, Edwin J. China in the Eyes of the Dutch, 1592-1685. Chicago 1964

V17 Vann, James A. The Swabian Kreis, 1664-1715: Parliamentary Politics and Feudal Privilege in the Holy Roman Empire. Harvard 1970

V18 Vann, John D., III. A Study of the Seigneurial Transactions and Possessions of the Temple in France (1120-1307). Yale 1965

V19 Van Ness, James S. The Maryland Courts in the American Revolution: A Case Study. Md 1968

V20 Van Orman, Richard A. Hotels in the Trans-Mississippi West, 1865-1890. Ind 1964

V21 Van Osdell, John G., Jr. Cotton Mills, Labor, and the Southern Mind, 1880-1930. Tulane 1966

V22 Van Slyke, Lyman P. Friends and Enemies: The United Front and Its Place in Chinese Communist History. Cal, Berkeley 1964

V23 Van Valen, Nelson S. Power Politics: The Struggle for Municipal Ownership of Electric Utilities in Los Angeles, 1905-1937. Claremont 1964

V24 Van Zijl, Theodore. Gerard Groote, Ascetic and Reformer (1340-1384). Cath 1963

V25 Vaporis, Nomikos M. The Controversy on the Translation of the Scriptures into Modern Greek and Its Effects, 1818-1843. Columbia 1970

V26 Varcados, Peter R. Labor and Politics in San Francisco, 1880-1892. Cal, Berkeley 1968

V27 Várdy, Steven B. Baron Joseph Eötvös: The Political Profile of a Liberal Hungarian Thinker and Statesman. Ind 1967

V28 Vaughan, Alden T. New England Puritans and the American Indian, 1620-1675. Columbia 1964

V29 Vaughn, William P. The Sectional Conflict in Southern Public Education, 1865-1876. Ohio 1961

V30 Vecchio, Alfred E. The Literary and Moral Personality of Leon Battista Alberti. NYU 1966

V31 Vecoli, Rudolph J. Chicago's Italians prior to World War I: A Study of Their Social and Economic Adjustment. Wis 1963

V32 Velde, M. Richard Ann, Sister. Muscovy in the Sixteenth Century: The Accounts of Sigismund von Herberstein and Antonio Possevino. Ind 1966

V33 Venables, Robert W. Tryon County, 1775-1783: A Frontier in Revolution. Vanderbilt 1967

V34 Ventry, Lance T. The Impact of the United States Committee on Public Information on Italian Participation in the First World War. Cath 1968

V35 Venza, James R., Jr. Federalists in Congress, 1800-1812. Vanderbilt 1967

V36 Vermes, Gabor P. Count István Tisza: A Political Biography. Stanford 1966

V37 Verstandig, Lee L. The Emergence of the Two-Party System in Maryland, 1787-1796. Brown 1970

V38 Vess, David M. French Military Medicine during the Revolution, 1792-1795. Ala 1965

V39 Vexler, Robert I. The Intellectual Origins of the French Labor Movement, 1852-1870. Minn 1965

V40 Veysey, Laurence R. The Emergence of the American University, 1865-1910: A Study in the Relations between Ideals and Institutions. Cal, Berkeley 1961

V41 Via, Anthony P. The Conflict in South Italy between Byzantium and the West in the Late Tenth and Early Eleventh Centuries. Wis 1966

V42 Viault, Birdsall S. The Peace Issue, 1939-1940. Duke 1963

V43 Vigil, Ralph H. Alonso de Zorita, Oidor in the Indies, 1548-1556. NM 1969

V44 Vigilante, Emil C. The Temperance Reform in New York State, 1829-1851. NYU 1964

V45 Viles, Perry. The Shipping Interest of Bordeaux, 1774-1793. Harvard 1965

V46 Villa, Brian L. A Case Study in Imperialism: Tunisia, 1881. Harvard 1969

V46a Vinz, Warren L. A Comparison between Elements of Protestant Fundamentalism and McCarthyism. Utah 1968

V47 Viola, Herman J. Thomas L. McKenney and the Administration of Indian Affairs, 1824-1830. Ind 1970

V48 Vipperman, Carl J. William Lowndes: South Carolina Nationalist, 1782-1822. Va 1966

V49 Viseltear, Arthur J. The Lithontriptic Medicines of the Eighteenth Century. UCLA 1965

V50 Visser, Derk. Thorstein Veblen's *Imperial Germany and the Industrial Revolution.* Bryn Mawr 1966

V51 Vocke, William F. The Athenian Heralds. Cincinnati 1970

V52 Voegeli, Victor J., III. The Northwest and the Negro during the Civil War. Tulane 1965

V53 Vogel, Dorothy C. Historiographical Analysis of the Baden Revolutions of 1848-1849. NYU 1970

V54 Vogel, Sally Ann H. A Political and Intellectual Biography of Sergei Mikhailovich Kravchinsky (Stepniak), 1851-1895. NM 1970

V55 Vogel, Virgil H. J. American Indian Medicine and Its Influence on White Medicine and Pharmacology. Chicago 1966

V56 Vogt, John L., Jr. Portuguese Exploration in Brazil and the Feitoria System, 1500-1530: The First Economic Cycle of Brazilian History. Va 1967

V57 Voight, Robert C. Defender of the Common Law: Aaron Goodrich, Chief Justice of Minnesota Territory. Minn 1962

V58 Volan, Denys. The History of the Ground Observer Corps. Colo 1969

V59 Volz, Carl A. Honorius Augustodunensis: Twelfth Century Enigma. Fordham 1966

V60 Von den Steinen, Karl. The Fabric of an Interest: The First Duke of Dorset and Kentish and Sussex Politics, 1705-1765. UCLA 1969

V61 Von der Heide, John T., Jr. Heinrich von Sybel and the Prussian School: A Study in Historical Interpretation. Northwestern 1963

V62 von Loewe, Karl F. The Lithuanian Statute of 1529: A Translation and Commentary. Kans U 1969

V63 von Wahlde, Peter H. C. Military Thought in Imperial Russia. Ind 1966

V64 Voorhis, Jerry L. A Study of Official Relations between the German and Danish Governments in the Period between 1940-1943. Northwestern 1968

V65 Vos, Howard F. The Great Awakening in Connecticut. Northwestern 1967

V66 Vuckovic, Milorad N. Parliamentary Opinion and British Foreign Policy, 1936-1938, with Special Reference to Germany. McGill 1966

W

W1 Wachtel, Dennis F. De Gaulle and the Invasion of North Africa. St L 1964

W2 Wack, John T. The University of Notre Dame du Lac: Foundation, 1842-1857. Notre D 1967

W3 Wade, Harry E. John Francis Bray: An Evaluation of His Place in the History of Socialist Thought. St L 1967

W4 Wade, James E. Persia: Britain's Pawn in India's Defense, 1797-1841. Ga 1968

W5 Wade, Rex A. War, Peace, and Foreign Policy during the Russian Provisional Government of 1917. Neb 1963

W6 Wade, Simeon M., Jr. The Idea of Luxury in Eighteenth-Century England. Harvard 1969

W7 Wagenvort-Regin, Deric. The Development of Schiller's Historical and Philosophical Thought. Columbia 1964

W8 Wagman, Morton. The Struggle for Representative Government in New Netherland. Columbia 1969

W9 Wagner, Edward J., II. State-Federal Relations during the War of 1812. Ohio 1963

W10 Wagner, Henry. Forgotten Hero: The Moses DeWitt Story. Syracuse 1965

W11 Wagner, Jonathan F. The Political Evolution of Gervinus. Wis 1969

W12 Wagner, Keith E. Economic Development in Pennsylvania during the Civil War, 1861-1865. Ohio 1969

W13 Wagnon, William O., Jr. The Politics of Economic Growth: The Truman Administration and the 1949 Recession. Mo 1970

W14 Wagoner, Harless D. The U.S. Machine Tools Industry from 1900 to 1950. Am 1967

W15 Wagstaff, Thomas. Andrew Johnson and the National Union Movement, 1865-1866. Wis 1967

W16 Wahl, James A. Baldus de Ubaldis' Concept of State: A Study in Fourteenth Century Legal Theory. St L 1968

W17 Waite, Mariella D. Political Institutions in the Trans-Appalachian West, 1770-1800. Fla U 1961

W18 Wakelyn, Jon L. William Gilmore Simms, the Artist as Public Man: A Political Odyssey, 1830-1860. Rice 1966

W19 Wakeman, Frederic E., Jr. Strangers at the Gate: Social Disorder in South China. Cal, Berkeley 1965

W20 Wakstein, Allen M. The Open-Shop Movement, 1919-1933. Ill 1961

W21 Waldman, Martin R. Henri Rochefort. Syracuse 1968

W22 Waldo, Gary M. Mussolini and the War, 1914-1919. Chicago 1969

W23 Walker, Barbara M. The Grandmesnils: A Study in Norman Baronial Enterprise. Cal, Santa Barbara 1969

W24 Walker, Claire B. A History of Factory Legislation and Inspection in New York State, 1886-1911. Columbia 1969

W25 Walker, Ernestine. Struggle for the Reform of Parliament, 1853-1867. Case W Reserve 1964

W26 Walker, Forrest A. The Civil Works Administration: An Experiment in Federal Work Relief, 1933-1934. Okla 1962

W27 Walker, Henry P. The Rise and Decline of High Plains Wagon Freighting, 1822-1880. Colo 1965

W28 Walker, Lawrence D. Hitler Youth and Catholic Youth, 1933-1936: A Study in Totalitarian Conquest. Cal, Berkeley 1965

W29 Walker, Sue S. Royal Wardship in Medieval England. Chicago 1966

W30 Wall, Donald D. National Socialist Policy and Attitudes toward the Churches in Germany, 1939-1945. Colo 1969

W31 Wall, Edward F., Jr. Joseph Lancaster and the Origins of the British and Foreign School Society. Columbia 1966

W32 Wall, Irwin M. French Socialism and the Popular Front. Columbia 1968

W33 Wall, Robert E., Jr. The Membership of the Massachusetts General Court, 1634-1686. Yale 1965

W34   Wallace, Andrew.   Soldier in the Southwest: The Career of General A. V. Kautz, 1869-1886. Ariz 1968

W35   Wallace, David H.   John Rogers, the People's Sculptor. Columbia 1961

W35a   Wallace, Harold L.   The Campaign of 1948. Ind 1970

W36   Wallace, John E.   The Case of Otto Abetz. S Miss 1969

W37   Wallace, Sylvia F.   Charles Kenneth Leith, Scientific Adviser. Wis 1966

W38   Wallace, Wesley H.   The Development of Broadcasting in North Carolina, 1922-1948. Duke 1962

W39   Wallenberger, Margaret K.   The Revolutions of the 1830's and the Rise of German Nationalism. Radcliffe 1962

W40   Wallenkampf, Arnold V.   The Herero Rebellion. UCLA 1969

W41   Waller, Robert A.   Congressman Henry T. Rainey of Illinois: His Rise to the Speakership, 1903-1934. Ill 1963

W42   Walsh, Evelyn M.   Effects of the Revolution upon the Town of Boston: Social, Economic and Cultural. Brown 1964

W43   Walsh, Francis R.   The *Boston Pilot:* A Newspaper for the Irish Immigrant, 1829-1908. Boston U 1968

W44   Walsh, James P.   The Pure Church in Eighteenth Century Connecticut. Columbia 1967

W45   Walsh, Justin E.   To Print the News and Raise Hell: A Biography of Wilbur F. Storey. Ind 1964

W46   Walsh, M. Madeline, Sister.   The Role of Dubois in French Foreign Affairs, 1715-1721. Fordham 1965

W47   Walsh, Margaret.   The Manufacturing Frontier: Pioneer Industry in Antebellum Wisconsin, 1830-1860. Wis 1969

W48   Walsh, Vincent J., Jr.   The Administration of the Poor Laws in Shropshire, 1820-1855. Penn U 1970

W49   Walter, Richard J.   University Reform and Student Politics in Argentina, 1918-1960. Stanford 1966

W50   Walterman, Thomas W.   Airpower and Private Enterprise: Federal-Industrial Relations in the Aeronautics Field, 1918-1926. Wash St L 1970

W51   Walters, Edward M.   The "Partnership" Philosophy: Australian-American Space-Tracking Relations. Ga 1970

W52   Waltmann, Henry G.   The Interior Department, War Department and Indian Policy, 1865-1887. Neb 1962

W53   Walton, Brian G. J.   James K. Polk and the Democratic Party in the Aftermath of the Wilmot Proviso. Vanderbilt 1968

W54   Walton, Clarence C.   Kiderlen-Wachter and the Anglo-German Problem, 1910-1912. Cath 1949

W55   Walton, Robert C.   Zwingli's Theocracy. Yale 1964

W56   Waltrip, John R.   Public Power during the Truman Administration. Mo 1965

W57   Waltz, James C.   Western European Attitudes toward the Muslims before the Crusades. Mich S 1963

W58   Walz, John D.   State Defense and Russian Politics under the Last Tsar. Syracuse 1967

W59   Walzer, John F.   Transportation in the Philadelphia Trading Area, 1740-1775. Wis 1968

W60   Wang, Chester C.   Wang Kuo-wei (1877-1927): His Life and His Scholarship. Chicago 1962

W61   Wang, Chi.   Young Marshal Chang Hsüeh-liang and Manchuria, 1928-1931. Georgetown 1969

W62   Wank, Solomon.   Aehrenthal and the Policy of Action. Columbia 1961

W63   Ward, Forrest E.   The Lower Brazos Region of Texas, 1820-1845. Tex U 1962

W64   Ward, James A., III.   That Man Haupt: A Biography of Herman Haupt. LSU 1969

W65   Ward, James E.   Franco-Vatican Relations, 1878-1892: The Diplomatic Origins of the *Ralliement.* Cornell 1962

W66   Ward, Stephen R.   British Veterans' Organizations of the First World War. Cincinnati 1969

W67   Warden, Gerard B.   Boston Politics, 1692-1765. Yale 1966

W68   Wardin, Albert W.   The Baptists in Oregon. Ore 1967

W69   Warholoski, Ronald A.   *Neudeutschland:* German Catholic Youth, 1919 to 1939. Pitt 1964

W70   Warken, Phillip W.   A History of the National Resources Planning Board, 1933-1943. Ohio 1969

W71 Warmund, Joram. Tschirschky in Office, 1906-1914: The Tschirschky Problem. NYU 1968

W72 Warner, Ted J. The Career of Don Félix Martínez de Torrelaguna: Soldier, Presidio Commander, and Governor of New Mexico, 1693-1726. NM 1963

W73 Warnicke, Retha M. William Lambarde, Elizabethan Antiquary. Harvard 1969

W74 Warnock, Henry Y. Moderate Racial Thought and Attitudes of Southern Baptists and Methodists, 1900-1921. Northwestern 1963

W75 Warren, Fintan B. Vasco de Quiroga and His Pueblo-Hospitals of Santa Fe. NM 1963

W76 Warren, Gordon H. The *Trent* Affair, 1861-1862. Ind 1969

W77 Warren, Robert D. The Life of Samuel Northrup Castle. Georgetown 1964

W78 Warshaw, Dan. Paul Leroy-Beaulieu, Bourgeois Ideologist: A Study of the Social, Intellectual and Economic Sources of Late Nineteenth Century Imperialism. Rochester 1966

W79 Warzeski, Walter C. Religion and National Consciousness in the History of the Rusins of Carpatho-Ruthenia and the Byzantine Rite Pittsburgh Exarchate. Pitt 1964

W80 Waskow, Arthur I. The 1919 Race Riots: A Study in the Connections between Conflict and Violence. Wis 1963

W81 Waswo, Barbara A. Landlords and Social Change in Prewar Japan. Stanford 1969

W82 Waters, John J., Jr. The Otis Family in Provincial and Revolutionary Massachusetts, 1631-1780. Columbia 1965

W83 Waters, Martin J. W. P. Ryan and the Irish Ireland Movement. Conn 1970

W84 Watkins, Holland D. Plutarco Elías Calles: *El jefe máximo* of Mexico. Tex Tech 1968

W85 Watson, Charles A. Britain's Dutch Policy, 1914-1918: The View from the British Archives. Boston U 1969

W86 Watson, Judge. The Economic and Cultural Development of Eastern Kentucky from 1900 to the Present. Ind 1963

W87 Watson, William B. A Common Market in Fifteenth Century Europe: The Structure of Genoese, Venetian, Florentine, and Catalan Trade with Flanders and England. Harvard 1963

W88 Watt, John R. Theory and Practice in Chinese District Administration: The Role of the Ch'ing District Magistrate in Its Historical Setting. Columbia 1967

W89 Watterson, John S., III. Dr. Thomas Burke: A Revolutionary Career. Northwestern 1970

W90 Watts, Eugene J. Characteristics of Candidates in City Politics: Atlanta, 1865-1903. Emory 1969

W91 Watts, James F. The Public Life of Breckinridge Long, 1916-1944. Mo 1964

W92 Watts, Sheldon J. The County of Northumberland, 1590-1635. Md 1965

W93 Wax, Darold D. The Negro Slave Trade in Colonial Pennsylvania. Wash U 1962

W94 Weakland, John E. The Pontificate of Pope John XXII: Problems of Church Reform and Centralization. Case W Reserve 1966

W95 Weatherhead, Richard W. Justo Sierra: A Portrait of a Porfirian Intellectual. Columbia 1966

W96 Weaver, Frederick H. Walter H. Page and the Progressive Mood. Duke 1968

W97 Webb, Allie B. W. A History of Negro Voting in Louisiana, 1877-1906. LSU 1962

W98 Webb, Stephen S. Officers and Governors: The Role of the British Army in Imperial Politics and the Administration of the American Colonies, 1689-1722. Wis 1965

W99 Weber, Christina M., Sister. The English Bishops, 1399-1413: Their Political Role in the Reign of Henry IV. Toronto 1962

W100 Weber, David J. The Taos Trappers: The Fur Trade from New Mexico, 1540-1846. NM 1967

W101 Weber, Richard K. Vincent of Beauvais: A Study in Medieval Historiography. Mich U 1965

W102 Webster, Anne K., Mother. The Impact of Catholic Hospitals in St. Louis. St L 1968

W103 Webster, Thomas S. Napoleon and Canada. Chicago 1961

W104 Wechsler, Howard J. Wei Cheng (A.D. 580-643) at the Court of T'ang T'ai-tsung. Yale 1970

W105 Weeks, John A. The Controversy over Chinese Labour in the Transvaal. Ohio 1968

W106 Wefald, Jon M. From Peasant Ideals to the Reform State: A Study of Norwegian Attitudes toward Reform in the American Middle West, 1890-1917. Mich U 1965

W107　Wegs, J. Robert.　Austrian Economic Mobilization during World War I, with Particular Emphasis on Heavy Industry. Ill 1970

W108　Wehn, Paul B.　Germany and the Treaty of Locarno, 1925. Columbia 1968

W109　Wehr, Paul W.　Samuel Hanna: Fur Trader to Railroad Magnate, 1817-1856. Ball State 1968

W110　Wehrle, Edmund S.　The Missionary Factor in Anglo-Chinese Relations, 1891-1900. Chicago 1962

W111　Weigold, Marilyn E.　National Security versus Collective Security: The Role of the *Couverture* in Shaping French Military and Foreign Policy (1905-1934). St John's 1970

W112　Weikel, Ann.　Crown and Council: A Study of Mary Tudor and Her Privy Council. Yale 1966

W113　Weiler, Peter H.　Liberal Social Theory in Great Britain, 1896-1914. Harvard 1969

W114　Weinberg, Julius.　Edward Alsworth Ross: An Intellectual Biography. Mich U 1963

W115　Weinberg, Sydney S.　Wartime Propaganda in a Democracy: America's 20th Century Information Agencies. Columbia 1969

W116　Weinberg, William M.　An Administrative History of the New Jersey State Board of Mediation. Penn U 1964

W117　Weinberger, Stephen.　Social and Economic Development in Provence, 972-1094. Wis 1969

W118　Weingartner, James G.　The *Leibstandarte Adolf Hitler*, 1933-1945. Wis 1967

W119　Weinman, Lois J.　Ecuador and Cacao: Domestic Responses to the Boom-Collapse Monoexport Cycle. UCLA 1970

W120　Weinstein, Fred.　Nihilism and Death: A Study of the Life of N. A. Dobroliubov. Cal, Berkeley 1962

W121　Weinstein, Minna F.　Jerusalem Embattled: Theories of Executive Powers in the Early Puritan Revolution. Md 1965

W122　Weir, Michael.　The Preparation of War in Medieval England, 1199-1307. Brown 1970

W123　Weir, Robert M.　"Liberty and Property, and No Stamps": South Carolina and the Stamp Act Crisis. Case W Reserve 1966

W124　Weisbord, Robert G.　African Zion: The Attempt to Establish a Jewish Colony in the East Africa Protectorate, 1903-1905. NYU 1966

W125　Weiss, Bernard J.　The Evolution of Britain's Military and Diplomatic Commitment to France, 1904-1914. Ill 1967

W126　Weiss, Nancy J.　"Not Alms, but Opportunity": A History of the National Urban League, 1910-1940. Harvard 1970

W127　Weiss, Richard.　The American Myth of Success, 1865 to the Present: A Study in Popular Thought. Columbia 1966

W128　Weiss, Robert M.　The Shock of Experience: A Group of Chicago's Writers Face the Twentieth Century. Wis 1966

W129　Weiss, Stuart L.　The New Deal and Collective Security, 1933-1936: The Origins and the Development of a Foreign Policy. Chicago 1961

W130　Weisser, Henry G.　The British Working Class and European Affairs, 1815-1848. Columbia 1965

W131　Weisz, Howard R.　Irish-American and Italian-American Educational Views and Activities, 1870-1900: A Comparison. Columbia 1968

W132　Weitekamp, Raymond.　Maurice Francis Egan: Writer, Teacher, and Diplomat, 1852-1924. Cath 1962

W133　Welborn, Max, Jr.　Victor Schoelcher's Views on Race and Slavery. Ohio 1965

W134　Welch, Allen H.　John Carvell Williams, the Nonconformist Watchdog (1821-1907). Kans U 1968

W135　Welch, James N.　Concepts Relating to Civil Rule in the Works of Saint Augustine and John Wyclif. St L 1963

W136　Weldon, Edward L.　Mark Sullivan's Progressive Journalism, 1874-1925: An Ironic Persuasion. Emory 1970

W137　Weleba, Shirley A.　Trial by Jury in Southern Rhodesia, 1900-1912. S Cal 1969

W138　Welisch, Sophie A.　The Sudeten German Question in the League of Nations. Fordham 1968

W139　Weller, Judith Ann.　A Study of the Regulation of the East Indian Indenture System in Trinidad, 1845-1917. Columbia 1965

W140　Wellmon, Bernard B.　The Parker Ranch: A History. Tex C 1969

W141 Wells, Damon. Man in Motion: The Last Years of Stephen Douglas, 1857-1861. Rice 1968

W142 Wells, Rebecca S. The Viennese Biedermeier Theater, 1815-1867. Miss S 1965

W143 Wells, Robert V. A Demographic Analysis of Some Middle Colony Quaker Families of the Eighteenth Century. Princeton 1969

W144 Wells, Ronald. A Portrait of Josiah Royce. Boston U 1967

W145 Wells, Samuel F., Jr. Anglo-American Friendship, 1904-1914: The Strategic Aspect. Harvard 1967

W146 Wells, Tom H. The Confederate Navy: A Study in Organization. Emory 1963

W147 Weltsch, Ruben E. Archbishop John of Jenstein (1348-1400): Papalism, Humanism and Reformism in pre-Hussite Prague. Colo 1961

W148 Welty, William M. Black Shepherds: A Study of the Leading Negro Clergymen in New York City, 1900-1940. NYU 1969

W149 Wemple, Suzanne F. Atto of Vercelli: Church, State and Society in the Tenth Century. Columbia 1967

W150 Wendel, Thomas H. The Life and Writings of Sir William Keith, Lieutenant-Governor of Pennsylvania and the Three Lower Counties, 1717-1726. Wash U 1964

W151 Wennersten, John R. A Reformer's Odyssey: The Public Career of Parke Godwin of the New York *Evening Post,* 1837-1870. Md 1970

W152 Werlich, David P. The Conquest and Settlement of the Peruvian Montaña. Minn 1968

W153 Werrell, Kenneth P. The Tactical Development of the Eighth Air Force in World War II. Duke 1969

W154 Wescott, Richard R. A History of Maine Politics, 1840-1856: The Formation of the Republican Party. Maine 1966

W155 Wesser, Robert F. Charles Evans Hughes and New York Politics, 1905-1910. Rochester 1961

W156 West, Delno C., Jr. Joachimism and Fra Salimbene. UCLA 1970

W157 West, Earl I. Religion and Politics in the Jacksonian Era. Ind 1968

W158 West, Franklin C. The Parties, the Princes, and the People: A Study of the German Referendum of June 20, 1926. Cal, Berkeley 1970

W159 West, Kenneth B. Tory Interpretations of the American Revolution. Wash U 1965

W160 West, Thomas R. Discipline and Energy: The Machine in American Literature, 1918-1941. Columbia 1965

W161 Westin, Richard B. The State and Segregated Schools: Negro Public Education in North Carolina, 1863-1923. Duke 1966

W162 Westrich, Sal A. The *Ormée* of Bordeaux. Columbia 1970

W163 Wetzel, Charles J. The American Rescue of Refugee Scholars and Scientists from Europe, 1933-1945. Wis 1964

W164 Whalon, Michael W. Maine Republicans, 1854-1866: A Study in Growth and Political Power. Neb 1968

W165 Whatley, George C. Jackson's Justices and the Federal System, 1830-1856. Ala 1969

W166 Whealey, Robert H. German-Spanish Relations, January-August 1939: The Failure of Germany to Conclude Military and Economic Agreements with Spain. Mich U 1963

W167 Wheaton, James O. The Genius and the Jurist: A Study of the Presidential Campaign of 1904. Stanford 1964

W168 Wheeler, Alice J. Society History in Eighteenth-Century Scotland. Emory 1966

W169 Wheeler, Douglas L. The Portuguese in Angola, 1836-1891: A Study in Expansion and Administration. Boston U 1963

W170 Wheeler, Earl M. The Role of the North Carolina Militia in the Beginning of the American Revolution. Tulane 1969

W171 Wheeler, Kenneth W. Early Urban Development in Texas, 1836-1865. Rochester 1964

W172 Wheeler, Mary E. The Origins and Formation of the Russian-American Company. NC 1965

W173 Wheeler, Penny M. The Twelfth-Century School of St. Victor. S Cal 1970

W174 Wheeler, William B. Urban Politics in Nature's Republic: The Development of Political Parties in the Seaport Cities in the Federalist Era. Va 1967

W175 Whisenhunt, Donald W. Texas in the Depression, 1929-1933: A Study of Public Reaction. Tex Tech 1966

W176 Whitaker, James W. The Rise and Development of Beef Cattle Feeding in Illinois and Iowa, 1840-1900. Wis 1965

W177 White, Ann B. The Hong Merchants of Canton. Penn U 1967

W178 White, D. Anthony. Mexico in World Affairs, 1928-1968. UCLA 1968

W179 White, Dan S. Hessen and the Reformulation of National Liberalism, 1880-1884. Harvard 1967

W179a White, Donald A. The Saxon Shore. Wis 1961

W180 White, John C. Pierre Victor Malouet: Administrator and Legislator (1740-1792). Duke 1964

W181 White, John L. The Christian Concept of Divine Providence and Arnold J. Toynbee's *A Study of History* and Subsequent Works. Cath 1969

W182 White, Leland R. The Development of More Open Racial and Ethnic Relations in British Honduras during the Nineteenth Century. Mo 1969

W183 White, Lonnie J. Arkansas Territorial Politics, 1819-1836. Tex U 1961

W184 White, Raymond E. Private Electric Utility Executives: Thoughts on Public Ownership, 1881-1960. Tex U 1965

W185 White, William B. The Military and the Melting Pot: The American Army and Minority Groups, 1865-1924. Wis 1968

W186 Whiteford, Daniel F. The American Legion and American Foreign Policy, 1950-1963. Md 1967

W187 Whitehouse, Eugene A. Prussian Policy towards the South German States, 1866-1870: A Study in Bismarckian Diplomacy. Mich U 1962

W188 Whiteside, Henry O. Kennedy and the Kremlin: Soviet-American Relations, 1961-1963. Stanford 1969

W189 Whitmore, Allan R. Beard, Boys, and Buckskins: Daniel Carter Beard and the Preservation of the American Pioneer Tradition. Northwestern 1970

W190 Whitmore, John K. The Development of Le Government in Fifteenth Century Vietnam. Cornell 1968

W191 Whitney, Harriet E. Sir George C. Gibbons and the Boundary Waters Treaty of 1909. Mich S 1968

W192 Whittaker, William G. American Labor Looks South: The Gompers Era, 1894-1924. Georgetown 1965

W193 Whitten, Dolphus, Jr. The State Delegations in the Philadelphia Convention of 1787. Tex U 1961

W194 Whitty, Michael D. Emil Mazey, Radical as Liberal: The Evolution of Labor Radicalism in the UAW. Syracuse 1969

W195 Wiberg, Charles E. A History of the University of Minnesota Chapter of the American Association of University Professors. Minn 1964

W196 Wickberg, Edgar B. The Chinese in Philippine Economy and Society, 1850-1898. Cal, Berkeley 1961

W197 Wickens, James F. Colorado in the Great Depression: A Study of New Deal Policies at the State Level. Denver 1964

W198 Wickman, John E. Political Aspects of Charles Wilkes's Work and Testimony, 1842-1849. Ind 1964

W199 Wickstrom, John B. The King's Chamber Ranks in Politics and Government, 1437-1485. Yale 1969

W200 Wickwire, Mary B. Lord Sandwich and the King's Ships: British Naval Administration, 1771-1782. Yale 1963

W201 Wiecek, William M. The Guarantee Clause of the United States Constitution: "A Sleeping Giant." Wis 1968

W202 Wiedemer, Jack E. Arms and Armor in England, 1450-1471: Their Cost and Distribution. Penn U 1967

W203 Wiener, Carol Z. Popular Anti-Catholicism in England, 1559-1618. Harvard 1969

W204 Wiener, Joel H. The Movement to Repeal the "Taxes on Knowledge," 1825-1840: A Study in British Working-Class Radicalism. Cornell 1965

W205 Wiener, Martin J. New and Untried Circumstances: The Intellectual Career of Graham Wallas (1858-1932). Harvard 1967

W206 Wightman, Joseph. Baldwin's Record in Foreign Affairs and Defense. SC 1961

W207 Wikramanayake, Ivy M. The Free Negro in Ante-Bellum South Carolina. Wis 1966

W208 Wilbur, W. Allen. Crisis in Leadership: Alexander Hamilton, Timothy Pickering, and the Politics of Federalism, 1795-1804. Syracuse 1969

W209 Wilcox, Carol H. The Franco-Russian Alliance, 1908-1911. Clark 1968

W210 Wilcox, Donald J. The Development of Humanist Historiography in Florence during the Fifteenth Century. Harvard 1967

W211 Wilensky, Norman M. The Republican Old Guard during Insurgency, 1908-1912. Yale 1961

W212 Wiley, George T. Educating the Children of England's Laboring Poor, 1850-1865. Case W Reserve 1965

W213 Wilhelm, Clarke L. William B. Wilson, the First Secretary of Labor. JH 1967

W214 Wilke, Ekkehard-Teja P. The German Government Crisis of 1896-1897. Ill 1967

W215 Wilkie, James W. The Mexican Revolution: Federal Expenditure and Social Change since 1910. Cal, Berkeley 1966

W216 Wilkinson, Ronald S. John Winthrop, Jr., and the Origins of American Chemistry. Mich S 1969

W217 Willertz, John R. National Socialism in a German City and County: Marburg, 1933 to 1945. Mich U 1970

W218 Willey, Thomas E. Back to Kant: The Revival of Kantian Idealism in Germany, 1870-1914. Yale 1965

W219 Willgoos, Robert G. G. D. H. Cole: His Guild Socialist Period, 1913-1927. Cath 1970

W220 Williams, Burton J. John James Ingalls: A Personal Portrait of a Public Figure. Kans U 1965

W221 Williams, Dalbert A. Colony Government in Jamaica, 1866-1914. Cath 1968

W222 Williams, David A. The Political Career of David C. Broderick. S Cal 1963

W223 Williams, Ernest R., Jr. The Florida Parish Ellises and Louisiana Politics, 1820-1918. S Miss 1969

W224 Williams, Harvey R. British Policy and Attitudes toward France, 24 February to 27 June, 1848. Chicago 1962

W225 Williams, John Adrian. Maori Society and Politics, 1891-1909. Wis 1964

W226 Williams, John Alexander. Davis and Elkins of West Virginia: Businessmen in Politics. Yale 1967

W227 Williams, John H. Dr. Francia and the Creation of the Republic of Paraguay (1810-1814). Fla U 1969

W228 Williams, Lance. Parliamentary General Enclosure from 1790 through the General Act of 1845. Ga 1970

W229 Williams, Lyle W. Struggle for Survival: The Hostile Frontier of New Spain, 1750-1800. Tex C 1970

W230 Williams, Max R. William A. Graham, North Carolina Whig Party Leader, 1804-1849. NC 1965

W231 Williams, Oscar R., Jr. Blacks and Colonial Legislation in the Middle Colonies. Ohio 1969

W232 Williams, Richard H. Politics and Reform: The California Democrats in the Cleveland Years. Yale 1968

W233 Williams, Robert C. The Culture of Political Despair: Russians in Germany, 1918-1923. Harvard 1966

W234 Williams, William H. The Priest in History: A Study in Divided Loyalties in the French Lower Clergy from 1776 to 1789. Duke 1965

W235 Williamson, Joel R. The Negro in South Carolina during Reconstruction, 1861-1877. Cal, Berkeley 1964

W236 Williamson, John G. Karl Helfferich (1872-1924): A Study of His Activities as Economist, Financier and Politician in Wilhelmine Germany. JH 1964

W237 Williamson, Samuel R., Jr. Anglo-French Military and Naval Relations, 1904-1914. Harvard 1966

W238 Williford, Miriam. The Reform Program of Dr. Mariano Gálvez, Chief-of-State of Guatemala, 1831-1838. Tulane 1963

W239 Willis, Edmund P. Social Origins of Political Leadership in New York City from the Revolution to 1815. Cal, Berkeley 1967

W240 Willis, Jean L. The Trade between North America and the Danish West Indies, 1756-1807, with Special Reference to St. Croix. Columbia 1963

W241 Willis, Jeffrey R. The Wehrmacht Propaganda Branch: German Miltary Propaganda and Censorship during World War II. Va 1964

W242 Willis, Leo S. E. Lee Trinkel and the Virginia Democracy, 1876-1939. Va 1968

W243 Willis, Richard E. The Politics of Parliament, 1800-1806. Stanford 1969

W244 Willke, Jean C. The Historical Thought of Adam Ferguson. Cath 1962

W245 Willman, Robert I.   Robert Harley and English Party Politics, 1689-1710. Harvard 1968

W246 Willson, John P.   Carlton J. H. Hayes in Spain, 1942-1945. Syracuse 1968

W247 Willson, Roger E.   The Truman Committee. Harvard 1966

W248 Wilshire, Leland E.   Boniface of Savoy, Archbishop of Canterbury, 1245-1270: His Role in English Politics. S Cal 1967

W249 Wilson, Constance M.   State and Society in the Reign of Mongkut, 1851-1868: Thailand on the Eve of Modernization. Cornell 1970

W250 Wilson, Everett A.   The Crisis of National Integration in El Salvador, 1919-1935. Stanford 1970

W251 Wilson, Harold A.   The Imperial Policy of Sir Robert Borden, 1911-1920: A Study in the Advancement of Dominion Status. Ia 1961

W252 Wilson, Iris H.   Scientific Aspects of Spanish Exploration in New Spain during the Late Eighteenth Century. S Cal 1962

W253 Wilson, James A.   Cattle and Politics in Arizona, 1886-1941. Ariz 1967

W254 Wilson, James H.   The Trial and Treason of General Custine. Mo 1966

W255 Wilson, Joan H.   The Role of the Business Community in American Relations with Russia and Europe, 1920-1933. Cal, Berkeley 1966

W256 Wilson, Joe F.   An Evaluation of the Failure of the Tacna-Arica Plebiscitary Commission, 1925-1926. Ga 1965

W257 Wilson, John B.   Mikhail Ivanovich Kalinin: The Revolutionary Years, 1875-1921. Boston U 1966

W258 Wilson, John S.   Norman Thomas, Critic of the New America. NC 1966

W259 Wilson, Lester N.   François de Callières, Diplomat and Man of Letters. Ill 1963

W260 Wilson, Major L.   An Analysis of the Ideas of Liberty and Union as Used by Members of Congress and the Presidents from 1828 to 1861. Kans U 1964

W261 Wilson, Raymond J.   In Quest of Community: The Critique of Individualism in America, 1860-1920. Wis 1964

W262 Wilson, Robert A.   A Study of the Political Institutions and Ranking Personnel of the New Meiji Government, 1868-1871. Wash U 1949

W263 Wilson, Theodore A.   Meeting at Argentia. Ind 1966

W264 Wilson, Theodore B.   The Black Codes of the South. Fla U 1962

W265 Wilson, Wesley C.   1946: General George C. Marshall and the United States Army Mediate China's Civil War. Colo 1965

W266 Wilson, William H.   The City Beautiful Movement in Kansas City, 1872-1914. Mo 1962

W267 Wilt, Alan F.   The Atlantic Wall: German Defenses in the West, 1941-1944. Mich U 1969

W268 Wilt, Paul C.   Premillennialism in America, 1865-1918, with Special Reference to Attitudes toward Social Reform. Am 1970

W269 Winchester, Betty Jo.   Hungarian Relations with Germany, 1936-1939. Ind 1970

W270 Winchester, Richard C.   James G. Blaine and the Ideology of American Expansionism. Rochester 1966

W271 Wines, Roger A.   The Franconian *Reichskreis* and the Holy Roman Empire in the War of the Spanish Succession. Columbia 1961

W272 Winfrey, Dorman H.   Julien Sidney Devereux and His Monte Verdi, Texas, Plantation. Tex U 1962

W273 Wingo, Horace C.   Race Relations in Georgia, 1872-1908. Ga 1969

W274 Wingo, Patricia W.   Clayton R. Lusk: A Study of Patriotism in New York Politics, 1919-1923. Ga 1966

W275 Winius, George D.   The Fall of Portuguese Ceylon, 1638-1656: Military, Diplomatic and Political Aspects in the Decline of an Empire. Columbia 1964

W276 Winkleman, Dean R.   New Zealand and the Policy of Sir George Grey. Case W Reserve 1964

W277 Winn, Wilkins B.   A History of the Central American Mission as Seen in the Work of Albert Edward Bishop, 1896-1922. Ala 1964

W278 Winnik, Herbert C.   The Role of Personality in the Science and the Social Attitudes of Five American Men of Science, 1876-1916. Wis 1968

W279 Winter, James H.   The Liberal Party and Parliamentary Reform, 1852-1867. Harvard 1961

W280 Winter, William.   The Villéle Ministry. Colo 1968

W281 Winters, Donald L. Henry Cantwell Wallace and the Farm Crisis of the Early Twenties. Wis 1966

W282 Winters, John D. The Civil War in Louisiana. LSU 1966

W283 Winters, Stanley B. Karel Kramář's Early Political Career. Rutgers 1966

W284 Wintterle, John F. John Dewey: Instrumentalism and Social Problems. Ore 1963

W285 Wirth, John D. Brazilian Economic Nationalism: Trade and Steel under Vargas. Stanford 1966

W286 Wiseman, John B. Dilemmas of a Party out of Power: The Democracy, 1904-1912. Md 1967

W287 Wiser, Vivian D. The Movement for Agricultural Improvement in Maryland, 1785-1865. Md 1963

W288 Witcher, Robert C. The Episcopal Church in Louisiana, 1805-1861. LSU 1969

W289 Witherell, Julian W. The Response of the Peoples of Cayor to French Penetration, 1850-1900. Wis 1964

W290 Witke, Roxane H. Transformation of Attitudes towards Women during the May Fourth Era of Modern China. Cal, Berkeley 1970

W291 Witt, Ronald G. The Education and Early Life of Coluccio Salutati. Harvard 1965

W292 Wittner, Lawrence S. The American Peace Movement, 1941-1960. Columbia 1967

W293 Woehrlin, William F. The World View of N. G. Chernyshevskii. Harvard 1961

W294 Woehrmann, Paul J. Fort Wayne, Indiana, Territory, 1794-1819: A Study of a Frontier Post. Kent 1967

W295 Wohl, Anthony S. The Housing of the Artisans and Laborers in Nineteenth Century London, 1815-1914. Brown 1966

W296 Wohl, Robert A. The Road to Tours: The Origins of the French Communist Party, 1914-1920. Princeton 1963

W297 Wolf, James B. Captain Hore's Mission: The London Missionary Society's Adventure to Lake Tanganyika, 1876-1888. UCLA 1968

W298 Wolf, Jerome. The Imperial Valley as an Index of Agricultural Labor Relations in California. S Cal 1964

W299 Wolfe, Robert D. The Origins of the Paris Commune: The Popular Organizations of 1868-1871. Harvard 1966

W300 Wolfe, William W. From Radicalism to Socialism: Men and Ideas in the Formation of English Socialist Theories, 1881-1889. Yale 1967

W301 Wolff, Gerald W. The Kansas-Nebraska Bill and Congressional Voting Behavior in the Thirty-third Congress. Ia 1969

W302 Wolff, Thomas. Inter-American Maritime Disputes over Fishing in the Twentieth Century. Cal, Santa Barbara 1968

W303 Wollman, David H. Parliament and Foreign Affairs, 1697-1714. Wis 1970

W304 Woloch, Isser. The Democratic Movement of the Year VI: The Evolution and Revival of Jacobinism in France, 1797-1798. Princeton 1965

W305 Woloch, Nancy S. The Self-Image of Antebellum Reformers: A Study of Nineteenth-Century American Autobiography. Ind 1968

W306 Wolters, Raymond R. The Negro and the New Deal Economic Recovery Program. Cal, Berkeley 1967

W307 Womack, John, Jr. Emiliano Zapata and the Revolution in Morelos, 1910-1920. Harvard 1966

W308 Wong, Frank Fe. Liang Ch'i-ch'ao and the Conflict of Confucian and Constitutional Politics. Wis 1965

W309 Wong, George H. China's Oppositions to Western Religion and Science during Late Ming and Early Ch'ing. Wash U 1958

W310 Wood, Allen H. The Gold Coins of the Great Kusāna. Georgetown 1965

W311 Wood, Charles T. The Apanages and the Growth of Royal Authority, 1224-1328: A Study in Family-Feudal Relations. Harvard 1962

W312 Wood, Douglas K. Men against Time: Studies in the Transcendence and Abolition of Time in Twentieth-Century European Thought. Yale 1967

W313 Wood, Forrest G. Race Demagoguery during the Civil War and Reconstruction. Cal, Berkeley 1965

W314 Wood, Gordon S. The Creation of an American Polity in the Revolutionary Era. Harvard 1964

W315 Wood, James B. The American Response to China, 1784-1844: Consensus Policy and the Origin of the East India Squadron. Duke 1969

W316 Wood, John E. The *Luftwaffe* as a Factor in British Policy, 1935-1939. Tulane 1965

W317 Wood, Joseph S. The Mormon Settlement in San Bernardino, 1851-1857. Utah 1968

W318 Wood, Thomas W., Jr. Influence of the *Paris Herald* on the Lost Generation of Writers. Okla 1966

W319 Woodall, John B. The *Ralliement* in France: Origins and Early History, 1876-1894. Columbia 1964

W320 Woodard, Nelson E. Postwar Reconstruction and International Order: A Study of the Diplomacy of Charles Evans Hughes, 1921-1925. Wis 1970

W321 Woodfin, Harold D., Jr. James VI and I and the Quest for Anglo-Scottish Unity: A Study of the Legal and Constitutional Issues. Tulane 1969

W322 Woodham, John E. Hipólito Unanue and the Enlightenment in Peru. Duke 1964

W323 Woodhouse, Caleb R. Religious Vitality in Fifteenth-Century England. Cal, Berkeley 1963

W324 Woodman, Harold D. King Cotton and His Retainers: A Study of Cotton Marketing in the South. Chicago 1964

W325 Woods, Frances Jerome, Sister. Mexican Leadership in San Antonio, Texas. Cath 1949

W326 Woods, Joseph M. Charles Stewart Parnell: An Interpretation. Harvard 1967

W327 Woods, Kenneth F. Samuel Guy Inman: His Role in the Evolution of Inter-American Cooperation. Am 1962

W328 Woodward, David R. The West and the Containment of Russia, 1914-1923. Ga 1965

W329 Woodward, Isaiah A. Arthur Ingraham Boreman: A Biography. W Va 1970

W330 Woodward, Margaret L. Spanish Apathy and American Independence. Chicago 1964

W331 Woodward, Ralph Lee, Jr. The *Consulado de Comercio* of Guatemala, 1793-1871. Tulane 1962

W332 Woodward, Robert C. Education in Oregon in the Progressive Era: Liberal and Practical. Ore 1963

W333 Woody, Kennerly M. Damiani and the Radicals. Columbia 1966

W334 Woodyatt, Lyle J. The Origins and Evolution of the New Deal Public Housing Program. Wash St L 1968

W335 Woolever, Anne E. Christopher Dawson: A Study in Anti-Democratic International Thought, 1920-1960. Toronto 1970

W336 Woolfolk, Sarah V. The Role of the Scalawag in Alabama Reconstruction. LSU 1965

W337 Woolley, William J. Poland in the League of Nations, 1932-1934. Ind 1969

W338 Wootten, William W. A Study of Henry I, King of England, 1068-1107. Minn 1964

W339 Worrall, Arthur J. New England Quakerism, 1656-1830. Ind 1969

W340 Wortham, John D. *Uraeus:* A History of British Interest in the Antiquities of Egypt in the Sixteenth, Seventeenth, Eighteenth, and Nineteenth Centuries. Tex U 1967

W341 Wortman, Marlene S. The Mugwump Movement in New York, 1865-1884: A Study of the Culture and Institutions of Reform. Chicago 1966

W342 Wortman, Richard S. The Crisis of Russian Populism. Chicago 1964

W343 Wosgian, Daniel S. Turks and British Rule in Cyprus. Columbia 1963

W344 Wotherspoon, James R. The San Francisco *Argonaut,* 1877-1907. Cal, Berkeley 1962

W345 Wou, Odoric. Militarism in Modern China as Exemplified in the Career of Wu P'ei-fu, 1916-1928. Columbia 1970

W346 Wozniak, John S. Hermann Wagener's Corporative Social Monarchy: German Conservatism at the Crossroads of the Social Question. Conn 1969

W347 Wright, Arthur E., Jr. The Writings of Jean-Baptiste de La Salle: His Religious Teachings. NM 1964

W348 Wright, James E. The Politics of Populism: Parties, Partisans, and Dissenters in Colorado, 1860-1912. Wis 1969

W349 Wright, James Z. Thomas Dixon: The Mind of a Southern Apologist. Geo P 1966

W350 Wright, Monte D. A History of Aerial Navigation to 1941. Duke 1970

W351 Wright, Richard J. Freshwater "Whales": A History of the American Ship Building Company and Its Predecessors. Kent 1968

W352 Wright, William J. Reformation Influence on Hessian Education. Ohio 1969

W353 Wright, Winthrop R. Argentine Railways and the Growth of Nationalism. Penn U 1964

W354 Wrigley, John E. Studies in the Life of Pierre Roger (Pope Clement VI) and of Related Writings of Petrarch. Penn U 1965

W355 Wrobel, Alfred J. The American Revolution and the Poland of Stanislaus Augustus Poniatowski (1763-1795). S Cal 1967

W356 Wrone, David R. Prairie Press in Transition: The East Central Illinois Newspaper Scene, 1830-1870. Ill 1964

W357 Wrong, Charles J. The French Infantry Officer at the Close of the *Ancien Régime*. Brown 1968

W358 Wu, Ellsworth Tien-wei. The Chinese Nationalist and Communist Alliance, 1923-1927. Md 1965

W359 Wu, Wei-ping. The Development and Decline of the Eight Banners: Case Study of the Decline of Alien Rule in Chinese History. Penn U 1969

W360 Wubben, Hubert H. Copperheads and Unionists: The Trial of Iowa Democracy, 1860-1865. Ia 1963

W361 Wussow, Walter J. French Freemasonry and the Threat of War, 1917-1939. Colo 1966

W362 Wyatt, David K. The Beginnings of Modern Education in Thailand, 1868-1910. Cornell 1966

W363 Wyatt, Loretta S. D. Carlota and the Regency Affair. Fla U 1969

W364 Wyatt-Brown, Bertram. Partners in Piety: Lewis and Arthur Tappan, Evangelical Abolitionists, 1828-1841. JH 1963

W365 Wyche, Billy H. Southern Attitudes toward Industrial Unions, 1933-1941. Ga 1970

W366 Wylie, Kenneth C. The Politics of Transformation: Indirect Rule in Mendeland and Abuja, 1890-1914. Mich S 1967

W367 Wyman, David S. American Policy toward Immigration of Refugees from Nazism, 1938-1941. Harvard 1966

W368 Wyman, Roger E. Voting Behavior in the Progressive Era: Wisconsin as a Case Study. Wis 1970

W369 Wynne, Robert E. Reaction to the Chinese in the Pacific Northwest and British Columbia, 1850 to 1910. Wash U 1964

W370 Wynot, Edward D., Jr. The Camp of National Unity and Polish Politics, 1936-1939. Ind 1970

Y

Y1   Yamamoto, Masaya (David). Image-Makers of Japan: A Case Study in the Impact of the American Protestant Foreign Missionary Movement, 1859-1905. Ohio 1967

Y2   Yaney, George L. The Imperial Russian Government and the Stolypin Land Reform. Princeton 1961

Y3   Yanow, Lilli A. Washington Irving as United States Minister to Spain: The Revolution of 1843. NYU 1969

Y4   Yarborough, Kemp P. *Chisholm* v. *Georgia:* A Study of the Minority Opinion. Columbia 1963

Y5   Yarnell, Allen L. The Impact of the Progressive Party on the Democratic Party in the 1948 Presidential Election. Wash U 1969

Y6   Yates, Stanley M. The Commune in French Historical Writing. Ill 1961

Y7   Yavenditti, Michael J. American Reactions to the Use of Atomic Bombs on Japan, 1945-1947. Cal, Berkeley 1970

Y8   Yedlin, Tova. The Political Career of Maxim Gorky. Alberta 1969

Y9   Yellowitz, Irwin H. Labor and the Progressive Movement in New York State, 1897-1916. Brown 1961

Y10   Yerushalmi, Yosef. Isaac Cardoso: A Study in Seventeenth Century Marranism and Apologetics. Columbia 1966

Y11   Yip, Ka-che. The Anti-Christian Movement in China, 1922-1927, with Special Reference to the Experience of Protestant Missions. Columbia 1970

Y12   Yoder, James D. Rural Pennsylvania Politics in a Decade of Discontent, 1890-1900. Lehigh 1969

Y13   Yodfat, Aryeh Y. The Jewish Question in American-Russian Relations (1875-1917). Am 1963

Y14   Yonce, Frederick J. Public Land Disposal in Washington. Wash U 1969

Y15   York, John M. Philip the Arab: The First Christian Emperor of Rome. S Cal 1964

Y16   Yost, John K. The Christian Humanism of the English Reformers, 1525-1555: A Study in English Renaissance Humanism. Duke 1965

Y17   Young, Chester R. The Effects of the French and Indian War on Civilian Life in the Frontier Counties of Virginia, 1754-1763. Vanderbilt 1969

Y18   Young, David N. The Mississippi Whigs, 1834-1860. Ala 1968

Y19   Young, George F. W. German Immigrants and Their Integration into Chilean Society, 1850-1930. Chicago 1969

Y20   Young, Katsu Hirai. The Japanese Army and the Soviet Union, 1936-1941. Wash U 1968

Y21   Young, Kenneth R. Nationalist Chinese Troops in Burma: Obstacle in Burma's Foreign Relations, 1949-1961. NYU 1970

Y22   Young, Lowell T. Franklin D. Roosevelt and Imperialism. Va 1970

Y23   Young, Marilyn B. American China Policy, 1895-1901. Harvard 1963

Y24   Young, Robert J. The English East India Company and Trade on the West Coast of Sumatra, 1730-1760. Penn U 1970

Y25   Younis, Adele L. The Coming of the Arabic-Speaking People to the United States. Boston U 1961

Y26   Younker, Daniel W. The Practical Origins of the Colonial Conference of 1887. Mich U 1968

Y27   Yuan, Tsing. Aspects of the Economic History of the Kiangnan Region during the Late Ming Period, ca. 1520-1620. Penn U 1969

Z

Z1 Zaccano, Joseph P., Jr. French Colonial Administration in Canada to 1760. Pitt 1961

Z2 Zacek, Joseph F. František Palacký and the Founding of Modern Czech Historiography. Ill 1962

Z3 Zacek, Judith C. The Russian Bible Society, 1812-1826. Columbia 1964

Z4 Zahniser, Marvin R. The Public Career of Charles Cotesworth Pinckney. Cal, Santa Barbara 1963

Z5 Zaller, Robert M. The Parliament of 1621: A Study in Constitutional Conflict. Wash St L 1968

Z6 Zangrando, Robert L. The Efforts of the National Association for the Advancement of Colored People to Secure Passage of a Federal Anti-Lynching Law, 1920-1940. Penn U 1963

Z7 Zaprudnik, Jan. Political Struggle for Bye-lorussia in the Tsarist State Dumas, 1906-1917. NYU 1969

Z8 Zaring, Philip B. In Defense of the Past: The House of Lords, 1860-1886. Yale 1966

Z9 Zarur, Claire A. Prince Napoleon (Jerôme) during the Second Empire. Georgetown 1965

Z10 Zegger, Robert E. John Cam Hobhouse at Westminster, 1818-1833. Columbia 1965

Z11 Zelechow, Bernard. Aesthetics and Social Ethics: A Study of the Bloomsbury Group. Harvard 1965

Z12 Zelman, Donald L. American Intellectual Attitudes toward Mexico, 1908-1940. Ohio 1969

Z13 Zelnik, Reginald E. Factory Labor and the Labor Question in Tsarist St. Petersburg, 1856-1871. Stanford 1966

Z14 Zemsky, Robert M. The Massachusetts Assembly, 1730-1755. Yale 1967

Z15 Zerner, Ruth. German Policy towards Austria, 1885-1890. Cal, Berkeley 1962

Z16 Zguta, Russell. Byliny: A Study of Their Value as Historical Sources. Penn S 1967

Z17 Zieger, Robert H. The Republicans and Labor: Politics and Policies, 1919-1929. Md 1965

Z18 Zilversmit, Arthur. Slavery and Its Abolition in the Northern States. Cal, Berkeley 1962

Z19 Zimdars, Benjamin F. A Study in Seventeenth-Century Peruvian Historiography: The Monastic Chronicles of Antonio de la Calancha, Diego de Córdova Salinas, and the *Compendio y Descripción* of Antonio Vazquez de Espinosa. Tex U 1965

Z20 Zimmer, Anne F. Y. Jonathan Boucher: Moderate Loyalist and Public Man. Wayne 1966

Z21 Zimmerman, Albright G. The Indian Trade of Colonial Pennsylvania. Del 1966

Z22 Zimmerman, Judith E. Between Revolution and Reaction: The Russian Constitutional Democratic Party, October, 1905, to June, 1907. Columbia 1967

Z23 Zimmerman, Loretta E. Alice Paul and the National Women's Party, 1912-1920. Tulane 1964

Z24 Zimmermann, Thomas P. Paolo Giovio and Cosimo I de'Medici, 1537-1552. Harvard 1964

Z25 Zinberg, Cecile. John Strype and the Sixteenth Century: A Portrait of an Anglican Historian. Chicago 1968

Z26 Ziros, Apostolos D. Cyprus in the United Nations Debates Since 1950. Ga 1969

Z27 Ziskind, Jonathan R. Aspects of International Law in the Ancient Near East. Columbia 1967

Z28 Zivajinović, Dragoljub R. The United States and Italy, April 1917-April 1919, with Special Reference to the Creation of the Yugoslav State. Penn U 1966

Z29 Zoghby, Samir M. The Impact of the Western Sudanic Empires on the Trans-Saharan Trade: Tenth to Sixteenth Century. Georgetown 1966

Z30 Zoltvany, Yves-François. Phillippe de Rigaud de Vaudreuil, Governor of New France (1703-1725). Alberta 1964

Z31 Zuber, Richard L. Jonathan Worth: A Biography of a Southern Unionist. Duke 1961

Z32 Zucker, Norman L. The Political Philosophy of George W. Norris. Rutgers 1961

Z33 Zucker, Stanley. Ludwig Bamberger and the Crisis of German Liberalism. Wis 1968

Z34   Zuckerman, Arnold. Dr. Richard Mead (1673-1754): A Biographical Study. Ill 1965

Z35   Zuckerman, Arthur J. The Jewish Patriarchate in Western Europe during the Carolingian Age. Columbia 1963

Z36   Zuckerman, Elliott. A Century of Wagner's *Tristan*. Columbia 1962

Z37   Zupko, Ronald E. A Dictionary of Medieval English Weights and Measures. Wis 1966

SUBJECT INDEX

Although this section is standard in form, a few explanations are in order. First, it embodies shortened cross references. For instance, it seems wasteful to repeat the word "railroads" in "see Civil War, railroads," when the latter word is the heading being consulted. Second, only the given name is included for titled nobility. Third, wherever a biography is involved, an effort has been made to associate the person with some country or a state with the United States. Fourth,

under state headings, to avoid repetition of numbers, each title is usually indicated but once under its major topical subheading. Quite obviously, under the subheading "biography" many subjects could be involved. Fifth, most phrases or terms used in the titles have been accepted as standard on the assumption that each authority selected them with some clear purpose in mind.

Abascal, José Fernando de, 019
Abbeys, T32
Abbott, Jacob, K84
Abbott, John, C189
Abdul Hamid II, G262, M416
Abetz, Otto, W36
Abjuratio Regni, R134
Abolitionism: Brazil, T105a; Cuba, K200; France, W133; Great Britain, S161; U.S., C241, F160, F198, J34, H425, L126, M82, M116, M132, M352, O2, P104, P211, R40, S424, S536, T52, W364; Venezuela, L220. *See also* anti-abolitionists; serfdom
Aborigines Protection Society, C302
Abraham Lincoln Battalion, R225
Absolutism: Bavaria, H77; France, B143, I23; Greece, P121; Prussia, F19; Russia, P124. *See also* monarchy
Abubakr of Katsina, H436
Abuja (Africa), W366
Abu Naddara, G63
Abundance, concept of, F166
Academic freedom, O33
Academies, H216, P168
Academy of Science: general, M108; Great Britain, H166; Paris, C132, H19, H67; Toulouse, P99
Academy of Sciences, Russia, G197
Acadia, R47
Accursuis, P101
Achaean League, P155
Acheh, D24
Acordada tribunal, M107
Acosta, Joaquín, D52
Action Française, D115, D187, S367
Action Libérale Populaire, D115, S604

Action Party, Italy, H296
Act of Supremacy, B468
Act of Uniformity, B137
Act of Union, Ireland, W321. *See also* Ireland
Acton, John E. E. Dalberg, B338, C186, H340, R282
Acton Circle, R282
Adam, William, G113
Adamic, Louis, L68
Adam of Dryburgh, H52
Adams, Brooks, C191, R37
Adams, Charles F., C213, F60, S428
Adams, Charles F., Jr., A158, B146, U11
Adams, Henry, B325, B373, B493, C191, H399, S240
Adams, Herbert, B325
Adams, John, A113, B347, C182, C310, F127, G302, H280, H398, H464, K285, L202, M259, P58, P130, R213, S559, W208
Adams, John (Confederate soldier), A22
Adams, John C., G280
Adams, John Q., D186, E94, W157
Adams, Samuel, B451, C310, M156, P58, S413, S559, T111
Adamson Act, S280
Addams, Jane, F27, H246, L142, Q1a
Ade, George, W128
Adler, Victor, F116
Admiralty, *see* navy
Adoption, R202
Adrian College, R140
Adriatic question, J32
Advertising, B79, H422, J22, S209
Aehrenthal, Alois von, W62
Aerial navigation, W350
Aerodynamics, research, K64. *See also* aviation

Aeronautics, *see* aviation
Afghan Convention of 1907, R10
Afghanistan, R10
Africa: general, B457, S85, W40; impact on colonial Argentina, C116; labor in, M91, W105; Roman, B186; and U.S., H167, O43, S150. *See also* colonial policy; colonial rivalry; colonization programs; education; exploration; frontier; imperialism; missionaries; nationalism; slave trade; trade; World War II; *countries by name*
African Reserves, S24
Agadir crisis, K49, W54
Agar, Herbert, C117, L68
Agassiz, Louis, D88, L228
Aged, *see* senior citizens
Agnostics, K182. *See also* secularism
Agobard of Lyons, B491
Agrarian theme, H17
Agrarian tradition, J39
Agricultural Adjustment Acts, C282, H341, H347, J79, K129, L15, P95, R256, S69, S138, S385. *See also* New Deal, farm programs
Agricultural Assn. (England), C377
Agricultural assns., G285, J50, P218. *See also* Farmers' Alliance; Granger movement
Agriculture: Brazil, E41, L201; Bulgaria, B149; Canada, S171; Chile, B103; China, Y27; Colonial Am., R17; Europe, P203; France, S128; Germany, B66, G10, L250; Great Britain, C377, L191, T20, W228; India, H253; medieval, B315, S128; Mexico, C338, D122; Peru, K60; Philippines, S189; Portugal,

S111; Roman, B200, J69; Russia, H39, N106, Y2; Santo Domingo, C197; Spain, M161. *See also* cotton; irrigation; plantations; tenant farmers
— *U.S.*: general, B120, B226, C351, J62, M329, M507, T167, W281; in Great Depression, C282, J79, K238, S138, S236; improvements in, B120, M217, W287; labor, C319, G210, G285, K119, M10, W98, W298; Middle West, D202; programs, M260, R256 (*see also* New Deal, farm programs); tariff, G317, L74. *See also* Agricultural Adjustment Acts; Agriculture, Dept. of; cattle industry; citrus industry; erosion; Farmers' Alliance; Farmers' Holiday Assn.; Granger movement; Great Plains; journalism; New South; Old South; peonage; Populist movement; reforms; vegetable industry; "agriculture" *under names of states; crops by name*
Agriculture, Dept. of, H329, K178, M41, S69, T167, W281
Agrippina, F59
Aguinaldo, Emilio, C380, G43
Aguirre Cerda, Pedro, H392
Ainsworth, Fred C., P170
Air Corps Tactical School, F118
Aircraft carriers, R98
Air force: France, F105, K262; Germany, W316; Great Britain, H143, J53; Italy, C47; U.S., B361, F118, F176, H266, H457, L279, M78, M466, N62, P27, R279, T14, W153. *See also* Douhet, G.
Air Force Academy, M344

Boker, George H., T104
Bolívar, Simón, H366, H421, K278
Bolivia, K223, M114, S249. *See also* Chaco War
Bologna, M275
Boloni-Farkas, Alexander, G39
Bolshevism, *see* Russian Revolution
Bombay, India, G307, K274
Bombing, *see* World War II
Bonald, Louis G. A. de, R53
Bonaparte, Jerome, Z9
Bonaparte, Joseph, C327
Bonaparte, Napoleon, *see* Napoleon I
Bonapartism, R249
Bond, Phineas, N25
Boniface VIII (Pope), M126, O25, S499
Boniface of Savoy, S299, W248
Bonílla, Policarpo, P82
Bonn, M. J., C153
Bonner, Edmund, S239
Book of the Order, S525
Books, B61, B110, J72, K84, M228. *See also* censorship; publishing
Boosterism, P126
Boot and Shoeworker's Union, B134
Borah, William E., A137, H281, M140, S51, S555, S614
Borchard, Edwin B., K85
Bordeaux, France, H467, V45, W162
Bordley, Stephen, M456
Bordon, Robert L., W251
Boreman, Arthur I., W329
Bormann, Martin, R246, S105
Borneo, P229
Bornu, Nigeria, B399
Bosnia-Herzegovinia, F76, I21, O97, W62
Bosses, political, A115, C15, D183, K66, M17, S488, T15
Boston, Mass.: in Am. Revolution, B451, C93, W42; charity, H428; Colonial Am., W67; demography, K203; economy, C335, M8, S433; education in, S134; intellectual, G167, M70, S205; journalism, F186, W43; Negro in, J21; police, K244, L31; politics, C69, H270, L42, M20, W174; religion, G283, M70, M316; social, K203; socialism in, C69; suburbs, M309
Boston and Albany Railroad, S21
Boston Pilot, W43
Botany, B168, C380, G303
Bothmer, Hans C., F81
Boucher, Jonathan, Z20
Bouelles, Charles de, M338
Bouillon, Duchy of, B242
Boulanger, George E. J. M., B536, H467, S159, W65

Boulangism, D187
Boulder Canyon project, M395
Boundaries, U.S., L118a
Boundary disputes, A41, I20, L198, O82. *See also* Alaska; Chaco War; Poland; Tacna-Arica; Venezuela
Boundary Waters Treaty, W191
Bourbons, New South and Reconstruction, B298, H126, M139, W97
Bourgeoisie, A123, J106, M155, N75, P40, W78. *See also* middle class
Bourne, Jonathan, Jr., B270
Bourne, Randolph S., B346, D210, M428
Boutwell, George S., B146
Bowell, Mackenzie, C189
Bowen, Francis, H397a, M213
Bowker, Richard R., M58
Bowles, Samuel, G69
Boxer rebellion, S247a
Boyd, David F., R57
Boyle, Robert, J19, J20, K33
Boy Scouts of America, W189
Bracciolini, Poggio, S173, S583
Braceros, C319, M10
Brackton, Henry de, S458
Bradish, Luther, G111
Bradlaugh, Charles, A132, K1, K257, N46
Bradley, Dan B., L236
Brahe, Tycho, K76
Brahmans, C274
Brahminism, India, D110, I15
Brandegee, Frank, S555
Brandenburg-Prussia, H387, J30
Braxton, Carter, S529
Bray, John F., W3
Brazil: general, C126, G199, G249; abolitionism, T105a; colonial, D26, D244, S141, T5 (*see also* colonial policy, Portugal); economy, D69, E41, G87, L201, R14, S369, W285; empire, B106, D30, E111, H70, H357; foreign relations, B408, B511, G87, H391, K9, M11, T47; frontier in, D30; intellectual, R5; politics, B118, C328, H20, K59, L148, L247, O74, P15, R5; settlement, P108a; social, L201. *See also* army; Catholic Church; church and state; education; immigration; imperialism; liberalism; nationalism; religion; trade
Brazos region, Texas, W63
Breche, Jean, F193
Breese, Sidney, M130
Brent, Charles H., P199
Brentanismus, M306
Brentano, Lujo, M306, S219
Brenz, Johann, C285, E99
Brest-Litovsk, Treaty of, W5
Brethren of the Common Life, V24

Brethren of the Free Spirit, M110
Breton, Robert, F193
Bretonne, Restif de la, P204
Bretton Woods Conference, E12
Breweries, D192a, P165
Briand, Aristide, C201, S604, T90. *See also* Kellogg-Briand Pact
Brick industry, C208
Briçonnet, Guillaume, H204
Bridges, Harry, M1
Bridges, Styles, P187
Brief Retrospect of the Eighteenth Century, A, S608
Briggs, Charles A., H142
Brinkerhoff, Roeliff, R92
Brinton, Daniel G., H36
Brisay, Jacques Réné de, L87
Brisbane, Arthur, F45, W305
Bristol, England, C61a, M193
Bristow, Joseph L., S614
British-American Union, M113
British and Foreign Anti-Slavery and Aborigines Protective Society, F194
British Columbia, P54, U17, W369
British Columbia Dragoons, R259
British Columbia Electric Railway Co., R258
British Commonwealth, *see* Commonwealth
British East Africa, P194, W124. *See also* East Africa
British East India Co., *see* East India Co.
British Empire, L137, S246. *See also* colonial policy, Great Britain; Commonwealth of Nations; imperialism
British Honduras, W182
British Legion, W66
British New Guinea, P217
British Quarterly Review, U9
British South Africa Co., M91, S24, S227
British West Africa, E67, S8, W289. *See also* West Africa
Brittany, H457a
Broadcasting, *see* radio
Broadhurst, Henry, P10
Brockdorff-Rantzau, Ulrich C. K. von, R217
Brockton, Mass., C251
Broderick, David C., W222
Brodrick, St. John, S41
Brogan, Denis, C153
Broglee, Jacques Victor Albert, duc de, G284
Broglie, Victor de, M129
Brook Farm, H336, S435, W151
Brookhart, Smith, S51
Brookings Institution, E2
Brooklyn, N. Y., G2
Brooks, Van Wyck, B346
Brophy, John, M478

Brown, John, O2
Brown, Joseph M., G1
Brown, Robert E., S310
Brown, William G., C202
Brown, Fort, M188
Browning, Gordon, M159
Brownlow, Louis, P176
Brownlow, William, F207
Brownlow, William G., L7
Brownson, Orestes A., G50, H336, M70, M211
Brownson's Quarterly Review, M70
Brownsville Affair, C366, L27
Brown Univ., H75, V14
Brown v. *The Bd. of Education of Topeka,* T101
Bruce, Philip A., S295
Brücke, Ernst, A77
Bruderzwist, S89
Bruere, Henry, C114
Brulart de Sillery, Nicholas, D130
Bruni, Leonardo, S173, S583
Brüning, Heinrich, D86
Brunner, Sebastian, S297
Bruno of Cologne, F151
Brunswick, Germany, R250
Brunswick Manifesto, B89
Brussels Conference (1937), A45
Brutê de Rêmur, Simon W. G., G135
Bryan, George, I12
Bryan, William J., B33, C164, C312, G279, K191, L146, M135, S644, W286
Bryce, James, C229, R39, S492, W145
Bucareli Conference, I2
Bucareli y Ursúa, Antonio M., C103
Bucer, Martin, B78, W352
Buchanan, James, M283, P84
Buchez, P. J. B., R53
Buchman, Frank N. A., H274
Büchner, Ludwig, H354
Buck, Solon J., N85
Buckalew, Charles R., H439
Buckingham, James S., P162
Bucknell Univ., P28
Buckner, Simon B., S558
Budberg, Andrei, G265
Buddhism, M393
Budi Utomo, N4
Buell, Bela S., L168
Buell, Don Carlos, C172
Buenderlin, Johannes, F155
Buenos Aires, Argentina, V15
Buenos Aires Conference, 1936, H115
Buenos Aires province, D164
Buffalo, N. Y., M50, M111, P12, S225
Buffalo (N. Y.) Historical Society, G172
Buganda, East Africa, R255
Bugeaud, Thomas R., R127a
Buhl (Henry) Foundation, L197

alliance systems; Concert of Europe; Paris, Conference of 1919; socialism; World War I, II
European Coal and Steel Community, M413, S188
European Commission on Human Rights, D195
European Defense Community, M267
European Free Trade Assn., C297
Eusebius Pamphili, D205
Evangelical and Reformed Church, H133
Evangelicalism, B438, C302, C311, E115, F75, L194, R88, R219, S151. See also revivals
Evangelical United Brethren Church, D44
Evans, John, K80
Evans, John G., H224
Evarts, William M., H466, P86
Everest, David C., K32
Everett, Edward, G167
Evolution, C358, D88, G279, G303, L146, L296, M99, M149, P96. See also Darwinism; fundamentalism
Ewart, John S., C247
Ewing, Thomas, F149
Exchequer Penal Laws, G316
Executive agreements, C204, H281, O11
Exempla virtutis, C121
Exeter, England, A106, C61a
Exhibitions, see expositions
Existentialism, H206, I30
Exner, Sigmund, A77
Expansion: of Brazil, T5; of China, L93; of Egypt, K2; of Germany, S107; Great Britain in North Am., J129, M62; of Greece, R251a; of Japan, M250, P248; of New Spain, H433, N107, T76, W252; of Rome, M387, R11; of Russia, B130, C362, F92, G261, H433, K122, K265, M170, M379, P80, R10, R146, S122, S582, S632, S637; Spain in Peru, W152; of U.S., B177, B384, H84, M268, P113, S243, T12, W270. See also imperialism; manifest destiny
Expatriates, G294, W318
Explorations: in Africa, R186; of Alaska, S243; of Pacific Ocean, M240; pre-Columbian, C16; scientific, S243; in Southeast Asia, R125; Spain in Am., C103, W152, W252; of U.S., C259, F106, J93, M45, S243, W198. See also Discovery, Age of; oceanography
Export-Import Bank, A18,

H310, M73, S443. See also investments abroad
Expositions, C374, M174, S262, S589
Expropriation, Mexico, I2, K209, L244
Extremists, see radicalism

Fabianism, W205
Fabian Society, S318, W300
Factories, see industry
Factors, H320
Factory committees, in Russian Revolution, A159
Factory laws, G88, W24
Fages, Pedro, N107
Fairbanks, Charles W., R144
Fair Deal, D7, L42. See also Truman, H.
Fair Employment Practices Board, B273
Fairfield, Conn., D16
Fair Labor Standards Act, M4, M57
Fairs, see expositions
Falconry, O32
Fall, Albert B., S555, T135
Fall Committee, L244
Fallen Timbers, Battle of, G90
Falloux Law, P3
Family, F180, G246, H80, J90, T116
Family of Love in England, M463
Family Welfare Assn., G83
Far East, C210. See also Great Britain, foreign relations; imperialism; Open Door policy; Southeast Asia
Farinacci, Roberto, F148
Farley, James A., N59
Farley, John M., S216
Farm bloc, G317, L238, M329
Farmer-Labor Party, G31, L238, S208, T142
Farmer-Labor Progressive-Federation, S467
Farmers, B226, K167. See also agriculture
Farmers' Alliance, B74, D116, G3, H126, M87a, N103. See also Populist movement
Farmers' Holiday Assn., D248, J79, K238
Farmers' Institute, R127
Farmers' Union, S138
Farm programs, see agriculture, U.S.
Farm Security Administration, H347
Farm tenancy, see tenant farmers
Farnam, Henry W., G287, M68
Fascism: Argentina, G68; France, A60, S425; Italy, B214, C404, F148, H237, L88, O4, R261, S39, S383, U14, V13; response to, D139, H237, S524, U14,

W335. See also anti-Fascism
Fascist International, L88
Fashoda affair, B453, H151, H188
Fauchet, Claude, H456
Faulkner, William, R237
Faÿ, Bernard, C153
February Revolution, see Russian Revolution, 1917
Fechner, Robert, P32, S2, S18
Federal Communications Commission, G82
Federal Emergency Relief Act, B108, H341, H347, J97, M261
Federal Farm Board, K178
Federalist Party: general, B154, C262, E66, F86, G148, G302, H219, H280, K105, K211, K225, K285, M435, M487, W174, Z4; in Congress, B350, V35; Conn., B268, B463; Del., B341; Md., B432, R90, V37; Mass., B50, B199, M20, R154; New England, A121, B430, W208; N.J., P226; N.Y., J110, T158; in Old South, B426, C342, R213
Federal Power Commission, B371, H203
Federal Republic of Germany, see West Germany
Federal Reserve System, B419, B512, E31, M269
Federal-state relations, M175, W9, W201. See also secession; states' rights
Federal Surplus Relief Corp., L15
Federal Theater Project, C60
Federal Trade Commission, D40, L141
Federal Water Power Commission, R235
Federal Writers Project, M102
Federation, of British Empire, S246. See also Commonwealth of Nations
Federation of American Zionists, F36
Feijóo y Montenigro, Benito G., A95
Feitoria system, V56
Feitosas family, C126
Fellowship of Reconciliation, C140, W292
Feminism, H335, S398. See also women; women's rights
Fénelon, François de Salignac de la Mothe, F13
Feng Yü-hsiang, S234
Fenton, Reuben E., M400
Ferdinand I (Austria), F66
Ferdinand I (Spain), L285, S537
Ferdinand II (Emperor), N67
Ferdinand VI (Spain), C14
Ferdinand VII (Spain), F32,

R95a
Ferguson, Adam, F7, W244
Ferguson, Howard, O50
Ferguson, James E., C5
Ferguson, Miriam A., C5
Fernald, Bert M., S555
Fernando, Y10
Ferrara Florence, Council of B476
Ferrer, Francisco, C278
Ferry Laws, S136
Fersen, Hans Axel von, B89
Fess, Simeon D., N48
Fessenden, William P., W164
Feudalism: general, B1, B7, B433; France, B147, B433, M434, W311; Great Britain, W23; Japan, B308; New France, R102; New Spain, A56; Swabia, V17. See also castles; knights; manors
Feurbach, Ludwig A., B385
Few, William P., P193
Fichte Society, E19
Fideism, L35, M411
Fielder, James F., M152
Fields, James T., T139
Fiennes, William, C393
Fifteenth Amendment, G104, S634. See also Reconstruction
Fifth Monarchy men, C230. See also millenarian thought
Fight for Freedom Committee, C117
Figueres, José, B151
Figueroa, Emiliano, N105
Finances: Confederacy, F50; Crusades, G281; France, S99, S127; Great Britain, D132, K4, M276, M505, N65; Italian city-states, K169; Mexico, W215; U.S., N28. See also Am. Revolution; banking; Currency Act; investments abroad; panics; taxation; war debts
Findley, William, I12
Fine arts, G167. See also art; dance; painting
Finland, C267, H45, K277. See also Russo-Finnish War; World War II
Finley, James B., T42
Finney, Charles G., H325, M258, P25, P158
Fire protection, G112, L19
Firestone Tire and Rubber Co., C119, N90
First International, A119
First Minnesota Infantry Regiment, I5
Fish, A59
Fish, Hamilton, M271
Fisher, Walter L., G182
Fisheries, see oyster industry
Fisheries question, B122, H461, P86, W302
Fishing disputes, W302

C320, S39; Japan, H153, M209; medieval, B262; Russia, A159, B395, F97, F219, G88, G311, M83, R208, Z13; Scotland, S567; Spain, C14; Sweden, M55; U.S., A11, A65, B160, B378, B406, C184, C351, D60, D123, D178, E73, F44, F47, G16, H132, H324, H379, K147, K269, L197, L205, P197, S445, S482, W24, W47, W160 (*see also* business; Great Depression; mobilization; regulatory agencies; steam engines; War Industries Board; *following industries:* airlines; automotive; barbed wire; breweries; brick; canning; cattle; cereal; citrus; coffee; furniture; glassworks; machine tools; oil; oyster; paper mills; phosphate; securities; sewing machines; shoe; silk; traction; uranium; vegetable; whiskey); Upper Silesia, S116. *See also* entrepreneurs; labor unions; *following industries:* coal; electrical; insurance; iron; lumber; naval stores; newspapers; railroads; shipbuilding; steel; sugar; textile; woolen

Infamia, L207

Infantry, I5, M461, W357

Inflation, U.S., B202, E28, H73

Influenza, N101

Ingalls, John J., W220

Ingersoll, Robert G., K182

Ingram, Orrin, T168

Inhamuns, C126

Inman, Samuel Guy, W327

Innocent III (Pope), A101

Inquiry, international, H282

Inquisition, M38, S480

Insanity, B259, C2, D3. *See also* mental health; mental hospitals; psychology

Inscriptions, Bengal, M449

Inspection laws, W24

Inspectors, French colonial, G32

Institute of Government Research, E2

Institute of International Education, H42

Institute of Pacific Relations, D41

Institutiones of Cassiodorus, E78

Insulae, P2

Insular Affairs, Bureau of, S474

Insurance, C306, E90, G205, H298, L241, P169. *See also* unemployment insurance

Insurgency movement, B59, D118, H352, W211

Integral Socialists, France, F217

Integration, D37

Intelligentsia: China, P222; Russia, P181, S214

Intendants, France, G291

Inter-American fisheries disputes, W302

Inter-American system, S443, W302. *See also* Pan American Conferences

Interchurch world movement, E92

Interferometer, S629

Interior, Dept. of, A52, F149, G66, G182, H350, M498, M511, O56, P85, P135, S104, T56, W52

Internal improvements, M128, M245, P30, P172, R59, S74, W230. *See also* canals; roads

Internal senses, S520

International African Assn., A86, K30, M323

International banking, *see* banking

International brigades, R120, R225

International commissions, *see* commissions

International Confederation of Free Trade-Unions, G150

International Control Commission, Vietnam, S37

International cooperation, S98

International Court of Justice, M284, P28. *See also* Permanent Court of International Justice

International courts, H120

International education, H42

Internationalism: Europe, C314 (*see also* Europe, union of); Germany, S200; Great Britain, W130, W335; U.S., B133, B245, D71, H246, H281, H301, J121, L79, M273, S574, T102, W292. *See also* Permanent Court of International Justice; public health; world federalism; world government

International Joint Commission, U.S.-Canada, R22

International Labor Defense, C83

International Labor Organization, D9, O89

International law, B102, B197, B332, B345, C183, D38, M284, O77, P28, P82, S286, W302, Z27. *See also* Nürnberg trials; Permanent Court of International Justice; Pious Fund case

International Longshoremen's Assn., N1

International organization, G150, G271, T19, W335. *See also* arbitration; collective security; League of Nations;

United Nations

International Red Aid, R291

International Refugee Organization, L239

International trade, *see* trade

International Workers of the World, C273, D210, F215

International Working Men's Assn., N68, S196

Inter-Parliamentary Union, C314

Interposition, B87

Interracial marriage, F162

Interstate Commerce Act, K229, P234

Interstate Commerce Commission, B248, C4, M165, U11

Interurbans, M48

Intervention: Europe in Latin Am., B257, O70; in Russia in 1918, K232, S334; U.S. in World War II, C117. *See also* French intervention; nonintervention policy; protectorates

– *U.S. in Latin Am.:* general, C86, C135, K15, L221, M474, M512, N18, Y22; in Cuba, H303, L29, M365; in Dominican Republic, C86, C411, M119; in Haiti, S100, S440; in Mexico, J73, K115; in Nicaragua, D147, D156, M7a, M366, N94; in Panama, M467

Invalid Corps, S607

Inventions, *see* patents; steam engines

Inventors, P178

Investment bankers, K37

Investments, U.S., G244, M60, S595

Investments abroad: Great Britain, C54, H24, M60, M464, O70, R29, R258; in Russia, M83; U.S., F57, K199, M493, P115, R206, S14, T164. *See also* banking, international; dollar diplomacy; U.S., foreign relations, economic aspects

Ionian Republic, M105

Iorga, Nicholas, O46

Iowa: agriculture, W176; biography, C254, W281; cities, B302, H108; economy, E87, T109; education, E77; land speculation, H108, S631; politics, C22, E87, M256; territory, B302. *See also* Civil War

Ipswich, Mass., P108

Iran, G37, M465, W4. *See also* Persia

Iraq, A83, M210

Ireland: 13th century, A75; and Am. Revolution, B516, M436; Boer War, F122; economy, O15; English Civil War,

B337, E52; English interests in, B337, B500, B516; home rule, B337, H263, K272, R172, S50, S55, S250, W83, W326; independence, *see* nationalism; land policy, L298; politics, B253, B258, B381, B500, B516, E103, G258, H24, O15, S638, W326; poor law, C290; rebellions, E52; Scots in, P89; travelers in, H450; union with Great Britain, G258, S250; and United Nations, M476; Wars of French Revolution, K96. *See also* Catholic Church; Irish

Irigoyen, Hipólito, G153

Irish: in England, L100; in Nova Scotia, L176; in U.S., B366, C185, C394, D220, F37, H89, M98, N70, O30, O36, R174, S602, T13, W43, W131

Irish Ireland movement, W83

Irish Parliamentary Party, S55

Irish World, R174

Ironclads, M311, S539

Iron industry, B416, D123, F220, N88, S448, T30

Iroquois Indians, G213, L87, V33

Irreconcilables, M140, S555

Irredentist movement, T17

Irrigation, C61, G130, G168, G220, H445, M166, S575

Irving, Washington, Y3

Isabella I (Spain), L285, S92, S537

Isabella II (Spain), H454, R222, Y3

Isherwood, Benjamin F., S326

Iskandar Muda, D24

Islam, *see* Muslims

Isolationism: Canada, C247; U.S., B52, C312, C394, D7, D159, D197, G31, G305, H60, H356, J123, K94, K220, L187, L238, M59, M415, S351, S352, T102. *See also* neutrality acts

Israel, G14, K256, S388. *See also* Palestine question; Zionism

Itagaki Taisuke, C226

Italian Catholic Action, A31

Italian-Ethiopian War, *see* Ethiopian War

Italian Nationalist Assn., D84

Italians, in U.S., A70, B114, B208, D139, D220, F62, I10, M111, N30, V31, W131

Italian Syndicalist Union, B214

Italy: 10th-11th centuries, V41; economy, C320, M155, S39; empire, L3; foreign relations, B496, C100, D29, D79, E70, F230, G183, L179, M44,

S215, S451, W91, Z28 (*see also* Triple Alliance); Greeks in, M462; industry, C320, S39; journalism, O4; Middle East, M292; politics, B214, B429, C320, D148, F148, L277, H296, H443, L277, M155, O4, O75, P51, V13; Reformation in, S137; and South Tyrol, F52; and Trieste, N98; unification, B398, B525, C400, E65, H91, H395, J118, L249, M46, M222, M355, R211, S152, S226; U.S. attitudes, D139, S383. *See also* air force; army; Austro-Sardinian War; Catholic Church; colonial policy; Ethiopian War; Fascism; Mussolini; nationalism; Renaissance; Rome; World War I, II

Italy, Kingdom of, B251, G306

Itanos, S465

Ito Hirobumi, N7

Iturbide, Agustín de, R180

Ivan III (Russia), O72

Ivan IV (Russia), E96, G268, H465, M340, P80

Ivanova-Voznesensk, Russia, G26

Iwakura Tomomi, M271

Izbrannaia rada, G268

Izvolsky, Alexander P., E82

Jackson, Andrew, B456, C46, D18, F192, M61, W157, W165

Jackson, Sheldon, H289

Jackson, T. J., M42

Jackson county, Mo., J45

Jackson (Miss.) *Daily News*, S311

Jacksonian democracy, C46, C107, D55, E94, F143, G12, G111, G148, M270. *See also* Jackson, A.

Jacksonian era, E94, F143, G151, M61, S42, T43, W157. *See also* Jackson, A.

Jackson Party, *see* Democratic Party

Jacobeans, H279, M62

Jacobins, H169, W304

Jagow, Gottlieb von, L253

Jamaica, K210, M207, R187, S59, W221

James I (England), A51a, A77a, B56, B239, B319, B448, C82, C258, C316, E84, G177, G228, G293, H66, J25, L134, L189, M62, M317, O27, P89, R178, S184, S548, S579, W92, W321, Z5

James II (England), B70, B81, B359, B446, D102, G228, H386, I4, L4, P138

James V (Scotland), E8, F53, S642

James VI, *see* James I

James, Duke of York, B357

James, Edmund J., R179, S624

James, Edwin, B168

James, George W., B344

James, Henry, R237

James, William, A42, B146, B493, F61, H28, K164, M352, W144

Jameson, J. Franklin, B266

Jammu Ladakh, India, S304

Jana Sangh, B112

Janes, Leroy L., M414

Jansenism, C206, W347

Japan: general, H125, H371, J99, S338, S427; Asian policy, F115, K20, Y20; China policy, F12, G96, G169, K220, M457, R24; economy, C122, H153; expansion of, K196, M250, P248; foreign relations, A136, B505, B517, C87, C158, D166, F12, F115, G96, G149, G169, G188, K20, M281, Y20 (*see also* Four Power Treaty); intellectual, B204, C130, D59, H154, H401, M393, P257, S427; journalism, A74; and Korea, H170, K20; Koreans in, M388; modernization, A7, C130, F203, H154, J99, M209, M385, M414, P257, S427, Y1; occupation of, S616; and Open Door, H81, I24; politics, A7, B204, C226, D245, F203, G252, H401, N7, N96, R24, S277, S437, T107, W262; social, B229, M419, S77, S338, W81. *See also* army; communism; immigration; industry; labor; Manchurian crisis; Meiji era; missionaries; nationalism; navy; occupation forces; religion; Russo-Japanese War; Sino-Japanese War; taxation; Tokugawa era; trade; Washington Disarmament Conf.; World War I, II

Japanese, in U.S., D19, H141, M394, P253, T156. *See also* immigration

Japanese-Soviet Neutrality Treaty, 1941, Y20

Jaurès, Jean Léon, S52

Java, M373, S329. *See also* Indonesia

Jay, John, B347, C310, G295, J64

Jay Treaty, C262, F24, R213

Jean, Count of Dunois, S533

Jeanin, Pierre, D130

Jean of Navarre, M235

Jebb, John, B321

Jefferson, Thomas, B136, B354, C351, E63, G302, K213, L222, M487, P130, P244, R262

Jefferson, territory of, R113

Jeffersonian democracy, A82, A147, G148, H382, K105, K213, O39, S218, T158

Jeffersonian-Republican Party, A6, A24, A147, B154, B201, B268, B407, B432, C99, C262, E63, E94, G156, G302, H211, K211, M435, M487, P120, P132, P226, R154, T158, V37

Jenkins, Edward, S381

Jennings, Edward, W98

Jenstein, John of, W147

Jerome, Saint, A21

Jerusalem, Kingdom of, A145, K234

Jesuits: in China, W309; and education, B17, P3; in France, B17, C206, P3; in Mexico, K239; in New Granada, F108; in North Am., B22, S498; in Peru, R182; in U.S., L243

Jewish Patriarchate, Z35

Jews: general, P191; in Argentina, A110; in Bulgaria, C137; in Europe, T64; in France, C144, H250, M206, R196 (*see also* Dreyfus affair); in Germany, F35; medieval, C144, F39; in North Africa, R196; in Poland, G116; in Russia, M298, N22, Y13; in Spain, F39; in U.S., B114, B194, B208, B355, D145, G171, H100a, K7, L149, N52, R171, R224, S177, S303, S602, Y13. *See also* antisemitism; Khazars; Marranism; Palestine question; refugees; Zionism

Jihād, S330

Jim Crow laws, *see* segregation

Joachim of Flora, D13

Joachite tradition, D13, W156

Joad, C. E. M., P59

Joaseiro, miracle of, D93

Jodl, Friedrich, H354

John (England), W122

John VI (Portugal), W363

John VIII Palaeologus, B476

John XXII (Pope), R240, W94

John, Lord Talbot, B414

John Birch Society, T112

John Donkey, C418

John of Jenstein, W147

John of Paris, R87

Johns Hopkins Univ., G83, R233

Johnson, Andrew, B109, B390, D146, H38, I19, L7, L131, M184, S264, T129, W15

Johnson, Bushrod R., C399

Johnson, Charles S., P74

Johnson, Hiram, B100, H155, L260, O47, S51, S555

Johnson, James W., E40

Johnson, John H., W148

Johnson, Louis, M59

Johnson, Nelson T., B482, H414, S483

Johnson, Reverdy, S380

Johnson, Samuel (Colonial Am.), E61, H440, M371

Johnson, Tom L., B411, J40

Johnson, William, V33

Johnson, William S., B172

Johnson Act, 1934, R104

Johnston, Albert S., C279, C402, S558

Johnston, Harry H., R186

Johnston, Joseph F., H106

Johnston, Samuel, S102

John Swinton's Paper, R236

Joint stock companies, B254

Jolof empire, C243

Jonas of Orléans, J37

Jones, Jenkin Lloyd, T55

Jones, Joseph, B387

Jones, Lloyd, O85

Jones, Morgan, S447

Jones, Samuel P., F189, P158

Jones, Thomas G., D42

Jones, Wesley L., F153

Jones, Sir William, S593

Jones, William (England), L25

Jones, William (U.S.), C326, E11

Jones Act (1916), S474

Jordan, David S., P139

Joseph, Archduke of Austria, B461

Joseph II (Austria), B193, D62, O5

Joule, James P., S506

Journal des Hommes Libres, F11

Journal de Trevoux, L35

Journalism: agricultural, K162, N91, S69; Canada, L41; Catholic Church, S363, S367; Civil War, M215, M446, S472; France, M266, S367, S408, W21; Germany, L70, W346; Great Britain, A142, L299, M346, O85, T72, T139; Ireland, W83; Italy, O4; Japan, A74; Netherlands, C360; religious, B379a, M266, R173; Russia, A79, B8, C345, S25; science, L138; U.S., D218, G122a, L51, R236, R288, S377, S472, S486, T71, W136 (*see also* columnists; muckrakers; news broadcasting; reporters). *See also* newspapers; periodicals

Jouvenel, Henry de, M351

Juárez, Benito, B209, M459, S130, W95

Judge, C418

Judges, B158, F163, R190, W88. *See also* courts

Judicial Reorganization Bill of 1937, D240, H368, P176

Laymen, S143

Lazarus, Emma, F36

Lea, Henry C., S480

Lead mining, G28

League for Independent Political Action, L68

League for Social Reconstruction, H375

League of Germandon Abroad, C373

League of Nations: Austria, A44; Belgium, K125; Chaco dispute, R252; drafting of, P200, R149; drug control, T19; France, G214, W111; Germany, W108; Great Britain, B245, M168, P174, S625, T61, W108; humanitarian work, S266; Memel question, S321; and minorities, F79, T64; Poland, W337; Rhineland, G147; slavery, C119, N90; and Saar, V4; social work, S266; and Sudetenland, W138; trade, P35; U.S., B245, B324, B366, B433, D174, D194a, D220, F196, J121, L146, L260, L261, M140, M380, N90, O89, P238a, S266, S486, S527, S555, T19, W320. See also Ethiopian War; Geneva Disarmament Conference; Manchurian crisis; mandates; sanctions

League of Nations Assn., J121

League of Nations Union, B245, C17, C229

League of the North, B408

League of Universal Brotherhood, T97

Learned, Rufus F., C359

Lease, Mary Elizabeth, C179

Leavenworth, Jesse H., U8

Leavitt, Joshua, D43, S424

Lebanon, M183, S261

Lebanon, Conn., S477

Le Bon, Gustave, N110

Lectures on Moral Philosophy, S153

Lee, Arthur, P208, R133

Lee, Ivy, R44

Lee, Jason, D77

Lee, Richard E., S416

Lee, Richard Henry, B347, C310, S559

Lee, Robert E., G94, M172

Lee, Roswell, C115

Lee, Samuel P., T110

Lee, Stephen D., H147

Leeds Working Men's Association, W3

Leer, G.A., V63

Leeser, Isaac, S177

Leeward Islands, R187

Lefèvre d'Etaples, Jacques, H204

Legendre, Charles W., C87

Legal profession, M104

Legal Tender Act, 1862, T145

Legal theory, G24

Legates, P101, U5. See also canon law

Legislative Commission of 1867, S306

Legitimists, France, C343, L209. See also Royalists

Leguía, Augusto B., K34

Leibnitz, Gottfried W. von, L66

Leibowitz, Samuel, C83

Leibstandarte Adolf Hitler, W118

Leicester House faction, M87

Leiden, Univ. of, R267

Leisure, H372, M469

Leith, Charles K., W37

Leland, Charles G., S371

Le Loi, W190

LeMans forgeries, G138

Lemke, William, B162, H202, P210, T154

Lemoine, Jean, S499

Lend Lease, C117, D49, H249, K141, L279, M141, M144

Lenglet Du Fresnoy, Nicolas, S168

Lenin, Vladimir I., B94, B288, D39, D73, H437, K157, L255, L290, M336, N106, R4, T117, W257. See also Russian Revolution

Leninism, L173

Leo XII (Pope), L13

Leo XIII (Pope), C21, H443, O75, S115, W319

Leo Frank Case, D145, R224

León, P212

Leonard, Daniel, B172

Leopold I (Austria), S271

Leopold I (Emperor), S207

Leopold II (Belgium), M323, S198

Leopold III (Belgium), K125

Leopold, Aldo, N13

Leopold, of Tuscany, G34

Leopoldina, Queen (Brazil), B106

LeRoy, Louis, G308

Leroy-Beaulieu, Paul, W78

Lerroux, Alejandro, C278

Lessing, Gotthold E., C309

Letcher, John, B317

Letelier, Valentin, S172

Leticia dispute, C174

Levant, M183

Levant Co., M62

Levant crisis, 1945, P110a

Levant trade, M62, P76

Levée en masse, R50

Leverett, John, K11

Leverrier, Urbain J. J., G280

Lévesque, René, H18

Levinson, Salmon O., D71

Lewes, George H., G142, M499

Lewis, C. Day, C281

Lewis, Charles F., L197

Lewis, John L., C88, M478. See also United Mine Workers

Lewis, Meriweather, M45

Lewis, Sinclair, M109, W160

Lewis, Tayler, D88

Lewis and Clark expedition, M45

Lewisohn, Ludwig, S303

Lex Agraria, B200

Liang Ch'i-ch'ao, H409, W308

Liao Chung-k'ai, W358

Liberal Arts, A139, C295, V14

Liberal Assn., J106

Liberal-Conservative Party (Canada), B216

Liberal Era (Russia), K14

Liberalism: Brazil, H357; Canada, C68; France, H130, S578; Germany, B115, H109, H184, K107, Z33; Great Britain, K42, M15, M30, M200, S402; Poland, B484; religious, B506; Russia, B167, B169, K14, K139, N49, T81; Spain, F32, K108; U.S., D53, H46, L56, L68, O78, V1. See also revolutions, of 1820-21, 1830, 1848

Liberal Party: Brazil, E111; Canada, L41, S530, S568; Colombia, D52, D98; Great Britain, A150, B211, B534, C17, E80, G67, H263, H396, K184, L188, L192, M160, R172, R242, S41, S58, S455, S475, W113, W279; Hungary, V36; Japan, C226; Mexico, A43, M516

Liberal Republicans, A32, D194, E105, G69, P175, T161

Liberal Unionist Party, Great Britain, E80

Liberator, The: Great Britain, W134; U.S., F41, F99, T52

Liber Floridus, F114

Liberia, C34, C119, D58, J98, M197, M221, N90, S279

Liberty, D95, H159, L32, T73, W260. See also freedom

Liberty and Property Defence League, S405

Liberty League, C263, G221

Liberty Party, U.S., H215

Librarianship, P23

Libraries, E17

Library List of 1783, S362

Libya, S170

Liddell Hart, B. H., R195

Liebknecht, Karl, B97, G159

Liebknecht, Wilhelm, G159

Life, C418

Li-Fournier convention, H406

Li Hung-chang, F134, S44

Lilienthal, David E., M35

Li Li-Sen, T74

"Lily Whites," C366, N24, W97

Lima, Peru, M223

Lima Conference, 1938, H115

Limousin province, B147

Linck, Wenzeslaus, D12

Lincoln, Abraham, B157, B327, C73, C172, C368, C412, D46, D146, D214, E36, H447, J84, N55, R161, R285, S75, S195, S240, S264, S296, S428, T56. See also Civil War; secession

Lincoln, Benjamin, C105

Lincoln, Levi, P120

Lincoln, Robert T., G136

Lincoln-Johnson Plan, B390

Lindamood, W. S., C208

Lindsey, Ben B., H156, H412

Lingard, John, F8, P219

Linguet, Simon N. H., L151, M314

Link, Arthur S., D165

Lippmann, Walter, B346, C25, D210, F61, K72, R93, S70, S580

Lipscomb, David, H363

Liquor business and controls, Q9

Lisa, Manuel, O35

Li Ta-chao, M289

Literature, see novelists

Lithographs, M228

Lithontriptic drugs, V49

Lithuania, S321, V62

Lithuanians, in U.S., A70, G235

Lithuanian Statute of 1529, V62

Little Colorado River Basin, P113

Little magazines, L190

Little Rock, Ark., R111

Little Steel industry, S401

Liu Chi, C125

Liu-Ch'iu, kingdom of, C148

Liudprand of Cremona, S611

Liu Hsiang, K28

Liu Ming-ch'uan, S444

Liu Shao-ch'i, O41

Liverpool, Robert J., K73

Livestock, L15, O35. See also cattle industry

Livingston, William, B202a

Livonia, U12

Livre du corps de policie, L273

Lleras, Lorenzo María, D52

Lloyd, Henry D., F189

Lloyd George, David, B508, C212, H396, K232, M505, R197, S50, S58, W54, Z8

Loans, see investments; investments abroad

Lobbying, D241

Local Governing Board, G315

Locarno, Treaty of, J23, T61, W108

Lochner, Louis, G286

Lochner v. *New York,* S508

Locke, John, H444, H468, R244

Loco-Focos, M63

Locomotives, F201

Lodge, Henry C., B373, B493, C370, H281, S555. See also

League of Nations, U.S.
Loeb-Leopold case, D210
Loehe, Wilhelm, H197
Logan, James, W150
Logan, John A., E37
Logan county, W. Va., C392
Logistics, in Civil War, G137
Loire province, S128
Loisy, Alfred F., R42
Lollards, F209
Lombardy, Republic of, G124
Lomonosov, Mikhail V., J94
London, Jack, D210
London, Meyer, B235
London, Bishopric of, L121, S239
London, England, B203, C61a, F23, F98, F156, H166, L100, M294, R2, S162, S183, S262, S341, S463, S505, W295
London Conferences: of 1827-32, S98; of 1912-13, L253, S98
London Economic Conference, F225
London Missionary Society, K174, P217, W297
London Naval Conferences, A100, B175, C3, I16, P22, R264, T152
Long, Breckinridge, F35, W91
Long, Huey P., B162
Long, Stephen H., B168
Long Parliament, M33, S387
Longshoremen, M1
López, Carlos Antonio, F113
Lopez, Francisco Solano, K228, O70
Lopez Contreras, Elezar, B495
Lopez de Cerrato, Alonso, S238
Lopez Mateos, Adolfo, W215
Lords, House of, F184, L284, S113, S548, Z8. See also Parliament
Lorimer, William, T15
Loris-Melikov, Michael T., K14
Lorraine, Cardinal of, N102
Los Angeles, Calif., B60, B83, D82, E20, F126, H390, L159, M394, V23
Los Angeles Times, M360
Losinga, Herbert de, A50
Los Santos Angeles de Guevavi, mission of, K111
Lossberg, von, Regiment, S320
Lost generation, see expatriates
Lotze, R. H., W218
Louis IX (France), G263, L203, P141, W311
Louis X (France), B433
Louis XII (France), S546
Louis XIII (France), B143, C222, S307
Louis XIV (France), B45, B143, B357, E44a, G6, G115, H82, H457a, K175, K292, O16, P149, R209, R247, S207, S421, S594, S638, T134,

W162
Louis XV (France), A1, H86, K99, P6, W46
Louis XVI (France), C7, C106, H169, R244, W357
Louis XVIII (France), B449, K71, M129, R95
Louisbourg, Fort, R47
Louisiana: general, C55, C70; agriculture, C19, H25, H341; economy, M364; French, S376; KKK in, A49, H99; politics, C55, D116, H25, H146, S121, W97, W223; progressive movement, S121; religion, P42, W288; settlement of, T124; slavery, M301; social, M426; Spanish, S376; T40; territory, C55, D23, H146, L85, M45, O35, U3; transportation, O18. See also Civil War; colonial policy, Spain; Negro; New Orleans; Reconstruction; secession
Louisiana, State Univ. of, R57
Louisiana purchase, F24, F29, K213, L85
Louis Napoleon, see Napoleon III
Louis of Guienne, L273
Louis Philippe, G164, K218, M129
Louisville, Ky., C269, F73, S600
Louisville, Cincinnati, & Charleston Railroad, S132
Louisville & Nashville Railroad, J59, S600
Louisville Courier Journal, S600
Louisville Daily Journal, C269
Lourenco, José, A90
Lourmarin, France, S231
Louvre, C277
Love, B217, F172, M463
Love, Alfred H., D160
Lovejoy, Arthur O., G287
Lovell, James, J100
Low, Seth, C114, D38, K294
Low-Church movement, England, B88
Lowe, Robert, B417
Lowell, A. Lawrence, H246
Lowell, Josephine S., R92
Lowell, Mass., S433
Lower clergy, French Revolution, W234
Lower Congo, S585
Lower Languedoc, R190
Löwith, Karl, R130
Lowndes, William, R274, V48
Lowther, James, M398
Loy, Matthias, F216
Loyalists, in Am. Revolution, B172, B424, B455, C6, G23, J96, L58, M104, M194, M312, M386, M390, N25, N93, O93, S366, S484, V33, W42, W159, Z20. See also

Spanish Civil War
Lubumbashi, Congo, F63
Lucca, B284, K4
Luce, Stephen B., H248
Ludendorff, Erich, B21, C357, P137
Ludlow, Louis, H356
Ludlow Amendment, B310
Ludolphus the Carthusian, B299
Ludovicus, see Louis IX
Ludwig I (Bavaria), G178
Ludwig II (Bavaria), E38
Luftwaffe, W316
Lugard, Frederick, H71
Lugo, province of, J61
Lumber industry, C72, C344, C359, C378, E44, F68, F87, G18, M432, P114, S347, T168. See also naval stores
Lunacharskii, Anatolii V., H355
Lusitania, M47
Lusk, Clayton R., W274
Luther, Martin, K173, S147, S185, S274, T35, W352. See also Reformation
Lutheran Evangelical Assn. of Finland, A35
Lutheran Laymen's League, G190
Lutherans: Austria, F155; Finland, A35; Germany, C285, E99, F161, R151, S471; U.S., F216, G190, H197, M226
Luther v. Borden et al., D103, S126, W201
Luttrell family, B440
Luxembourg gallery, C277
Luxemburg, Rosa, B97, R115
Luxury, idea of, W6
Luzon, P. I., L46
Lyautey, Hubert, C300
Lyceum, M257
Lyell, Charles, M99, P5
Lynching, Z6
Lyon, Lucius, S253
Lyon, France, A119, B224, G229
Lyon (France) Mission to China, L8
Lyonnais, France, S128
Lytton Commission, D159, N94

Mabillon, Jean, B184
McAdoo, William G., B419, S10
Macarius, Metropolitan, M340
MacArthur, Arthur, G43
MacArthur, Douglas, D215, H111
Macaulay, Catherine, B321
McBryde, John M., C224
McCabe, E. P., T100
McCall, Nathaniel, G237
McCarthy, Joseph R., G259, H65, K82, T112
McCarthyism V46a
McClellan, George B., H121
McClelland, Robert, F149
McClure's Magazine, S181,

S205, S221, S511
McCormack, Arthur T., J5
McCormack, Joseph N., J5
McCoy, Frank R., N94
McCoy, Isaac, S133
McCulloch, J. R., E64a
McCulloch v. Maryland, 113
McDonald, Forrest, L294
Macdonald, James R., F5
Macdonald, John A., H190, M427
Macdonald, John S., H312
MacDonald, Ramsay, B425, M160, T60, T62
McDowell, James, C256
Macedonia, D92, H9, H12, S470, T86
McElroy, Robert M., B266
Macer, F114
McFarlane, Peter B., A161
McGarrity, Joseph, T13
McGee, William J., H36
McGilvra, John J., D162
McGreevy-Langevin scandal, L41
Mach, Ernst, B261, K164
Machado y Morales, Gerardo, J3
Machajski, Jan W., S214
Machakos Kamba, M490
McHenry, James, M259
Machiavelli, Niccolo, A93
Machine, and civilization, W160
Machines, see bosses, political
Machine tools industry, U.S., C115, W14
McIntire, Carl, V46a
McKay, Douglas, M151
McKean, Thomas, R254
McKelway, Alexander J., B379a
McKendree, William, E114
McKenney, Thomas L., V47
Mackenzie, Alexander, H190, M427
MacKenzie, Ranald S., N80
McKim, James M., C241
McKinley, William, F46, H303, K191, M135, M501, S240, V2
McKinley Tariff, T36
Mackintosh, James, N21
McLaughlin, Andrew C., B266
McLean, Angus M., U6
MacLeish, Archibald, D53
McNabb rule, K82
McNary, Charles L., J74
McNary-Haugen Act, M329
McNutt, Paul V., N26
Macon, Nathaniel, H211
Macon, S374
Macon county, Ga., J41
Macon's Bills, H211
McPherson, Aimee Semple, E20
McRae, Colin J., F50
MacReynolds, James C., S87
MacVeagh, Isaac Wayne, O58
Macy, Jesse, C254
Madagascar, H188, K103, L124, M252
Madero, Francisco, B138, B469,

M324, S27, T135, V10, W215
Madiera River, D30
Madison, James, B350, C99, E66, K138, S362
Magazines, *see* periodicals
Magdeburg Centuries, R151
Maginot Line, C195, H431, R286, W111
Magistrates, *see* judges
Magnolia Oil Co., K152
Magón, Ricardo Flores, A43
Magyars, B294, K112, S456
Mahan, Alfred T., B178, D38, G54, H248, K35, L154, R37
Mahan, Dennis H., G250, H16
Maharashtra state, India, C96
Mail, *see* Post Office
Maimonides College, S177
Main Currents in American Thought, M308
Maine: general, B49, S124; Colonial Am., L105; economy, S347; labor, S149; politics, B49, H447, O28, S149, S187, W154, W164; religion, L105. *See also* Am. Revolution; Civil War
Maine, Henry J. S., B102
Mainz, Elector of, K292, T66
Maiorescu, Titu, G257
Maistre, Joseph de, L86, R53
Maitland, Peregrine, Q3
Majority Socialist Party (SPD), *see* Social Democratic Party, Germany
Majthenyi, Joseph, G39
Makarios III, Archbishop, Z26
Maklakov, V. A., D34
Malawi Kingdoms, L37
Malaya, F48, R8
Malaysia, P229
Mali, Z29
Malin, James C., B153
Mallet du Pan, Jacques, N8
Mallory, Stephen R., M311, S539, W146
Malon, Benoît, F217
Malouet, Pierre-Victor, W180
Mamlūk Empire, B4
Man: concepts of, H434, S601; image of, M497; nature of, H381, K164; theory of, P96
Man, Hendrik de, H74
Management and labor, M112. *See also* employers
Manchu dynasty, *see* Ch'ing dynasty
Manchuria, B274, L93, W61
Manchurian crisis: general, M457, R24, W61; Great Britain, G273, H183, M168; League of Nations, D159, D174, N94, S527; U.S., C3, D159, D174, H183, H414, I14, M18, M168, O89, P72, S527
Mandates, A154, B295, B473, D198, G21, G84, L137,

M183, M351, S261
Mandel, Georges, S242
Mandingo states, Q7
Manifest destiny, B527, G50, K83, R124, U3
Manigault family, C381
Manila trade, Q5
Manitoba, Canada, C189, C390
Mann, Heinrich, G275
Mann, Horace, F45, M257
Mann, Thomas, Z36
Mann-Elkins Act, K229, M218
Manning, Henry E., C186
Manors, England, G231
Manteuffel, Otto von, G108
Mantua, Italy, P8
Manuel II (Palaeologues), B63a
Manufacturing, *see* industry
Manumission, M460. *See also* emancipation
Manuscripts, Texas, K126
Manwaring, Roger, S387
Maoris, W225
Mao Tse-tung, D39, L255, O41, S174, T57, W358
Maramic Iron Works, N88
Maranhão e Grão Para, G278
Maratha War, S461
Marathon Paper Mill Co., K32
Marble, Manton M., M79
Marburg, Theodore, H246
Marburg, Germany, W217
Marcantonio, Vito, K18, L12, S65
March retreat, 1918, H232
Marcuse, Herbert, R166
Maréchal, Ambrose, M509
Maret, Abbé, S363
Mariana Islands, P248
Mariátegui, José Carlos, C141
Maria Theresa, B193, B386, K29
Marie Antoinette, B89
Marie de Médicis, V5
Marines, U.S., M7a
Marion county, Mo., F160
Maritain, Jacques, A78
Maritime history, B105. *See also* merchant marine
Marius, Gaius, M254
Marketing, U.S., P197, W324
Markham, Edwin, F189
Marković, Svetozar, M25
Marne, battle of, M252
Marne-Rhine Canal, H57
Marranism, Y10
Marriage, F162, H208, J90, O66, R177, T116
Marseilles, France, C168, G229
Marshall, Charles B., K13
Marshall, George C., H308, L225, S501, W265
Marshall, Humphrey, T34
Marshall, John, B503, T127
Marshall, Louis, R224
Marshall, Stephen, W121
Marshall College, B64
Marshall Islands, P248
Marshall Plan, R147

Marshals, U.S., B43
Marti, José, T137
Martin, Josiah, G23, W170
Martin, Thomas S., G52, H327, K43, L52
Martineau, Harriet, M499
Martínez, Hernándes, W250
Martínez, Mariano, M375
Martínez, de Torrelaguna, Felix, W72
Martin v. *Hunter's Lessee,* T127
Martyrs of Cordoba, C246
Marx, Karl, C37, F210, G62, R201, S569, V61. *See also* Marxism
Marxism, C379, E43, E81, H200, H206, K157, L255, M370. *See also* communism
Mary I (England), C347, H221, S239, W112
Maryland: agriculture, W287; biography, C99; cities, M456; Colonial Am., C64, C190, D102, E53, G127, J116, M241, M456, N53, S310, Z20; Confederation Era, M143; economy, B464; politics, B432, C99, M29, R90, S380, V37; progressive movement, C375; religion, D102, G135, H127, M208, M509. *See also* Am. Revolution; Baltimore; Civil War
Maryland State Colonization Society, C34, M221
Mary of Guise, S642
Mary of Lorraine, S642
Maso degli Albizzo, Messer, M401
Mason, Charles, T109
Mason, James M., W76
Masonic Order, *see* Freemasonry
Masons, medieval, S222
Massachusetts: general, B384, M167, T138; antislavery movement, J34; biography, B176, C177, E14, T97; cities, C251, F212, G246, L211, M94, P108, R234, S433 (*see also* Boston); Colonial Am., B99, B260, B286, B336, B488, D144, F154, F157, K11, K46, L164, L211, M94, M104, M300, M312, M337, M508, P108, R7, R33a, R133, S118, S294, W33, W67, W82, W216, Z14; Confederation era, H34; economy, C251, C335, M8, R234, S433; intellectual, C167, M70, S205; labor, B134; lawyers, G48, M104; and Maine, B49; New Deal, G176, M232; newspapers, F186, W43; politics, A3, A12, B50, B199, B283, B384, B430, C69, G156, H89, H254, H270, L42, M20, M58, M232, M352,

P120, P250, R153, R154, R234, S47, W174; progressive movement, A12; railroads, S21; religion, C69, G283, M70, M316, W339 (*see also* Puritans); slavery, Z18; social, F30, K203, R223; socialism, B134; women's suffrage, K87. *See also* Am. Revolution; Civil War; education, U.S.; Negro
Masséna, André, H384
Masses, F99
Mass-transit, H192
Masters, Edgar Lee, K12
Matebeleland, S24
Matanuska colony, Alaska, M359
Maternity laws, C152
Mathematics, G5, H67, K156, M120, S532
Mather, Cotton, B259, R33a
Mather, Richard, B494
Mathias, Archduke, S89
Matter, nature of, G161
Mattheus de Acquasparta, M238
Matthews, Brander, F228
Maupeou, René-Nicolas-Augustin de, H417
Maura, Antonio, C278
Maurain, Jean, C37
Maurice, Frederick D., C305
Maurus of Salerno, S11
Maury, Matthew F., S249, T110
Maximilian II Emanuel (Bavaria), G6
Maybank, Burnet R., C43
Maybury, William C., A115
Mayer, Wilhelm, M332
May Fourth movement, China, C147, K56, K291, M234, S57, W290
Mayhew, Thomas, J70, L163
Maynard, John, L25
Mayo, Nathan, L10
Mayorga, Martín de, G118
Maysville Road Bill, G12
Mazarin, Jules Cardinal, M319, R275
Mazey, Emil, W194
Mazzini, Giuseppe, F189
Meacham, Alfred B., P136
Mead, Richard, Z34
Meaux, France, H204
Mechanical engineers, C18
Mechanics, laws of, H67
Mechanization, H8, H379
Mediation: international, P207, R252, W256; labor, W116
Medical Assn. of the State of Mo., E35
Medical Institute of Philadelphia, R122
Medicare, P169
Medici, Cosimo I de', Z24
Medicine: Am. Revolution, C93; ancient, R126, S60; China, C371; Civil War, B387; Colonial Am., W216; Dutch,

Nature, and mathematics, K156

Naumann, Friedrich, F161

Nauvoo, Ill., F107, S252

Navajo Indians, K75, R184

Naval Accords, *see* London Naval Conf.; Washington Disarmament Conf.

Naval stores, C72, P105. *See also* lumber industry

Naval strategy, A133, O31

Naval War College, S441

Navarro, Sanchez (family), H105

Navigation: general, P34; Acts, M39, S563 (*see also* trade, Colonial Am.); aerial, W350; system, M480

Navy: Austro-Hungarian, G54; Chile, S40; Confederate, B412, M311, S539, W146; France, B241, P149, S638; Germany, K77, L165, R264, S54, W54; Great Britain, A133, B101, B111, B139, B241, F21, H241, P182, R264, S563, W54, W145, W200, W315; Japan, D143, P103; in Mediterranean, H40; Russia, M105; Spain, F178; U.S., A100, B175, B232, B483, B485, C259, D143, D204, E74, H15, H125, H241, H332, K35, K172, L154, O63, P157, P213, S223, S326, S374, S441, T14, T110, T152, W145, W315 (*see also* Am. Revolution, naval aspects; Civil War, U.S., naval aspects; Navy, Dept. of). *See also* disarmament; London Naval Conf.; Mahan, A. T.; Washington Disarmament Conf.; World War I, II, naval aspects

Navy, Dept. of, C219, C303, E11, F55, H56, H248, M137

Navy Board, Great Britain, P182

Nawab Wazier, of Oudh, I8

Nazi Germany: agriculture, L250; architecture, L28, T26; Austria, L82, M362 *(see also Anschluss);* and Balkans, O76; and Belgium, K125, K205; colonialism, S107; concept of state, B475; and Czechoslovakia, A88, M236, S335; disarmament, D86; Finland, C267; foreign relations, B195, B498, C267, D6, D166, F165, G180, H194, J35, L82, O29, O76, P22, R227, W166, W269; and France, J35; Great Britain, F5, M255, N19, P22, V66; Hungary, W269; ideology, N92, R246; Japan, D166; Middle East, M292; music, E57; opposition to, B287, H339; Papacy, D136;

Poland, G272, L144, R227; politics, A67, L28, M81, N27 (*see also* National Socialism); programs, N27; propaganda, E57, K288, P246; Romania, F165; Soviet Union, B195; Spain, P236, W166; Sudetenland, A88, S335; trade, B104, H285; U.S., B104, B355, B498, D6, F231, G180, K54, M496, O29; and Wagnerism, H252; youth movements, H201, W28, W69. *See also* antisemitism; German-Am. Bund; Hitler, A.; labor; Munich crisis; Nürnberg trials; refugees; S.S.; World War II

Near East, *see* Middle East

Nebraska: general, C336, M175; agriculture, B173, C61, P39; cities, C171; economy, D76; New Deal, B173; newspapers, B351, C164; politics, B117, B351, C164, D7, L275, P39, P63; territory, M175

Nebraska, Univ. of, H75

Nebular hypothesis, N104

Necker, Jacques, N8

Negro: and Africa, C287; in British Honduras, W182; in Colonial Am., W231; in Jamaica, K210; in New Spain, B368, P11; in Peru, B353; in Venezuela, L220. *See also* race; racial concepts and theory; slavery; slave trade

— *in U.S.:* general, F222; in Ala., C83, G277, J85, K227, S233a, W336; and army, W185; attitudes toward, B215, F207, G217, H378, N81, W74; in Boston, J21; in Calif., D82, F171; and Catholic Church, G22; in Chicago, S438, S577; in Civil War, B15, B210, C146, E14, G76, V52, W264; in Detroit, K40; in Ga., M253, S192, W273; ideology, F222; in Ind., C145, L257; in La., F89, H25, K192, W97; and Mark Twain, P125; in Mass., J21; in Mich., K40; migration, F171, L257; in Miss., H116, H348, S17; in Mo., M380, S322; and New Deal, K129, W306; in New South, B523, D14, F207, G41, G46, H378, N24, N81, W161, W273, W349; newspapers, S322; in N.Y. City, F195, O87, S78, W148; in N.C., B510, R198, W161; in Ohio, G89; in Okla. territory, T100; in Pa., N36; politics, C366, N24, T18, W97; Reconstruction, A32, C252, H38, H116, H240,

N81, R119, W264, W313, W336; and religion, F4, G22, R77, S562, W148; rights of, L104; social, K192; as soldiers, B211, F85, F112, P134; in S.C., C315, E113, S31, T36a, W207, W235; in Tenn., A110a, G194; in Texas, B74, C366, G121, L27, R106; in Va., B489; in World War I, B52a, F85. *See also* Brownsville Affair; civil rights; Civil War; colonization programs; desegregation; education; emancipation; Fifteenth Amendment; Fourteenth Amendment; free Negro; Great Depression; Ku Klux Klan; National Association for the Advancement of Colored People; National Urban League; segregation

Neill, Charles P., B42

Nelson, Knute, B252

Nelson, Leonard, S584

Nelson, Thomas A. R., L7

Nelson, Thomas H., R230

Nelson, William R., M32

Németh, László, L252

Neo-Kantianism, W218

Neo-socialism, G282

Nepean, Evan, N43

Neptune, G280

Nerchinsk, Treaty of, M170

Nero, F59

Nesiotic League, S308

Nesselrode, Charles-Robert, G265

Netherlands, C360, D62, D233, F127, G115, L97, M339, M354, P205, S389, V16, W85. *See also* New Netherlands

Netherlands West India Co., C268

Neubacher, Hermann, R148

Neudeutschland, W28, W69

Neufmarché, Bernard de, N40

Neufville, Nicolas de, D130

Neuilly, France, O9

Neuilly-sur-Seine, Treaty of, D203

Neurath, Constantin F. von, H194

Neuroanatomy, A77

Neurophysiology, A77

Neutralism, G75

Neutrality: Civil War, O77; Mexican Revolution, H334; Thirty Years' War, H387; War of 1812, E29; World War I, C312, H331, J47, K130, K214, L118, M286, R89

Neutrality Accord, 1902, S215

Neutrality Acts, B370, H60, K85, L187, M59, T118

Neutral rights, M311, W76

Neuzeit, Austria, B304

Nevada, L177, R113, S556

Nevada City, Calif., M177

Nevin, John W., B64, F183

New Abolitionism, P159

New Amsterdam, *see* New Netherlands

Newark, N.J., G15, H295

Newcastle Educational Commission, W212

Newcomb, Simon, W278

New Deal: general, B396, C304, G226, J8, M73, R68, S296a, V1, W70; Ark., H341; art programs, C288, M358; banking, B512; business, C263, T80; Catholic Church, F120; child labor, M4; civil liberties, A148; coal industry, J66; Colo., W197; and Congress, B73, G226, H53, H69, P56, P176, S142, S201, S385, W41; continuation of, H288; farm programs, B173, G285, H341, L15, S69, S138, T167 (*see also* Agricultural Adjustment Acts); foreign policy, W129 (*see also* Good Neighbor policy; Hull, Cordell; Neutrality Acts; World War II, coming of); Ga., C291, H347; and Great Britain, D150; housing, W334; Ill., J97; and Indians, P135; and isolationism, L187; and journalists, O78; labor, A92, A148, B219, H311, L12, M57, R12; La., H341; Mass., G176, M232; Minn., K216; Miss., H341; N.C., M185, M417; Ohio, M261; opposition to, A109, B73, B524, C263, D7, F200, L197, L233, M68, N99, O78, P56, P210, S65, S203, S351, S478, T80, T154, W258; Pa., S488; and progressives, D6, G198, S284; relief, M102, M103, M433, W26 (*see also* Civilian Conservation Corps; Civil Works Adm.; Federal Emergency Relief Act; Public Works Adm.; Works Progress Adm.); reorganization of, P176; resettlement programs, H341, M359; S.C., C43; Supreme Court, H368, P176, S87; taxes, L16; Tenn., G194; and towns, A131; Va., H195; Virgin Islands, G215. *See also* Great Depression; Negro; Reciprocal Trade Agreements; Roosevelt, F. D.; Securities and Exchange Commission; social security

New Economic Policy, U.S.S.R., F97, M475

New England: in Am. Revolution, K150; Colonial Am., B388, B430, B494, C72, C75, C237, C324, F83,

R286; naval aspects, L165; Near East, R212; Negro in, B52a, F85; observers, M286; and Oklahoma, L291; opposition to, M361; peace movements, B310, C140; peace negotiations, *see* Paris Conference of 1919; peace proposals, H244, V42; Prussia, H373; and psychologists, C20; religion, M115a, M205; revisionists, C240, K85, K94, T133; Russia, G49, G240, H319, I7, P142, W5; socialists, B235, M201; soldiers in, B41; Straits question, L44; strategy, G304; Sweden, K214; transportation, K110; Turkey, C98, L44; Ukraine, H319, P142; U.S., B41, B126, B155, B235, B281, B310, B389, C20, C140, C209, C229, C293, C312, C394, C395, F84, F85, F164, F176, F230, G165, G183, G239, G286, G287, H33, H94, H234, H331, J47, J49, J50, K110, K275, L291, M47, M115a, M286, M361, R70, R93, W115, Z28 (*see also* Congress, U.S.). *See also* Armistice; blockade; mobilization; neutrality; preparedness; propaganda; public opinion; reparations; revolutions, of 1918; veterans; war debts

World War II: Africa, B263, C323, J28, W1; air power, B361, H143, H266, L279, M78, W153; Argentina, P258; armored forces in, C195; Australia, R58; Austria, L82; Balkans, M379, O76, R148; Belgium, K202, K205; and Berlin, P67; bombing, B361, H266, M78; Brazil, M11; Bulgaria, C137; Canada, B124; Caribbean, H292; censorship, W241; chemical warfare, B240; China, F64, L225, S174, S375b; coming of, B195, B370, B505, C175, C210, D53, D79, G233, H242, K220, M11, M18, M141, M144, N19, S553, U18, W166, Y20 (*see also* Munich Crisis); Czechoslovakia, J38, M236; Denmark, V64; diplo-

macy, B19, C204, G4, G114, G180, H54, H107, H292, L82, L279, M199, O17, R58, S34, S468, W263 (*see also* Yalta Conference); Egypt, J28; Finland, C367, K277; France, C67, C317, G51, H330, H472, J51, M295, N100, P68, R96, R286, S291, T90, W36; Free French, M183, T90; Germany, A23, B25, C323, G180, H358, K31, K202, L73, L82, M53, N92, P246, V64, W30, W217, W241, W267; Great Britain, H143; Greece, H359, R148; Hungary, F51, K31, M9; Iceland, H449; Indo China, K8; Italy, H296, H351, S345; Japan, B361, K17; Jews, C137; Kenya, S256; labor, E28, G165, G238, H358, K226, M478, S450; Latin Am., G219, H310; medicine, L107; Mexico, S34; and Middle East, M292; military aspects, B25, B148, B240, C323, H157, H308, L73, S345, S501, T160, W1, W267; Morocco, B263; naval aspects, R98; Netherlands, S389; Nigeria, O61; Norway, C180; pacifists, W292; peace efforts, V42; Philippines, S514; Poland, B195, H54, M144, T63; postwar planning, G64; prisoners of war, P167; religion, A53; revisionists, K95; Romania, F165; Soviet Union, A53, B25, G4, G143, L73, L279, M379, O17, T160; Spain, B76, H43, P236, W246; strategy, B148, H107, H157, H308, L73, M75, P37; surplus, S517; surrender terms, M53; Sweden, C180; Turkey, B19, L82; U.S., B124, B240, C117, C204, E28, E79, G4, G122a, G143, G165, G180, H292, H308, K226, L279, M244, M394, O17, P167, P253, S34, T156, W70, W115, W153, W163 (*see also* atomic bomb; Congress, U.S.; draft; Lend Lease; reconversion); and Western Hemisphere, G114, H310; women, G238. *See also* collaboration; mobilization; occupation forces;

preparedness; propaganda; public opinion; refugees; resistance movements; Vichy France; Yalta Conference
Worth, Jonathan, Z31
Wright, Elizur, Jr., F198
Wright, Frank Lloyd, T169
Wright, Hendrick B., C406
Wright, Henry C., W305
Wright, Joseph A., C353
Wright, Luke E., C221
Wright Act, M166
Wriston, Henry M., V14
Writers Project, WPA, M102
Wu, Emperor, O73
Wu Chih-hui, G40
Wu Mi, R216
Wu P'ei-fu, W345
Württemberg, C285, D100, E99, H318, H448, M334, W187
Wu San-kwei, K113, T141
Wu T'ing-fang, S247a
Wyclif, John, T16, W135
Wydeville family, M142
Wyer, Malcolm G., P23
Wyncoop, Edward W., U8
Wyndham family, B440
Wyoming: biography, S518; cities, S518; politics, C304; territory, G184, G300, H350
Wyville, Granville, B321

Xántus, John, G39
Xenophon, T91
XYZ Affair, K285, Z4

Yager, Arthur, C193
Yale College, S109, T146
Yalta Conference, C205, M379, P67, S637, T46
Yamagata Aritomo, N7
Yamamuro Gumpei, B14
Yancey, William L., D206
Yangban, S418
Yangtze River Valley, P48, Y27
Ya'queb Sanu', G63
Yazoo-Mississippi Delta, B379
Yellow fever, C70, E59
Yellow River Administration, H407
Yellowstone National Park, H58
Yenan province, S174
Yesler, Henry L., F77
Yi dynasty, S418
Yogaku, M393
Yokoi Shōnan, M414
Yorke, Joseph, M339
Yorkshire, England, C77, K204, K254
Yorubaland, P129

Yosemite National Park, H58
Youmans, Edward L., L138
Young, Art, F99
Young, Brigham, M97, R60a
Young, Ewing, H345
Young, Owen D., H430
Young Egypt Party, J28
Young Hegelians, B385
Young Men's Association, S112
Young Men's Christian Assn., A110a, F75, G36
Young Plan, H430
Young Turks, S621. *See also* Turkey
Youth: in Elizabethan England, E95; in 16th century London, B203; in U.S., F102
Youth movements, Germany, A58, H201, W28, W69
Ypsilanti, Mich., H264
Yrigoyen, Hipólito, F58
Yuaikai, L45
Yuchi Indians, M150
Yueh Fei, K23
Yugoslavia, G53, I1, N98, O97, R185, S635, Z28
Yugoslavs, in U.S., A70
Yung-cheng Emperor, H408, S360
Yunnan province, J78, S360

Zabern affair, M95
Zacatecas, Mexico, G33
Zachariad dynasty, E97
Zambia, R158
Zanzibar, D226
Zapata, Emiliano, D122, W307
Zaporogians, M186
Zehrer, Hans, S584
Zelaya, José Santos, M366, P82
Zell, Catherine, K180
Zell, Matthew, K180
Zemsky Sobor, H465
Zemstvo, A66, D157, K14, M163, R105, S64, S485, T81
Zeppelins, S374
Zéspedes, Vicente M. de, T8
Zimmermann, Wilhelm, F210
Zion City, Ill., C298
Zionism, D161, F36, F173, S388, W124. *See also* Israel; Palestine question
Zola, Emile, H455
Zollverein, H145
Zorita, Alonso de, V43
Zosimus, S62
Zubatov, Sergei V., S111a
Zurich, Switzerland, S490
Zweig, Stefan, S509
Zweigert, Erich, M36
Zwingli, Huldrych, W55

ERRATA TO *DISSERTATIONS IN HISTORY, VOLUME I (1873-1960)*

Inadequate records account for most of the errors in *Dissertations in History, 1873-1960,* although some in the index section represent editorial mistakes.

Title Section

A105   *Correct title is:* Church and State in the Reign of Louis Philippe, 1830-1848.

C328   *and* C339a *are the same person. The second entry is correct.*

D142   *Date of degree is* 1959.

F88   Anonymi *should be italicized.*

R383   *Correct title is:* The United States Army's Currency Management in World War II.

T55   *Author's name is spelled* Temperley.

Incomplete records at Catholic University at the time of the first compilation prevented any full or accurate listing of authors and titles. Professor Manoel Cardozo has conducted a thorough search which allows a more complete record. The following numbers represent substantive changes where titles varied considerably. Where variations in wording or spelling were minor no corrections are included.

A51   *Correct title is:* The Catholic University of America, 1887-1896: John J. Keane as First Rector.

B274   *Date of degree is* 1949.

B360   *Correct title is:* Hibernian Crusade: The Story of the Catholic Total Abstinence Union of America.

B665   *Date of degree is* 1935.

C127   *Date of degree is* 1959.

D18   *Date of degree is* 1944.

H325   *Date of degree is* 1948.

K226   *Date of degree is* 1941.

L365   *Date of degree is* 1944.

M78   *Correct title is:* Joseph McKenna, Associate Justice of the United States. *Date of degree is* 1946.

M423   *Correct title is:* The *Noticias Secretas de América* in the Light of Contemporary Evidence. *Date of degree is* 1956.

M689   *Date of degree is* 1948.

M692   *Correct title is:* Rufinas of Aquileia: His Life and Works. *Date of degree is* 1944.

N100   *Correct title is:* The Most Reverend Francis P. Kenrick, Third Bishop of Philadelphia, 1830-1851. *Date of degree is* 1949.

P156   *Correct title is:* The Historical Thought of Philippe Buchez (1796-1865). *Date of degree is* 1958.

P167   *Correct title is:* Manton Marble of the New York *World.*

R17   *Date of degree is* 1953.

R287   *Date of degree is* 1933.

S5   *Correct title is:* Paul Albar of Cordoba: Studies on His Life and Writings.

W30   *Correct title is:* The Chronicles of Saint Antonius, Archbishop of Florence, 1389-1459.

Index Section

Caprivi: *First name should be* Georg Leo.

Church and state, France: *add* A105.

Delcassé *should not be italicized.*

Intervention: *second entry should read* U.S. in Latin Am.

Landour *should read* Landaur.

Navy: *delete cross-reference to* Civil War, naval aspects.

Paris Peace Conference, *delete* C96.

Revolutions: *add* Mexican *to cross references.*

Veterans: *add* Civil War *to cross references.*